Social Enterprise

New organizations, driven by an entrepreneurial spirit but focused on social aims, are emerging throughout Europe. This important new text develops a comparative European analysis within a multidisciplinary framework to explore social enterprises. Breaking new ground, *Social Enterprise* combines theory with a rigorous analysis of 160 social enterprises across 11 EU countries to provide the reader with a thorough understanding of these complex organizations.

The text is structured around a number of key themes (multiple goals and multiple stakeholders, multiple resources, trajectories of workers, public policies) and developed through a pan-European analysis. Each theme is illustrated with short country experiences that reflect the diversity of welfare models across Europe. *Social Enterprise* is essential reading for all those who want to learn more about social enterprise.

Marthe Nyssens is a professor at the Department of Economics of the Catholic University of Louvain, Belgium, where she is the co-ordinator of a research team on third sector and social policies (CERISIS). All the contributors are members of the EMES European Research Network (www.emes.net).

Routledge Studies in the Management of Voluntary and Non-Profit Organizations

Series editor: Stephen P. Osborne

Social Enterprise

At the crossroads of market,
public policies and civil society

Edited by Marthe Nyssens
with the assistance of
Sophie Adam and Toby Johnson

LONDON AND NEW YORK

First published 2006
by Routledge
2 Park Square, Milton Park, Abingdon, Oxon OX14 4RN

Simultaneously published in the USA and Canada
by Routledge
270 Madison Ave, New York, NY 10016

Routledge is an imprint of the Taylor & Francis Group, an informa business

Reprinted 2008, 2009

Typeset in Baskerville by
Florence Production Ltd, Stoodleigh, Devon
Printed and bound in Great Britain by
MPG Books Ltd, Bodmin, Cornwall

British Library Cataloguing in Publication Data
A catalogue record for this book is available from the
British Library

Library of Congress Cataloging in Publication Data
A catalog record for this book has been requested

ISBN10: 0–415–37878–8 (hbk)
ISBN10: 0–415–37879–6 (pbk)

ISBN13: 978–0415–37878–9 (hbk)
ISBN13: 978–0415–37879–6 (pbk)

Contents

Illustrations

Tables

Figures

Contributors

Mike Aiken is at the Open University, UK, where he is researching the organizational values of voluntary organizations, the employment role of social enterprises and a management learning programme on outcomes. He previously worked in the voluntary sector for 20 years and remains active in citizen action groups.

Ingo Bode has a doctoral degree from the University of Duisburg-Essen, Germany. As well as being a private lecturer at that institution, he has researched and taught in France, Canada and the UK. His research interests are the sociology of organizations, social policy and the non-profit sector, including international comparisons. His latest book is *Die Dynamik organisierter Beschäftigungsförderung*, Wiesbaden 2005.

Carlo Borzaga is Professor of Economic Policy and Dean of the Faculty of Economics, University of Trento, Italy. He is the President of ISSAN (Institute for the Development of Non-profit Organizations). His main fields of research include analysis of the labour market and economic roles of non-profit organizations and co-operatives. He has carried out and co-ordinated numerous research projects in these fields.

Elisabetta Bucolo is a sociologist and a researcher at the Centre de Recherche et d'Information sur la Démocratie et l'Autonomie (CRIDA) in Paris. Her work, in France and in Europe, focuses mainly on the third sector and civil society, social enterprises, organizations in the social and solidarity-based economy and public policies that support them.

Sara Campi (Ph.D. in Service Management) is a researcher at the Research Centre for Not-for-profit Organizations (Cenpro) of the University of Genoa and a research associate at the Centre d'Economie Sociale, University of Liège. Her research and publications are on social enterprise, the relationship between NPOs and public agencies, the multi-stakeholder nature of social enterprises and corporate social responsibility.

Núria Claver is a sociologist. Her main professional activity focuses on the analysis of town planning policies and their economic and social impact. She also acted as a research assistant to the CIES (Centro de Investigación de Economia y Sociedad) in Barcelona, where she was chiefly concerned with the EMES projects.

Jacques Defourny is Professor of Economics at the University of Liège and director of the Centre d'Economie Sociale. He has chaired the EMES European Research Network for the last ten years. His work focuses on conceptual and quantitative approaches to social enterprise and the third sector in general.

Adalbert Evers is Professor for Comparative Health and Social Policy at the Justus Liebig University in Giessen, Germany. He researches and publishes on the interlinkages between public policies and civil society in the field of welfare services, including issues of welfare mixes, the third sector and democratic governance.

Laurent Gardin is a lecturer in Sociology at the University of Valenciennes and a researcher at the LISE laboratory of CNAM/CNRS (Conservatoire National des Arts et Métiers/Centre National de la Recherche Scientifique) in Paris. His work focuses mainly on civil society, social enterprises, organizations in the solidarity-based economy and public policies that support them.

Olivier Grégoire worked as a research fellow at the Centre d'Economie Sociale (University of Liège, Belgium) after completing his graduate studies in economics. He took part in multidisciplinary and international research on the performance of non-profit organizations in developed and developing countries. He is currently a programme officer for UNAIDS, the Joint United Nations Programme on HIV/AIDS.

Lars Hulgård is Associate Professor and International Co-ordinator of 'Civil Society and New Forms of Governance in Europe' (CINEFOGO), a Network of Excellence funded by the EU's Sixth Framework Programme. His research interests include civil society theory, the relation between social capital and welfare, the impact of institutions on the formation of social capital and social entrepreneurship.

Jean-Louis Laville is Co-director of the LISE laboratory of the CNRS (Centre National de la Recherche Scientifique), and a professor at the CNAM (Conservatoire National des Arts et Métiers) in Paris. His research centres on civil society and economic sociology, and he is the author of 'The Third Sector in Europe' (with Adalbert Evers).

Andreia Lemaître is a research fellow of the FNRS (Fonds National de la Recherche Scientifique, Belgium) and a member of the CERISIS research centre and of the Development Studies Institute of the Catholic

University of Louvain, Belgium. She is studying for her Ph.D. and has been awarded several scientific prizes for her work on the social economy, social enterprises and public policies.

Monica Loss graduated in Economics at Trento University. She teaches a post-graduate course in 'Management of Non-profit Organizations and Social Co-operatives' at ISSAN, University of Trento, and is the Dean of the administrative staff of this institute. She carries out research in the work integration of disadvantaged workers, work integration social co-operatives and social enterprises.

Susana Nogueira is a sociologist whose main professional activity is in the public social security services, working with homeless people, women experiencing domestic violence and abused/neglected children. She also acts as research assistant at the Centro de Estudos para a Intervenção Social (CESIS) in Lisbon, concerned with the EMES projects.

Marthe Nyssens is Professor in the Department of Economics of the Catholic University of Louvain, Belgium, where she is the co-ordinator of a research team on the third sector and social policies. Her work focuses on conceptual approaches to the third sector, both in developed and developing countries, as well as on the links between third sector organizations and public policies.

Mary O'Shaughnessy is a lecturer in the Department of Food Business & Development and the Centre for Co-operative Studies at the National University of Ireland, Cork (UCC). Her research interests include rural development and rural social enterprise. She contributed to the mid-term review of Ireland's CAP Rural Development Plan (2000–06).

Pekka Pättiniemi is the Principal of the People's Cultural and Educational Association in Finland, as well as serving on the boards of the Finnish Association for Co-operative Research and the Swedish Association for Co-operative Research, and chairing the board of Coop Finland. He has publications to his name on co-operative and social enterprises, in both Finnish and English.

Heloísa Perista is a senior researcher at the Centro de Estudos para a Intervenção Social (CESIS) in Lisbon. Social enterprises are among her research interests. She has published several articles and working papers on this issue as an outcome of her participation as the Portuguese partner in the EMES projects.

Alexis Platteau has a master's degree in Economics. He has worked as a research fellow at CERISIS (University of Louvain, Belgium), and taken part in several research projects on work integration social enterprises.

Andreas Schulz is a former research fellow at the Institute for Comparative Health and Social Policy at the Justus Liebig University, Giessen, Germany. His research covers issues linked to labour market policy, welfare organizations and social services.

Roger Spear is Chair of the Co-operatives Research Unit, founder member and Vice-President of the EMES research network, and teaches organizational systems and research methods in the Centre for Complexity and Change at the Open University (UK). He has conducted numerous research studies on co-operatives and social enterprises (see http://systems.open.ac.uk/page.cfm?pageid=RogerShome).

Yohanan Stryjan is a sociologist and Professor of Business Administration at Södertörn University College (Stockholm). His research covers issues of social entrepreneurship and co-operative organization in changing institutional landscapes. He is also a board member of the Stockholm Co-operative Development Agency and vice-chairman of the International Co-operative Alliance Research Committee.

Isabel Vidal is Professor of Economic Theory and Director of the Research Centre on Citizenship and Civil Society at the University of Barcelona, and President of the Research Centre on Economy and Society. Her areas of research are social enterprise, social economy and third sector, corporate social responsibility, labour market and active employment policies.

Acknowledgements

This book represents the results of work undertaken within the European Community's Fifth Framework Programme for Research, Technological Development and Demonstration Activities. Researchers from 11 EU countries, forming the EMES European Research Network (www.emes.net), worked from the autumn of 2001 until the end of 2004 on the research project entitled 'The Socio-Economic Performance of Social Enterprises in the Field of Integration by Work' (HPSE-CT2001–00092).

I want particularly to thank Dorotea Daniele from DIESIS (Brussels) and Enzo Pezzini from Confcooperative (Brussels) who provided me with outstanding assistance in the co-ordination of the Network. They took charge of all the administrative and technical matters related to the project. Moreover, they organized all the joint working sessions, which were held twice yearly throughout Europe.

I am also grateful to Sophie Adam (Centre d'Economie Sociale, Liège) who did a heroic job as the editorial assistant for the preparation of this volume. The final product also owes much to Toby Johnson, who carefully executed the final linguistic editing. My thanks also go to the Centre for Civil Society, Department of Social Policy, London School of Economics, which hosted me for several months when I was working on this book.

Finally, I wish to express my warm thanks to all the junior and senior researchers who have been involved in this project over all these years as well as to the organizations and enterprises that were visited or surveyed in each country.

Marthe Nyssens

Introduction

1 Defining social enterprise

Jacques Defourny and Marthe Nyssens

Overview

The objectives of this chapter are to outline the concept of 'social enterprise' as used in this book and to compare it with other approaches. The core hypotheses and the empirical field of the research project upon which this book is based are also presented. After reading this chapter, the reader should:

- have an understanding of the different approaches to the concept of social enterprise;
- identify the core hypotheses around which the research project is articulated;
- identify the subset of social enterprises on which the research project is based, namely work integration social enterprises (WISEs).

---

1 The origin of the concept of 'social enterprise' and its evolution

The increasing acknowledgement of the third sector in Europe, together with the broader interest in non-conventional entrepreneurial dynamics addressing current challenges, led to the emergence of the new concept of 'social enterprise'. Whereas a dozen years ago this concept was rarely discussed, it is now making amazing breakthroughs on both sides of the Atlantic. In the US, it first met with a very positive response in the early 1990s[1]. In 1993, Harvard Business School launched the 'Social Enterprise Initiative', one of the milestones of the period. Since then, other major universities – including Columbia, Stanford and Yale – and various foundations have set up training and support programmes for social enterprises or social entrepreneurs.

However, in the United States the social enterprise remains a very broad and often quite vague concept, referring primarily to market-oriented economic activities serving a social goal. The social enterprise is then viewed as an innovative response to the funding problems of non-profit organizations, which are finding it increasingly difficult to solicit private donations and government and foundation grants (Dees 1998). The concept is also used to highlight the innovative side of certain types of projects, as well as the financial risks they are taking (Young 2001). In this latter case, the concept of social enterprise includes a wide spectrum of organizations, from for-profit business engaged in socially beneficial activities (corporate philanthropy) to non-profit organizations engaged in mission-supporting commercial activity (Kerlin 2005).

In Europe, the concept made its first appearance in the early 1990s, at the very heart of the third sector, following an impetus that was first Italian, linked closely with the co-operative movement. More precisely, in 1991, the Italian parliament adopted a law creating a specific legal form for 'social co-operatives'; the latter went on to experience an extraordinary growth. These co-operatives arose primarily to respond to needs that had been inadequately met, or not met at all, by public services (Borzaga and Santuari 2001).

In a second phase, European researchers noticed the existence of similar initiatives, though of a substantially lesser magnitude, and taking a variety of labels and legal forms, in various other European countries. In 1996, some of these researchers decided to form a network to study the emergence of social enterprises in Europe. Covering all of the 15 countries that then made up the European Union, this group, named the EMES European Research Network, carried out its initial research work over a four-year period and gradually developed a common approach to the study of social enterprises (Borzaga and Defourny 2001).

In 2002, there was a sudden acceleration of the debate around social enterprise in the United Kingdom. The Blair government launched the 'Social Enterprise Coalition' and created a 'Social Enterprise Unit' to improve the knowledge of social enterprises and, above all, to promote social enterprises throughout the country. Within the same framework, the Department of Trade and Industry, which supervises the Unit, has put forward its own definition of social enterprise and a new legal form, the 'Community Interest Company', was voted by Parliament in 2004. Even though the concept of social enterprise is still imprecise in British usage, two characteristics appear to form part of the identity of this kind of enterprise: they are driven primarily by social objectives and they achieve sustainability through trading (DTI 2002).

In the European public debate, the concept may have various meanings. One school of thought stresses the social entrepreneurship dynamic exemplified by firms that seek to enhance the social impact of their productive activities. In this area, the literature quite often highlights the innovative approach to tackling social needs that is taken by individuals in fostering business (Grenier 2003), mainly through non-profit organizations, but also in the for-profit sector (Nicholls 2005).[2] In this latter case, this idea has to do, at least partially, with the 'corporate social responsibility' debate. Another stream only uses the concept of social enterprise for organizations belonging to the third sector and therefore builds on the specificities of the latter. In such social enterprises, generally of the non-profit or co-operative type, the social impact on the community is not only a consequence or a side-effect of economic activity, but its motivation in itself. The previous EMES book, *The Emergence of Social Enterprise* (Borzaga and Defourny 2001), paved the way for such a framework and this book relies on the same 'building blocks'.

Social enterprises have been defined by the EMES Network as organizations with an explicit aim to benefit the community, initiated by a group of citizens and in which the material interest of capital investors is subject to limits. Social enterprises also place a high value on their autonomy and on economic risk-taking related to ongoing socio-economic activity.

The EMES definition of social enterprise

The EMES definition distinguishes between, on the one hand, criteria that are more economic and, on the other, indicators that are predominantly social. These indicators, such as they can be found in the works published by the Network,[3] are presented below.

To reflect the economic and entrepreneurial dimensions of initiatives, four criteria have been put forward:

a) *A continuous activity, producing and selling goods and/or services*
   Social enterprises, unlike some traditional non-profit organizations, do not normally have advocacy activities or the redistribution of financial flows (as do, for example, grant-giving foundations) as their major activity, but they are directly involved in the production of goods or the provision of services to people on a continuous basis. The productive activity thus represents the reason, or one of the main reasons, for the existence of social enterprises.

b) *A high degree of autonomy*
   Social enterprises are created by a group of people on the basis of an autonomous project and they are governed by these people. They may depend on public subsidies but they are not managed, directly or indirectly, by public authorities or other organizations (federations, for-profit private firms, etc.). They have the right to take up their own position ('voice') as well as to terminate their activity ('exit').

c) *A significant level of economic risk*
    Those who establish a social enterprise assume – totally or partly – the risk of the initiative. Unlike most public institutions, their financial viability depends on the efforts of their members and workers to secure adequate resources.

d) *A minimum amount of paid work*
    As in the case of most traditional non-profit organizations, social enterprises may combine monetary and non-monetary resources, volunteering and paid workers. However, the activity carried out in social enterprises requires a minimum level of paid work.

To encapsulate the social dimensions of the initiative, five criteria have been proposed:

e) *An explicit aim to benefit the community*
    One of the principal aims of social enterprises is to serve the community or a specific group of people. In the same perspective, a feature of social enterprises is their desire to promote a sense of social responsibility at local level.

f) *An initiative launched by a group of citizens*
    Social enterprises are the result of collective dynamics involving people belonging to a community or to a group that shares a well-defined need or aim; this collective dimension must be maintained over time in one way or another, even though the importance of leadership – often embodied in an individual or a small group of leaders – must not be neglected.

g) *Decision-making power not based on capital ownership*
    This generally refers to the principle of 'one member, one vote' or at least to a decision-making process in which the voting power in the governing body with the ultimate decision-making rights is not distributed according to capital shares. Moreover, although the owners of the capital are important, decision-making rights are generally shared with the other stakeholders.

h) *A participatory nature, which involves the various parties affected by the activity*
    Representation and participation of users or customers, stakeholder influence on decision-making and participative management are often important characteristics of social enterprises. In many cases, one of the aims of social enterprises is to further democracy at local level through economic activity.

i) *Limited profit distribution*
    Social enterprises not only include organizations that are characterized by a total non-distribution constraint, but also organizations which – like co-operatives in some countries – may distribute profits, but only to a limited extent, thus avoiding profit-maximizing behaviour.

Source: Defourny 2001: 16–18.

It has to be underlined that, rather than constituting prescriptive criteria, these indicators describe an 'ideal-type' that enables researchers to position themselves within the 'galaxy' of social enterprises. Without any normative perspective, they constitute a tool, somewhat analogous to a compass, which can help the researchers locate the position of certain entities relative to one another, and which may enable researchers to establish the boundaries of the set of organizations that they will consider as that of social enterprises.

2 The concept of social enterprise: a bridge between co-operatives and non-profit organizations

Several concepts have been used to define a set of organizations and initiatives that are neither public nor private for-profit ones. It may be said that two theoretical approaches to the third sector have gradually spread internationally, accompanied by statistical work aiming to quantify its economic importance.[4] On the one hand, the 'non-profit school' approaches this sector via the statutory ban on the distribution of profits in these organizations. On the other hand, the concept of the 'social economy', which brings together co-operatives, mutual societies and associations (and, with increasing frequency, foundations), stresses the specificity of the mission of these organizations, namely, their aim to benefit either their members or a larger collectivity rather than generating profits for investors. This approach also highlights the presence of a democratic decision-making process within the organizations and the prevalence of people and labour over capital in the distribution of incomes. Our approach to the social enterprise does not seek to supplant existing concepts of the third sector – such as the concepts of the social economy, the non-profit sector or the voluntary sector. Rather, it is intended to enhance third sector concepts by shedding light on *particular dynamics within this sector*.

Theoretically, the social enterprise concept can also be seen as a tool for building bridges between distinct components of the third sector. As a matter of fact, when apprehending the third sector, two sources of tension appear to be recurrent and sometimes difficult to overcome. One source of tension originates in the gap between enterprises offering their entire output for sale on the market (as do most co-operatives), on the one hand, and associations whose activities are usually deemed to have a weak economic character (such as youth movement activities) and whose resources are totally 'non-market' (grants, subsidies, etc.), or even non-monetary (volunteering), on the other hand. A second tension arises between mutual interest organizations (co-operatives, mutual societies and a large number of associations) which, at least in principle, aim to serve their members, and general interest organizations, serving the broader community (such as organizations combating poverty and exclusion, or those involved in development co-operation, environmental protection and so on).

These two sources of tension are partly illustrated in Figure 1.1. The first source of tension is represented by the coexistence of two quite distinct spheres: the left sphere represents the co-operative tradition (which has generated a specific literature and schools of thought); the right sphere represents the tradition of associative initiatives and movements (which has also inspired numerous sociologists and political scientists and found particular impetus in North American research works on non-profit organizations). The second source of tension may also be discerned in this figure, although only partly: it is found within each of the two spheres, where general interest organizations tend to be located towards the centre, whereas mutual interest organizations tend to be located either on the left or on the right of the diagram (although some advocacy non-profit organizations may, of course, be of general interest).

The unifying role of the social enterprise concept resides primarily in the fact that it generates a mutual attraction between the two spheres. It accomplishes this by attaching itself to certain organizations within each sphere; these organizations are then drawn to and included in a single group of organizations, because they are, in the last analysis, very close to each other, and whether they choose a co-operative legal form or an associative legal form depends primarily on the legal mechanisms provided by national legislations.

On the one hand, compared to traditional associations, social enterprises place a higher value on economic risk-taking related to an ongoing productive activity (in the world of non-profit organizations, production-

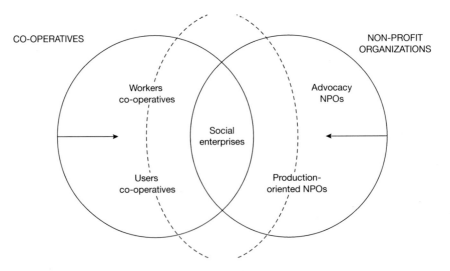

Figure 1.1 Social enterprises, at the crossroads of the co-operative and the non-profit sectors

Source: adapted from Defourny (2001: 22)

oriented associations are certainly closer to social enterprises than are advocacy organizations and grant-making foundations). On the other hand, in con-trast to many traditional co-operatives, social enterprises may be seen as more oriented to the whole community and putting more emphasis on the dimension of general interest. Moreover, social enterprises are said to combine different types of stakeholders in their membership, whereas traditional co-operatives have generally been set up as single-stakeholder organizations. These contrasting elements, however, should not be over-estimated: while social enterprises as we have defined them are in some cases new organizations, which may be regarded as constituting a new sub-division of the third sector, in other cases, they result from a process at work in older experiences within the third sector. In other words, it can be said that the generic term 'social enterprise' does not represent a conceptual break with institutions of the third sector but, rather, a new dynamic within it – encompassing both newly created organizations and older ones that have undergone an evolution. Such a dynamic perspective explains why the landscape of social enterprises can only be suggested by dotted lines.

Finally, although most social enterprises take the form of co-operatives or associations, there is nothing to prevent them from adopting other legal forms. This is even truer in countries that have designed completely separate legal forms for at least some social enterprises, such as the new 'community interest company' legal form in the United Kingdom. This explains why the set of social enterprises in our diagram goes beyond the frontiers of both spheres. As to the intersection between the latter, it can be illustrated by new legal frameworks combining a limitation on the distribution of profit and the major features of the co-operative legal form. The 'co-operative society of collective interest' (*société coopérative d'intérêt collectif*) in France, the 'social purpose company' (*société à finalité sociale* or *vennootschap met sociaal oogmerk*) in Belgium and the pioneering Italian legal form for 'social co-operatives' (*cooperative sociali*) may be analysed along such lines.

3 Three key research questions

The above-mentioned previous book by the EMES Network traced the most significant developments in social enterprises emerging in Europe (Borzaga and Defourny 2001). The final chapters of that book also presented an initial attempt to outline a theory of social enterprise: according to these contributions, an 'ideal-typical' social enterprise could be seen as a 'multiple-goal, multi-stakeholder and multiple-resource enterprise'. However, these theorized features remained untested and paved the way for further research. The main objective of the PERSE[5] research project, upon which this book is based, was to explore more deeply such hypotheses and to further develop a theory of social enterprise through a comparative analysis of social enterprises in Europe.

More precisely, the research project was articulated around three main theoretical axes:

1 Social enterprises usually have a complex mixture of goals (Evers 2001). The first hypothesis put forward in this research project regarding social enterprises' mission is that the latter would include at least three different categories of goals: social goals, connected to the particular mission of social enterprises to benefit the community; economic goals, related to the entrepreneurial nature of social enterprises; and socio-political goals, referring to the fact that social enterprises are often rooted in a 'sector' traditionally involved in socio-political action. This last goal can be analysed in the wider perspective of 'producing social capital', where social capital is understood as referring to 'features of social organizations such as networks, norms and trust that facilitate co-ordination and co-operation with mutual benefit' (Putnam 1993). Concretely, the pursuit of a 'social capital goal' by social enterprises may translate not only into a will to co-operate with economic, social and political actors through the development of various networks but also into the implementation of democratic decision-making processes, in specific working conditions (flat hierarchy, workers' participation, trusting atmosphere, etc.), or in the promotion of volunteering (Davister 2004). As a matter of fact, within these organizations, the production and mobilization of social capital can be goals in themselves and not only tools/instruments for achieving other objectives (Evers 2001).

Moreover, regarding these multiple goals, another hypothesis had been put forward: multi-stakeholder ownership (Bachiega and Borzaga 2001) might be an efficient way for social enterprises to achieve their overall mission, and the representation of different types of stakeholder on the board might be a way to combine the various goals of the enterprise, thanks to the various sensibilities of the stakeholders.

2 The second hypothesis put forward in this project was that social enterprises mobilize different kinds of market and non-market resources to sustain their public benefit mission: they trade goods and services in the market; public financing generally supports their public benefit mission; and, finally, social enterprises can also rely upon volunteer resources. These latter resources could be seen as a result of the mobilization of social capital. According to Laville and Nyssens (2001), social capital is a fully fledged production factor within social enterprises since it is part of the production process and it improves it, mainly by reducing the transaction costs (trust among the agents makes co-ordination easier and increases their motivation) and by reducing the production costs (by the use of donations, volunteers and a better involvement of users). By following Polanyi (1944) and his 'substantive approach' to the economy, we argue that social enterprises combine the economic principles of market, redistribution and

reciprocity and hybridize these three types of economic exchange so that they work together rather than in isolation from each other.

3 Social enterprises are embedded in the political context. Public policies in the field of social enterprises are the result of interactions between the promoters of the latter and representatives of public bodies. We put forward the hypothesis that this dynamic of institutionalization can lead to the development of innovative public schemes and at the same time to a movement of 'isomorphism' on the part of social enterprises, towards public organizations or for-profit enterprises.

These core ideas can be examined within the landscape of theories seeking to explain the behaviour and the 'raisons d'être' of third sector organizations as well as of the (quite limited) existing literature dealing specifically with social enterprises. Coupled with the EMES criteria discussed above, our hypotheses propose a theoretical corpus that is really specific to social enterprises, although it still needs empirical support. More precisely, compared to the dominant approach of the rationale of social enterprises in the US and UK contexts, such hypotheses may be seen as innovative on four central points.

First, our framework emphasizes the multidimensional mode of governance of social enterprises. As Young and Salamon state: 'In Europe, the notion of social enterprise focuses more heavily on the way an organization is governed and what its purpose is rather than on whether it strictly adheres to the non-distribution constraint of a formal non-profit organization' (2002: 433). This point of view is, indeed, richer than that based solely on the non-distribution constraint or the limitation on profit distribution, which constitutes the central feature on which the greatest part of the non-profit literature has been built (Hansmann 1980). As a matter of fact, although our definition of social enterprise also includes this feature by its 'limited profit distribution' criterion, it goes further than that, by incorporating other aspects that are central to characterising social enterprise's governance structure. These include, among other aspects, the existence of a collective dynamic of entrepreneurship involving people belonging to a community or to a group that shares a well-defined need or aim. This view also contrasts with the emphasis put on social entrepreneurship (Dees 2001), 'which reflects a shift towards focusing on individuals and away from traditional emphasis on the community and collective found in community development and the co-op movement' (Grenier 2003: 4). Our approach does not exclude the possibility for some leader or charismatic entrepreneur to play a key role in the enterprise, but generally these persons are supported by a group whose members are responsible for the public benefit mission of the social enterprise. The EMES definition also stresses the involvement of different stakeholders in the governance of the organization through formal channels (membership of the board) or less formal ones. To that extent, we can argue that our approach to social enterprise remains more in line with and rooted in the third sector literature, especially that part of it focusing on community development and the social economy.

A second important point of divergence between our framework of analysis and most literature on social enterprise is the fact that, in our approach, the economic dimension does not necessarily mean that the social enterprise must achieve economic sustainability through a trading activity. Indeed, even if 'definitions of social enterprise differ in terms of the amount of the income that must be generated through trading' (Haugh 2005: 3), a clear emphasis is generally put on the importance of resources coming from commercial activities, as the DTI stresses: 'A social enterprise is, first and foremost, a business. That means it is engaged in some form of trading, but it trades primarily to support a social purpose' (DTI 2002: 13). On the contrary, our central idea is rather that the financial viability of the social enterprise depends on the efforts of its members to secure adequate resources to support the enterprise's social mission, but these resources can have a hybrid character and come from trading activities, from public subsidies and from voluntary resources obtained thanks to the mobilization of social capital.

The third point is related to the nature of the production activity of the social enterprise. Although this is not explicitly mentioned in the EMES list of criteria, the production of goods and/or services should, in itself, constitute (not only indirectly, through the income it generates) a support for the social mission. In other words, the nature of the economic activity must be connected to the social mission: if the mission of the social enterprise is to create jobs for low-qualified people, the economic activity itself supports the work integration goal; if the mission of the social enterprise is to develop social services, the economic activity is the delivery of these social services, and so on. By contrast, in the US or UK conception of the social enterprise, the trading activity is often considered simply as a source of income, and the nature of the trade does not matter (Dees 1998).

Finally, an innovative aspect of our framework stems from the analysis of the interactions between the organizations and public policies. This question has traditionally been approached through the analysis of organizations (DiMaggio and Powell 1983). From this perspective, the objectives and practices of organizations are partially shaped by their external environment, which includes the legal and regulatory framework within which they operate. Such a perspective fails to take into account a fundamental fact that the PERSE research project sought to explain in its analysis: the relationship between social enterprises and public policies is not one-sided, and social enterprises are not mere 'residual' actors, filling the gaps left by the market or the state and under the control of public regulation. Social enterprises actually also influence their institutional environment, and they have contributed to the development and shaping of institutions and public policies.

Social enterprises can be said to be located in an intermediate space (Evers and Laville 2004), at the crossroads of market, public policies and civil society. Even though the concept of civil society is rather polysemic, most analysts would probably agree that it refers, today, to actors who belong to

> the arena of uncoerced collective action around shared interests, purposes and values. In theory, its institutional forms are distinct from those of the state, family and market, though in practice, the boundaries between state, civil society, family and market are often complex, blurred and negotiated.
>
> (LSE 2004)

This way of considering social enterprises contrasts with the usual representation, emerging from third sector literature, of a 'residual sector' facing market and government failures (Steinberg 2004) and tending to 'put the state, the market and the third sector in separate boxes' (Lewis 2004: 172). Social enterprises mix different logics: they trade in the market, but not with an aim of maximizing the financial return on investment for their shareholders; they receive public support through public policies which they contribute to shaping; they are embedded in civil society through the development of voluntary collective action around common goals characterized by a public benefit dimension.

4 Work integration social enterprises (WISEs) in Europe: a wide spectrum of organizations in different countries

Social enterprises are active in a wide variety of fields, including the fight against the structural unemployment of groups excluded from the labour market, personal social services, urban regeneration, environmental services, and the provision of other public goods or services. However, in order to develop our analysis on a reliable empirical base, we have had to focus on a rather limited field of activity that has allowed meaningful international comparisons and statistical analysis. In this perspective, we have chosen the field of 'work integration', which is emblematic of the dynamics of social enterprises and constitutes a major sphere of their activity in Europe. The major objective of 'work integration social enterprises' (WISEs) is to help disadvantaged unemployed people, who are at risk of permanent exclusion from the labour market. They integrate them back into work and society, in general through productive activity.

The persistence of structural unemployment among some groups, the difficulties traditional active labour market policies face in integrating them and the need for more active integration policies have naturally raised questions as to the role that social enterprises can play in combating unemployment and fostering employment growth. Indeed, although the rate of employment[6] varies greatly among European countries (with high rates of participation in the UK and Nordic countries and the lowest ones in Spain, Italy and Belgium), all EU countries are characterized by low rates of employment for some groups, for instance women, non-European workers, older people and/or low-skilled workers (see Table 1.1). For example, in all countries except the Nordic countries and Portugal, among people with at most a lower secondary education, less than one person out of two is working. Women's employment rates are very low in Italy and Spain. Rates of employment of non-European people are low everywhere, even in the Nordic countries.

If we now look at WISEs, they are clearly unevenly distributed throughout Europe. In some countries (such as Italy), there are thousands of organizations active in the field of work integration of long-term unemployed and disadvantaged people. In other countries the number of work integration social enterprises is relatively low. There is also a significant heterogeneity – both among countries and within each country – in the ways WISEs function. There are great variations, finally, as to WISEs' activities, origins, legal forms and level of visibility, and as to the public schemes supporting them. But WISEs are basically present in all European countries and are thought of as important tools of active labour market policies.

Table 1.1 Rates of employment in EU countries (population from 15 to 65 years old) (%)

Country	Rate of employment	Rate of employment of women	Rate of employment of non-European people	Rate of employment of people between 50 and 64 years old	Rate of employment of people with at most a lower secondary education (population under 60)
Belgium	59.7	51.3	30.4	41.2	42.4
Denmark	76.4	72.6	49.7	67.2	61.9
Finland	69.1	67.0	54.6	60.8	51.1
France	62.9	56.6	43.4	51.6	47.8
Germany	65.4	58.9	51.0	50.4	43.8
Ireland	65.0	55.3	58.5	55.3	48.1
Italy	55.4	42.1	n/a	40.4	46.5
Portugal	68.6	61.1	76.1	59.7	67.9
Spain	58.4	43.8	67.2	47.3	53.7
Sweden	74.0	72.5	49.6	74.0	59.2
UK	71.5	65.1	57.2	62.2	48.6
EU	64.2	55.2	52.6	52.0	50.1

Source: European Social Statistics – Labour force survey results 2002.

In one of its previous research projects, the EMES Network identified 44 different types of WISE[7] (see Appendices 1 and 2 to this chapter). All these address, through various modes of integration, the problems of long-term unemployment and occupational inactivity of disadvantaged people in the labour market. Davister *et al.* (2004) have identified four main groups, which they describe as follows.

The first group includes enterprises offering occupational integration supported by permanent 'subsidies'. This group includes mostly the oldest forms of WISE, i.e. those for the handicapped. These organizations exist in most European countries and aim to remedy the discrepancy between the productivity required by the 'classical' labour market and the capacities of the handicapped. Nowadays, these organizations, most of which are recognized and subsidized by public authorities, offer open-ended work contracts. Owing to their increasing professionalization, these WISEs generally mobilize few volunteers, and the share of their resources that comes from the market is ever-increasing. Among these WISEs, we can mention sheltered employment (Ireland and Portugal), sheltered workshops (Belgium and Denmark) and the Samhall network of sheltered workshops (Sweden). Work care centres and social workshops (Belgium) also belong to this group; it should be mentioned that these two types of WISE are practically the only organizations in Europe offering sheltered employment to people considered as socially handicapped, although with no mental or physical disabilities.

A second group is constituted by the types of WISE that provide permanent, self-subsidized employment, i.e. stable jobs, economically sustainable in the medium term, to people who are disadvantaged in the labour market. In the initial stage, public subsidies are granted to make up for the lack of productivity of the target group. These subsidies are often temporary, and they taper off until the workers become competitive in the mainstream labour market. After this subsidized stage, these WISEs must pay the workers in integration from their own resources. These initiatives, which include community businesses and social firms in the UK and social firms and some types of co-operatives in Germany, are generally of more recent origin than sheltered workshops. Most often, they offer open-ended work contracts. The pressure to be profitable is, here, generally higher than in any other type of WISE.

A third, large group comprises the types of WISE that mostly aim to (re)socialise people through productive activities. We can, for example, mention centres for adaptation to working life in France, sheltered employment centres in Spain and social co-operatives in Sweden. These WISEs target able-bodied workers with serious psycho-social problems or handicapped people. They generally do not provide real work but, rather, sheltered employment, and not a work contract as such (food and, most often, shelter in exchange for work, for example). Volunteering is significant and resources from the market are rather limited.

The fourth group – the largest among the WISEs studied – comprises initiatives offering transitional employment or traineeships. These enterprises, even though they all share a common goal – namely, to help workers in integration find work in the mainstream labour market – are sometimes very different in the way they implement this goal. For example, Belgian on-the-job training enterprises offer qualifying training, while French work integration enterprises provide a real job, of one year's duration. These differences generate a different mobilization of resources. Some of these WISEs survive nearly exclusively on subsidies. Conversely, others are practically independent of any public subsidy. The importance of volunteering also varies greatly. The handicapped or people with serious social problems are generally not targeted by these organizations. The main reason for this is that the goal in these WISEs is a relatively quick reintegration of the workers into the mainstream labour market. Consequently, most work or traineeship contracts are fixed-term contracts. We can include in this fourth group labour co-operatives (Finland), temporary work integration enterprises (France), intermediate labour market organizations (UK) and local community enterprises offering traineeship and temporary work integration (Denmark).

Finally, it should be mentioned that several types of WISE are difficult to classify in any of these four main groups because they implement simultaneously several modes of integration. For example, B-type social co-operatives in Italy and neighbourhood enterprises in France pursue several integration goals for very varied target groups.

5 The sample of the PERSE project

Empirical evidence on WISEs in the EU countries exists, but almost all available information is limited to basic quantitative data (number of enterprises, of workers employed, of consumers). Unfortunately, very limited information is available on the way in which social enterprises operate, on how they mobilize and mix productive resources, on their mode of governance and on the quality of the jobs provided. To develop our research questions, 162 WISEs, located in 11 European countries,[8] were selected.

It was decided to leave aside social enterprises for the disabled, which pioneered the field in the 1960s, in a majority of European countries. As a matter of fact, in most cases, these initiatives have been heavily regulated by public bodies and now constitute a field of their own. However, some WISEs integrate disabled persons besides other persons who are at risk of permanent exclusion from the labour market; this kind of organization is represented in our sample.

The sampling of work integration social enterprises for the PERSE project

For the empirical research of the PERSE project, we selected a subset of 15 work integration social enterprises (WISEs) to be studied in depth in each country.

Former studies (such as Borzaga and Defourny 2001) have clearly shown that the field of WISEs is more complex than the ideal-type of social enterprise depicted by the EMES criteria might suggest. Given this heterogeneity, the choice of the 15 cases was guided by the following rationale.

The first criterion was the representativeness of the WISE (even though it did not fully reflect the EMES criteria) in the whole land-scape of WISEs of the country. Far from being rooted in statistical theory, such a representativeness could be linked to the fact that WISEs of this type:

- were numerous or were growing in number or social important-ance;
- represented a major path of organizational development;
- were typical with respect to national or regional labour market policies or social actors' strategies.

A second criterion was the closeness of the WISE to the ideal-type of social enterprise described by the EMES criteria, although it appeared necessary not to be too rigid in applying these criteria: for example, an organization could (still) be close to the EMES criteria, but it could also happen that *some* distinctive elements, which had been present in the beginning of the organization, had subsequently faded away.

The sample constituted in this way is not statistically representa-tive. It includes, in addition to WISEs typical of each country, some WISEs that are not necessarily typical but which appear to be good examples of the ideal-type of social enterprise.

The WISEs in the sample are active in a wide spectrum of activities (see Table 1.2). Some WISEs produce public goods, i.e. goods that are non-rival in consumption (the use of the good by one person does not prevent its use by others) and non-excludable (there is a technical diffi-culty in charging individuals for the consumption of the good or the service). This is a well-known case of market failure, which implies inter-vention by the state. Therefore, it is not surprising that these WISEs rely, for their financing, on contracts with public bodies. Eighteen per cent of

Table 1.2 Type of production of WISEs*

Type of production	No. of WISEs	Percentage of WISEs
Social services	29	19
Recycling	28	18
Services for enterprises	19	12
Personal services	14	9
Gardening and urban regeneration	12	8
Processing industry	10	6
Building industry	9	6
Restaurants and hotels	8	5
Traffic and telecommunication	7	5
Culture and leisure	7	5
Education	5	3
Commerce	3	2
Placement services	3	2
Agriculture	1	1
Total	155	100
n/a	7	

*The data in the tables in this book come from PERSE database if not specified.

the WISEs in the sample are active in recycling and 8 per cent in gardening and urban regeneration (not all the activities in this latter sector are public goods; for example, gardening in a private house is not).

Other WISEs produce individual goods or services, i.e. goods whose consumption is clearly divisible, such as restaurant or childcare services. However, we can make a further distinction, among individual goods and services, between pure private goods and quasi-public goods. The latter, despite their divisible nature, give rise to collective benefits beside the private benefits; they produce collective externalities, i.e. the activity of the WISE has indirect effects that affect the whole community.[9] For example, childcare services produce private benefits for the child's parents and, at the same time, they produce positive impacts on the community by facilitating the access of women to the labour market, by fostering social cohesion in distressed areas, and so on. For these reasons, childcare can be considered as a quasi-public good. Some goods or services are also quasi-public goods as a result of the type of consumers addressed. For example, a restaurant for needy people which sells its products at low prices produces a quasi-public good. As a consequence of these externalities, market mechanisms cannot produce an optimal level of this kind of good. This is the rationale behind the public regulation of social services. Nineteen per cent of WISEs in the sample are active in social services (childcare, elderly care, second-hand shops for needy people, delivery of meals, shopping, transport for people with reduced mobility, etc.). Three per cent of WISEs are active in the education sector and 5 per cent in the culture and leisure sector (community centres, theatres, recreation centres, tourism projects, etc.). Some of these latter services can be considered as quasi-public goods. Therefore, it can be considered that more or less one-quarter of WISEs produce quasi-public goods.

The remaining WISEs produce pure private goods. Twelve per cent of them deliver services to enterprises (subcontracting, industrial cleaning, developing infrastructure for enterprises, consultancy, etc.). Nine per cent provide personal services (house cleaning, shopping, etc.) to households. Unlike social services, these personal services do not produce, at least not to the same degree, collective benefits. The 'traffic and telecommunication' sector includes services such as transport (taxis, bus, etc.) and information technology services, messaging and radio – 5 per cent of WISEs in the sample are active in this field. Other sectors are the building industry and the processing industry (wood, clothing, painting, carpentry, metal, etc.), restaurants and hotels, commerce, placement services, agriculture. All these activities can be considered as private goods.

6 Plan of the book

The book is divided into four parts. The first two parts focus on the rationale underpinning social enterprises such as it emerged from the analysis of the information collected on 162 European social enterprises. The third part analyses the profiles and trajectories on the labour market of a sample of almost 1,000 WISE participants. Finally, the role of public policies is at the core of Part IV. In each part, one or two chapters are devoted to transversal European analysis. These transversal chapters are illustrated by shorter chapters focusing on specific countries that reflect the diversity of social enterprise patterns and welfare models across Europe.[10]

Part I is devoted to the analysis of the governance of social enterprise. According to our 'multiple goals – multiple stakeholders' hypothesis, the analysis of Campi, Defourny and Grégoire (Chapter 2) aims to elucidate the specific objectives WISEs pursue and the role the involvement of stakeholders plays within them. More specific insights into this twofold dimension of WISEs are proposed by Hulgård for Danish social enterprises (Chapter 3), by Bucolo for French social enterprises (Chapter 4) and by Borzaga and Loss for Italy (Chapter 5). As social capital may be seen not only as a resource, but also as a goal of the social enterprise, Hulgård and Spear (Chapter 6) analyse its key role for social entrepreneurship. They adopt an institutional perspective, based upon the premise that social capital must be examined in the context of changing institutional configurations.

Contributions to Part II analyse how social enterprises mix different kinds of resources to sustain their multiple goals. Gardin (Chapter 7) invites the reader to go beyond the approach according to which these enterprises mobilize only two types of resources: market resources, like any enterprise, and non-market resources from the public sector, aimed at making up for the lack of productivity and the guidance and training needs of their workers in integration. According to the hypothesis put forward, European social enterprises use a complex mix of resources based on four types of economic relations: the market, redistribution, but also the socio-politically embedded market and reciprocity. More specific analysis of the resource mix of WISEs is proposed for Irish WISEs by O'Shaughnessy in Chapter 8, for Spanish WISEs by Vidal and Claver in Chapter 9 and, finally, for Finnish social enterprises by Pättiniemi in Chapter 10.

The major objective of WISEs is to integrate people who are at risk of permanent exclusion from the labour market back into work, and society in general, through productive acivity. Therefore, Part III is devoted to the analysis of the data that have been collected regarding the profiles and trajectories of 949 disadvantaged workers who entered European WISEs in 2001. Borzaga and Loss (Chapter 11) examine the profiles of these workers with a particular focus on their employment experience and on the channels of entry to the social enterprises. Afterwards, they identify their different integration paths. This flow analysis grasps the evolution in the personal condition of the disadvantaged workers, particularly in terms of income and human capital. Country analyses regarding the trajectories of beneficiaries of WISEs are developed for Portugal by Perista and Nogueira in Chapter 12, for Sweden by Stryjan in Chapter 13 and for Belgium by Nyssens and Platteau in Chapter 14.

The field of social enterprises has been characterized by a movement of institutionalization in the framework of public policies across Europe, even though it varies from one country to the other. Part IV is shaped around the hypothesis that this dynamic of institutionalization can lead to the development of innovative public schemes and, at the same time, to a movement of 'isomorphism' on the part of social enterprises. Bode, Evers and Schultz (Chapter 15) develop an analytical framework in order to grasp the historical dynamics and the possible trends toward isomorphism of this organizational field. Aiken develops this theme in the field of UK social enterprises in Chapter 16. Laville, Lemaître and Nyssens (Chapter 17) show how public policies in the field of social enterprises are the results of interactions between the promoters of the latter and representatives of public bodies. They also depict the different models of public policies to support the mission of social enterprises that exist across Europe. In Chapter 18, Bode, Evers and Schultz analyse the historic dynamic between social enterprises and public policies in Germany.

In the concluding chapter (Chapter 19), Nyssens draws lessons regarding the core hypotheses of the research and tries to develop some guidelines that might be useful to policy makers beyond the wide variety of contexts which always have an important influence on the way social enterprises can emerge and grow across Europe.

Review questions

- Why could one say that social enterprise, as defined by the EMES network, could be seen as a bridge between co-operatives and non-profit organizations?
- How does the ideal-type of a 'multiple goals–multiple resources' social enterprise differ from the image of social enterprise viewed as a business with a social aim?
- Identify some work integration social enterprises in your country and classify them according to the typology suggested in Section 4 of Chapter 1.

Appendix 1 Modes of integration in WISEs*

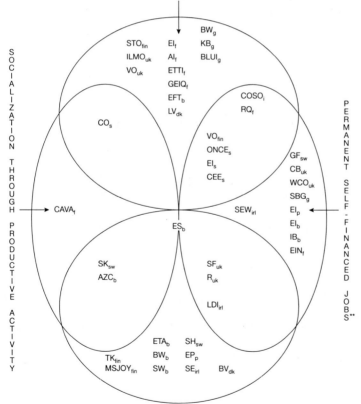

Source: adapted from Davister *et al.* (2004).

* See Appendix 2 for legend.   ** Sometimes supported by short-term subsidies.

Appendix 2 The 44 categories of WISEs and their abbreviations

The categories of WISEs are first mentioned in the language of the concerned country and then in English.

Belgium

EI_b entreprises d'insertion (integration enterprises)

ETA_b entreprises de travail adapté (adapted (*or* sheltered) work enterprises)

EFT_b entreprises de formation par le travail (on-the-job training enterprises)

ES_b entreprises sociales d'insertion non reconnues (work integration social enterprises not accredited by public authorities)

SW_b sociale werkplaatsen (social workshops)

IB_b invoegbedrijven (integration enterprises)

BW_b beschutte werkplaatsen (sheltered workshops)

AZC_b arbeidszorgcentra (work care centres)

Denmark

LV_{dk} lokalt orienterede sociale virksomheder som tilbyder uddannelse og midlertidig beskæftigelse (local community enterprises offering traineeship and temporary work integration)

BV_{dk} beskyttede værksteder (sheltered workshops)

Finland

STO_{fin} sosiaalinen työosuuskunta (labour co-operatives)

VO_{fin} vajaakuntoisten osuuskunta (co-operative social firms for disabled people)

TK_{fin} työkeskus (work centres)

$MSJOY_{fin}$ muut sosiaalialian järjestöjen omistamat yritykset (other enterprises owned by associations for the disabled)

France

$CAVA_f$ centres d'adaptation à la vie active (centres for adaptation to working life)

EI_f entreprises d'insertion (work integration enterprises)

AI_f associations intermédiaires (intermediate voluntary organizations)

RQ_f régies de quartier (neighbourhood enterprises)

$ETTI_f$ entreprises de travail temporaire d'insertion (temporary work integration enterprises)

GEIQ$_f$ groupements d'employeurs pour l'insertion et la qualification (employers' organizations for work integration and training)

EIN$_f$ entreprises insérantes (long-term work integration enterprises)

Germany

SBG$_g$ soziale Betriebe und Genossenschaften (social firms and co-operatives)

KB$_g$ kommunale Beschäftigungsgesellschaften (municipally owned social enterprises)

BW$_g$ Beschäftigungsgesellschaften von Wohlfahrtsverbänden (social enterprises organized by welfare organizations)

BLUI$_g$ Beschäftigungsgesellschaften von lokalen, unabhängigen Initiativen (social enterprises organized by independent local initiatives)

Ireland

SE$_{irl}$ sheltered employment

LD$_{irl}$ local development work integration social enterprises

SEW$_{irl}$ Social Economy (National Programme) work integration social enterprises

Italy

COSO$_i$ co-operative sociali di tipo b (B-type social co-operatives)

Portugal

EI$_p$ empresas de inserção (integration companies)

EP$_p$ emprego protegido (sheltered employment)

Spain

CEE$_s$ centros especiales de empleo (special employment centres)

CO$_s$ centros ocupacionales (sheltered employment centres)

ONCE$_s$ empresas de la Organización Nacional de Ciegos de España (ONCE) (enterprises of the Spanish National Organisation for the Blind)

EI$_s$ empresas de inserción (social integration enterprises (for people at risk of social exclusion))

Sweden

SK$_{sw}$ sociala arbetskooperativ *or* socialkooperativ (social co-operatives)

SH$_{sw}$ Samhall (Samhall network of sheltered workshops)

GF$_{sw}$ grannskapsföretag (community enterprises)

United Kingdom

WCO_{uk}	worker co-operatives
CB_{uk}	community businesses
SF_{uk}	social firms
$ILMO_{uk}$	intermediate labour market organizations
R_{uk}	Remploy (large quasi-state enterprise)
VO_{uk}	voluntary organization with a work integration objective

Source: adapted from Davister *et al.* (2004)

Notes

1 Since the early 1980s, however, Ashoka, an organization founded by B. Drayton, had supported individual entrepreneurs with a social mission who were called 'social entrepreneurs'.

2 See also the definition of social enterprise by the Harvard Business School, http://www.hbs.edu/socialenterprise/whatis.html.

3 The first works by EMES were published in 1999 but this set of criteria had already been identified in the interim reports (EMES Network 1997 and 1998) which were used by the OECD (1999).

4 For an extensive review of these concepts, see Defourny (2001).

5 PERSE is the acronym for the name of the project in French; a translation of the project's full name would be: 'The Socio-Economic Performance of Social Enterprises in the Field of Integration by Work.' This research project was carried out from September 2001 to March 2004; the project was undertaken within the framework of the 'Key Action Improving the Socio-economic Knowledge Base' programme of the European Commission (Research DG, Fifth Framework Programme).

6 We chose the rate of employment as an indicator of the degree of underemployment in European countries, as the rate of unemployment is very sensitive to institutional factors that may vary a lot among countries (for instance, some groups in identical situations may be considered on or out of the labour market, depending on national administrative rules).

7 This project, entitled ELEXIES and carried out in collaboration with the European federations CECOP and ENSIE, had a mainly descriptive objective: it aimed to list and describe the main features – legal frameworks, support and financing organizations, target groups, types of professional training, etc. – of WISEs in 12 member states of the European Union. The results of this work were published in the EMES *Working Papers Series* (www.emes.net).

8 Belgium, Denmark, Finland, France, Germany, Ireland, Italy, Portugal, Spain, Sweden and the UK.

9 Externalities arise when the actions of certain agents have an impact – be it positive or negative – on the well-being of other agents not regulated by the price system. Externalities are collective in nature when they concern the community as a whole, for example when they involve social cohesion, public health or local development.

10 Extensive country reports are available in the EMES *Working Papers Series*, EMES European Research Network: see www.emes.net.

Bibliography

Bachiega, A. and Borzaga, C. (2001) 'Social Enterprises as Incentive Structures', in Borzaga, C. and Defourny, J. (eds) *The Emergence of Social Enterprise*, London and New York: Routledge, 273–95.

Borzaga, C. and Defourny, J. (eds) (2001) *The Emergence of Social Enterprise*, London and New York: Routledge.

Borzaga, C. and Santuari, A. (2001) 'Italy: from Traditional Co-operatives to Innovative Social Enterprises', in Borzaga, C. and Defourny, J. (eds) *The Emergence of Social Enterprise*, London and New York: Routledge, 166–81.

Davister, C. (2004) 'Le capital social dans l'économie sociale d'insertion', *Reflets et perspectives de la vie économique*, XVLII, 2004, 3: 63–72.

Davister, C., Defourny, J. and Grégoire, O. (2004) 'Work Integration Social Enterprises in the European Union: an Overview of Existing Models', *Working Papers Series*, 04/04, Liège: EMES European Research Network.

Dees, J.G. (1998) 'Enterprising Nonprofits', *Harvard Business Review*, January–February, 55–67.

Dees, J.G. (2001) 'The Meaning of Social Entrepreneurship'. Available at www.fuqua.duke.edu/centers/case/leaders/resources.htm.

Defourny, J. (2001) 'From Third Sector to Social Enterprise', in Borzaga, C. and Defourny, J. (eds) *The Emergence of Social Enterprise*, London and New York: Routledge, 1–28.

DiMaggio, P.J. and Powell, W.W. (1983) 'The Iron Cage Revisited: Institutional Isomorphism and Collective Rationality in Organisational Fields', *American Sociological Review*, 48: 147–60.

DTI (2002) *Social Enterprise: a Strategy for Success*, London: Department of Trade and Industry. Available at www.sbs.gov.uk/SBS_Gov_files/socialenterprise/SEA StrategyforSuccess.pdf.

EMES European Research Network (1997) *Semestrial Progress Report*.

EMES European Research Network (1998) *Semestrial Progress Report*.

EMES European Research Network (1999) *Semestrial Progress Report*.

Evers, A. (2001) 'The Significance of Social Capital in the Multiple Goal and Resource Structure of Social Enterprises', in Borzaga, C. and Defourny, J. (eds) *The Emergence of Social Enterprise*, London, New York: Routledge, 296–311.

Evers, A. and Laville, J.-L. (eds) (2004) *The Third Sector in Europe*, Cheltenham and Northampton, MA: Edward Elgar.

Grenier, P. (2003) 'Reclaiming Enterprise for the Social Good: the Political Climate for Social Entrepreneurship in UK', paper presented at the *32nd Annual ARNOVA Conference*, Denver, CO.

Hansmann, H. (1980) 'The Role of Nonprofit Enterprise', *Yale Law Journal*, 89: 835–901.

Haugh, H. (2005) 'A Research Agenda for Social Entrepreneurship', *Social Enterprise Journal*, 1, 1: 1–12.

Kerlin, J. (2005) 'Social Enterprise in the United States and Europe: Understanding and Learning from our Differences', paper presented at the *First European Conference of the ISTR and EMES Network on the Concepts of the Third Sector: The European Debate*, Paris.

Laville, J.-L. and Nyssens, M. (2001) 'The Social Enterprise. Towards a Theoretical Socio-economic Approach', in Borzaga, C. and Defourny, J. (eds) *The Emergence of Social Enterprise*, London and New York: Routledge, 312–32.

Lewis, J. (2004) 'The Third Sector, the State and the European Union', in Evers, A. and Laville, J.-L. (eds) *The Third Sector in Europe*, Cheltenham and Northampton, MA: Edward Elgar, 169–87.

LSE (2004) 'What is civil society?', London: London School of Economics, Centre for Civil Society. Available at www.lse.ac.uk/collections/CCS/what_is_civil_society.htm.

Nicholls, A. (2005) 'Measuring Impact in Social Entrepreneurship: New Accountabilities to Stakeholders and Investors?', *Seminar on Social Enterprises*, Milton Keynes University, Milton Keynes.

OECD (1999) *Social Enterprises*, LEED Programme, Paris: OECD.

Polanyi, K. (1944) *The Great Transformation; the Political and Economic Origins of our Time*, New York: Farrar and Rinehart.

Putnam, R. (1993) 'The Prosperous Community: Social Capital and Public Life', *The American Prospect*, 13: 35–42.

Steinberg, R. (2004) *The Economics of Nonprofit Enterprises*, Cheltenham and Northampton, MA: Edward Elgar.

Young, D. (2001) 'Social Enterprises in the United States: Alternate Identities and Forms', *International Conference on Social Enterprise*, Trento.

Young, D. and Salamon, L. (2002) 'Commercialization, Social Ventures, and For-Profit Competition', in Salamon, L.M. (ed.) *The State of Nonprofit America*, Washington, DC: Brookings Institution, 423–46.

Part I

The governance of social enterprise

2 Work integration social enterprises: are they multiple-goal and multi-stakeholder organizations?

Sara Campi, Jacques Defourny and Olivier Grégoire

Overview

The objective of this chapter is to analyse the multi-stakeholder and multiple-goal structures of social enterprises on the basis of the data collected on 160 WISEs. After reading this chapter, the reader should:

- understand the theoretical frameworks supporting the 'multiple-goal, multi-stakeholder' social enterprise ideal-type;
- grasp the extent to which empirical evidence confirms this ideal-type;
- identify further lines of empirical analyses to understand the dynamics of stakeholders.

Introduction

A multi-stakeholder character and a multiple-goal nature are claimed to be important aspects of social enterprises as they were previously analysed by the EMES European Research Network (Borzaga and Defourny 2001). However, although these features have been underlined by various authors in theoretical terms, empirical evidence of their existence is still rather limited. This chapter, therefore, aims to take a step forward by conducting a deeper analysis of multi-stakeholder and multiple-goal characters in work integration social enterprises (WISEs) across Europe.

In the following pages, we first consider the multiple-goal aspect, providing some theoretical elements that are useful in interpreting its origins and its differentiating potential. Theories are then tested against the data collected during the PERSE project. The second section starts with a brief overview of the economic and organizational literature on multi-stakeholder topics; it also presents the approach we chose and the data we collected to check whether or not WISEs are multi-stakeholder enterprises. The third section examines the reasons that could explain the involvement of various categories of stakeholder in the ownership structure and the decision-making process of such organizations.

1 The multiple-goal nature of WISEs

1.1 Theoretical insights

Third sector literature often stresses, explicitly or implicitly, the fact that non-profit organizations (NPOs) are more likely and better able to combine several objectives than traditional for-profit firms which, in neo-classical economic theory, are generally supposed to have one single major goal, i.e. profit maximization, dominating all other possible achievements (Weisbrod 1988; Ben-Ner and Van Hoomissen 1991; Hansmann 1996, among many others). In their attempt to provide 'building blocks' for a socio-economic theory of social enterprises, Laville and Nyssens (2001) went further by suggesting that such a combination of different goals is embedded in the very nature of social enterprises as conceptualized by the EMES European Research Network. In their view, social enterprises pursue at least three different categories of goal:

- *Social goals*, connected to the particular mission of social enterprises, i.e. to benefit the community. This 'general' goal can be expressed as a number of more specific ones, such as meeting the social needs of a particular category of citizens (socially excluded people, families with children or elders to look after, immigrants, people with specific health problems, etc.) or improving life quality in deprived areas.
- *Economic goals*, connected to the entrepreneurial nature of social enterprises: ensuring the provision of specific goods or services, achieving financial sustainability in the medium/long run, efficiency, effectiveness, competitive advantage, etc.
- *Socio-political (civic) goals*, connected to the fact that social enterprises come from a 'sector' traditionally involved in socio-political action: proposing and promoting a new model of economic development; promoting the democratization of decision-making processes in economic spheres; promoting the inclusion of marginalized parts of the population, etc.

It should be noticed that although these categories of goal may seem clearly separated in some cases, in other cases the boundaries are rather blurred. For example, when the production activity deals with services that are clearly of public interest (as in the case of recycling activities, environmental services, elderly care, etc.), social and economic goals cannot easily be separated one from the other.

A difference between traditional third sector organizations and social enterprises lies in the fact that the multiple-goal nature of the latter has an intrinsic character. In traditional third sector organizations, the co-existence of various categories of goals is not so clearly marked: in most traditional associations, the commercial dimension and the commitment to economic goals are usually significantly lower than in social enterprises, whereas traditional co-operatives do not generally pursue the general interest in the same way as social enterprises do (Borzaga and Santuari 2003).

When social enterprises are engaged in the occupational and social integration of disadvantaged people, as is the case for those analysed here, the simultaneous presence of different goals is expected to be particularly evident, since these enterprises are supposed to combine goals of the training and work integration of disadvantaged people, the production of goods and services (whether of public or private interest), as well as the promotion of more socially inclusive and labour-intensive economic development (Evers 2001).

If we now look at the managerial literature on organizational goals, things appear much less clear. As early as in the late 1930s, for example, Barnard (1938) showed that, from an organizational point of view, the for-profit or non-profit nature was not a good indicator of organizational diversity since each organization – independently of the distribution of profits – could be seen as a 'co-operative system' within which the entrance and permanence of actors was due to the balance between incentives and contributions they exchanged with the system. In other words, all individuals in an organization have personal goals that need to be satisfied through the pursuit of the organizational mission, thus determining the need for the organization to take into account such a diversity of individual objectives to guarantee its survival. Such a line of thought has been particularly elaborated by authors such as Freeman (1984) who developed the idea that organizations have various stakeholders, whose 'stakes' have to be considered by managers in developing organizational processes. Others, such as Mintzberg (1983), have also stressed the existence, within all organizations, of a system of social and economic goals.

Many other authors, especially those linked to the 'new institutional economics', underline the interpretative poverty of the simple profit-maximization objective in analysing modern enterprises, which are increasingly compelled by market dynamics to take into account stakeholders' specific needs (Milgrom and Roberts 1992).

Finally, from an operational perspective, it can be noted that increasing numbers of traditional enterprises claim concern for goals other than pure economic ones. In this way, 'corporate social responsibility' (CSR) practices are put forward to demonstrate enterprises' commitment to attend not only to economic goals but also to the social and environmental needs of stakeholders and the community.

This brief literature overview suggests that social objectives are not unusual in traditional for-profit enterprises or, in other words, that in terms of goals the border separating traditional enterprises from social enterprises is not a clear-cut one. Nevertheless, the economic objectives of social enterprises are expected to focus on the production of goods and services per se, as responses to addressed needs – or, in the specific case of WISEs, as a means to achieve the work integration of disadvantaged workers – and on financial sustainability rather than on profit maximization and financial return. As a corollary, social objectives are supposed to be incorporated at the very core of social enterprises' goals, whereas they appear as more 'peripheral' in for-profit enterprises.

1.2 Empirical evidence

The existence of a multiple-goal structure was analysed in the PERSE project by asking managers of the 158 WISEs that formed the sample to indicate the goals pursued by their organization. More precisely, interviewees were asked to identify such goals within three categories of objectives defined on the basis of some previous EMES work referring specifically to WISEs (Evers 2001): occupational and social integration of the workers; production of goods and services; and advocacy and lobbying. A fourth category was also available to allow for any other kinds of goal.

At this first level, the 'multiple-goal' hypothesis finds a very strong support: 154 organizations out of 158 were considered by their manager to have at least two objectives.[1] More precisely, 97 per cent of the organizations in the sample pursue an objective of occupational and social integration as well as an objective of production of goods or services, and nearly 90 per cent also mentioned an advocacy and lobbying objective. Only 10 per cent of the WISEs surveyed declared that they had goals they classified in the 'other' category: community renewal through solidarity and self-help, environmental protection, innovation in the provision of social services, promotion of entrepreneurial behaviour within the community, etc.

Of course, it was necessary to go beyond such a superficial view, and especially to look at the *relative importance* the interviewees gave to the various categories of goals. This was done from two different perspectives. First, managers were requested to rank the categories of goal, from one to four in order of decreasing importance.

As shown in Table 2.1, the results suggest a quite clear order of importance: the social and occupational integration of disadvantaged workers is considered as the most important objective by 77 per cent of the WISEs surveyed, the production of goods and services is cited as the second most important goal by 55 per cent and advocacy and lobbying as the third objective by 69 per cent.

Second, the respective weights of the various goals were computed to take into account information such as the fact that the production objective, although second in most cases, comes first for 30 per cent of WISEs.

Table 2.1 Goal ranking in European WISEs (%)

Goal	Rank 1	Rank 2	Rank 3	Rank 4	Total
Occupational and social integration	77	18	5	0	100
Production	30	55	15	0	100
Advocacy and lobbying	5	19	69	7	100
Other	25	19	25	31	100

The results of such calculations, as presented in Table 2.2, show that the respective weights of the two major categories of goal come closer: on average, at the European level, their weights are then 41 per cent for the occupational and social integration objective and 35 per cent for the production goal, while the advocacy and lobbying objective matters for 21 per cent (significantly more than the 'other' category, which weighs only 3 per cent).[2] This picture is confirmed by the analysis at the national level: these weights stay within the same range and never go beyond 47 per cent for a single goal when they are calculated within each national sample of WISEs.

However, such a strict ranking still does not provide any information about the distance between objectives nor about the relations between the different goals. It is why the survey tried to fine-tune the results by focusing

Table 2.2 The respective weights of goals within European WISEs* (%)

	Occupational and social integration	Production	Advocacy and lobbying	Other	Total
Belgium	39	36	20	4	100
Denmark	43	28	28	1	100
Finland	34	39	24	3	100
France	43	34	23	0	100
Germany	43	30	27	1	100
Ireland	34	42	21	3	100
Italy	46	38	15	2	100
Portugal	47	35	18	0	100
Spain	43	32	20	4	100
Sweden	44	32	16	8	100
United Kingdom	35	39	23	3	100
Average	41	35	21	3	100

* The number of organizations that declared that they pursued the goal was weighted by the value of the rank attributed to the goal (values being respectively 4, 3, 2 and 1 for ranks 1, 2, 3 and 4). The results were then converted into percentages of the total.

on the way WISEs balance their production goal and their work integration objective.[3]

Answers here reveal that 50 per cent of managers consider both objectives as equally important while 34 per cent see the production activity as subordinated to the work integration goal. This latter situation is particularly true for a majority of WISEs in countries such as Denmark, Germany or France, where most public subsidies they receive seem clearly linked to active labour market policies and/or to specific profiles of disadvantaged unemployed persons. However, in some cases where the work integration goal prevailed at first, a tendency to better balance both objectives was observed as WISEs were increasingly pushed towards the private market. Such a trend is clearly identified in Italy (see Chapter 5 of this book).

On the other hand, the production goal may be expected to be particularly important when WISEs produce public or quasi-public goods or services, for instance within contracts with local or regional public authorities. As a matter of fact, a subgroup of WISEs insist on the fact that their core mission is to participate in local development, especially in disadvantaged communities, by delivering a range of goods and services and that, *in this process*, they create training and employment opportunities for marginalized groups in the local labour market. Therefore, for this kind of social enterprise, the mission of 'integration of disadvantaged workers through a productive activity', while important, remains in the background of their mission. This is the case, for example, for local development initiatives in Ireland (O'Hara and O'Shaughnessy 2004) or community businesses in the UK (Aiken and Spear 2005). However, on the basis of the data collected during the PERSE project, it was not possible to find any significant correlation between the relative importance of goals and the nature of the goods and services produced.

In spite of such diversity, all these results strongly confirm the hypothesis according to which a majority of European WISEs have a multiple-goal structure, characterized by quite an equal relevance of the two major objectives hypothesized as typical of this specific kind of social enterprise, namely the occupational and social integration of disadvantaged people and the production of goods and services.

Finally, when asked about the origin or source of their WISEs' goals, practically all managers referred to the original intentions of the founders, which appeared to be strongly related to community needs (82 per cent) and labour market problems (78 per cent).[4] Such a frequent reference to the needs of the community as a source of the organization's mission is certainly in line with the hypothesis put forward by Evers (2001), according to whom the multiple-goal structure of social enterprises is, above all, dominated by the intention to serve the community, this latter vocation itself being a key element of the EMES definition of social enterprise.

2 Are WISEs multi-stakeholder organizations?

2.1 A brief conceptual overview

The idea of the multi-stakeholder nature of organizations can be found in several parts of the literature on the third sector: it appears in the economic literature analysing the reasons for the existence of the third sector (Ben-Ner and Van Hoomissen 1991; Hansmann 1996; Krashinsky 1997), its evolution over time and its comparative advantage (Borzaga and Mittone 1997) and the specific characteristics of its organizations (Gui 1991; Pestoff 1995); it also appears in more managerial and organizational analyses, focusing on more practical aspects, such as stakeholders' participation in the decision-making processes, stakeholders' role in boards, outcomes of participation etc. (Middleton 1987; Cornforth 2003). As a matter of fact, various books have been published to provide social entrepreneurs with tools to develop initiatives and to deal with a diversity of stakeholders.[5]

What is a multi-stakeholder structure?

Nowadays, one of the most widely used definitions of stakeholders is the one by Freeman (1984), who stresses the need for management to be responsive to stakeholders, that is to 'any group or individual who can affect or is affected by the achievement of an organization's purpose' since they have 'some inalienable rights to participate in decisions that substantially affect their welfare or involve their being used as a means to another's ends' (as quoted by Evan and Freeman 1993: 82).

As already stated by Thompson (1967), the existence of a multiplicity of subjects affected by the organization's action and able to affect it is typical of all organizations, in the perspective of open systems. Therefore, in such a broad approach, all organizations might be considered as being multi-stakeholder. Moreover, as observed by Donaldson and Preston (1995), anyone looking into this large and evolving literature with a critical eye will observe that the concepts of stakeholder, stakeholder model, stakeholder management, and stakeholder theory are explained and used by various authors in very different ways and supported (or critiqued) with diverse and often contradictory evidence and arguments.

In the third sector literature, however, there is a quite clear idea about the innovation embedded in the multi-stakeholder approach: the innovation consists in the 'internalization' of the stakeholders, i.e. the shift from a traditional view of stakeholders as external subjects (often generating costs for the organization) to a new one, which focuses on the participation of these subjects as internal components (Pestoff 1995). Various categories of stakeholder can easily be identified in third sector organizations, although they are not all necessarily 'internalized': workers, managers, volunteers, donors, consumers or users, public authorities, the local community, unions, other third sector organizations, private firms or any other category having specific interests or relations with the organization.

Regarding the nature of stakeholders' involvement, various approaches may be found in the literature, but it seems useful here to point out two distinct perspectives:

- On the one hand, Pestoff (1995) stresses, above all, the involvement of stakeholders in the organizational decision-making process. The absence of reference to membership means that the multi-stakeholder feature is connected to the possibility for stakeholders to participate in the decision-making process, be it as formal members of the organization or as subjects who are not necessarily members but are formally involved in the board.
- On the other hand, Borzaga and Mittone (1997) as well as Laville and Nyssens (2001) explicitly define the multi-stakeholder structure as a structure in which various stakeholders are supposed to be members and therefore co-owners of the organization. In such a perspective, the membership-ownership structure is the key indicator to be analysed in order to identify the various categories of stakeholders.

How does a multi-stakeholder structure work?

According to the literature, the practical functioning of multi-stakeholder organizations depends on a variety of factors, first of all the categories of stakeholder involved in the decision-making processes (Jordan 1990), the nature of their stake, the intensity and duration of these stakes (Pestoff 1995) and the balance of incentives and contributions connected with their participation.

In analysing the concrete functioning of multi-stakeholder organizations, it seems important to consider the characteristics of participation arrangements (Jordan 1990; Helmig *et al.* 2004). Are the stakeholders involved in the decision-making process also members of the organization? What are the rules of access to the decision-making process? What are the relative weight and influence of each category of stakeholder? Is the decision-making process democratic? What is the relative importance of formal and informal processes in decision-making participation?

Informal elements of participation seem to be particularly important in third sector organizations, where it is not unusual to find groups of members interacting outside meetings to discuss board business without the participation of stakeholders who, although formally involved in the decision-making process, are not part of the informal network 'governing' the organization (Middleton 1987); and conversely, there might be people who take part in this informal network without being members and without being involved in the formal decision-making process.

2.2 Empirical evidence

Single- versus multi-stakeholder WISEs

For its empirical work, the PERSE project first adopted the approach put forward by Borzaga and Mittone (1997), according to whom the multi-stakeholder nature of a social enterprise is connected with its membership and ownership structure. With this idea in mind, managers of all 158 European WISEs were asked to characterize the membership-ownership structure of their organization. Although it was not easy to make the notion of 'stakeholders' understood exactly in the same way by all interviewees, the emphasis was clearly put on the existence, or not, of different categories of stakeholders among members/owners. Answers to this first question indicate that a majority of European WISEs (58 per cent) are seen as multi-stakeholder structures while 42 per cent are characterized as single-stakeholder organizations. As shown in the first column of Table 2.3, WISEs in the second group are particularly numerous in two countries: in Portugal, all WISEs in the sample have a single stakeholder, which is generally a larger organization that founded the WISE as a contribution to top-down public strategies against unemployment; these founding bodies may be private social solidarity institutions, *misericordias* linked to the Catholic Church, mutual benefit associations or co-operatives (Perista and Nogueira 2004); in Spain, the same explanation holds for foundations in the case of six WISEs, and a single-stakeholder category was also identified in three workers' co-operatives and three other initiatives launched by groups of citizens (Vidal and Claver 2004).

Table 2.3 Distribution of WISEs according to the number of stakeholder categories involved (%)

	Single-stakeholder organizations	2 different categories	3 different categories	4 different categories	5 different categories	6 different categories	More than 6 different categories
Belgium	0	67	13	13	7	0	0
Denmark	23	15	15	0	15	31	1
Finland	43	14	29	14	0	0	0
France	36	21	21	7	14	0	1
Germany	50	36	14	0	0	0	0
Ireland	17	25	17	33	8	0	0
Italy	20	53	20	7	0	0	0
Portugal	100	0	0	0	0	0	0
Spain	80	13	0	7	0	0	0
Sweden	40	13	27	7	7	6	0
United Kingdom	33	8	17	33	8	0	1
Total	42	25	15	10	5	3	0

As far as WISEs' legal forms are concerned, 64 per cent of the WISEs surveyed proved to be co-operatives or associations, which is not surprising since social enterprises were defined from the outset as third sector organizations.[6] In order to find out whether WISEs' legal forms constitute an indicator of their single- or multi-stakeholder nature, we cross-analysed the data on both variables. Remembering that co-operatives have a single-stakeholder tradition,[7] and that, even nowadays, their statutes often admit but do not usually impose the participation of the various stakeholders,[8] we could have expected this legal form to be more frequently associated with the single-stakeholder character. However, analysis at the national level reveals that legal status constitutes a weak indicator of whether a WISE has a single- or multi-stakeholder nature: the choice of a multi-stakeholder status instead tends to depend on the autonomous decision of its founders (more generally, members/owners) within legal frameworks that often permit – explicitly or implicitly – but do not require the involvement of more than one category of stakeholders.[9]

Coming back now to the 58 per cent of WISEs described as multi-stakeholder organizations, it appeared that the diversity of legal forms and requirements across countries made an aggregate analysis of more precise features quite difficult, at least with the membership-ownership approach adopted so far. Therefore, we chose to go further with multi-stakeholder structures by looking at the composition of boards, and asked managers to identify categories of stakeholders within their board. In doing so, we in a way combined and balanced the two above-mentioned conceptual approaches to stakeholder involvement. The results, as shown in the remaining columns of Table 2.3, indicate that the number of stakeholder categories ranges from two to six, with an average of 3.1. Among interesting results, one can mention the fact that about half of Danish WISEs appear to have a very high number – five or six – of distinct categories of stakeholders. As a matter of fact, Chapter 3 of this book clearly explains that WISEs in Denmark often involve a large number of partners in their founding and development process.

The functioning of multi-stakeholder WISEs

The data collected during the PERSE project also allow us to analyse several aspects of the practical functioning of WISEs, especially those with a multi-stakeholder structure. First, as far as the rules governing the decision-making process are concerned, an overwhelming majority of multi-stakeholder WISEs (87 per cent) appear to have democratic decision-making processes, i.e. the 'one member, one vote' rule is applied in their governing bodies, including their general assembly. This suggests that the involvement of stakeholders leads to their having a real voting power – and not just a symbolic one – in the organization. Such a statement, however, only refers to the formal level and, as already underlined, third sector organizations can be characterized, probably more than other kinds of enterprises, by a high degree of informality, often affecting the decision-making processes as well. This means that a formal presence in democratic boards or assemblies might prove insufficient to participate in decisions taken outside the institutional bodies by the most influential persons or groups. This is why the PERSE research project also tried to collect information on the actual influence of stakeholders.

In order to do so, managers were asked to evaluate the impact, in the decision-making process, of each category of stakeholder represented in the board of their WISE.[10] The number of board members belonging to each category was also taken as an indicator of its relative importance. Combining both sources of information, percentages were computed to reflect, although with clear limits, the actual influence of the various categories of stakeholder.

These results, as presented in Table 2.4, first suggest that staff and volunteers are the most influential groups (21 per cent and 20 per cent of the 'total influence' respectively) when WISEs from all countries are taken together, while private consumers and participants – i.e. workers in the integration process – are the weakest (5 per cent and 7 per cent respectively).[11] At the level of each country, the analysis also suggests the prevalence of one or two groups, but these may vary significantly:

- *volunteers* in France (36 per cent), Germany (25 per cent) and Spain (44 per cent);
- *staff* in Belgium (24 per cent), Finland (26 per cent), Italy (55 per cent) and Sweden (24 per cent);
- *participants* in Sweden (24 per cent);
- *business organizations* in the United Kingdom (25 per cent);
- *government representatives* in Denmark (25 per cent).

However, the most interesting result from Table 2.4 lies in the fact that in all countries but one (Italy), the actual power seems to be shared among several stakeholder categories, none of these being deemed to have an overwhelming influence on the boards.

Finally, it is also possible to investigate whether or not the influence of the various stakeholder categories is related to the type of decisions to be taken. Information collected from managers does not show significant changes in the estimated influence of each group when decisions refer to the production process, to the work integration mission or to advocacy and political matters.

To sum up, the results presented in this section tend to support two major ideas. First, the multi-stakeholder structure of WISEs is not just a theoretical characteristic of an 'ideal-type' of social enterprise: in the field of work integration, a majority of social enterprises as surveyed in our project seem to confirm such a feature, even though it is also clear that a

Table 2.4 Influence of stakeholder categories in multi-stakeholder WISEs* (%)

	Users/ customers	Volunteers	Staff	Participants	Business	Government	NPOs	Other**	Total***
Belgium	1	13	24	10	9	10	19	15	100
Denmark	9	7	17	7	13	25	18	5	100
Finland	0	6	26	21	10	10	15	13	100
France	10	36	10	3	10	10	13	10	100
Germany	0	25	12	18	10	18	18	0	100
Italy	4	29	55	1	3	0	1	6	100
Spain	0	44	28	0	4	0	15	9	100
Sweden	12	6	24	24	9	15	3	8	100
UK	3	13	4	0	25	19	19	17	100
Average	5	20	21	7	10	13	14	10	100

*Portugal is not included in this analysis since all the organizations surveyed in this country were single-stakeholder (see Table 2.3).

**This category includes: private individuals (other than consumers), local community representatives, private financing bodies, experts, etc.

***Totals may differ from 100 per cent owing to rounding.

significant proportion of WISEs are better described as single-stakeholder organizations; this is, in particular, true of WISEs whose creation was due to a 'mother' structure, in a top-down strategy. Second, the existence of several stakeholder categories, when confirmed, is not only formally reflected in the composition of the boards, but also generally means a real sharing of voting power and actual influence among these categories.

3 Reasons for the existence of multi-stakeholder WISEs

The literature has put forward several possible reasons to account for the existence of multi-stakeholder organizations.[12] Rather than seeing them as hypotheses to be tested empirically here, we will review some of these theoretical views and just refer briefly to some of our data when feasible.

3.1 *Ensuring organizational stability and resources*

From an organizational perspective, some authors view the board as the institutional level whose task is to manage the interdependencies between the organization and its environment; external parties are then involved in the decision-making process in order to ensure organizational stability. In other words, multi-stakeholder structures are an organizational answer to the needs of involvement of the social actors that are necessary for the birth and the survival of social enterprises.[13] In this perspective, a multi-stakeholder board can (Middleton 1987):

- better ensure resources (including legitimacy) to the organization through the participation of governmental bodies, donors and other subjects capable of delivering strategic resources;[14]
- accelerate the internal adjustments needed to meet evolving environmental demands, thanks to the involvement of clients and other third sector organizations;
- reduce external constraints by influencing external conditions to the advantage of the organization, by internalizing stakeholders such as governmental bodies (in charge of policy making), users and other third sector organizations (potential partners in lobbying projects).

As to the idea of better ensuring resources, we cross-analysed the results of the study of WISEs' resource mix (see Chapter 7 of this book) and those deriving from our analysis of boards' composition. Along with the five types of WISE defined on the basis of their resource mix, we identified, through hierarchical clustering (Ward algorithm), six different types of board according to the prevalent group(s) of stakeholders which might be seen in this context as major actors or channels for key resources.[15] The analysis shows very little correlation between the resource mix of WISEs and the composition of their boards. However, such a statistical exercise does not allow us to discard the hypothesis according to which the presence within boards of specific categories of stakeholders constitutes a means of better ensuring the organization's resources: just the presence of a stakeholder category in the board might be more important than its actual weight or prevalence for securing a specific type of resource.

The other two arguments refer to the boards' capacity to avoid threats to organizational stability, which could be improved by involving particular categories of stakeholder. These two points, however, do not really differ from the former argument when it comes to threats that are strongly related to the availability of resources. As far as other types of threat are concerned, there appear to be serious obstacles to translating such an idea into testable hypotheses: not only would the threats to be avoided not be easy to observe, but it would also probably be even harder to establish a clear relation of causality with the involvement of specific categories of stakeholder.

3.2 Multi-stakeholder structures as an instrument to manage the mix of goals

Extending to social enterprises a line of reasoning developed by Tirole (1994) for government institutions, Bacchiega and Borzaga (2001) note that the presence of multiple – potentially conflicting – objectives is more likely when control rights are shared among different categories of stakeholder. This, of course, is also true for non-profit organizations in general. In such a perspective, the multiplicity of organizational objectives and the involvement of a variety of stakeholders may be regarded as being tightly connected. Going a step further, Evers (2001) suggests that involving diverse stakeholder categories in the decision-making process is a valid instrument to manage the balance between multiple goals as well as to safeguard commitments to a set of goals of different types in the organization; this balance would be unlikely to be achieved in a homogeneous board, composed of few categories of stakeholders, and where the degree to which diverse opinions are expressed is low (Middleton 1987).

One empirical way, among others, to look at this hypothesized relation between multiple-goal and multi-stakeholder features of social enterprises is to compare the goal structure of single-stakeholder and multi-stakeholder WISEs. Such a comparison is provided in Table 2.5 on the basis of the relative importance of goals in both types of WISEs. However, these results do not show any significant difference in the goal structures of single- and multi-stakeholder organizations.[16]

Apart from the limits of our empirical survey, such an absence of difference might be explained by the strength of what is shared by all stakeholder categories or by those that are most influential: while conflicting interests may be easily identified between shareholders, managers, workers, unions and other stakeholders in for-profit companies, social enterprises are often founded on the basis of a vision, a mission and values widely shared by the stakeholders involved. Constraints on the distribution of profits, which lead to their reinvestment for the achievement of the organization's mission and thus reduce the range of possible uses of the residual income (Hansmann 1996), as well as democratic rules in the main controlling bodies, probably express and, at the same time, reinforce such a

Table 2.5 Relative importance of goals in single-stakeholder and multi-stakeholder WISEs* (%)

Multi- or single-stakeholder nature	Occupational and social integration	Production	Advocacy and lobbying	Other	Total
Single-stakeholder WISEs	42.4	34.4	21.2	2.0	100
Multi-stakeholder WISEs	39.8	35.5	21.7	3.0	100
All WISEs (single-and multi-stakeholder)**	41.0	35.0	21.4	2.6	100

*The respective weights of the various goals have been calculated as explained in the note to Table 2.2.

**The results in the bottom line are the same as those presented in Table 2.2 but they have been calculated here as the weighted average of the results for single-stakeholder organizations and multi-stakeholder ones.

process of convergence among stakeholders. Chapter 4 of this book, which analyses the functioning of French WISEs, supports this view: although practically two-thirds of WISEs surveyed in France were seen as multi-stakeholder organizations, this chapter underlines the importance of these common grounds and values among stakeholders from the founding of the organization.

This, of course, should not be understood as meaning that conflicting interests do not exist in WISEs; for instance, customers' requirements as to the quality of goods or services and delivery times may well come in opposition to the workers' interests in terms of time needed for learning and acquiring technical skills. However, these two categories, which are the most likely to have conflicting goals, are most often weakly represented in boards, as shown in Table 2.4. And as far as the other stakeholder categories are concerned, it seems likely that they are more aware of the need to balance the two main goals of WISEs and to see them as intrinsically connected. In other words, board members may have been deemed to belong to different categories on the basis of their 'status' towards the WISE (customers, participants, etc.); but such a perception may have hidden the fact that their actual stakes are not necessarily divergent and that in many cases they are very convergent.

In any case, the analysis of WISEs in our sample tends to demonstrate that single-stakeholder organizations and multi-stakeholder ones (which, as already mentioned, account respectively for 42 per cent and 58 per cent of the sample) in fact share many organizational features: they are similar in terms of legal status, goals and decision-making rules. Moreover, the multi-stakeholder character of more than half the WISEs surveyed does not seem to be connected to their multiple-goal character, which is in fact shared by those WISEs described as single-stakeholder organizations.

To go further, it would be necessary to collect and analyse data about the informal participation of stakeholders. This might be done in two directions at least. First, it would be interesting to conduct a deeper analysis of the real, actual influence of stakeholders in the decision-making processes. In this perspective, stakeholders' participation should be examined not only on the basis of managers' – as in this project – but also of other stakeholders' perceptions, in order to have a broader view as well as to analyse informal coalitions of members, circulation of information, emergence of leadership, etc. A second path would lead outside the formal governing bodies in order to observe the informal ways and influences through which WISEs are related to the local community, customers, beneficiaries, public authorities, partners, etc., without these formally participating in the board. This, of course, would be particularly crucial to better understand the governance and the behaviour of those WISEs described here as single-stakeholder organizations.

Finally, another way to test the existence of significant differences between single- and multi-stakeholder WISEs would be to compare their social and economic performance, i.e. the extent to which their goals are actually achieved. Indeed, indicators of performance would help to see whether organizations involving only one category of stakeholders in their board would be able to achieve a different level of performance from multi-stakeholder ones through continuous and informal contacts with interested parties (consumers, public bodies, other third sector organizations, etc.) which are not formally part of the decision-making process.

3.3 Involvement of stakeholders as a result of a cost-benefit analysis

The participation of a category of stakeholders implies costs and benefits, both for the organization and for the stakeholders considered. From an organizational perspective, it is thus possible to consider the issue of the balance between contributions and incentives for all subjects participating in the organization. This perspective, in fact, seems useful in trying to interpret the emergence of multi-stakeholder structures as an organizational answer to the needs of involvement of the social actors that are necessary for the birth and the survival of social enterprises. Moreover, it also seems to be functional to evaluate and interpret the presence of some actors and the absence of others in organizations (Jordan 1990): both the stakeholders and the organization decide to participate/ask for participation according to the balance between contributions and incentives.

Major works in this field of investigation are those conducted by Ben-Ner and Van Hoomissen (1991) and by Hansmann (1996). Analysing the emergence of non-profit organizations, the first two authors suggest that such organizations will be owned and controlled by those stakeholders for whom the net expected benefits of ownership are higher than the net benefits they might expect from alternative solutions. As to Hansmann, he distinguishes between the 'costs of market contracting' and the 'costs of ownership'. Involving a stakeholder in an organization's ownership reduces the costs of market contracting, especially in some situations (such as the production of services that have some characteristics of quasi-public goods, as is the case for work integration services). On the other hand, it increases the costs of ownership, in particular as regards the decision-making process, since the interests of the various categories of stakeholders may become more conflicting. The extent to which these costs will vary depends upon the stakeholders involved and the degree of heterogeneity of their interests. Comparing such costs to advantages to be received from being involved can lead each stakeholder to decide to become an owner or not. At a theoretical level, Hansmann goes on to state that the organizational form chosen for an enterprise should be the one that minimizes the costs of market contracting and the costs of ownership for all stakeholders concerned by the enterprise's activities. Although Hansmann seems to consider that only one stakeholder category will finally become involved, he paves the way for the same kind of analysis in cases where several different stake-holders do actually share the ownership and control of an organization.

Such a line of thought does not lead easily to testable hypotheses, as the outcomes of multi-stakeholder structures appear to be, like any other social phenomenon, very complex and multifaceted. General considerations include, for instance, the fact that the multiplicity of opinions in the boards can sometimes be interpreted as a positive element, because it stimulates innovation both in social and economic patterns (Laville and Nyssens 2001), but also as a negative feature, since it may cause inefficiency within the board. In other words, the heterogeneity of the board's membership actu-ally makes the decision-making process longer and more complex (Borzaga and Mittone 1997; Hirschman 1980), sometimes leading to the phenome-non of 'noisy boards', which has consequences not only on efficiency but also on the ability to deal with crucial business and to support operational management activities (Middleton 1987); but on the other hand, the hetero-geneity of the board also has 'trust generation effects', emerging in a multi-faceted social environment where conflict is replaced by fruitful discussions and social capital creation (Laville and Nyssens 2001).

Conclusions

The first achievement of our research has been to strongly confirm the multiple-goal structure of European WISEs: nearly all the organizations in the sample analysed declared that they had more than one goal. Moreover, these objectives, as had been hypothesized, belong in an over-whelming majority of cases to three main categories: occupational and social integration, production of goods and services, and lobbying and advocacy. The most distinctive feature of WISEs, however, is probably the fact that the first two categories of goal are quite equally embedded in most organizations in the sample. Indeed, such an integration of social and economic objectives seems to draw a line between social enterprises, on the one hand, and for-profit companies, on the other, although the latter increasingly claim they are concerned with social and environmental objectives and not just profit maximization.

These results come from the analysis of both single-stakeholder organiza-tions and multi-stakeholder ones, thus confirming that it is a characteristic of all the social enterprises engaged in the social and occupational integra-tion of disadvantaged people. As regards WISEs' goals structure, it is also noteworthy that the multiplicity of objectives in these organizations can derive not only from the existence of social and occupational integration goals and production ones but also from the nature of the productive activ-ity: when WISEs aim to serve the community through the production of public interest goods rather than private ones, the general social aim to serve the community is translated concretely into different goals: integration of disadvantaged people, on the one hand, and production of general interest goods/services (environmental ones, for instance), on the other.

As to the hypothesized multi-stakeholder nature of WISEs, it also found empirical support as 58 per cent of the organizations in the sample involve more than one category of stakeholder in their decision-making process. Moreover, the data collected seem to indicate that the participation of stakeholders in these WISEs leads to the exercise of a real influence within boards. Indeed, according to the indicators developed, the analysis shows, in the majority of the WISEs surveyed, quite a balanced governance structure, where the involvement of stakeholders is made real and effective by democratic decision-making processes and by a rather balanced distribution of influence among various groups.

Coming finally to the reasons explaining the multi-stakeholder structure of many WISEs, we identify three major lines of theory. They all seem relevant and probably complementary, although not easy to test empirically. Further research is thus clearly needed to explore in more depth the determinants as well as the outcomes of such a structure of ownership and management. More fundamentally, as illustrated by the various models identified by Cornforth (2003)[17] in boards of non-profit organizations, it would also be fruitful to examine the governance of social enterprises through other perspectives than stakeholder theory.

Review questions

- In which cases could one say that the social goal of social enterprises is twofold?
- What different reasons could explain the involvement of a variety of stakeholders in social enterprises?
- How could you explain the fact that both multi-stakeholder and single-stakeholder social enterprises appear to be multiple-goal organizations?

Notes

1   Four organizations pursue only one goal: a Finnish co-operative and an English recycling organization declared a single goal of production of goods and services, a German organization stressed only an objective of work and social integration and, surprisingly, an English co-operative claimed it was only engaged in promoting the co-operative movement (classed in the 'other' category).

2   Interestingly, the advocacy and lobbying goal is the least important for Italian WISEs, probably because they have the strongest federal bodies (local and national consortia) which take charge of most of these functions.

3   More precisely, managers were asked whether the production of goods and services was subordinated to the work integration goal, balanced with it or dominated work integration.

4 Interviewees were requested to tick all relevant items in a list.
5 See, for example, Pearce (2003), Dees *et al.* (2002) or the publications by 'Social Enterprise London'.
6 Of course, the relative importance of these two legal forms vary a lot among countries: 80 per cent of the WISEs surveyed in France were associations, while 80 per cent of WISEs in Sweden and all WISEs in Italy were co-operatives.
7 Jordan (1990) reports the failed attempt of the French co-operative movement to introduce the multi-stakeholder status during the first ICA (International Co-operative Alliance) meeting in 1895. The position of the Alliance today still favours a traditional single-stakeholder membership.
8 The Italian law on social co-operatives (L. 381/91), for example, explicitly permits (but does not make compulsory) the inclusion in the ownership structure of volunteers, participants (whenever it is possible) and legal persons whose statutes provide for the financial support or development of social co-operatives.
9 One of the very few exceptions is the legal framework of 'integration enterprises' (*enterprises d'insertion*) in the Walloon Region (Belgium): generally registered as co-operatives with a social purpose, they are obliged by law to offer their workers, hired as disadvantaged unemployed people, formal membership within a certain period of time. In the same way, a law recently passed in Italy (June 2005) paves the way for rules concerning 'social enterprises' (not just social co-operatives) which would impose the formal involvement of workers and users/customers in the decision-making process.
10 For the sake of simplicity, the influence of each category had to be described as strong, weak or insignificant. We are fully aware of the limits of such an approach that relies solely on the managers' perceptions, especially as the latter may actually in many cases be the most powerful agent in the organization.
11 With the exception of two or three countries, it seems that WISEs often encounter difficulties or are reluctant to involve 'participants' in the decision-making process. Of course this may be explained by the profile of these workers (often with a low qualification or sometimes a mental handicap) as well as by their desire or obligation to leave some specific types of WISE after a certain period.
12 Petrella (2003) provides an interesting survey of the 'raisons d'être' of multi-stakeholder organizations, especially referring to new institutional economic theory.
13 Jordan (1990) refers, for example, to the *in extremis* involvement of staff, which is usually necessary in case of crisis in consumer co-operatives.
14 Pfeffer (1973), in his study of religious and private non-profit hospitals, underlines that, in his sample, the more dependent on external resources an organization is, the more participative its board is.
15 WISEs in the overall sample were divided among the following categories: mixed boards, boards dominated by NPOs, boards dominated by workers, boards dominated by participants, boards dominated by volunteers and boards dominated by representatives of the public authorities.
16 Moreover, single-goal organizations are almost as frequent among multi-stakeholder organizations as among single-stakeholder ones: four organizations in the project sample, two of which are single-stakeholder and two multi-stakeholder, declared that they had one only goal.
17 Analysing how boards function in non-profit (and public) organizations, Cornforth (2003) identifies five models in addition to the stakeholder model: a compliance model, based on agency theory; a partnership model, based on stewardship theory; a co-optation model, linked to resource dependency theory; a democratic model and a 'rubber stamp' model, based on managerial hegemony theory.

Bibliography

Aiken, M. and Spear, R. (2005) 'Work Integration Social Enterprises in the United Kingdom', *Working Papers Series*, 05/01, Liège: EMES European Research Network.

Bacchiega, A. and Borzaga, C. (2001) 'Social Enterprises as Incentive Structures', in Borzaga, C. and Defourny, J. (eds) *The Emergence of Social Enterprise*, London and New York: Routledge, 273–95.

Barnard, C. (1938) *The Functions of the Executive*, Cambridge, MA: Harvard College.

Ben-Ner, A. and Van Hoomissen, T. (1991) 'Nonprofit Organizations in the Mixed Economy', *Annals of Public and Cooperative Economy*, 62, 4: 520–50.

Borzaga, C. and Defourny, J. (eds) (2001) *The Emergence of Social Enterprise*, London and New York: Routledge.

Borzaga, C. and Mittone, L. (1997) 'The Multi-stakeholder Versus the Nonprofit Organization', *Discussion paper*, 7, Trento: Department of Economics, University of Trento.

Borzaga, C. and Santuari, A. (2003) 'New Trends in the Nonprofit Sector in Europe: the Emergence of Social Entrepreneurship', in OECD, *The Nonprofit Sector in a Changing Economy*, Paris: OECD.

Cornforth, C. (ed.) (2003) *The Governance of Public and Non-profit Organisations*, London and New York: Routledge.

Dees, J.G., Emerson J. and Economy P. (2002) *Strategic Tools for Entrepreneurs: Enhancing the Performance of Your Enterprising Nonprofit*, Indianapolis, IN: Wiley.

Donaldson, T. and Preston, L.E. (1995) 'The Stakeholder Theory of the Corporation: Concepts, Evidence, and Implications', *Academy of Management Review*, 20, 1: 65–91.

Evan, W.M. and Freeman, R.E. (1993) 'A Stakeholder Theory of Modern Corporation: Kantian Capitalism', in Beauchamp, T. and Bowie, N. (eds) *Ethical Theory and Business*, Englewood Cliffs, NJ: Prentice Hall.

Evers, A. (2001) 'The Significance of Social Capital in the Multiple Goal and Resource Structure of Social Enterprises', in Borzaga, C. and Defourny, J. (eds) *The Emergence of Social Enterprise*, London and New York: Routledge, 296–311.

Freeman, R.E. (1984) *Strategic Management: A Stakeholder Approach*, Boston, MA: Pitman.

Gui, B. (1991) 'The Economic Rationale for the Third Sector', *Annals of Public and Cooperative Economics*, 62, 4: 551–72.

Hansmann, H. (1996) *The Ownership of Enterprise*, Cambridge, MA: Harvard University Press.

Helmig, B., Jegers, M. and Lapsley, I. (2004) 'Challenges in Managing NPO: A Research Overview', *Voluntas*, 15, 2: 101–16.

Hirschman, A.O. (1980) *Shifting Involvements – Private Interest and Public Action*, Princeton, NJ: Princeton University Press.

Jordan, J.E. (1990) 'The Multi-stakeholders Concept of Organization', *Yearbook of Co-operative Enterprise 1989*, Oxford: Plunkett Foundation.

Krashinsky, M. (1997) 'Stakeholder Theories of the Non-profit Sector: One Cut at the Economic Literature', *Voluntas*, 8, 2: 149–61.

Laville, J.-L. and Nyssens, M. (2001) 'The Social Enterprise. Towards a Theoretical Socio-economic Approach', in Borzaga, C. and Defourny, J. (eds) *The Emergence of Social Enterprise*, London and New York: Routledge, 312–32.

Middleton, M. (1987) 'Nonprofit Boards of Directors: Beyond the Governance Function', in Powell, W.W. (ed.) *The Nonprofit Sector. A Research Handbook*, New Haven, CT: Yale University Press.

Milgrom, P. and Roberts, J. (1992) *Economics, Organization and Management*, Englewood Cliffs, NJ: Prentice Hall.

Mintzberg, H. (1983) *Power in and Around Organizations*, Englewood Cliffs, NJ: Prentice Hall.

OCDE (1999) *Les entreprises sociales*, Paris: OCDE.

O'Hara, P. and O'Shaughnessy, M. (2004) 'Work Integration Social Enterprises in Ireland', *Working Papers Series*, 04/03, Liège: EMES European Research Network.

Pearce, J. (2003) *Social Enterprise in Anytown*, London: Calouste Gulbenkian Foundation.

Perista, H. and Nogueira, S. (2004) 'Work Integration Social Enterprises in Portugal', *Working Papers Series*, 04/06, Liège: EMES European Research Network.

Pestoff, V.A. (1995) 'Local Economic Democracy and Multi-stakeholders Cooperatives', *Journal of Rural Cooperation*, XXIII, 2: 151–67.

Petrella, F. (2003) 'Une analyse néo-institutionnaliste des structures de propriété multi-stakeholder: une application aux organisations de développement local', Thèse de doctorat, 434/2003, Faculté des sciences économiques, sociales et politiques, Université Catholique de Louvain, Louvain-la-Neuve.

Pfeffer, J. (1973) 'Size, Composition and Function of Hospital Boards of Directorates', *Administrative Science Quarterly*, 18, 3: 349–64.

Thompson, J.D. (1967) *Organizations in Action*, New York: McGraw Hill.

Tirole, J. (1994) 'The Internal Organisation of Governments', Oxford Economic Papers, 46: 1–29.

Vidal, I. and Claver, N. (2004) 'Work Integration Social Enterprises in Spain', *Working Papers Series*, 04/05, Liège: EMES European Research Network.

Weisbrod, B. (1988) *The Nonprofit Economy*, Cambridge: Cambridge University Press.

3 Danish social enterprises: a public–third sector partnership

Lars Hulgård

Overview

This chapter analyses the dynamic of stakeholders upon which Danish social enterprises rely, as well as the way in which these WISEs balance their various objectives. After reading this chapter, the reader should:

- identify the role of each type of stakeholder in Danish WISEs;
- understand the crucial role of public–civil society partnership in the field of Danish WISEs.

Introduction

The landscape of WISEs in Denmark is dominated by local community enterprises offering traineeship and temporary work integration (*lokalt orienterede sociale virksomheder som tilbyder uddannelse og midlertidig beskæftigelse*).[1] The public sector and the third sector are absolutely dominant stakeholders in the 13 WISEs that make up the Danish sample, while the private sector plays a less significant role. Danish WISEs are both similar to and different from European social enterprises as they have been depicted in the PERSE study. On the one hand, Danish social enterprises fit the general European picture of social enterprises in that they have a strong entrepreneurial component, while remaining strongly embedded in the associative or co-operative world; indeed, most WISEs in the Danish sample were founded by local actors, often in close co-operation with third sector organizations. On the other hand, many Danish social enterprises distinguish themselves from most European WISEs as regards the extent of public sector involvement: Danish WISEs, though formally autonomous, are under pressure from public authorities, which often determine their objectives (Riis 2003).

In Denmark, there is no specific legislation for co-operatives or social co-operatives, and WISEs only rarely adopt an associative (non-profit organization) legal form. Among the variety of legal forms adopted by

Danish WISEs, the prevailing one is that of the 'self-owning institution'. The term self-owning institution refers to the legal status of a wide range of cultural, environmental, educational and social institutions and organizations providing various public goods under subcontract, especially within the field of welfare provision – day-care, cheap meals, work integration, rehabilitation, nursing homes, hostels, emergency centres, etc. – and within the private school sector. Riis (2003) estimated that there were 9,000 self-owning institutions operating in the social area in Denmark.

The strength of the ties between these organizations, on the one hand, and national, regional and local public bodies, on the other hand, varies from one organization to another. The Danish sample reflects this diversity, as it includes a wide spectrum of organizations, from WISEs that are more or less integrated parts of the local public welfare system to organizations under little or practically no direct supervision from public authorities.

Besides the 'self-owning institutions', which account for 46 per cent of the cases, the Danish sample includes foundations (31 per cent of the WISEs studied) and registered associations (15 per cent), the remaining 8 per cent being represented by a limited company. It thus appears that third sector-oriented legal forms (associations and foundations) come in second place, whereas legal forms connected to the private sector are rarely found. However, the rather ambiguous category of self-owning institutions makes it hard to base our stakeholder discussion on the legal forms adopted by the WISEs. In other words, there could be a continuous blurring of boundaries between public and third sector actors – and their respective institutional logics – in the 13 WISEs of the Danish sample.

1 Multiple stakeholders

The concept of the multi-stakeholder structure may help us to understand the internal and external dynamics of the organizations in the Danish sample. Indeed, all WISEs in the sample have been established as a direct result of co-operation between a multiplicity of local actors, and often as a direct result of a long history of co-operation between these local actors, engaged either specifically in the provision of work/social integration or in other related fields, such as community development.

1.1 Founding actors as an indication of the stakeholder structure

The WISEs in the Danish sample were founded by an association of citizens (58 per cent of cases), government representatives (17 per cent) or representatives of third sector organizations (17 per cent); actors from the private sector hardly played any role in the founding of WISEs. Although, as just mentioned, 58 per cent of the organizations studied state that the most important actors in the founding of the organization were citizens or groups of citizens, we strongly question this kind of result. As a matter of fact, the interviews suggest that these 'citizens' are indeed often representatives and professionals from a wide range of local public and third sector organizations. It can thus be said that most WISEs are the product of intense networking between various local organizations, interest groups and public authorities.

There is no obvious relation between the legal form and the balance between actors from the public and third sectors in the founding stages of the organizations, although some slight trends can be identified: according to the qualitative data, foundations and associations can be seen as a more direct result of networking activity among actors from the third sector or groups of citizens, whereas the establishment of the self-owning institutions in the sample was more dominated by the presence of actors from the public sector.

1.2 The composition of boards

Looking at the board members of all 13 WISEs (Table 3.1), we find that the types of stakeholders identified as possible stakeholders in the framework of the PERSE project are all represented; permanent staff members, representatives from the public sector and representatives from the third sector are the stakeholder categories most often represented among the WISEs in the Danish sample, followed by representatives of the private sector, private persons/users and participants. Twenty-three per cent of the 13 WISEs have volunteers as board members.

The composition of boards can also be studied from the point of view of the number of members that come from each stakeholder category. As

Table 3.1 Stakeholders and boards of Danish WISEs (%)

Categories of board members	Proportion of boards in which the category is present	Proportion of all board members	Influence on decision-making
Users/private persons	33	6	3
Volunteers	23	6	9
Permanent staff	62	17	34
Participants	31	6	9
Representatives of the private sector	38	14	9
Representatives of the public sector	62	26	16
Representatives of the third sector	46	20	9
Other		5	11
Total		100	100

shown in the third column of Table 3.1, the dominant groups of actors in the boards of the 13 organizations are representatives of the public sector and the third sector. Although the private sector did not play a significant role in the founding of the WISEs in the sample, it provides a significant 14 per cent of the board members. Another key feature is the presence on the boards of internal actors in the form of members of the permanent staff.

1.3 The influence of stakeholders

The last column of Table 3.1 shows how the managers of the 13 WISEs estimate the influence of the different categories of board members on the organization.

The data strongly suggest that the dominant board members are to be found among the permanent staff members, but representatives from the public sector also exert a significant influence on decision-making. Moreover, 38 per cent of managers estimate that the role of representatives from the public sector will become even more important in the future.

Finally, the influence of the different categories of stakeholder can also be looked at as regards the various activities of the organizations (work integration, production activities and political activities). Permanent staff members appear to have a dominant position concerning work integration and production, whereas representatives from both the public and the third sector seem more influential concerning the lobbying and advocacy activities of the WISEs.

The way in which participation in decision-making is achieved varies among the WISEs studied. In one enterprise, participation is limited to 'briefings where we inform participants about their responsibilities and their possible benefits'. In others, there is a more solid structure of participation in the decision-making process; a manager explained: 'We have a programme committee with two or three persons deciding a programme for two or three months.' There is no clear connection between the ownership structure and the decision-making structure, since the only privately owned enterprise is also an enterprise with one of the most participatory decision-making structures in planning the activities of the enterprise.

2 Multiple goals

In conjunction with the overall picture of European WISEs as described in Chapter 2 of this book, the multiple-goal structure is a very dominant feature among Danish work integration social enterprises. All 13 organizations have multiple goals; they mix, to varying degrees, the following goals: social integration, work integration, individual – and to some extent collective – empowerment, production of goods and services, and lobbying.

Table 3.2 Goal structure of Danish WISEs (%)

Goals	Ranked 1st	Ranked 2nd	Ranked 3rd
Work and social integration	**92**	8	0
Production of goods and services	0	**54**	46
Advocacy and lobbying	8	38	**54**

According to the managers interviewed, work and social integration is clearly the prominent objective among Danish WISEs, with 92 per cent of organizations viewing integration as their primary objective (see Table 3.2). It is also interesting to note that none of the organizations declares the production of goods and services to be its primary objective; this goal is ranked only third in importance, after advocacy and lobbying activities, by slightly less than half of the managers.

2.1 Work integration

Work integration schemes provided by Danish WISEs can roughly be divided between 'occupational training' and 'educational activities'; the dominant approach is to offer the participants occupational training. The activities offered are generally viewed as alternatives to conventional and traditional state-initiated projects and methods. As one manager put it:

> We have had participants who have been through nearly every scheme the local municipality had to offer – and who had almost given up the idea of finding a job. After joining us most of them found a real job or went on to get further education.

This quotation reflects a widespread opinion among leaders of Danish WISEs. Although the schemes vary from organization to organization, it is commonly acknowledged that the WISE status creates means to develop schemes that are very successful compared to those provided by the national or local authorities.

2.2 Production activity

Production is to be understood in two manners: the first type of production is the job offer or the specific kind of work integration activity sold by the WISE to public authorities. This includes the production of various public goods such as counselling, education and training. As regards this type of production, the WISE is a provider of services financed by public authorities. The second type is the production, by the participants and staff members of the WISE, of goods and services sold to customers.[2]

The first type of production is an important feature in all the Danish cases studied, whereas the production of goods and services for the private market can be found in 62 per cent of the WISEs of the sample. Among the latter, there is a great diversity in the way the WISEs mix the two production types. Two examples – Sydhavns-Compagniet and Kulturgyngen – perfectly illustrate such diversity. In Sydhavns-Compagniet work and social integration services (type 1) are by far the dominant production type, as opposed to the small-scale production of goods and services, delivered mainly through the organization's second-hand shop. At the other end of the spectrum, Kulturgyngen is illustrative of the growing focus on production of goods and service (type 2) as opposed to a strict focus on work integration. The production activities of this WISE include three branches: 'Gyngen' runs a café, a restaurant, online catering, and a stage for live music; 'City Sleep-In' runs a youth hostel; and 'Kultursats' runs an advertising agency.

When asked to identify the balance between the work and social integration activities and the production of goods and services, just over half of the organizations in the sample state that the production of goods and services is subordinated to the goal of work and social integration, and 38 per cent of organizations view the production of goods and services as being in balance with the objective of work integration. There is no significant relation between the way the production and integration activities are balanced and the type of production carried out.

Although type-2 production plays a minor role in most Danish WISEs in terms of earnings, it carries a high symbolic value and it represents a vital means in the creation of effective and 'meaningful' work integration schemes and programmes. The general organizational point of departure, especially for WISEs intensively engaged in both production types, is to strive towards creating a working climate as close as possible to that of a private enterprise. The general underlying goal behind this approach is to motivate participants and cultivate their skills in a way that raises their capability to hold a normal job. A manager expresses this view as follows:

> We are not a normal enterprise, because of the capabilities of the participants, but we try as hard as possible to create a sense of professionalism. One can say that our primary objective is the social dimension (work integration), but we try to do this work 'behind the scenes'. . . . Of course this is a challenging task, but we find it mandatory that the work integration process build on respect for the capabilities and resources of the individual participant.

2.3 Lobbying and advocacy

Lobbying and advocacy are practised in two ways by Danish WISEs: as lobbying for the interests of the enterprise and as advocacy for the interests of participants in job training. These two types of lobbying are not identical.

Lobbying for the interests of the enterprise

Most enterprises are fully aware that lobbying is a necessity, and that their connections to politicians and public authorities are crucial to sustaining their activities and scaling up the enterprise in the long run. Connections to politicians, in the form of formal and informal relationships through boards and networks, provide the enterprises with a voice in local – and occasionally even national – politics. Connections to local public authorities are necessary as a way to secure a supply of people to undertake work experience and training. In social capital and network theory, such close contacts to local actors are what help the enterprises get by, while contacts to local and national politicians help the enterprise move ahead (Briggs 1998).

Although all enterprises are aware of the need to lobby, especially in the local political arena, some do better than others in this regard. The qualitative data show that there exists a difference in the level of lobbying activity between those organizations that have strong formal ties with local public authorities, on the one hand, and the more autonomous WISEs in the sample, on the other: the former usually lobby less than the latter. This seems to accord with the typologies we have discussed in relation to WISEs' legal forms. Third sector-oriented organizations (foundations and associations) with no direct institutionalized ties, in the form of public servants on their boards or direct supervision, need to maintain their ties to local public authority actors constantly. In contrast, WISEs classified as self-owning institutions operate with a higher level of institutionalized ties to the public sector and do not stress this lobbying activity in the same manner. This trend is illustrated by the following statement by the manager of a WISE in the sample:

> As opposed to other initiatives more closely related to – or even initiated by – the municipality of Copenhagen, our status and autonomy force us to use a lot of resources to facilitate our relationship with public servants. . . . Competition in this field is strong, and we often have to compete with the municipalities' own projects. . . . Our relations with key local politicians have a lot of impact, but the relationship with people in administration is equally important, if not even more crucial.

The following quotation from the manager of another WISE underlines the value of the institutionalized ties between the WISE and local and regional public authorities:

> Because of our status (legal form) we have a close relationship with multiple administrators through our connection to the regional network formed by . . . county authorities within the field of psychiatry. . . . The network increases the visibility of our organization. . . . [It is] by

far our most important network because of the supervision that goes on, but also because of the relationships we build with top-level officials from the administration.

Advocacy for the participants

Advocating the interests of the participants refers to the collective and individual empowerment of the latter. This is about supporting and facilitating participants' right to have a say not only in matters that affect their everyday life, but also in politics. The ways in which WISEs advocate the interests of their participants do not follow any particular systematic strategy; they are varied, but three main types can be distinguished: micro-level, meso-level, and macro-level advocacy.

MICRO-LEVEL ADVOCACY – TRAINING

Micro-level advocacy is closely related to individual empowerment. Here there is no specific intention to relate the empowerment of the individual participant to larger socio-economic changes, or to reflect on how power structures influence the individual's opportunities for inclusion.

MESO-LEVEL ADVOCACY – DEMONSTRATION OF A THIRD WAY

Meso-level advocacy aims to show, through the very example of the WISE, how the social enterprise model, based upon new balances between 'traditional' employment and new forms of production subsidized by public authorities, is a third way between unemployment and full employment in the normal labour market. Meso-level advocacy is also related to 'the everyday life approach', where solidarity with the participants and respect for their life are important features of the organization.

MACRO-LEVEL ADVOCACY – POLICY ENGAGEMENT

Macro-level advocacy is more related to the overall goal of relating the activities of the social enterprise to the ambition to build social movements in order to change the current power structures in the direction of serving the interests of socially excluded groups. As indicated by the managers, this concern plays hardly any role, although it was the driving force in the first period of social enterprises, and may be the reason why the organizations formed at that time gained a lasting influence on the Danish welfare society.

Conclusion

The most striking features of the field of WISEs in Denmark such as it emerged from the PERSE study are the strong dependency of Danish work integration social enterprises upon the public sector, and the general transition towards more professionalised approaches reported by the WISEs in the sample. Indeed, the empirical results indicate that Danish WISEs are highly dependent on contracts with the public sector; moreover, they enjoy less autonomy today than they did previously. They also consider their work integration activities to be more important than advocacy, and are moving in the direction of more professionalised management structures. Overall, a tendency towards institutional isomorphism prevails (see Chapter 15 of this book). All these factors may lead to a loss of Danish WISEs' capacity to act as watch dogs advocating the interests of their original constituencies.

Review questions

- Why could one say that Danish social enterprises are both similar to the 'general' European picture of social enterprises as organizations strongly embedded in the third sector, and different from the picture of pure third sector organizations?
- What are the different objectives behind the lobbying and advocacy activities of Danish WISEs?

Notes

1   The field of WISEs also includes sheltered workshops (*beskyttede værksteder*), but these initiatives were not included in the sample of WISEs constituted for the purpose of the PERSE project.
2   It should be underlined that the Danish sample is the only one in the PERSE study to include WISEs with no production of type 2. It was requested that all WISEs included in the study have a continuous activity of the production of goods and services, but there are very few 'real' WISEs – such as defined for the PERSE study – in Denmark, and the criteria could thus not be applied too strictly in the case of this country.

Bibliography

Briggs, X. de Souza (1998) 'Moving Up Versus Moving Out: Neighbourhood Effects in Housing Mobility Programs', *Housing Policy Debate*, 8, 1: 195–234.
Riis, K. (2003) *De selvejende sociale institutioner, hvad skal vi egentlig med dem?*, Odense: Center for Frivilligt Socialt Arbejde.

4 French social enterprises: a common ethical framework to balance various objectives

Elisabetta Bucolo

Overview

This chapter shows how French social enterprises balance social, economic and lobbying goals through the development of a specific type of management. After reading this chapter, the reader should:

- grasp the common ethical framework shared by the different stake-holders in French WISEs and its crucial role in balancing various objectives;
- identify and understand both the internal and external processes implemented by these WISEs in order to achieve balance among their objectives.

Introduction

In the 1980s, an unexpected rise in unemployment in France led to a social crisis that culminated in the marginalization of a broad stratum of society that had been discarded by the labour market. Labour market integration mechanisms had to adapt to this change. Work integration initiatives of this period sought to maintain these individuals in work settings, so that they would not lose hope of eventually returning to work in an ordinary company.

From the 1990s on, the economic recession weakened the social fabric. Social exclusion resulted in a loss of autonomy and generated new target populations – mainly individuals increasingly cut off from the labour market, who had no hope of entering this market and consequently needed more focused social support and personalized career coaching than the previous generation of excluded workers.

The solidarity-based programmes designed to help this particular group to deal with their problems have taken many forms – direct assistance, mutual aid and grassroots action. However, WISEs are often the only organizations capable of providing these individuals with labour market re-entry training. For some of these workers, WISEs represent the 'last chance'; for others, they constitute the first step in an integration process.

Overall, the 'individuals with major difficulties' (without differentiating on the basis of sex or background) still constitute the main target group of most of the organizations making up the sample constituted for the PERSE project. A great many of these individuals are young people with social problems who have never, or hardly ever, worked, or unskilled women who have been unemployed for a long time.

1 The sample of French WISEs

While there is no universally accepted definition of the WISE concept in France, a whole range of organizations function and perceive their economic and social challenges in a similar way.

The sample of French WISEs constituted for the PERSE project (on which this chapter is based) includes the following types of social enterprises: one centre for adaptation to working life (*centre d'adaptation à la vie active*, or CAVA); three work integration enterprises (*entreprises d'insertion*, or EI); three intermediate voluntary organizations (*associations intermédiaires*, or AI); and two temporary work integration enterprises (*entreprises de travail temporaire d'insertion*, or ETTI). It also includes initiatives working in the area of work integration that have not been officially accredited by the government for this purpose: three neighbourhood enterprises (*régies de quartier*, or RQ) and two long-term work integration enterprises (*entreprises insérantes*).[1] The sample is presented in more detail in Table 4.1.

2 The main goals

One of the characteristics of social enterprises is that they combine multiple goals; the main goals are integration, production and lobbying. In the sample studied, it appears that the vast majority of WISE activities are geared primarily towards the social and labour market integration of individuals with major problems and whose needs are not met by any other organization. The work integration goal is coupled with the necessity to develop activities of production of goods and services in order to ensure this integration. Managers get involved in lobbying networks only subsequently, for reasons linked to the sustainability of the enterprise and to advocate their workers' rights.

2.1 Integration

In terms of social and occupational integration, WISEs' main purpose is to allow individuals excluded from the labour market and from society at large to find a new role through an economic activity and personalized social coaching.

Table 4.1 The PERSE sample of French WISEs

Type	Work integration	Activity
3 intermediate voluntary organizations	Work-based social integration, preparation for work by placing unemployed persons at the disposal of businesses, municipal administrations, social housing organizations and individuals	Services in the framework of local development. The services have low added value due to employees' low skill levels (housework, ironing, gardening, odd jobs)
Long-term work integration enterprise no. 1	Long-term employment contracts in problem zones that help integrate women into the labour market	Selling ethnic food to promote cross-cultural understanding
Long-term work integration enterprise no. 2	Work-based social integration through long-term employment contracts	Processing waste
2 temporary work integration enterprises	Social and professional monitoring of individuals with a view to securing employment for them	Temporary placements and putting the workers at the disposal of private businesses
1 centre for adaptation to working life	Social coaching and training prior to placement in a business	Manufacturing, packing and assembling parts for private companies
Work integration enterprise no. 1	Development of activities and creation of jobs through long-term contracts within the framework of a collective project	Restaurant and catering; sewing
Work integration enterprise no. 2	Trial period for individuals, many of whom have never worked, through short-term contracts	Environmental services (recycling) and educational programmes for schools
Work integration enterprise no. 3	Giving mentally ill individuals the opportunity to be useful by participating in a work group and to relate to others, through long-term contracts	Restaurant
3 neighbourhood enterprises	Promotion of projects for the labour market integration of residents of the neighbourhood; the projects increase their collective responsibility through training for ordinary skilled employment	Improving the living environment and social cohesion in neighbourhoods with high unemployment through home care, mediation, environmental improvements, clean-up, renovating social housing

Some of these organizations see their activities as a transitional period, somewhere between unemployment and work in the labour market – an intermediary stage of training and social re-adaptation. They allow individuals who have been excluded from work for very long periods to get used again to certain work habits, such as fixed work schedules, certain types of tasks and responsibilities and working in a team. In conventional work environments, these individuals may find it difficult to re-acquire these work habits; a transition period in a labour market integration activity provides them with smooth, gradual integration. WISE activities take place in a framework based on a management style that is flexible enough to adapt to this specific population. This flexibility helps the workers find their bearings again, not only in terms of economic activity but also as regards their social integration problems. The social coaching, housing, legal support and health services serve as a transitional stage, enabling these individuals to surmount the initial period of isolation and distress and to give themselves the means to deal more effectively with work and work-related constraints.

In temporary work integration enterprises (ETTIs), for example, the aim of the founders is to create conditions that will allow workers to get back to work in the mainstream labour market. Training organized within the enterprise is thus adapted to market demands, in order to encourage the workers, as far as possible, to join the mainstream labour market. In this sense, many people see the WISE as the only way to acquire an income and some work experience that will help them in their search for a first job. Indeed, many low-qualified workers applying for a job find that proving that they have already worked is the only way to obtain the job. Those WISEs that specialize in temporary work or in outsourcing their workforce deal especially with this target group, which seeks not only specific guidance but a first contact with the labour market.

For other WISEs, getting individuals back to the labour market is not the priority. Instead, they focus on individuals who are experiencing severe social exclusion, providing them with the tools they need to reorient and rebuild their lives socially and psychologically through, among other things, a salaried work activity. When these workers leave the WISE, labour market re-entry constitutes one of several possible options available to them. In fact, these WISEs aim to offer each disadvantaged worker a chance to reassess the role of work in their lives by supporting them while they gain control over their own personal project. These individuals develop an awareness of their previous inactive status, to which they do not want to return.

For example, young jobseekers entering one of the work integration enterprises (EIs) studied found themselves, previous to joining the WISE, in situations of very serious exclusion; most of them were homeless and found in the enterprise a place where they could regain a grasp on their life as a member of society. In this type of organization, integration is more about access to civic rights and learning about the civic rights and duties of everyone than integration into the mainstream labour market. Indeed, upon completing the integration path within the WISE (whose duration is strongly limited by legal restrictions), integration in the labour market still seems very difficult to achieve.

2.2 Production

The objective of producing goods and services takes priority over the integration objective in only a small minority of cases – primarily organizations in which the original associative project was based on activist motivations: ecological motives in the case of environmental activities, compassionate motives in the case of services to individuals in difficulty and civic awareness in the case of organizations fighting unemployment. In their way of thinking, providing services to users or, more broadly, defending a cause, takes priority and subsequently generates a reflection on the integration of individuals in difficulty.

For example, two organizations whose main activity is sorting and processing waste are the only ones in the French sample to give production activities priority over other objectives. These organizations obviously aimed primarily to promote a form of activity with a specific goal; taking action to help disadvantaged groups came second.

Conversely, the other organizations of the sample first aimed at the integration of disadvantaged workers, and then had to look for market activities that could ensure the viability of their integration projects. They have had to find niches for goods and services whose production requires no specific skills and that can thus be produced by workers with very weak qualifications. For the centre for adaptation to working life (CAVA) studied, which aims to integrate very young women experiencing social exclusion due to abandonment or family breakdown, the primary objective is to resocialise these women and subsequently to integrate them into real occupational activities. In order to achieve this goal, the commercial department of the organization mainly focuses on finding non-competitive market niches where the production of goods or services only requires manual competencies, such as making boxes or decorative objects, affixing labels, etc.

Where feasible, they give preference to the production of services over the production of goods, because of the added social value service provision generates. As a matter of fact, they value the relational aspect of service provision, which constitutes a pedagogical element of the integration programme. The examples of catering and the door-to-door collection of recyclables are good illustrations of this: restaurant work allows the workers to come into contact with clients and improve their communication skills; likewise, direct contact with residents who deposit their recyclable wastes at the kerbside improves the standing of the disadvantaged workers in their community by giving them a new role in the eyes of others.

2.3 Advocacy and/or lobbying

The importance of the third broad objective, namely advocacy and/or lobbying, appears to vary from one WISE to another, but it is not a major priority in any of the WISEs surveyed. The managers know how important lobbying is for the long-term survival of their organizations and for the promotion of their specific working methods with disadvantaged workers or for the defence of a specific cause, but their commitment to lobbying and advocacy depends on the time that remains available once they have attended to production and management. When it is possible for the WISE to devote time to real advocacy and lobbying, their main goal obviously remains to promote an environmental, social, civic or analogous cause and in particular to put pressure on public authorities, since, beyond the reason motivating the lobbying, this can directly affect the productive activity of the WISE. As a matter of fact, local para-public networks working in the field of integration through economic activity are the most effective fora for making contacts and setting up networks and partnerships to ensure the local embeddedness of activities.

Similarly, as far as lobbying is concerned, WISEs want to demonstrate that it is possible to set up sustainable activities of production of goods and services while working with target groups in great difficulty and aiming to integrate them socially. Faced with the public authorities' difficulty in finding solutions to rising unemployment, the issue for WISEs is to demonstrate the contribution of their economic and social projects and to propose alternative points of view on social exclusion, with a view to putting forward a political societal project.

In this sense, some WISE managers may be directly involved in political action within a political party or, more broadly, within local authorities. Such an involvement increases their capacity for bargaining and adaptation to market forces and public policies. Finally, it can be said that overall political objectives are always in the background, even when WISEs do not explicitly pursue advocacy and lobbying goals, since WISEs' distinctive activities serve as a vehicle for advocating an individual's right to attain dignity through work. This social commitment is the force that drives social enterprises and, through their actions, they are a vehicle for this type of social awareness in the public arena.

3 Balancing objectives

On the basis of the interviews conducted with WISE managers, it appears that in order to find the proper balance among the various objectives (social, economic and advocacy-related goals), a specific type of management is required, that the enterprises develop over time. In this perspective, several axes are often underlined.

In order to pursue what most work integration enterprises consider to be their main goal, namely the integration of disadvantaged workers, WISEs must produce goods and services that will ensure their existence in the long run and create as many jobs as possible for the individuals in integration. The organization must simultaneously remain economically viable, surviving on competitive markets or ensuring its activities without entering into direct competition with private enterprises. To maintain the balance between work integration and production, WISEs must always be on the lookout for new market niches. The specific target group of WISEs requires case-by-case adjustments and flexible work arrangements on the part of the organizations, so that all the workers in integration can find their own pace while completing their tasks. This means adapting timetables, work methods and the allocation of tasks, and providing supervision of the production tasks and social follow-up of the workers.

Nevertheless, to make such a balance sustainable, there first needs to be, from the inception of the organization, a common ethical framework behind all its actions. This common ethical framework translates into shared values that provide a common bond, and institutional and organizational standards to which the actors constantly refer. The values of sharing and solidarity are fundamental to the activities of all the organizations studied. Even before an organization affirms the value of the work itself, it holds up the right to work as a fundamental human right. Work is most often not viewed as a value in itself but, rather, as an indispensable means of achieving human dignity and social integration. Overall, we may view these values as providing the most effective procedural foundation for the success of the integration programme. More particularly, they heavily influence each integration organization's internal operating methods and the way WISEs form their external networks and gain their territorial footing.

In order to achieve a fecund balance of their three main objectives, WISEs rely both on internal processes (namely specific personnel recruitment methods and the formal and informal democratic participation of stakeholders) and on external ones (the mobilization of networks). In the following, these processes, which appear to be specific to WISEs, will be described in more detail.

3.1 Methods of recruiting staff and workers in integration

When hiring permanent staff, WISEs often pay equal attention to the candidate's personal values and his/her technical abilities. However, it is usually the commitment to the values advocated by the organization that determines which person will be chosen. That said, certain organizations have had to demonstrate flexibility in this regard in order to meet production requirements. This is the case of the centre for adaptation to working life (CAVA) studied, which had to bring commercial managers into its team in order to find new markets; another example is that of an integration enterprise which hired a cook whose professional skills were needed to sustain its restaurant.

Candidates willing to work for an organization that gives priority to respect for the individual must demonstrate conviction and commitment to the project. Accepting this principle is fundamental for all candidates; since they come from a wide variety of professional environments, it is important that they understand that they need to adjust the methodologies and techniques of their previous work experience to the needs of a very fragile population. As a matter of fact, this population needs greater care and support than other workers, whose autonomy derives from self-confidence in their own abilities. For this reason, WISEs often take much greater care in recruiting staff for low-level positions (these staff often being in closer and permanent contact with the individuals in integration schemes) than they may do for other positions.

To get round this difficult adaptation required of permanent staff, some organizations prefer to hire individuals whose trajectory is analogous to that of the workers in the integration programme, and who, given their previous work situation, share in principle the organization's values. However, only a minority of organizations apply this practice; in most cases, the desire to ensure competent and skilled monitoring prevails.

Thus, some of the permanent staff were unemployed for a long time before being hired by the WISE, while the majority have no specific profile. Staff teams can include employees who were hired by the organization after having spent some time within the organization in an integration project. Depending on the available positions and their abilities, individuals frequently obtain permanent positions through internal hiring channels.

Staff teams also include employees who originally came from other professions and who, through their commitment to this new profession, over the years become real social work experts. This holds true for most WISE founders, who often came from conventional career paths or were originally hired because of their specific skills.

To sum up, two main types of profiles coexist within WISEs' staff teams: activists who become social entrepreneurs, on the one hand, and professionals who, through their commitment to the organization, may adopt an activist stance.

In general, the first profile corresponds to the individuals who initiate the integration projects. Activists for a particular cause, such as protecting the environment or fighting social exclusion, they are the organizations' founders and perpetuate the values of the original project. Their commitment and their presence in the teams serve as a point of reference for all involved – both workers in integration and permanent employees. As inventors of methods specific to their activity, they develop a professionalism that is peculiar to their field. This is even truer in organizations in which the production of innovative services and goods aims not only at the work integration of the disadvantaged workers but also at benefiting the users.

This 'specific career', which we may name that of 'social entrepreneur', characterizes many WISE founders.

As the organization grows – and as the number of workers in integration proportionally increases – new positions must be created to develop other administrative, business or human resource services. Staff teams thus grow, incorporating personnel with new, more professional profiles who are hired for their particular skills in performing specific tasks. Although such a second wave of staff is characterized by more specific professional skills, the value system to be shared by these individuals and their capacity for teamwork remain important, although more implicitly.

Beyond typologies, another key feature of all WISE teams is the fact that they are embedded in their local environment. They generally have an extensive knowledge of local needs, of residents experiencing difficulties and of the jobs available. This allows the WISEs to adequately meet these needs by adapting their coaching and production activities.

As to the mechanisms for selecting the workers for the integration programme, they vary according to the organization. Most of the time, selection criteria take into account the individual's motivation for embarking on a coaching programme with a social enterprise. Usually, the skills required are very rudimentary. In fact, the institution generally has practically no special requirements, given that its first aim is to teach basic work practices: punctuality, how to present oneself, respect for rules, working with others and so on.

Indeed, the main concern of WISEs is to guarantee basic guidance, because true occupational training is only possible in the framework of other guidance mechanisms or within a traditional enterprise in which the worker will be integrated. In other words, learning an actual trade is deemed to be feasible only at a later stage, in another framework. Finally, it can be said that the social enterprise's margin for selection is very narrow: the type of workers referred to them by social services cannot be placed in any other structure.

3.2 *Democratic participation by stakeholders*

Another mechanism implemented by WISEs to balance their objectives consists in the promotion of democratic participation by the stakeholders. Our survey allows us to say that numerous collective in-house mechanisms have been established to facilitate participation by both workers and permanent staff. Such active participation in the work of the enterprise falls within the domains of both participatory management and training.

In terms of more direct participation in the decision-making process, the legal forms of all the WISEs surveyed – most of them are registered as non-profit organizations (*associations* under the law of 1901) – allow for participation by stakeholders, though it is not compulsory. Consequently, the participation of various categories of stakeholders (volunteers, salaried workers and users) in the decision-making process is not so much the result of the organization's legal form as of the internal operational rules it sets for itself. In the sample studied, it was very rare for all these three categories of actors to be really involved in the decision-making process regarding the orientation of the WISE. Only in one of the long-term work integration enterprises of the sample are the salaried workers actually represented on the board of directors and thus have a vote. The salaried workers obtained this right after extensive negotiations, but this case constitutes an exception rather than the rule. In all the other cases examined, only the volunteer members of the board have the right to vote, on a 'one person, one vote' basis. In general, the board's composition reflects the networks to which the founders belong. When the organization is characterised by a strong local embeddedness, and especially when the functioning of the organization strongly depends on its good relationships with the public authorities, prominent local citizens form the majority on the board. Otherwise, this too is a marginal phenomenon. The board is generally made up mostly of representatives of the non-profit sector, volunteer board members representing no organization and third-sector representatives, especially from citizen associations supporting the organization's militant activities. In general, WISEs encourage representatives of private enterprise to serve on the board so as to increase partnerships with this sector.

The only multi-stakeholder form bringing together users and volunteers – mainly residents, local public authorities and service purchasers, but only very rarely workers – is that of neighbourhood enterprises. Their charters provide that three types of stakeholders participate on their boards: the municipality, social housing owners and residents. Other non-profit organizations and – more rarely – employees, can also be included on the board.

WISEs have set up other mechanisms to promote participation by the staff and the disadvantaged workers; these mechanisms differ from one WISE to another. All WISEs scrupulously comply with labour law and, whenever the size of the enterprise allows it, representation bodies for the personnel are set up (staff representatives, works councils, etc.). They all hold regular formal meetings to prepare proposals for the organization's board; the proposals deal with operations, problems occurring during the course of activities or, more generally, project implementation. In sum, all WISEs have mechanisms facilitating broader participation by permanent staff in work organization and activity management. These mechanisms range from team self-management to daily meetings of the group. While these bodies do not actually make official decisions, they are in some way the spokespeople of the salaried workers and of the workers in integration to the board.

Indeed, although the decision-making process is formally based on the principle of 'one person, one vote', effective management is often in the hands of one or two board members along with the managers. The managers of WISEs who are employed by the organization have no vote on the board, but they are often invited to board meetings since they have access to all important information. Therefore, they play a crucial role in decisions of the board, which often simply implements the manager's proposals.

Workers in integration are rarely involved in the decision-making process. Some organizations have set up representative bodies to allow for increased worker involvement in internal operations. This translates into meetings with workshop or department heads, the assignment of representatives with the right to vote (calculated according to the number of hours worked), etc. Some organizations hesitate to include workers in the decision-making process, especially during periods of crisis. This is true, for example, of organizations mainly targeting mentally handicapped workers. Although they point out the participatory and collective nature of the organization, there remain certain doubts about the real possibility of allowing these workers to participate in decisions or even meetings.

3.3 Mobilizing networks to achieve the three priority objectives

To varying degrees, WISEs are involved in networks that eventually – and indirectly – help them meet their priority objectives. Their involvement with networks exists at three levels: local, regional and national.

According to all organizations, it is the local networks that provide results in the mid- to long-term. Local embeddedness is necessary for WISEs, and it is easier to mobilize personnel at this level. WISEs often mobilize managers within urban communities, employment services, local missions and community centres providing integration services. The long-term sustainability of WISEs' activities is linked to their embeddedness in a particular territory (this is even truer in rural areas). WISEs' local networks serve as a basis for the development of the production activities, because they provide more accurate information on the demand for goods and services. At the same time, WISEs try to increase awareness of people's right to work and to social integration within the public or private local institutions that are supposed to send them their disadvantaged workers. To achieve this, it is very important to establish relationships based on trust and mutual knowledge. WISEs find it easier to bring their activities to public attention when their sector of activities is very limited and specific; this is, for example, the case of the work integration enterprises active in the field of recycling that have played a role in educating the local population on environmental protection issues – and this is true in small villages as well as in large towns. For example, one big-city integration enterprise became known locally thanks to its activist commitment. Through general environmental education and pedagogical activities in schools, this WISE helped create an informal network at the local level. The network then grew as a result of a contract with the town council to collect paper and cardboard in the city. Since then, thanks to this project (which was only experimental at first), the WISE has become known locally, and participates actively in sustainable development networks and local work integration networks.

On an intermediate level, there are regional networks. In general, these are networks bringing together similar types of WISEs. Regional networks group together work integration organizations with similar characteristics in terms of legal forms, and sometimes even in terms of priorities or values. These networks are also activist organizations created with a view to gaining official recognition for their members. Many WISE managers are involved in these networks and in many cases hold managerial or decision-making positions. Belonging to these networks allows WISEs to implement projects that they could not have supported on their own, and even to carry out co-ordinated actions at the regional level which go beyond their local framework.

Managers get involved less frequently within organizations at the national level, for obvious reasons of distance and usefulness. Their participation in, and hence their contribution to, national bodies is rarer and only concerns a minority of WISE managers. This participation takes the form of sporadic meetings, thematic symposiums or formal exchanges. In our view, involvement in these networks is more useful in terms of recognition of the WISE and sense of belonging than for developing activities. But belonging to a national movement or activist organization can enhance a WISE's actions in a way that goes beyond strictly practical considerations and which is linked more specifically to the promotion of certain values.

In general, participating in networks in the area of work integration allows WISEs to advocate both social and occupational integration within the framework of a productive unit, and gives them the right to be better taken into account by public policy, given their direct contribution to the integration of the unemployed.

Conclusion

The studies conducted in France reveal the specificity of WISEs regarding their ability to effectively articulate multiple goals that may seem contradictory but that, on the whole, blend well and generate activities that are economically, socially and politically sustainable. In order to achieve this, WISEs implement internal processes of broad participation and shared values of solidarity, and also make use of external partnership and advocacy networks.

Even though, as it appeared from the analysis of the WISEs studied, mechanisms of broad participation of the multi-stakeholder type only exist in neighbourhood enterprises (RQs), where the users are formally present on the board of the organization, a major concern of all WISEs is to implement informal mechanisms ensuring the broadest possible participation of salaried workers and users. Consequently, beyond what is provided for in the statutes of non-profit organizations (*associations*), which give formal voting power to the members of the organization and its elected board members, other procedures, whose natures vary from one WISE to another, exist to allow the stakeholders to democratically express themselves. Similarly, regarding more specifically the three levels of intervention in the public arena (namely, the local, regional and national levels), the analysis has revealed the importance of this type of embeddedness, which enables WISEs to set up networks that can ensure their sustainability, in ways that differ according to the level concerned.

Beyond the specific goals of each WISE, no enterprise in the sample focuses exclusively on a social role, and the priority remains to combine purely social activity with a sustainable productive activity. WISEs remain a necessary step, coming before training, professionalization and stable work, for a category of workers who cannot directly enter traditional employment, which is becoming increasingly specialized because of technological progress.

All WISEs claim to be professional in the field of work integration or simply in their productive activities and underline the social utility and the collective benefits produced in their various fields of activity. However, the seriousness of their work is not matched by their image among public sector and private sector interlocutors, which obliges WISEs to limit their action to inappropriate fields or to adapt to unachievable constraints. This underlines the difficulty WISEs have in gaining recognition of their specificity – a specificity which lies in the fact that they combine professionalism with commitment to the rights of disadvantaged workers.

Finally, through the multiplicity of goals considered and the specific means implemented, WISEs play a major societal role: through setting up forms of democratization of the economy, they demonstrate that beyond the traditional market, other forms of economy are possible.

Review questions

- Why do the majority of French WISES rank the work integration of disadvantaged workers as their priority goal?
- In which cases does the production goal take priority over the integration objective?
- What roles do networks play in the development of French WISEs?

Note

1   Only one of the types of WISE identified in France (see Chapter 1, Appendix 2 of this book) was not included in the present sample: employers' organizations for work integration and training (*groupements d'employeurs pour l'insertion et la qualification*, or GEIQ).

5 Multiple goals and multi-stakeholder management in Italian social enterprises

Carlo Borzaga and Monica Loss

Overview

This chapter explores the evolution of the social co-operative movement in general, and of work integration (i.e. B-type) social co-operatives in particular, in Italy. After reading this chapter, the reader should:

- understand the reasons for the emergence of social co-operatives in the landscape of Italian public policies;
- grasp the main evolutions in the field of B-type social co-operatives regarding their goals and their multi-stakeholder ownership.

Introduction

'Work integration social co-operatives' (also referred to as B-type social co-operatives, or *cooperative sociali di tipo b*) are the only type of WISEs identified by the PERSE project in Italy. Indeed, although other types of organization aimed at integrating disadvantaged people into work exist, they are not significant.

Unlike other European countries that witnessed a considerable development of sheltered workshops, this model never succeeded in Italy. On the contrary, the social co-operative model, based on the twofold principle of both work and social integration, was preferred.

The role of the social co-operatives evolved over the years: initially they supported public social services aiming to integrate disadvantaged people, but later on they gained increasing autonomy in the definition of the goals pursued. This process was favoured by the coming into force of the national legislation regulating social co-operatives, but also by an outstanding development of entrepreneurial behaviour and practices within these WISEs.

After a brief description of the national system of protection of weak groups as regards work integration, this chapter will explore the evolution of the social co-operative movement in general, and of work integration (i.e. B-type) social co-operatives in particular. The characteristics of the latter in terms of organizational forms and role played in the balance between labour market and social policies will be singled out, with particular reference to the sample of work integration social co-operatives surveyed by the PERSE project.

1 A general framework

In the last two decades, stagnation of employment rates, rising unemployment associated with considerable demographic changes, massive female participation in the labour market, slower productivity growth, computerisation and demand for highly skilled workers have all been factors that have paved the way for problems such as long-term unemployment, exclusion of unskilled workers from the labour market and subsequent high risks of social exclusion. As regards Italian labour policies (in general and especially for hard-to-employ people), at the beginning of the 1990s, they were mostly characterized by their passive nature and heterogeneous coverage of the problem.

During the 1990s, labour policies were mainly oriented to the control of wage growth, through general tripartite agreements (the so-called *concertazione*, among trade unions, associations of employees and the government) and to the introduction of rules to make the labour market more flexible, such as part-time contracts, fixed-term contracts, temporary jobs (and the related placement agencies). New forms of employment, characterized by contracts mixing characteristics of salaried work and freelance work (the so-called *collaborazioni coordinate e continuative*), were also widely adopted. Finally, labour policies were reoriented away from passive policies and the resources were transferred to the budget of more active policies, whose main measures were the introduction of training contracts (fixed-term two-year contracts with reduced social security contributions); the reform of the employment services to allow private companies to operate as employment agencies matching labour demand with supply; the provision of various kinds of employment subsidies for firms employing long-term unemployed people and, finally, the strengthening of vocational training.

As regards policies and interventions designed for disabled people, Law 482 of 1968 established a quota system that required firms and public bodies with more than 35 employees to hire a quota of disabled people equal to 15 per cent of the overall workforce. But this system proved too strict and not very effective, and very often induced firms to evade the compulsory employment of disabled people. After several unsuccessful attempts, Parliament reformed the law in 1999 (Law 68 of 1999). The new law reduces the compulsory quota of disabled workers for firms with more than 50 employees from 15 per cent to 7 per cent; firms with 35 to 50 employees must employ two disadvantaged workers and firms with 15 to 35 employees must employ one disadvantaged worker.

Public policies aiming at the work integration of disadvantaged people other than the disabled have not been very effective so far either. The effectiveness of the active labour market programmes that have been developed during the last decade has been neither evident nor immediate, owing in part to a decrease in employment opportunities and to the increasing selectiveness of the demand for workforce. The problem is even more complicated and difficult to solve when unemployment is associated with other disadvantages, such as social exclusion, disability or low skills.

2 Work integration social co-operatives: characteristics and development

2.1 The first initiatives

In Italy innovative experiences of co-operatives targeting the work integration of disadvantaged people started to develop during the 1980s. These initiatives were rooted both in the process of de-institutionalization (closing down or capacity reduction of institutions for people affected by mental disorders, but also for young people with domestic problems, and orphans) and in the development of the demand for work integration for disabled people who, in the previous years, had followed educational and training paths. The effects of these factors were reinforced by the strict limits of the compulsory quota legislation supporting disabled people, which was based on an excessively bureaucratic management system: it ignored a large weak segment of the population, such as drug addicts and people with mental trouble, while, at the same time, people not in need could benefit from the law.

The new forms of initiative were created with the aim of giving disadvantaged people a remunerated stable job (if possible). Unlike what was the case in protected workshops, the proportion of disadvantaged employed was rather low at the outset. From the very beginning, the legal form adopted by most of these organizations was the co-operative. Sectors of activity differed according to the local economic context; they included services (laundry, green area maintenance, restaurants and food provision in general), manufacturing and handicrafts (glass, wood working, etc.).

These 'social' co-operatives started to develop in the northern regions first, while in the south their spread is a more recent phenomenon. This is mostly due to the socio-economic context, characterized in the north by a low unemployment rate and a high degree of economic development, and in the south by higher unemployment rates and a society more based on family networks, which have until recently attempted to deal with most of their social needs internally. As a consequence, social co-operatives created in the northern regions mainly attempt to satisfy collective needs such as childcare, services to the elderly, support to families with minors, etc., while in the southern regions they are often self-employment or self-entrepreneurial initiatives, in which the original intention of the founders (mainly disadvantaged people themselves) is to create job opportunities for themselves; the activities carried out are mainly activities to answer private needs such as gardening, cleaning and laundry.

2.2 A-type and B-type social co-operatives: Law 381 of 1991

After some years of free development, these organizations were recognized by Law 381 of 1991 (*Disciplina delle cooperative sociali*), which also established a distinction between A-type and B-type social co-operatives: according to the legislation, A-type social co-operatives are supposed to supply educational and social services, while B-type social co-operatives pursue production activities aimed at both providing job opportunities to disadvantaged workers and promoting the social integration of the latter by means of professional and personal development. In other words, the experience inside the social enterprise must allow the workers to improve their professional skills and also their personal abilities in terms of personal relations, behaviour, and autonomy in everyday life.

The law precisely defines the categories of disadvantaged people targeted by B-type social co-operatives. They are: people with physical or mental disabilities, drug addicts, alcoholics, minors with family problems and prisoners on probation. A public authority (municipality, public health agency, region or labour office) must certify the disability. The certification of disadvantage made by the public administration indicates a period of time; the disadvantage is thus supposed to be temporary, except for people with a certified permanent disability. At least 30 per cent of the total labour force engaged in B-type social co-operatives must be disadvantaged. The law provides for exemption from social security contributions for all the disadvantaged workers employed (provided, as mentioned, that the disability is certified by a public authority).

As regards economic and financial matters, the law states that public bodies, in derogation from the law on contract procurement by the public administration, may – for some categories of activities also defined by the law (provision of services such as cleaning, laundry, gardening) – conclude agreements with B-type social co-operatives without issuing calls for tenders. Besides, in calls for tenders in which the total amount of the contract is under the threshold established by European Union legislation, public administrations are allowed to include in the contract a so-called 'social clause', according to which the provider must employ a certain number of disadvantaged people (on this subject, see Chapters 7 and 17 of this book). Moreover, the workers employed must also enter a formalised work integration scheme.

The law thus explicitly recognizes an affinity of mission between public bodies and social co-operatives, and emphasizes the possibility of collaboration between them. However, the implementation of this principle has led to many difficulties, mainly regarding financial matters, due to frequent delays in payment by the public administrations. Recently, the resource mix of B-type social co-operatives and the way in which they mobilize these resources have changed. In order to ensure greater autonomy from subsidies, social co-operatives tend to seek to develop their entrepreneurial dimension and to increase the share of their market resources through the development of economic relationships, be it with the private market or with public bodies.

2.3 Scope of the movement

As concerns the extent of the whole movement in Italy, the first social co-operatives were created towards the end of the 1970s; they developed during the 1980s, but the strongest development occurred during the 1990s, and mainly after the approval of Law 381 of 1991. Table 5.1 (based on INPS[1] data) shows this development for the period between 1993 and 2000.

From 1993 to now, there has been a substantial development of work integration social co-operatives, both in terms of the number of organ-

Table 5.1 B-type social co-operatives (1993–2000)

	1993	1994	1995	1996	1998	1999	2000
Number of co-operatives	287	518	705	754	1,463	1,787	1,915
Annual rate of growth (%)		80.5	36.1	6.9	39.3	22.1	7.2
Total employment	4,501	7,115	9,837	11,165	23,104	28,079	32,939
Annual rate of growth (%)		58.1	38.3	13.5	43.8	21.5	17.3
Disadvantaged workers employed	1,675	3,204	4,686	5,414	11,319	12,310	13,569
Annual rate of growth (%)		91.3	46.2	15.54	54.5	8.8	10.2
Average number of employees per co-operative	15.7	13.7	13.9	14.8	15.8	15.7	17.2
Average number of disadvantaged workers per co-operative	5.8	6.2	6.6	7.2	7.7	6.9	7.1
Disadvantaged workers in total workforce (%)	37.2	45.0	47.6	48.5	49.0	43.8	41.2

Source: National Institute of Social Security (INPS).

izations and of the number of people employed. The rate of growth of B-type social co-operatives was very high in the early 1990s, because of the process of separation into two co-operatives (one A-type and one B-type) undertaken by several organizations which were managing both the provision of social services and work integration activities before the approval of the 1991 law.

It is also interesting to note the substantial and continuous growth of the number of co-operatives, of total employment and of the number of disadvantaged workers employed;[2] according to a recent study on social co-operatives (Marocchi 2005), the growth has been confirmed for subsequent years, although there might be some stabilization after 2002. Other sources (data from the General Directorate for Co-operatives – DGC – and estimates from Federsolidarietà) seem to confirm these trends. No less remarkable is the stability of the average size of these co-operatives in terms of total number of employees and number of disadvantaged workers and the consequent stability of the percentage of disadvantaged workers in the total workforce (around 40 per cent).

As a final remark, it is clear that B-type social co-operatives have become an important phenomenon: they now employ more than 18,000 disadvantaged workers, and their total workforce probably reaches 45,000.

2.4 The key role of consortia

In the years of their development and consolidation, many changes have occurred in the organizational and governance framework of work integration social co-operatives. After the period of pioneering experiences, the law of 1991, which set up the legal framework for social co-operatives, represented an important input not only for the development of this legal form, but also for the establishment of a clear distinction between those co-operatives oriented to the provision of social services and those aimed at providing job opportunities to disadvantaged workers. During the 1990s the movement developed a networking system, which helped social co-operatives to maintain a small dimension: instead of increasing the size of single co-operatives to match the growing demand for services, the main strategy has been to spin off new initiatives, thereby also pursuing a specialization strategy and allowing the advantages of large size to be reaped by grouping co-operatives into local consortia. The latter are formed mainly at the provincial level and they themselves form overall consortia at the national level.

Consortia now constitute an integrated entrepreneurial system. They perform one or more of the following functions:

- delivering support services to individual co-operatives, mainly in the form of training services, technical and administrative services, and knowledge and information transmission services;

- representing the interests of co-operatives: the consortium acts as a lobby for the development of policies and guidelines supporting the creation and expansion of social co-operatives;
- promoting joint economic strategies: consortia take various forms of action to foster the productive activities of their members.

In 2000 the regional registers listed a total of 207 such consortia in Italy, which represented an increase of 50 per cent on the 1998 figures. These consortia have developed mainly in the northern region, where 52 per cent (107 organizations) of them are located, followed by the south (59 consortia or 28 per cent of the total) and the centre (41 consortia or 20 per cent of the total).

3 The sample of WISEs surveyed

As already said, B-type social co-operatives in Italy represent the only organizational model of WISEs meeting the criteria of the EMES Network. The major challenge for building the sample to be surveyed was thus to choose 15 social co-operatives out of an overall population of some 2,000 organizations. The choice of co-operatives to be investigated was supported by the most important national consortium – Consorzio Nazionale 'Gino Mattarelli' – which brings together a significant number of social co-operatives and has all the relevant information regarding the co-operatives operating at a local level that was needed to select interesting cases.

The detailed criteria taken into account to build the sample were the following: type of work integration services offered (training, stable or transitional jobs); single or multiple economic activities; homogeneous territorial distribution; types of disadvantaged people targeted; size; and historical evolution of the co-operative. It was agreed by various parties involved in the sample selection process that the territorial distribution of the co-operatives was an important differentiation element, as were the origin of the organization, the original intention of the founders, the dynamics of development experienced, the governance and the sectors of activity. The sample was constituted so as to reflect the diversity of the field of B-type social co-operatives in these regards.

The sample comprises 15 organizations, equally distributed from a territorial point of view: seven in the north, seven in the south and islands and one in the centre. The majority of these social co-operatives carry out several economic activities in several economic sectors and employ various kinds of disadvantaged workers. Only four organizations pursue just one economic activity and employ only one category of disadvantaged workers.

3.1 Multiple goals

Analysis of the data collected from the social co-operatives surveyed reveals that most of them were founded with the main goal of creating work integration. At the outset, production activity was considered as only ancillary to this social goal. However, the pattern of development followed by social co-operatives in Italy has led to a reinforcement of the production activity, because of market pressure. Today, it seems that both dimensions are of equal importance.

The social co-operatives in the sample are involved in a wide variety of production activities. Some Italian WISEs provide services, such as the maintenance of green areas, cleaning and laundry; others produce and commercialize agricultural products, wood and metal handicrafts, or assemble industrial products. The activities carried out are obviously connected with and strongly influenced by the territorial and geographical location of the organizations; this is particularly true of the production of goods (the agricultural sector prevails in the south, the industrial sector in the north).

B-type social co-operatives were initially characterized by a high dependence on public resources. Today, WISE resources may come from various sources and many social co-operatives have a twofold orientation, towards both the private market and the public one (see Chapter 7 of this book). The trend in the last few years has been towards an increase in sales to the private market, especially for co-operatives providing services. There is even a social co-operative in the Lombardy region which, ever since its foundation, has worked only with private enterprises. As the only exception in the sample, another social co-operative, also located in the north, can be pointed out: since its foundation, at the initiative of a public social service, this social co-operative has operated using exclusively public resources.

The main aim of the work integration activities carried out by the social enterprises in the sample obviously remains to secure permanent jobs for their disadvantaged workers, but the way this goal is pursued has evolved over time: while social co-operatives initially sought to provide stable jobs for the disadvantaged workers inside the social enterprise itself, they now tend rather to provide the workers with training activities (of both vocational and general educational type) in order to enable them to find a stable job in the 'open labour market'. For some co-operatives, particularly in the southern regions, the main goal of the integration path is to provide disadvantaged workers with basic working instruments; their action is based on the assumption that a job is an effective treatment to escape marginalization and social exclusion. Target groups of the work integration services are mainly drug addicts and people with mental disorders, but also new categories of disadvantaged people, such as prisoners, alcoholics and socially marginalized people. Most social co-operatives in the sample focus on several categories of disadvantaged workers, although some southern social co-operatives employ only former drug addicts and northern social co-operatives usually have a specific focus on either people affected by mental disorders or ex-prisoners.

3.2 Multi-stakeholder enterprises

As far as managerial and entrepreneurial aspects are concerned, social co-operatives have specialized and they have improved their managerial skills and competences in order to better meet market requirements and to better answer the increasing demand for more specific services and products.

The governance framework has also changed, evolving towards a wider involvement of the different stakeholders: only 20 per cent of the Italian WISEs surveyed are single-stakeholder organizations, while a large majority of them (80 per cent) declare that they have a multi-membership nature or a multi-stakeholder structure:[3] 53 per cent involve two categories of stakeholders, 20 per cent three categories and 7 per cent four categories. These organizations consider that, since they were created to give an answer to community needs, it is quite natural to involve many actors from the community in the decision-making process even though, in some cases, the co-existence of these different actors can create problems for the management of the enterprise.

The most influential category of stakeholders in multi-stakeholder social co-operatives (see Table 2.4 in this book) is that of staff members (55 per cent), followed by volunteers (29 per cent). The interviewees consider governmental representatives to have no influence at all, while private individuals, business representatives, participants and representatives from non-profit organizations exert only a low influence (respectively 4 per cent, 3 per cent, and 1 per cent for the two last).

The adoption of a multi-stakeholder structure may enable the member workers undergoing a work integration programme to sit in the general assembly or in the board of directors. However, as we have just seen, this is not very common, because these individuals may experience self-control difficulties. In one social co-operative, such difficulties led to the removal of a disadvantaged worker from the board of directors. But very often, solutions are implemented to promote other forms of participation by these workers in the economic and managerial life of the organization: informal participation is made possible through internal meetings, working groups on specific issues, as well as involvement in the enterprise's activities. In recent years social co-operatives have tended to develop and increase their multi-stakeholder nature, involving many different categories of stakeholders in the organization's 'life' – both those who are interested by the activities carried out by the social co-operatives (i.e. public administrations, local institutions) and those whose involvement is interesting for the social co-operative itself (associations, credit institutions such as credit co-operatives, etc.).

The number of volunteers has been reduced, compared to the early development period, but nowadays they still represent 10 to 15 per cent of members. If, in the early stage of the co-operative movement's development, volunteers formed the core of the organizations (volunteers and volunteer-workers played a very important role in the development of the first social co-operatives, which were very similar to voluntary organizations: their entrepreneurial aspect was not very developed) and were active in all spheres of activity, their role has evolved over time, and most volunteers nowadays are members of the board of directors and have a more 'honorific' role than a really operative one. This is probably due mainly to the efforts made by social co-operatives to ensure their economic sustainability, which seem to lead them to favour the participation of stakeholders who are able to facilitate the access to funding. Deeper investigation is needed regarding this general trend, which seems to emerge from the current debate on the role of volunteers in the life of social co-operatives.

This evolution appears to be particularly evident in the regions of the south, which have witnessed a late and slow development of the social co-operative movement, compared to the northern and central regions of the country. This slower development is mainly due to the south's socio-economic condition: this region is characterized by low economic growth, high criminality and extremely high unemployment. In this context, finding a job is difficult even for workers who are not 'disadvantaged', and integrating the disadvantaged appears to be a real challenge; the main contribution of social co-operatives to the economic development of this region is the creation of new employment. More than in other areas of the country, the economic sustainability of an enterprise depends – besides market and other factors (such as criminality) – on its internal functioning, and more particularly on its financial management; consequently, the fact that social co-operatives involve few volunteers does not significantly reduce their effectiveness in integrating their members, nor their democratic governance. Rather, it can be considered as a consequence of a different distribution of tasks among different actors of the third sector in the southern regions.

In general, the community orientation of governance may take the form of a number of processes, such as democratic decision-making procedures that encourage all stakeholders to participate dynamically; the involvement in the organization's governance of different stakeholders (workers, volunteers, users, etc.) and the absence of proportionality between voting rights (or weight in the decision-making process) and share capital.

In none of the 15 WISEs in the sample did we find representatives of public agencies as members of the board. This probably results from the process of 'entrepreneurialization' and specialization undergone by a significant number of social co-operatives. Besides this category, participants in integration programmes and representatives of the private business sector and the third sector are the categories least represented on boards of directors. Conversely, the categories most frequently present are member-employees and volunteers, especially those assuming key roles, such as president or auditor. The interviews also show a strong involvement of these two categories in both the work-integration activity and the production of goods and services, which tends to confirm the equal importance social co-operatives place on their social and economic dimensions.

Conclusions

Notwithstanding the evolution B-type social co-operatives have undergone over the last years as to the importance of their economic activities (which has resulted, for example, in an increase of manufactured goods and services supplied and in the evolution towards a multiple-goal structure), the original mission pursued seems to firmly remain: Italian WISEs still aim to offer work opportunities to people at risk of social exclusion. The original idea of the founders – namely that work integration and vocational training are the most effective tools to tackle social exclusion – is still challenging and well-grounded.

In recent years things have changed in many ways, and the social co-operative model has specialized and reached an important – even though not yet very well recognized – role in the Italian socio-economic system. Thanks to their flexible organization, to their ability to bring a quick and adequate answer to the needs expressed by the local community, to the networking system they have developed to support small enterprises, and to the important impulse given to the employment of both able and disadvantaged people, B-type social co-operatives can now be considered as labour policy tools, rather than merely as supporting devices for social inclusion programmes. The main social objective, namely supporting disadvantaged people in finding a job, still persists as a major goal of these organizations, which, in doing so, are able to combine, probably better than other organizational forms, the two goals of social inclusion and economic production of goods and services.

Review questions

- What are the differences between B-type social co-operatives in the north of Italy and those in the south of the country?
- Why have consortia played a crucial role in the development of the social co-operative movement?

Notes

1 INPS is the National Institute of Social Security, to which work integration social co-operatives have to communicate the number of disadvantaged people they employ (in order to get the above-mentioned exemption).

2   The INPS data underestimate the number of disadvantaged people employed in B-type social co-operatives. This is due to the fact that the enterprise can benefit from social security exemption only for the employment of disadvantaged people as defined by law. If they employ, for instance, long-term unemployed people (who are not defined as disadvantaged by law), they are not entitled to this fiscal benefit.

3   As explained in Chapter 2 of this book, the definition of the term 'multi-stakeholder' used by the PERSE project is that proposed by Borzaga and Mittone (1997), according to whom the multi-stakeholder nature is connected with the ownership structure.

Bibliography

Bandini, F. (2003) *Manuale di economia delle aziende non profit*, Padua: CEDAM.

Borzaga, C. (1994) 'La cooperazione sociale di inserimento lavorativo: una analisi empirica dell'efficacia e dei fattori di successo', *Rivista della Cooperazione*, 18, September–October.

Borzaga, C. (ed.) (2000) *Qualità del lavoro e soddisfazione dei lavoratori nei servizi sociali*, Rome: Fondazione Italiana per il Volontariato.

Borzaga, C. and Defourny, J. (eds) (2001) *L'impresa sociale in prospettiva europea*, Trento: Edizioni 31.

Borzaga, C. and Mittone, L. (1997) 'The Multi-stakeholder versus the Nonprofit Organization', *Discussion Paper*, 7, Trento: Department of Economics, University of Trento.

Borzaga, C. and Santuari, A. (eds) (1997) *Servizi sociali e nuova occupazione: l'esperienza delle nuove figure di imprenditorialità sociale in Europa*, Vol. 1, Trento: Regione Trentino Alto-Adige.

Borzaga, C. and Zandonai, F. (2002) 'I contenuti del terzo rapporto sulla cooperazione sociale', in *Comunità cooperative*, Turin: Edizioni della Fondazione Giovanni Agnelli.

Centro Studi CGM (ed.) (1997) *Imprenditori sociali. Secondo rapporto sulla cooperazione sociale in Italia*, Turin: Edizioni della Fondazione Giovanni Agnelli.

Demozzi, M., Loss, M. and Valenti, G. (2000) *The work integration of disadvantaged people*, research report, Trento: ISSAN.

Fazzi, L. (2003) *Costruire Politiche Sociali*, Milan: Franco Angeli.

Hansmann, H. (1996) *The Ownership of Enterprise*, Cambridge, MA: Harvard University Press.

ISTAT (2001) *Le istituzioni nonprofit in Italia. I risultati della prima rilevazione censuaria. Anno 1999*.

Loss, M. (1999) *Active employment policies and labour integration for disabled persons: estimation of the net benefits*, research report, Trento: ISSAN.

Loss, M. (2004) *The Individual Benefits for Disadvantaged Workers Employed in Work Integration Social Enterprises. European Analysis*, PERSE research report, Liège: EMES European Research Network.

Loss, M. and Borzaga, C. (2002a) 'National Profiles of Work Integration Social Enterprises: Italy', *Working Papers Series*, 02/02, Liège: EMES European Research Network.

Loss, M. and Borzaga, C. (2002b) *The Socio-economic Performance of Social Enterprises in the Field of Integration by Work*, intermediate research report, Trento: ISSAN.

Loss, M. and Borzaga, C. (2003) *Labour Integration, Social Enterprise and Local Development*, Trento: Agenzia del Lavoro.

Marocchi, G. (1999) *Integrazione lavorativa, impresa sociale, sviluppo locale*, Milan: Franco Angeli.

Marocchi, G. (2002) 'L'inserimento lavorativo nelle cooperative social', in *Comunità cooperative*, Turin: Edizioni della Fondazione Giovanni Agnelli.

Marocchi, G. (2005) *Le traiettorie di sviluppo della cooperazione sociale italiana in Beni comuni, Quarto rapporto sulla cooperazione sociale in Italia*, Turin: Edizioni Fondazione Giovanni Agnelli.

Musella, M. (2005) 'Cooperazione sociale e Mezzogiorno', in *Beni comuni. Quarto rapporto sulla cooperazione sociale in Italia*, Turin: Edizioni della Fondazione Giovanni Agnelli.

Spear, R., Defourny, J., Favreau, L. and Laville, J.-L. (eds) (2001) *Tackling Social Exclusion in Europe*, London: Ashgate.

6 Social entrepreneurship and the mobilization of social capital in European social enterprises

Lars Hulgård and Roger Spear

Overview

This chapter adopts an institutional approach to analysing the dynamic of social entrepreneurship and the way in which social entrepreneurs make use of social capital. This chapter aims to:

- show the difference between the voluntarism and the institutional approaches to social capital;
- give a sense of the different patterns of social entrepreneurship;
- identify the different channels through which social enterprises can develop social capital.

Introduction

During the last two decades, starting in the mid-1980s, a remarkable connection between features usually considered as belonging to the sphere of civil society and characteristics usually related to market economics has evolved as a trend in the not-for-profit sector: the emergence of social entrepreneurship. Concepts and understandings related to social science all of a sudden ended up intertwined with the vocabulary of market economics: 'entrepreneurship', 'innovation', 'capital' and so on. Social entrepreneurs, it is said, are the equivalents of business entrepreneurs 'but they operate in the social, not-for-profit sector, building "something from nothing" and seeking new and innovative solutions to social problems'.[1]

In the EU and in European countries in general we find widespread evidence of the existence of social enterprises; this phenomenon reflects changes in the way social cohesion, social integration and social policy are thought of and dealt with. These changes have been pinpointed in numerous publications from the viewpoint that a certain degree of entrepreneurial orientation is mandatory for all types of not-for-profit organisations today: 'a degree of entrepreneurial orientation would then be imperative for each and every organization today, irrespective of its location in one or the other "sector"' (Evers 2001: 297).

In his speech to the European Co-operative Convention in Brussels in February 2002, President of the European Commission Romano Prodi dealt with social entrepreneurship in a way that covered both sides of the issue: *market orientation*, and *organized civil society / social capital*. Mr Prodi stressed that co-operatives are social enterprises that form an important part of the European social economy: they are important contributors both to the economy and to the generation of social capital. They demonstrate 'that the spirit of solidarity which is at the root in no way clashes with an entrepreneurial outlook' (Prodi 2002). What makes social enterprises and co-operatives special to the President of the European Commission is the combination of innovation and entrepreneurial orientation with the added value caused by their identity as being 'schools of participation and active citizenship'.

This vision is quite similar to the formulations in current social capital research where social capital, being defined as networks of trust relations and norms of reciprocity that provide an important asset for co-operation for mutual benefit (Putnam 2000), is seen as crucial in the making of sustainable communities.

Current views of social capital can be divided into two basic discourses: the 'voluntarism discourse', on the one hand, and the 'institutional discourse', on the other. The major distinction between the two concerns the relationship between civil society and the two remaining sectors of modern society, namely the public sector and the for-profit market sector. The question is whether social capital is mainly produced in networks of mutual trust relations among civic engaged individuals (as argued in the voluntarism discourse) or through changing institutional configurations between actors and institutions from all three spheres of modern society – the public sector, the for-profit market sector as well as civil society (which is the point of view advocated by the institutional discourse). The voluntarism discourse emphasizes the role of family and community networks, whereas the institutional discourse stresses relations and intersectoral links between institutions. In the institutional view, it is the institutional configurations between actors and institutions engaged in specific policy problems that determine the outcome of certain actions.

Thus, the voluntarism discourse emphasizes the role of rational individuals and groups making bonds and bridges of social capital based upon voluntary individual actions. This view is powerful in American discussions of civil society and social entrepreneurship. Key figures in American discourses on civil society and social entrepreneurship have emphasized how individual social engagement has been surrendered to the welfare state. They have further argued that problems of social cohesion can only be solved by encouraging voluntarism (civil society action) and by strengthening linkages between individuals from the non-profit and the for-profit sectors in collaborative social enterprise initiatives (Schambra 1997; Dees 2001).

This chapter adopts the institutional approach; it seeks to identify and analyse the specific institutional configuration of actors and institutions from state, market and civil society. It focuses on socially embedded rules and structures, and their roles in shaping individual and collective action. Though major differences exist among theorists within the frame of this approach, all supporters of the institutional discourse share one common view: they do not consider the public sector and civil society as necessarily being opposed to each other (this is another major difference between the institutional approach and the voluntarism one). According to the institutional perspective the historic relationship between civic organizations and the government sector is one of complementarity rather than of opposition (Skocpol 1997, 2003; Selle 1999; Rothstein 2001; Hulgård 2004). Some scholars working within the institutional view further stress the possible synergy effect between public sector and civic engagement (Woolcock 2000).

The distinction between voluntarism and institutionalism, as will be shown now, relates to the distinction between 'bonding' and 'bridging' social capital.

Bonding social capital is produced when people who share some basic identities interact in situations based on networks, norms and trust. Bonding social capital is not necessarily a policy issue, and it is easily produced in homogeneous associations based on a commonly shared background, e.g. ethnicity, status or gender.

Bridging social capital involves the creation of 'bridges' between individuals and groups who are different. Bridging social capital is produced within social networks among people who previously might not even know each other, but who come to share some institutional experiences. Both forms of social capital have important societal functions; however, it is empirically much easier to create bonding social capital than bridging social capital. While bonding social capital almost produces itself, wherever people meet as equals, bridging social capital often needs to be facilitated with some level of institutionalization and formal organization which can usefully be considered in a policy context and in a welfare context. Bridging social capital encourages people to generate generalized trust (Rothstein and Stolle 2002).

The voluntarism discourse tends to emphasize bonding social capital, with its focus on 'agency' by private individuals and groups in civil society; it recognizes the value of bridging social capital, but its failure to take account of how the difficulties of bridging social capital can be overcome through institutional measures, and its hostility to the state influencing the institutional context, leads to it being rather a weak perspective for understanding bridging social capital.

On the other hand, the institutional approach to social capital emphasizes structural (institutional) features of the context, and recognizes the role the state can play in establishing a facilitative institutional context; thus it is a useful perspective for addressing the complex relation between micro-level interaction (bonding) in strong networks, and the possibility for co-ordination and social cohesion on the macro level based upon the existence of generalized trust (bridging). The perspective guiding the social capital part of the PERSE research project was that more or less institutionalized and sustainable networks linking individual and collective actors in mutual trust relations constitute a resource that WISEs can mobilize to achieve their objectives; it is thus closer to the 'institutional discourse'.

This institutional approach also informs the other main theme of this chapter – social entrepreneurship – since, as we shall see, entrepreneurship operates not just at the organizational level (creating a new social enterprise), but also at the institutional level (creating a facilitative context). The two fields of social entrepreneurship are intimately interlinked, and we adopt a dynamic perspective to reveal their interrelation in the development of the social enterprise over time, from its formative phase to its established phase, and its subsequent phases of adaptation.

In the introductory section of this chapter, we have tried to map out the major frames of analysis which can be used to study how social enterprises make use of social capital. In the next section (Section 1), we examine some of the conceptual issues that are currently emerging in the study of social entrepreneurship and social capital in the formative stage of social enterprises. This is followed in Section 2 by an examination of empirical evidence on this formative phase, drawing on 17 in-depth case studies from the PERSE project. In Section 3 we examine in some depth the different ways in which social capital is used and reproduced in the established phase of all the cases of the PERSE sample (this amounts to around 150 social enterprises). Before concluding, we develop in Section 4 an institutional perspective on this extensive European experience, and we examine the micro–macro linkages – demonstrating the specific institutional configurations that mediate relations between actors, institutions and policies in the different countries studied.

1 Social entrepreneurship and social capital in the formative phase of social enterprises – overview

Social entrepreneurship is empirically interesting as a field where the mobilization of social capital can be explored. It appears to succeed against the odds, since it often operates in difficult sectors marked by low levels of available resources but where such a lack may possibly be compensated by the use of social capital. Theoretically it is interesting since it represents a challenge to conventional thinking about entrepreneurship, which tends to emphasize the individual, whereas in social entrepreneurship there often seems to be a more collective dimension, where the social entrepreneur is embedded in a network of support/advice that helps this model of entrepreneurship succeed.

This section of this chapter draws on small and medium enterprise (SME) literature on entrepreneurship, the literature from not-for-profit studies and social enterprise studies, and the institutional perspective on social capital to construct an understanding of our in-depth case study data. This study is exploratory; it attempts to reveal what is distinctive about social entrepreneurship in the WISE sector. Evidence (both anecdotal and in the literature) suggests that social entrepreneurship may have some features that differentiate it from entrepreneurship in the conventional business sector.

First, institutions have often played key roles in the entrepreneurial process in non-profits and co-operatives (Cornforth *et al.* 1988). Several examples bear testimony to this: in the Mondragón co-operative movement, in northern Spain, it is clear that the co-operative bank, Caja Laboral Popular, has played a central role in nurturing and supporting entrepreneurs developing co-operatives; in Italy the growth of social co-operatives during the last two decades has been supported by consortia of local co-operatives providing management services; in the UK and Sweden, co-operative development agencies have been the focus of entrepreneurial activity for worker co-operatives. These institutional forms of support for entrepreneurship may help to compensate for deficiencies; indeed, some authors consider that third sector organizations suffer some weaknesses: for example, Abell (1983) argues that co-operatives suffer an entrepreneurial problem, while Salamon and Anheier (1997) note that non-profits do not seem to have effectively responded to opportunities in new welfare markets. Thus, while all entrepreneurship is institutionally configured, social entrepreneurship develops a distinctive kind of relation to its institutional context, with organizations frequently playing a facilitating role. And in the case of WISEs the role of public institutions is particularly important both in terms of access to financial resources, and in terms of how bridging social capital may be used.

Second, purely economic theories of entrepreneurship indicate that the 'heroic individual' is unlikely to choose to form an enterprise that has a collective form of ownership (Abell 1983). This points to the need to consider other motivations than those of these 'heroic individuals', such as social rewards, in the initial motivation of social entrepreneurs. It is also likely that more collective forms of entrepreneurship will result in collective forms of ownership – such as those often adopted in social enterprises – and collective ownership is a form of mobilization of social capital. This collective dimension of entrepreneurship is not very well developed in any of the literature on entrepreneurship, and even less in the not-for-profit literature, where entrepreneurship is rarely a topic of research. However, there is some relevant literature: Young (1987) describes several cases of collective entrepreneurship, though he does not bring this out as a distinctive factor of entrepreneurship. Van de Ven (1993), in a theoretical paper that maps out a research agenda for studying the infrastructure for entrepreneurship, argues that 'the process of entrepreneurship is a collective achievement requiring key roles from numerous entrepreneurs in both the public and private sectors'. Casson (1995) argues that entrepreneurship can be a distributed process across the public/private divide. But besides a few exceptions such as these, in general the collective dimension of entrepreneurship is under-theorized in the SME and non-profit literature.

Both the institutional dimension (in particular, the specific role played by institutions in facilitating organizations) and this collective dimension of social entrepreneurship point to distinctively different models of entrepreneurship in this sector. The processes operating collectively and institutionally may be distributed outside the boundaries of the social enterprise, for example to include public sector or the wider social economy sector.

A third distinctive feature of social entrepreneurship is still more directly linked to social capital, since it concerns the potential use made of social capital in social entrepreneurship. Although one should not overstate the importance of this feature, since undoubtedly there is evidence of individualist entrepreneurs forming social enterprises, social capital can play a more important role in social enterprises than in other enterprises for three reasons:

- Social capital fits well with social enterprise: the multiple-goal structure that characterizes social enterprises, and which typically is not just concerned with economic goals, would seem to allow a wider range of relations to be developed regarding the other, non-economic goals. Indeed, it appears that many social enterprises have a community orientation and carry out, to a significant level, networking and lobbying activities (see Chapter 2 of this book), above and beyond those required for purely instrumental economic benefit, and these activities are very likely to use and generate social capital. The creation of social capital can even be a goal in itself for the social enterprise.
- The multi-stakeholder structure of social enterprises, with boards representing diverse groups, facilitates multiple linkages within the social enterprise and between the social enterprise and its environment (see Chapter 2 of this book). Such linkages create and generate social capital, both through the multiple-stakeholder board, via internal interactions among its members, as well as through the increase of links with its environment.
- The use of volunteers illustrates how social capital can be translated into other resources within the enterprise (see Chapter 7 of this book).

2 Analysis of social entrepreneurship case studies in the formative phase

The evidence in this section is drawn from a subset (17 case studies from five countries: Belgium, Denmark, Germany, Italy and the UK) of the data collected in the framework of the PERSE project. By and large, the main sectors in which WISEs operate are local and community services, some of which are delivered under contract to the public authorities, while others are sold directly to individuals.

Drawing on the first two distinctive features of social entrepreneurship presented in the previous section (namely, the importance of the institutional context and the collective dimension of social entrepreneurship), we first take an institutional perspective to develop a new view of social entrepreneurship; on this basis, we then outline the distinctive characteristics of three models of social entrepreneurship found empirically. The third distinctive feature of social entrepreneurship is developed in Section 3, where a more detailed analysis of the forms of social capital used and reproduced in established European WISEs is provided.

2.1 Institutional contexts for social entrepreneurship

European WISEs are highly heterogeneous, in terms of the various institutional contexts in which they have developed and which have contributed to shaping them. However, in broad terms, these initiatives also share many similarities: they all need to establish relations with different institutions to ensure their resources – different arms of the state for subsidies and contracts, the private sector for sales in the market, and the community and like-minded networks for social capital. They manage these relations both directly – through lobbying-type activities – and indirectly – through participation in networks, drawing on social capital.

In several countries there are quite well-established institutional forms and strongly patterned institutional relations that social entrepreneurs can take up to facilitate the process of social entrepreneurship. The types of WISEs and their contexts differ in terms of degree of recognition of the organizational form (the highest level of recognition being the creation of a new, specific legal form), the level of maturity of lobbying/negotiating networks, the degree of standardization of grant/subsidy funding packages available to them, etc.

There appear to be three main types of institutional context that shape social entrepreneurship:

- new legal forms or new specific policies within structured public frameworks (see Chapter 17 of this book);
- self-labelling forms and networks;
- ad hoc constructed contexts (with new types of social enterprise sometimes adapted from other institutional forms).

The first type of context is typified by the case of Italy, where legal forms specific to WISEs have existed for over 20 years, with well-established models of subsidy and contracts, and well-developed relations between municipalities and social enterprise networks. Belgium also illustrates this case: early development of some pioneering initiatives led, after a long process of institutionalization, to the creation of some new specific public schemes through a gradual evolution of the public policies for specific subsidy and support. Many subsequently created WISEs could take advantage of this institutional niche, which resulted in a boom in such initiatives.

The second type of institutional context – self-labelling forms and networks – can be seen in countries such as the UK, where social enterprises take the form of several different types that have emerged and self-labelled over the years, such as community businesses or intermediate labour market organizations. Each of these has its own network, its own organizational form, and has a patterned access to different types of resources.

Finally, the third type of context refers to the ad hoc constructed contexts, where each new social enterprise is created by drawing on generalized institutional elements (such as the market or public/associative partnership), rather than institutional contexts specific to social enterprise such as either of the two above forms. This type includes innovative developments in some countries (possibly where social enterprises are not so well-developed), such as Denmark.

Thus the first two types of institutional context arise first from the creation and recognition of a new social enterprise identity; from the parallel development of institutional relations related to this – including public policy frameworks, support structures, professional advisers (knowledgeable about this new institutional form); and from the development of relevant formal networks (see the second part of Section 3.2 – entitled 'Networking and bridging social capital' – of this chapter). As described above this patterning of institutional contexts has a longitudinal dimension – typically, it evolves over a period of time, and it continues to evolve as the population/sector of social enterprises develops (with the possible emergence of isomorphic tendencies, as described in Chapter 15 of this book) and as features of the institutional context (such as the markets, policies on subsidies or the role of relevant civil society players) evolve. Thus, for example, in Germany, the social movements of the 1970s shaped new non-profit/public partnerships for work integration, which gradually became institutionalized in formal organizations, dominated by business rationales and professionalization processes (see Chapter 18 of this book for more details). To summarize, institutional contexts of social enterprise develop and evolve over the years: activists embedded in social movements or leading community action create new social enterprise; they then, through bridging social capital and lobbying activities, go on to shape the institutional context – acting in concert with state actors as civic entrepreneurs.

As regards the level of innovation (in the Schumpeterian sense of the term), it can be expected to differ according to the type of context. In terms of Schumpeterian entrepreneurship, there is innovation when a new form of organization or a new institutional context is created – as happened at some past point for the first and second types of context, and is still under way in the case of the third type of context. In other words, innovation is expressed, on the one hand, through the setting up of a new hybrid structure or organizational form, which links together people and resources in a distinctive way (for example, multi-stakeholder governance, use of social capital – including volunteers and high trust networks – and integration of multiple sources of resources) or, on the other hand, through the creation of new institutional arrangements that mesh with and support the new social enterprise. In this sense, the level of innovation is probably much lower when a new social enterprise is created in the already well-established first or second types of context than in the third type (other things – such as markets or products – being equal).

2.2 Collective dimension and models of entrepreneurship

As explained above, much conventional literature (which also informs popular images of entrepreneurship in the media) makes an unquestioned assumption that entrepreneurship takes the classic form of the 'heroic individual'. There might well be an overemphasis on the individual in the SME sector; and in the social economy, where collectivist values are much stronger, it is very unlikely that such a model is dominant. As Spear (2006) argues in a small-scale study of entrepreneurship in worker co-operatives, individualistic entrepreneurship in these enterprises is the exception rather than the rule. Instead, more collective models – which, because of their collective dimension, are associated with a higher level of social capital – are the norm: joint (leader and supporters) or team-based entrepreneurship.

In the 17 cases of European WISEs on which Section 2 is based, three types or models of entrepreneurship can be distinguished, almost all of which are clearly collective forms:

- organizational (sponsored) entrepreneurship in nine cases;
- citizens' entrepreneurship in six cases;
- joint entrepreneurship in two cases.

Organizational (sponsored) entrepreneurship (nine cases) takes the form of organizations leading or sponsoring[2] the creation of the new enterprise – these organizations can be trade unions, voluntary organizations, municipal departments and so on. This model also covers partnership initiatives (four cases among the 17 studied here) led by subgroups from an organization (such as professionals from a municipality) in collaboration with other organizations or groups of stakeholders.

Citizens' entrepreneurship (six cases) takes several forms: first, informal collective volunteer activity for disadvantaged groups, then partnership initiatives between volunteers and disadvantaged groups, and, finally, initiatives by groups of disadvantaged people.

Joint entrepreneurship (two cases) takes, in our sample, the form of two rather different types: in one of the two cases, an individual entrepreneur played a role in the merger between two organizations, which resulted in the creation of the new social enterprise; in the other case, a small group of three entrepreneur managers created a new social enterprise. Although the former case could be classed as individualistic, it is classed here as joint, because two social enterprises were involved, with the leaders of the second social enterprise playing a role; the latter case is clearly collective.

Thus in our subset of case studies, the collectivist model of entrepreneurship was clearly predominant, and consequently these social enterprises can logically be expected to use and generate a comparatively high level of social capital.

Among the 17 WISEs studied, a distinction can also be established between sponsored entrepreneurship and self-help entrepreneurship (the above-defined category of organizational entrepreneurship clearly falls within the sponsored entrepreneurship form; as far as citizens' and joint entrepreneurship are concerned, these could be either sponsored or self-help entrepreneurship, or a mix of both forms); this corresponds to the traditional distinction, within the social economy, between charity, on the one hand, and mutuality (or co-operation), on the other. Some WISEs also mix these two orientations. Sponsored patterns of social entrepreneurship may be particularly prominent among WISEs concerned with employing disadvantaged participants as opposed to providing welfare services for them. This orientation (towards sponsored entrepreneurship or self-help entrepreneurship) influences, in turn, the ways in which the social enterprise is subsequently structured – in particular the composition of the board and the participation or involvement of entrepreneurial stakeholders. This is relevant for our purpose since, as we shall see in Section 3, it has implications for the patterns of social capital – bonding and bridging – that emerge. Thus, for example, initiatives by groups of disadvantaged people, in the self-help mould, will tend to lead to a board where they are represented, and a higher level of internal participative involvement, i.e. high bonding social capital, and relatively low bridging social capital. Conversely, a highly sponsored pattern of social entrepreneurship, in the charitable mould, will tend to create space on the board for its sponsors (professionals and members of the municipality), with less space for staff and disadvantaged participants; as a consequence, bonding social capital, in such a case, will tend to be relatively low, while the level of bridging social capital will be high.

Evidence from these 17 case studies also contributes to our understanding of subsequent episodes of social entrepreneurship, and the role of social capital. In some cases, social capital seems to play a role: thus in many social enterprises there is a clear orientation to giving something back to the community – i.e. a reciprocation, and this leads in some cases to providing additional services to the community as the social enterprise grows and develops. And, significantly, in well-networked social enterprises, the locus of entrepreneurial activity is not always only within the social enterprise, thus in some cases network or partnership activity leads to new initiatives. At the institutional level, in some cases, such as in Italy, growth has clearly arisen from entrepreneurial activity through bridging networks to improve the institutional context. Finally, while changes in external conditions (such as pressure from the market) can lead to the development of the enterprise, continually adapting to the changing policy context is frequently quoted as one of the difficult entrepreneurial challenges faced by the social enterprises – we return to this issue in the final section of this chapter.

To summarize, the institutional perspective, which states that social capital is produced mainly through institutional configurations linking actors from the three main spheres of society (the public, private for-profit and non-profit sectors), has revealed three types of contexts that appear relevant to understanding patterns of social enterprise development. We have also specified three models of entrepreneurship; we noted how these models are intimately intertwined with social capital and influence the structures chosen and developed, and the forms of social capital that are reproduced in the newly established social enterprise. In Section 3, we will analyse the use of social capital in subsequent stages of development of WISEs, once the social enterprise is established.

3 Social capital in established European WISEs

Three forms of social capital have been identified in the framework of the PERSE research project:

- social capital as norms and values: the normative dimensions of the organization inhibit or enhance social capital (this is developed in Section 3.1);
- social capital as networks and social relations within the realm of the social enterprise (this is addressed in the first part of Section 3.2.);
- social capital created in the external linkages between actors and organizations belonging to different spheres – non-profit, for-profit and public sector (this bridging dimension of social capital is the subject of the second part of Section 3.2).

For the first two sections, we rely on quantitative data[3] collected in more than 150 WISEs across Europe. Since we have no reliable quantitative data presenting the types and numbers of networks European WISEs are engaged in, the third section is based on the results from the national case studies.

The PERSE study examined both the bonding dimension of social capital, i.e. networks and trust relations generated within social enterprises, among homogeneous actors, and its bridging dimension, i.e. relations among board members of multi-stakeholder WISEs and networks generated between social enterprises and actors from different sectors. In this chapter, both forms are examined, although we focus more particularly on the role of bridging social capital, drawing on the institutional discourse. As already mentioned, the institutional perspective considers that bridging social capital is created when links are created between institutions and actors belonging to sectors that are different (e.g. state, market and civil society).

3.1 Social capital as norms and values

This section reviews the norms and values of the WISEs studied and examines the extent to which the former may be considered to enhance or inhibit the development of social capital. The norms and values guiding the majority of European WISEs studied in the PERSE project can apparently be traced back, in many cases, to the original orientations expressed by the founding members: 32 per cent of all WISEs state that the source of their goals is derived from the original intentions formulated by the founders. Other sources of goals cited include response to community needs (26 per cent), reaction to labour market problems (22 per cent), networks (18 per cent) and umbrella organizations (only 3 per cent).

Bode *et al.* (2003) identified five main types of norms and values in German WISEs:

- strong religious values;
- response to and implementation of municipal policy guidelines;
- a utopia of 'new work';
- linkage of social and entrepreneurial orientations;
- social protection and promotion.

At the European level, although religious values are not as manifest in some countries as in others, a strong value-based orientation related to norms and intentions originally expressed by the founders is generally important as a 'moral foundation' of many WISEs. The main values of WISEs are, broadly speaking, to address inequalities and provide social justice for disenfranchised groups – both of which values are likely to enhance the creation of social capital.

When it comes to daily practices, however, the picture is more blurred, and a strong moral code gives way to a more pragmatic one. In the words of German sociologist Max Weber, we observe a transition from ideas and values to interests and purposes in professional and bureaucratic organizations as triggers of action. Indeed, despite the declared importance of the original intentions formulated by the founders, these intentions seem to have no significant impact on the current goals of social enterprises and on the way they currently perform; in other words, the actual goal structure is based upon more pragmatic interests and purposes, with consequences for processes of institutional isomorphism. The production schemes, the management structure, the working climate and the decision-making processes in European WISEs are more deeply influenced by other factors (such as extensive professionalization of the organization and the evolution of production methods towards the private sector – see Chapter 15 of this book) than by the values laid down by the founders.

Again Germany provides a clear example: the authors of the German study note that most of the WISEs interviewed have no special, formal instruments to achieve a good working climate promoting internal democracy. This results in the working climate being, in most cases, similar to that of a normal enterprise in the first labour market. And pragmatic considerations concerning the temporary nature of many participants' involvement with the organization may reinforce this. Internal democracy is introduced only by special laws or is based on a 'club culture' in small initiatives (Bode *et al.* 2003). Professionalisation and adoption of private sector management structures and working climate seem to replace participative decision-making and social capital as primary objectives in many European social enterprises – resulting in a downgrading of the importance of social capital. This is a problem that is confirmed by other empirical research on the relation between third sector organizations and social capital (Selle 1999). If organizations in the social economy (WISEs included) serve as schools of democracy, it is due to their participatory structure where identities are forged in collaborative arenas.

Turning now to the relative importance of the different goals of the WISEs, advocacy has a particular importance for social capital. The ways in which European WISEs advocate the interests of their participants differ. At the micro level this takes the form of improving the participants' labour market worth and individual empowerment; meso-level advocacy aims to show the value of the social enterprise model, based upon new balances between 'traditional' employment and new forms of production subsidized by public authorities; while macro-level advocacy relates to the ambition to build social movements in order to change the current power structures in the direction of serving the interests of socially excluded groups. But the overall picture of the PERSE study shows that advocacy is not the most prominent goal of WISEs: work integration and social integration are the prominent objectives, while only 5 per cent of organizations mention goals concerning advocacy and lobbying as their primary objective (see Chapter 2 of this book).

In terms of social capital this could be a problem since norms, trust and networks as triggers for action could be, as we have just seen, relatively unimportant in social enterprises simply engaged in the 'production of work integration' within a paradigm of being as close as possible to the private sector. Advocacy activities could make up for this lack of production of social capital. In WISEs where advocacy processes are well established, the level of social capital could be higher, compared to WISEs that prioritize the production of work integration, even though both goal structures would enhance the interests of the excluded (participants).

3.2 Social relations and networks: bonding and bridging forms of social capital

Social enterprises are generally considered as often being short of direct access to financial capital and therefore dependent on social capital, both in networks outside the enterprise and within the enterprise:

> While social entrepreneurs are seeking to attract resources for the social good, rather than for financial returns, they rely ... on a rich network of contacts that will provide them with access to funding, board members, and management and staff, among other resources.
>
> (Austin *et al.* 2003: 9)

Bridging and bonding social capital within the WISE

In this section, the participatory board in a single-stakeholder organization refers to bonding social capital, while in organizations with a multi-stakeholder nature, the participatory board serves as a focus for bridging social capital, since the multi-stakeholder character implies that the actors concerned belong to heterogeneous groups.

It is an obvious hypothesis that there would be a strong participatory democracy in European WISEs since they are, by definition, part of the social economy, whose organizations, as noted in the introductory section of this chapter, often function as schools of participation and active citizenship. Another reason for the 'participatory-democracy thesis' is based upon the notion that social enterprises are locally embedded, with the ambition of benefiting the community. And as we have seen their strong value-based orientation, derived from their founders, forms a 'moral foundation' for many WISEs. However, the results we are going to present here draw a more complex picture than the participatory-democracy hypothesis might suggest.

As far as decision-making is concerned, the Portuguese part of the PERSE study offers a good example of the discrepancy between the norms and the actual structures of decision-making:

As to the mobilization of social capital, some WISEs explicitly referred to the promotion of a democratic, flexible and informal structure. However, the role of the participants in the decision-making process is rather limited. The management boards of the promoting body usually make the most important decisions.

(Perista and Nogueira 2003: 33)

The creation of social capital can, nevertheless, be analysed considering that the participation of homogeneous categories of stakeholders on WISEs' boards and the strong presence of 'insider' categories, within multi-stakeholder boards, are indicators of a high level of bonding social capital, whereas the participation of actors belonging to different categories, within a multi-stakeholder board, creates and uses bridging social capital, especially when the actors involved in the board belong to 'outsider' categories that are not normally represented in the enterprise (such as users or representatives from other organizations).

The single- or multi-stakeholder nature of European WISEs is studied in detail in Chapter 2 of this book. The single-stakeholder character (42 per cent of WISEs) indicates strong bonding social capital, but weak bridging social capital. The majority (58 per cent) of the WISEs studied are multi-stakeholder, and these have a strong presence of staff or volunteers on the board (see Table 6.1) – one or other of these insiders is the dominant stakeholder in all cases except the UK. Again, this indicates strong bonding social capital. Thus, on the one hand, at the European level, the dominant category of stakeholders is permanent staff, and this may indicate the existence of an isomorphic tendency (Cornforth *et al.* 1988); on the other hand, analysis of the situation at the national level reveals

Table 6.1 Presence of stakeholder categories in multi-stakeholder organizations (%)

	Users/ custo-mers	Volun-teers	Perma-nent staff	Partici-pants in schemes	Private business sector	Govern-ment agencies	Third sector	Other	Total
Belgium	3	6	22	10	9	10	22	18	100
Denmark	6	10	27	13	9	16	12	7	100
Finland	0	4	24	10	15	12	9	26	100
France	7	45	21	0	2	5	17	2	100
Germany	6	32	12	22	6	10	12	0	100
Ireland	16	34	4	0	4	24	14	4	100
Italy	7	38	37	3	5	0	2	7	100
Spain	12	19	21	5	9	7	23	5	100
Sweden	15	5	22	13	7	18	5	15	100
UK	3	3	10	0	24	22	21	16	100
Average	7	18	21	8	9	13	14	11	100

that in four countries, volunteers are strongly influential, indicating that institutional factors can, in some cases, resist such tendencies.

In general, in the multi-stakeholder WISEs, there is also a significant level of outsider influence – business, government, third sector – thus demonstrating good bridging social capital. But with the average number of categories of stakeholder on the board being around three, and insiders generally prominent, we see a degree of selectiveness in bridging. Although the picture reveals a wide involvement of stakeholders, social enterprises appear to have less participatory decision-making for users and participants than one might have expected from a social capital perspective. The low level of influence of participants in most countries (Germany constituting an exception to this general trend) indicates a decline in founding moral values (isomorphic tendencies).

In theory, third sector organizations are intermediary organizations that contribute to a democratic society in two different ways: 'they have "external" effects on the larger polity, and they have "internal" effects on participants themselves' (Putnam 2000: 338). Insofar as WISEs do not use to the full extent the social capital represented by participants in the composition of boards and strategic decision-making, they miss the opportunity to be 'schools of democracy' for the most vulnerable part of the population. However, they may still be effective providers of social services.

Networking and bridging social capital

In social capital theory a high degree of participation in both formal and informal networks is an indication of a high degree of social capital. In the PERSE project we have examined bridging social capital as networking between the WISEs and other actors and institutions. Our analysis is based on data collected on the following factors:

- formal and informal networks to which WISEs belong;
- federations grouping them;
- relations with public authorities and political parties;
- relations with economic actors;
- forms of support received from other organizations.

As an idea, or even as a value, 'networking' has a high priority for all WISEs. However, when it comes to actual participation in networks, differences appear among WISEs and among countries. Some social enterprises have a high degree of membership in local, regional and even national networks, while in other WISEs, networking primarily takes place on a local (sometimes even only informal) level. There is a trend to a greater degree of participation in formal networks with national impact in some countries than in others. To a large extent these differences can be explained by the degree of institutionalization of the context in which social enterprises operate in each country.

Formal networking at the local and/or regional level, and even at the national level, is for example common among Belgian and Italian WISEs – both countries in which, as we have explained, WISEs operate in a well-established institutional framework. The local networks are generally created by WISEs themselves or by a support organization. At the regional level, networks constitute both real advocacy groups with the political actors and an important meeting place for WISEs. The degree of commitment of WISEs to these regional networks is weaker than in networks at the local level (even though some WISE directors are administrators of the networks). In Italy social co-operatives join networks and umbrella organizations at both the local and/or national levels. These sorts of network organizations are composed of social enterprises and, in some cases, also by advocacy associations:

> As a result of their participation in networks or umbrella organizations, social co-operatives are asked to contribute to the organizations' activity through a membership fee, participation in meetings, collaboration in network projects that involve other social enterprises, maintenance of the organization, etc. . . . Most of the co-operatives of the sample analysed are members of local consortia within the national consortium CGM (Consorzio Gino Mattarelli).[4] Local consortia are supposed to represent member co-operatives at the local level and they contribute to building up social policies. They normally provide co-operatives with a number of specific services such as: general contracting, administrative counselling, fiscal assistance, training and project planning.
>
> (PERSE project – Italian team 2003: 19)

In other countries, networking mainly occurs on an informal basis. Although there is a strong emphasis on the value of networking in Danish WISEs, for example, they seem to be among the least formal European WISEs in their networking strategies, and most organizations hope that this field of activity will be developed in a more formal and strategic manner in the future. Most local networking in Denmark tends to have an ad hoc basis. Such informal relations serve as channels for information about business opportunities and give overall access to knowledge about the local community and the needs of specific target groups. Informal relations also play a significant role for the organizations' visibility in local political contexts, through 'gentlemen's agreements' between different actors to promote each other whenever possible. But whereas participation in such informal networks plays a significant role, participation in, and membership of, umbrella organizations are rare.

If participation in local and/or regional networks, be they formal or informal, is considered as essential by the WISEs studied, relations with the public authorities and the political actors are just as important. But the connections between WISEs and the various political and public institutions at the level of the boards are not particularly strong (13 per cent presence – see Table 6.1). However, informal connections to powerful actors on both administrative and political levels are seen as facilitating vital access to local public institutions and associated resources. The managers of the WISEs studied described these relations as good and necessary for the development (or maintenance) of the activities of their enterprise. Regular contacts between WISEs and public authorities are channels for exchanging information on the progress of grant applications (such as those for integration-linked subsidies), and reinforcing co-operation for the achievement of common goals (for example, some WISEs in Belgium maintain close links with the local 'public centre for social aid' (CPAS/OCMW) in order to enable the employment of the people requiring this public service).

Relations between WISEs and for-profit private enterprises seem less developed. When a WISE co-operates with this type of economic actor, the collaboration usually does not go beyond the commercial aspects (sale of goods and services produced by the WISE). Moreover, some managers of WISEs underlined that they did not publicise the fact that they were a social enterprise because they wanted to be considered as producers just like any other enterprise.

4 Institutional configurations of European WISEs

Regarding the specific relations between actors and institutions involved in the production of various forms of social capital, the micro–macro link becomes a question of specific institutional configurations between actors, institutions and policies instead of a priori conceptions of autonomous individuals or pre-social structures (Healey 1997: 55).

The institutional discourse is based upon the premise that social capital must be regarded in *policy contexts of changing institutional configurations*. The state may thus play a role in the production of bonding and bridging social capital, through creating – in a top-down action – a facilitating context for social entrepreneurship.

The institutional approach captures many of the activities and rationales related to social enterprises and social entrepreneurs. We further examine this perspective by reviewing two contrasting cases from Denmark and the UK.

The first case is that of Create, a British social enterprise. The institutional configuration outlined in Figure 6.1 depicts the web of relational embeddedness that is necessary for a successful social enterprise in a complex society. This social enterprise has quite a high dependence on public subsidies for its work integration. Developing durable and direct contacts with public authorities (from local city council officials to regional/national authorities, etc.) is often crucial to sustaining such activities in the long run, especially when funding from any single public source may dry up.

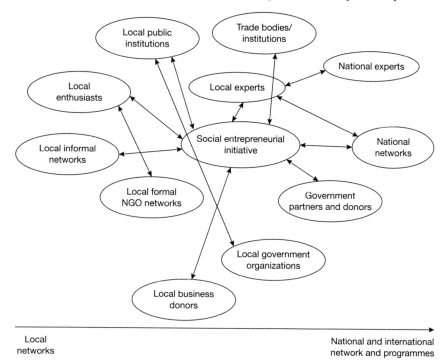

Figure 6.1 Institutional configuration of Create

But subsidies are a minor part of its total income; market income from diverse sources – individuals, third sector and business – provides its dominant income, and gives it credibility. The case of Create illustrates some of the strategic dilemmas faced by a social enterprise operating in a mixed resource framework as it deliberates issues of sustainability. This WISE recognizes the transaction costs associated with diversifying funding sources, but to avoid over-dependency on a single source of income, the enterprise requires a diverse mixture of funding and network contacts to actors from all three spheres of society (thus ensuring public, private and social capital resources). This dense network of relations is not only valuable because of the bridging social capital it embodies, but also because it provides the basis for improving access to other funding sources, thereby sustaining the institutional capacity of the social entrepreneurial initiative.

This British case may be contrasted with that of the Bridge, a Danish social enterprise, founded by stakeholders from the public sector and local voluntary associations in Esbjerg. It mainly relied on a single source of funds – the local municipality funded 81 per cent of its annual income – and had limited relations to donors, contracts and deals. Its social capital derived from enthusiasts, participants, and volunteers, and its lack of involvement in formal networks at a regional or national level meant that it was short of bridging social capital in a vertical sense,[5] which left it vulnerable and eventually unsustainable. When local politicians decided to stop their engagement with the Bridge, there was no time to develop new opportunities and contacts with people and networks that would provide alternative deals, and the enterprise disappeared. This experience shows the vulnerability of social enterprises that do not work on a broad-based approach involving contacts and deals with several donors through the use of bridging social capital networks in all three spheres of contemporary society.

Comparison between the two cases also indicates a role for public authorities in influencing the policy context for generating social capital, and preventing similar situations from developing into a crisis of legitimacy. Public authorities can change their relations with social enterprises by creating a climate of partnership and collaboration, and advising them to broaden their portfolios and networks in order to improve sustainability. Social enterprises can similarly seek to develop their social capital by continually monitoring the extent to which their networks contribute to a diverse and sustainable portfolio of deals and activities.

Conclusion

The PERSE research project has attempted in an exploratory way to examine different types of entrepreneurship among European WISEs. Since social capital – in the forms of norms, mutual trust and networks – is an important resource in the social economy, it was considered important to study the role of norms and of formal and informal networks and support structures in this entrepreneurial process.

Within social capital theory, two main discourses can be distinguished: a voluntarism discourse and an institutional discourse. According to the voluntarism discourse, the key actors are private individuals, and social capital is considered as being generated through a bottom-up process, whereas the institutional discourse is based upon the premise that social capital must be regarded in policy contexts of changing institutional configurations. Our analysis leads us to suggest that the distinction between bonding and bridging social capital is useful for developing an institutional approach to social capital in WISEs.

This institutional perspective has revealed three types of contexts that appear relevant to understanding patterns of social enterprise development: new legal forms or new specific policies within structured public frameworks; self-labelling forms and networks; and ad hoc constructed contexts (with new types of social enterprise sometimes adapted from other institutional forms). In a subset of 17 WISEs, we have also distinguished three models of entrepreneurship: organizational (sponsored) entrepreneurship was the prevailing model, followed by citizens' entrepreneurship, while joint entrepreneurship only occurred in a minority of cases. And we have argued that the dominant forms of entrepreneurship (sponsored or self-help) interlink with social capital to influence the ways in which the social enterprise is subsequently structured – in particular, the composition of the board and the participation or involvement of entrepreneurial stakeholders; sponsored entrepreneurship tends to lead to strong bridging social capital, and self-help entrepreneurship tends to lead to strong bonding social capital.

With regard to norms and values in European WISEs, while a strong value-based orientation is apparent at the founding stage, professionalization imposes a new set of practices that may circumscribe participation and the use of social capital in some cases, and thus raise issues of institutional isomorphism.

Most European WISEs are fully aware that social capital-generating activities such as lobbying and networking are a necessity in their relations with politicians and public authorities. In social capital and network theory such close contacts with local actors are what helps the enterprises get by on a daily basis, while contacts to local and national politicians help the enterprise to scale up and sustain its activities (Briggs 1998; Woolcock 2000; Austin *et al.* 2003). Analysis of the data collected in the framework of the PERSE project reveals that, while social capital activities (advocacy and participatory decision-making) have a lower priority in European WISEs than production and work-integration activities, such activities are clearly valued.

In terms of bonding social capital, the data collected show that the degree of involvement of participants (i.e. the workers engaged in an integration process) is low within European WISEs' boards, and permanent staff are the most influential category of stakeholders overall. This might be interpreted as an indicator of a low level of bonding social capital in the case of participants, but high in the case of staff. This may reflect the isomorphic trend to more professionalization and weakening of the influence of norms and values such as the importance of democracy in the workplace.

With regard to networking activities and related bridging social capital, we have shown that the presence of a variety of stakeholders on the board of a WISE is a channel for developing links with actors who are external to the WISE, and consequently enhance the development of bridging social capital, and that high levels of formal networking activity can be institutionalized, particularly in countries (such as Italy) where social enterprises are well-developed and established. Evidence from other countries shows that informal networking can also be functional for the organization in a number of ways: for accessing business opportunities, legitimising an intermediary role for a community or specific target group, and sustaining a social enterprise's institutional capacity by improving its relations with a variety of resources.

Review questions

• Why is the institutional approach more relevant than the voluntarism one in analysing social capital in the field of social enterprises?
• How can one analyse the multi-stakeholder dynamic within social enterprises in the perspective of the mobilization of social capital?
• How can one explain the low involvement of disadvantaged workers in WISEs?

Notes

1 The British Community Action Network – www.can-online.org.uk/
2 It should be noted that some of these sponsored social enterprises also fit well with the model referred to in business literature as the 'spin-off' model.
3 Note that social capital may be understated, since many enterprises tend to underestimate voluntary contributions and their impact, as well as the extent of their networking strategies.
4 The Gino Mattarelli Consortium is the largest social co-operative consortium at the national level in Italy. It brings together some 1,300 B-type and A-type social co-operatives.
5 It should be noted that some theorists (such as Woolcock 1998) refer to such links with positions of power and resources as 'linking social capital'.

Bibliography

Abell, P. (1983) 'The Viability of Industrial Producer Co-operatives', in Crouch, C. and Heller, F. (eds) *International Yearbook of Organisational Democracy*, Chichester: Wiley.

Ackerman, S.R. (1997) 'Altruism, Ideological Entrepreneurs and the Non-profit Firm', *Voluntas*, 8, 2: 120–34.

Austin, J., Howard, S. and Wei-Skillern, J. (2003) 'Social Entrepreneurship and Commercial Entrepreneurship: Same, Different, or Both?', *Social Enterprise Series*, 28, Working Paper, Division of Research, Harvard Business School.

Badelt, C. (1997) 'Entrepreneurship Theories of the Non-profit Sector', *Voluntas*, 8, 2: 162–78.

Baumol, W.J. (1993) 'Formal Entrepreneurship Theory in Economics: Existence and Bounds', *Journal of Business Venturing*, 8, 3: 197–210.

Bode, I., Schulz, A. and Evers, A. (2003) 'Multiple Goals and Social Capital', *Working Papers Series*, Liège: EMES European Research Network (draft).

Briggs, X. de Souza (1998) 'Moving Up versus Moving Out: Neighbourhood Effects in Housing Mobility Programs', *Housing Policy Debate*, 8, 1: 195–234.

Casson, M. (1995) *Entrepreneurship and Business Culture*, Aldershot: Edward Elgar.

Cornforth, C., Thomas, A., Lewis, J. and Spear, R. (1988) *Developing Successful Worker Co-operatives*, London: Sage.

Dees, J.G. (2001) 'The Meaning of "Social Entrepreneurship"'. Available at www.fuqua.duke.edu/centers/case/documents/dees_SE.pdf.

Evers, A. (2001) 'The Significance of Social Capital in the Multiple Goal and Resource Structure of Social Enterprises', in Borzaga, C. and Defourny, J. (eds) *The Emergence of Social Enterprise*, London and New York: Routledge, 296–311.

Gartner, W.B. (1989) '"Who is an Entrepreneur?" is the Wrong Question', *Entrepreneurship Theory and Practice*, 13, 4: 47–68.

Healey, P. (1997) *Collaborative Planning – Shaping Places in Fragmented Societies*, London: Macmillan.

Hulgård, L. (2004) 'Entrepreneurship in Community Development and Local Governance', in Bogason, P., Kensen, S. and Miller, H. (eds) *Tampering with Tradition: The Unrealized Authority of Democratic Agency*, Lanham, MD: Lexington Books.

Johannisson, B., Alexanderson, O., Nowicki, K. and Senneseth, K. (1994) 'Beyond Anarchy and Organization: Entrepreneurs in Contextual Networks', *Entrepreneurship and Regional Development*, 6: 329–56.

Perista, H. and Nogueira, S. (2003) *Multiple Goals and Social Capital*, Portuguese report, Liège: EMES European Research Network (unpublished).

PERSE project – Italian team (2003) *Multiple Goals and Social Capital*, PERSE research first draft report, Liège: EMES European Research Network.

Prodi, R. (2002) 'Co-operative added value', speech to the *European Co-operative Convention*, Brussels, 13 February 2002. Available at http://europa.eu.int/rapid/pressReleasesAction.do?reference=SPEECH/02/66.

Putnam, R.D. (2000) *Bowling Alone: the Collapse and Revival of American Community*, New York: Simon & Schuster.

Rothstein, B. (2001) 'Social Capital in the Social Democratic Welfare State', *Politics & Society*, 29, 2: 206–40.

Rothstein, B. and Stolle, D. (2002) 'How Political Institutions Create and Destroy Social Capital: An Institutional Theory of Generalized Trust', paper presented at the *98th Meeting of the American Political Association*, Boston, MA, 29 August–2 September.

Salamon, L.M. and Anheier, H.K. (eds) (1997) *Defining the Non-profit Sector – a Cross-National Analysis*, Manchester: Manchester University Press.

Schambra, W.C. (1997) 'Local Groups are the Key to America's Civic Renewal', *The Brookings Review*, 15, 4: 16–19.

Schumpeter, J.A. (1934) *The Theory of Economic Development*, Cambridge, MA: Harvard University Press.

Selle, P. (1999) 'The Transformation of the Voluntary Sector in Norway: a Decline in Social Capital?', in Van Deth, J., Maraffi, M., Newton, K. and Whiteley, P. (eds) *Social Capital and European Democracy*, London and New York: Routledge.

Skocpol, T. (1997) 'Building Community Top-down or Bottom-up?', *The Brookings Review*, 15, 4. Available at www.brookings.edu/press/review/fall97/skocpol.htm.

Skocpol, T. (2003) 'Voice and Inequality: The Transformation of American Civic Democracy'. Available at www.apsanet.org/imgtest/Skocpol.pdf.

Spear, R. (2006) 'A different model?', *International Journal of Social Economics*, 33, 5 & 6.

Stryjan, Y. (undated) 'Sweden: Multiple Goals and Social Capital', *Working Papers Series*, Liège: EMES European research Network (unpublished).

Van de Ven, A.H. (1993) 'The Development of an Infrastructure for Entrepreneurship', *Journal of Business Venturing*, 8, 3: 211–30, New York: Elsevier.

Woolcock, M. (1998) 'Social Capital and Economic Development: Toward a Theoretical Synthesis and Policy Framework', *Theory and Society*, 27, 2: 151–208.

Woolcock, M. (2000) 'Social Capital: The State of the Notion', in Kajanoja, J. and Simpura, J. (eds) *Social Capital. Global and Local Perspectives*, Helsinki: Government Institute for Economic Research.

Young, D. (1987) 'Executive Leadership in Nonprofit Organisations', in Powell, W.W. (ed.) *The Nonprofit Sector: A Research Handbook*, New Haven, CT: Yale University Press.

Part II

The balance of resources in social enterprise

7 A variety of resource mixes inside social enterprises

Laurent Gardin

Overview

The objective of this chapter is to analyse, on the basis of the substantive definition of the economy (elaborated in the footsteps of Polanyi), the various types of resources mobilized by European social enterprises. European social enterprises use a complex mix of resources based on four types of economic relations: the market, redistribution, the socio-politically embedded market, and reciprocity. A European typology of WISEs is put forward, in order to understand these enterprises' dynamic across national borders. After reading this chapter, the reader should:

- understand the rationale underpinning each type of economic relationship;
- be aware that an agent can support the mission of social enterprises through different economic relationships;
- identify the different patterns of mixing resources among European social enterprises.

Introduction: social enterprise in a plural economy

We put forward the hypothesis that social enterprises are not only 'multiple-goal' and 'multiple-ownership' enterprises, but that they are also 'multiple-resource' organizations. Social enterprises mobilize different kinds of market and non-market resources to sustain their goals. They sell goods and services in the market. Public financing generally supports their public benefit mission. Finally, social enterprise can rely upon volunteer resources. Therefore, in terms of resources, as well as in other ways, social enterprises are located in an intermediate space, at the crossroads of the market, the state and civil society.

The economic approach of social enterprises in general and of WISEs in particular is based on the substantive definition of the economy, which was elaborated in the footsteps of Karl Polanyi's works. According to Polanyi *et al.* (1957: 243):

> The substantive meaning of economic derives from man's dependence for his living upon nature and his fellows. It refers to the interchange with his natural and social environment, in so far as this results in supplying him with the means of material want satisfaction.

This approach allows us to highlight the diversity of economic principles, which are not limited to the market principle or the principle of redistribution, but also include household economy and the principle of reciprocity. The latter appears to us as central in characterising social enterprises but it is often neglected by economic analysts because, in most cases, it belongs to the non-monetary economy. Polanyi defines reciprocity on the basis of the anthropological principles of permanent gifts and counter-gifts and shows that 'reciprocity demands adequacy of response, not mathematical equality' (Polanyi *et al.* 1957: 73). The importance of reciprocity in primitive societies then leads to dispute over the natural character, in men, of the 'propensity to barter, truck and exchange one thing for another' (Polanyi 1944: 45) highlighted by Adam Smith.

It is on this hypothesis of a plurality of economic principles that the concept of the social enterprise was based, giving a central importance to reciprocity. This conceptualization relies on the distinction between the three main types of economic principle: the market, redistribution and reciprocity. 'Throughout history, various combinations of these three basic principles have arisen. The specific combination reflected by the contemporary economy may be divided into three poles:

- The market economy. Here, the market has the prime responsibility for the circulation of goods and services. This should not be taken to mean that the market economy is the product of the market alone but it gives priority to the market and a subordinate role to non-market and non-monetary relations' (Laville and Nyssens 2001: 324–5). In other words, the market economy mixes market and non-market resources, and even non-monetary resources.
- The non-market economy. This is an economy in which the prime responsibility for the circulation of goods and services falls within the jurisdiction of the welfare state.
- The non-monetary economy. 'This is an economy in which the circulation of goods and services depends primarily on reciprocity. Although it is true that a certain number of the reciprocal relationships adopt monetised forms (such as donations), it is really within the non-monetary economy that one observes the main effects of reciprocity – in the form of self-production and in the household economy' (Laville and Nyssens 2001: 325). The monetary economy as a whole is not based on reci-

procity; for example, when a local authority puts premises at the disposal of an organization free of charge, this is rather a form of redistribution. It is mainly through defining a value for volunteer work that the mobilization of reciprocity-based resources in social enterprises can be highlighted.

Laville and Nyssens conclude:

> According to plural conceptualization of the economy and to an ideal type methodology, it is possible to argue that the capacity to sustain a social enterprise in accordance with its initial logic presupposes its ability to *continuously hybridize the three poles of the economy so as to serve the project.* [. . .] Hybridization not only means relying on the three types of economic relations over a long period, it also means balancing these economic relations through negotiations among the partners in a manner consistent with the goal of the project.
>
> (Laville and Nyssens 2001: 325)

Reciprocity is thus actually at the very heart of definitions of social enterprise.

In order to make reciprocity visible, a first important step consists in apprehending non-monetary resources. This definition of a value for non-monetary elements allows us to highlight reciprocity-based resources which, in most cases (and as is the case for volunteering) do not take a monetary form; it is also a means to highlight some types of support given by redistribution and which are often forgotten, such as exemption from social security contributions, personnel secondments and use of premises. Monetary resources appear in the balance sheets and profit and loss accounts of initiatives, but directly linked non-monetary elements do not always do the same; taking them into account would allow us to obtain a more accurate vision of the economy of these initiatives. We should also assess the extent to which reciprocity influences the other types of economic relations, and more specifically determine the extent to which it allows market exchanges to be re-embedded in solidarity networks; in other words, what has to be studied is the way in which the exchanges of goods and services take into account the social and socio-political goals of WISEs.

The purpose of the study of the economy of the organization is to try to understand how it fits into the different economic logics that Polanyi brought to the fore: the market, redistribution, reciprocity. This is a difficult undertaking, which requires us to understand:

- *the origin* of the resources (e.g. from private customers, from the private sector, from the public sector, from the third sector);
- *the purpose* of those resources: to buy services and/or to fulfil objectives linked to work integration as well as socio-political objectives;

- *the type of allocation (different economic logics)* of those resources (e.g. the sale of services, public subsidies, gifts and volunteering).

Thus, this study cannot content itself with merely crunching numbers even though, as far as monetary resources are concerned, a budgetary analysis is required. One must, then, seek to understand how the socio-economic organization works, by interviewing its leaders, and thus resolve the issues at stake. This approach was used for a total of 146 enterprises on the basis of the analysis of their accounts for the year 2001 and of a comprehensive approach based on interviews of WISE managers.

A number of methodological difficulties must be signalled prior to unveiling the results of this research. Some of these arise from the difficulty of evaluating indirect aid in monetary terms, especially where such aid takes the form of exemption from taxes and social contributions, owing to the complexities of certain national mechanisms. Also on the subject of non-monetary services, a quantitative evaluation proved difficult to achieve for certain WISEs: those with little experience of this type of analysis were sometimes reluctant to divulge too much. Furthermore, the qualitative interviews were conducted with WISE representatives and it was difficult for them to answer questions dealing with the motivations of resource providers. This difficulty accounts, for example, for the 28 per cent non-answer rate for the question concerning the social and socio-political motivations of actors in the various sectors when purchasing a service. Finally, on the one hand, with an average of 14 enterprises studied per country, we are wary of painting a nationwide picture of the state of resource hybridization; but on the other hand, this work is useful in identifying the general characteristics of the resource mix in European WISEs and it provides an initial transnational typology of the difficulties experienced and the diverse forms that these resources can take, mindful of the particular nature of WISEs.

1 Diverse economic relationships and socio-economic agents

Averaging 62 per cent of monetary resources, the sale of goods and services is the main type of resource for WISEs. Subsidies account for 35 per cent of their monetary resources, with gifts and subscriptions accounting for only 3 per cent of the latter. The importance of non-monetary resources should not, however, be underestimated, representing as they do an average of 12 per cent of total resources. These non-monetary resources comprise indirect aid, principally from redistribution (exemptions from social contributions, tax deductions and loans of equipment and services) and from reciprocity as regards the mobilization of voluntary workers. This valuation of non-monetary resources puts the importance of the sale of goods and services into perspective. As shown in Table 7.1, although these sales

Table 7.1 General resource mix (%)*

Type	From individuals	From the private sector	From the public sector	From the third sector	Total
1 Monetary resources	16	15	51	6	88
1.1 Sales	15	15	19	4	53
1.2 Subsidies	0	0	32	0	32
1.3 Gifts	1	0	0	1	2
2 Non-monetary resources	5	0	5	2	12
2.1 Indirect subsidies	0	0	4	2	6.5
2.2 Voluntary work	5	0	0	0	5.5
Total	21	15	56	8	100

*Figures in the tables in this chapter have been rounded.

are the leading type of resource for WISEs, on average they only represent 53 per cent of their total resources.

Aside from placing a value on the non-monetary elements, the other distinctive feature of our approach is the attention paid to the origin of the resources. This method highlights the predominance of the public sector within the economic equilibrium of these initiatives, with more than half (56 per cent) of WISE resources coming from the public sector. A superficial examination of initiatives' accounts would lead one to the conclusion that public subsidy – or redistribution – accounts only for 32 per cent of WISEs' resources; but 19 per cent of their total budgets come from the purchase of goods and services by public bodies, and redistribution provides a further 4 per cent in the form of non-monetary aid. Our approach shows how the public sector, as well as being the primary source of subsidy funding, also provides indirect aid and is a purchaser of goods and services.

The general characteristics of WISEs' resources might be summed up as follows: as already mentioned, most resources are generated through the sale of goods and services (53 per cent), with most resources coming from the public sector (56 per cent); non-monetary resources are not negligible but are undervalued. Overall, these enterprises mix all types of resources even though, as we shall examine later, it is possible to distinguish between various categories of WISE on the basis of their resource mix.

After this general presentation of the characteristics of WISEs' resource mix, we may now proceed to analyse how the actors in these situations manage to achieve these resource mixes, and how they feel about the relationships they have built with the various resource providers.

1.1 Market and socio-politically embedded market resources

Sales – which, as already mentioned, represent 53 per cent of total resources – constitute these enterprises' main resources. The fact that a majority of resources are market-based confirms that WISEs have an undoubted presence in the market in order to ensure their economic equilibrium. However, these market resources have a number of specific characteristics regarding their origins and the way in which they are generated, due to the importance of networks in their mobilization as well as to the way in which purchasers take into account social enterprises' social and socio-political objectives. Sales to households and those to the private sector each represent 15 per cent of total resources, i.e. 30 per cent taken together. The exact extent of the share of private sector or individual-based resources is directly linked to the nature of the activity undertaken. For example, the Portuguese initiatives studied are concerned with services to individuals, and sales to private individuals account for all sales of services (37 per cent of resources). Conversely, in Italy, the growth in industrial activities undertaken by social co-operatives indicates a high level of co-operation with the private sector (29 per cent of resources, as opposed to only 6 per cent from households).

Meanwhile, sales of goods and services to the public sector represent 19 per cent, a total that is higher than sales to the private sector or to households; these sales are made primarily to municipalities (12 per cent of total resources). Finally, sales to the third sector account for 4 per cent of the total budget.

When questioned about the way in which sales to the various sectors were made, European WISE managers stressed the importance of social networks in the mobilization of resources, including market-based resources:

> All WISEs involved in the sales of goods and services to persons and to the private sector emphasize that being connected to local formal as well as informal networks plays a significant role in the mobilization of these resources, as well as pointing out key members of the organizations and external actors as vital for their reputation and campaigns for products and services.
>
> (Hulgård and Bisballe 2004: 9)

More specifically, the researchers questioned managers about buyers' recognition of social enterprises' social and socio-political goals when making purchases (see Table 7.2). This recognition takes a number of forms: it can be based either on integration targets or on productive output (as in the case of environmental factors).

There was a high rate of non-response (28 per cent) to this question, but clear differences emerge between households and the private sector on the one hand, and the public and third sectors on the other. Managers consider that a relative majority of all purchasers, namely 41 per cent (57 per cent when non-responses are excluded), do not take social and socio-political objectives into account; but this trend is more predominant for purchases made by households (59 per cent) and the private sector (61 per cent). Such purchases are thus overtly market-based, and although they have their

Table 7.2 Recognition of social enterprises' social and socio-political goals (%)

Type of sale	Sale to				
	Individuals	*Private sector*	*Public sector*	*Third sector*	*Total*
Sale with social and socio-political motivation	14	16	**47**	**66**	31
Sale without social and socio-political motivation	**59**	**61**	15	16	41
No answer	26	22	38	18	28
Total	100	100	100	100	100

origins to some extent in social networks, they are primarily founded on issues of quality and price of the goods and services. However, clients may also be motivated by the nature of the activity, as is the case, for example, with the sale of environment-friendly products. A WISE's integration mission is rarely a priority motivation for the purchase of services by the private sector, except in relatively rare cases (such as one case in Italy). On the other hand, in almost 47 per cent of public sector purchases and two-thirds of purchases by the third sector (respectively 75 and 80 per cent if the non-responses are ignored), the social and socio-political objectives of the social enterprise feature among the criteria for choosing the service provider. But although these motivations may lead the public authorities to prioritize WISEs, this does not prevent them from being demanding in terms of quality and price of the goods and services. This type of economic relationship is referred to as a 'socio-politically embedded market':

> The partners from the market sector attach more importance to the quality of the products, to the flexibility and to the lower costs of products and services from WISEs compared with other normal firms. Partners from the public and the third sector, being themselves organizations which are not guided by the profit-motive, seem to have however different priorities. Here, non-economic purposes for supporting the WISE by purchasing their products and services and by concluding contracts with them are reported as being important.
>
> (Bode *et al.* 2004: 12)

The main public sector purchasers are municipal institutions, followed by regional institutions. Italy shows the highest level of sales to the public sector (notably to municipalities), and in that country managers consider that a very marked majority of purchasers take the social and socio-political goals of WISEs into account. In this country, aside from sales originating in social networks, we can observe a strong level of recognition of social enterprises' social and socio-political goals by purchasers from the public and third sectors.

1.2 *The diversity of subsidies*

With 56 per cent of total resources, the public sector is the largest provider of funds to WISEs. Besides sales, which account for 19 per cent of the total resources of WISEs as analysed previously, public resources also take the form of subsidies (32 per cent of total resources) and indirect aid (which represents 4 per cent of total resources but whose total amount is under-valued owing to the difficulty some teams experienced in assessing its level).

Regarding subsidies, they are the main source of public finance. Forty-six per cent of subsidies are delivered by national bodies, and another 22 per cent are delivered at the regional level. The local level, whose share is very significant in the purchase of goods and services, accounts for only 17 per cent of public subsidies. Seventy-nine per cent of subsidies are linked to goals relating to the labour market, primarily through financing fixed-term contract employment opportunities (35 per cent), permanent job creation (16 per cent), placement services (7 per cent) and consultancy and support (5 per cent). These public subsidies may be allocated on the basis of key criteria unilaterally set by governmental agencies ('supervisory regulation') but also as a result of negotiations between governmental agencies and the organization ('negotiated agreement'). Fifty-four per cent of subsidies are attributed in supervisory form and impose criteria such as client profiles and payment methods. To a lesser extent, subsidies may also be attributed in negotiated form at both the national and local levels. It is sometimes difficult to assess whether or not a public subsidy is nego-tiated in nature. Although a grassroots organization may receive a subsidy in supervisory form, at the regional and national levels social enterprise networks can negotiate with public authorities on the mechanisms for obtaining financing.

Regarding indirect public sector financing, this mainly targets activities designed to stimulate the labour market. Forty-six per cent of these resources take the form of secondment of personnel, 18 per cent are in the form of equipment loans (primarily premises) and 35 per cent take the form of reduced social contributions, tax deductions, etc. Although the stated amount is far from insignificant, the figures are undervalued. A distinction is made between non-monetary aid attributed on the basis of negotiations with municipalities, in the form of equipment loans and personnel secondments, and those attributed essentially at the national level by the state in supervisory form, which take the form of exemptions from social contributions and taxes.

1.3 *Reciprocity-based resources*

Donations and non-monetary aid

The analysis of the results revealed that the third sector was the sector most likely to make purchases motivated by social enterprises' social and socio-political goals, and that these purchases were proportionally higher even than those made by the public sector. Third sector actors would therefore seem to be the allies of WISEs, despite the fact that their purchases account for only 4 per cent of total resources. The third sector's status as an ally of WISEs is also evidenced through donations and subscriptions (which represent 1.4 per cent of total resources) and non-monetary aid (1.7 per cent of total resources), that primarily takes the form of equipment loans and personnel secondments. This support, driven by a sense of mutual aid, is almost always provided subsequent to negotiation and covers every aspect of the social enterprises' projects. Third sector donations are highest in Italy (11 per cent of resources); they are driven by goals centred on community mutual aid, but this should not mask another goal (which might be characterized as corporatist), namely the recognition of co-operative and third sector consortia by public authorities:

> The analysis of the data of the sample confirms that there exists a strong relationship among the social co-operatives working in the same community and particularly in the same sector of activity. This relation is even stronger if the social co-operatives considered are members of the same local consortia. The relationship does not rely on social motivations only; it is also market-orientated. In order to better meet the needs of the community where they operate, social co-operatives work in network, offering a wide and complete range of services. This is also a good way to reinforce the trust of the public administration towards the activities of the private sector. . . . Donations are coming from third sector institutions and normally have mutual-help motivations. Non-profit organizations which make donations to social co-operatives are, in most cases, religious organizations or large foundations. Private (non- or for-profit) enterprises can donate instruments, vehicles or other stuff that they do not use anymore or that they buy and then donate to the social co-operative because of 'social responsibility policies'. However, this kind of resources does not constitute a consistent part of the resources of the enterprises.
>
> (Borzaga and Loss 2004: 12)

The third sector comes well ahead of the private sector, whose contributions in terms of monetary gifts and indirect aid account for no more than 0.2 per cent and 0.4 per cent of resources, respectively. Private individuals hardly ever contribute via indirect aid, but via their donations they do provide 0.6 per cent of monetary resources. The reciprocal involvement of the private individual is expressed primarily through volunteering.

Evaluating voluntary work

Voluntary work accounts for 5 per cent of WISEs' resources. Volunteers supply 34 per cent of this input, staff members 28 per cent and board members 26 per cent. Forty per cent of voluntary participation is rooted in mutual solidarity, 30 per cent in charitable work and 17 per cent in a political choice. Furthermore, 39 per cent of WISEs are seeking to increase their use of volunteer labour; this might seem to conflict with the top priority of WISEs, namely job creation. This overall trend regarding volunteering should not mask very significant variations among countries – in Ireland, for example, 80 per cent of the enterprises studied encourage the development of voluntary activities – and among the different types of initiative.

2 Types of resource mobilization

2.1 National differences: resource hybridization as a reality

Mechanisms for resource hybridization vary greatly from country to country (see Table 7.3). Sales represent three-quarters of the resources of Finnish enterprises, but under 30 per cent of WISE resources in Germany and Ireland.

Monetarily evaluated voluntary participation accounts for a share of resources that ranges from 0 per cent in Portugal[1] to 17 per cent in Germany. It thus appears that WISEs do not rely solely on market- and non-market-based monetary resources, but also on non-monetary resources, partially reciprocity-based.

Analysis of the origin of resources in the various countries surveyed (see Table 7.4) confirms the vital importance of the public sector in ensuring the economic equilibrium of WISEs. In seven out of the 11 countries, over half of all resources were provided by the public sector, and in three other countries public sector resources are quantitatively the first to be mobilized; only in Finland do public sector resources come behind those derived from households and the private sector.

2.2 Five types of resource mobilization

The first section of this chapter analysed the overall average (so to say, the 'average of averages') of WISEs' resources in the sample as a whole. This approach, which has the advantage of highlighting the presence, within WISEs, of a multiplicity of economic principles, nonetheless tends to underplay the differences among countries and groups of enterprises in terms of resource mix. Given that each national sample included 14 case studies, a national classification seemed difficult to achieve and it was felt more valuable to construct a transversal typology, based on the whole sample, in order to understand the enterprises' dynamic across national borders. The typology we established was based on the following criteria: first, the mobilization or not of reciprocity-based resources; then, the respective importance of

Table 7.3 Types of resources by country (%)

Type	Germany	Ireland	Portugal	Sweden	Denmark	France	Belgium	UK	Italy	Spain	Finland	Average
Sales	25	29	38	42	52	58	60	65	71	71	75	53
Subsidies	53	60	62	38	35	27	19	31	6	16	6	32
Gifts	0	2	0	3	3	1	0	1	11	5	0	2
Indirect subsidies	5	2	0	14	5	12	13	1	8	2	10	7
Voluntary	17	7	0	2	5	2	8	1	4	5	8	6
Total	100	100	100	100	100	100	100	100	100	100	100	100

Table 7.4 Origins of resources in each country (%)

	Germany	Sweden	Denmark	UK	Portugal	Ireland	France	Spain	Italy	Belgium	Finland	Average
From persons	15	11	20	20	36	33	11	25	10	22	**30**	21
From private sector	7	17	7	8	0	2	21	25	28	24	**30**	15
From public sector	**76**	**68**	**66**	**64**	**64**	**63**	**56**	**46**	**45**	**39**	29	**56**
From third sector	3	5	7	8	0	2	12	5	17	15	11	8
Total	100	100	100	100	100	100	100	100	100	100	100	100

market- and socio-politically embedded market-based resources, on the one hand, and of redistribution-based resources, on the other. Based upon these criteria, we were able to distinguish five broad types of WISE in terms of mobilization of resources (see Table 7.5). Out of the 146 WISEs surveyed during this research, 38 per cent[2] call upon almost no reciprocity-based resources, whereas a very large majority (62 per cent) mobilize reciprocity as well as, in differing proportions, redistribution and the market. We shall now look in greater depth at the socio-economic characteristics of these different types of WISE.

A minority of WISEs not mobilizing reciprocity-based resources

Fifty-six WISEs adopt an almost exclusive market or redistribution approach, or else combine these two economic approaches but without incorporating reciprocity-based resources, or only in a very marginal manner. We can therefore identify three categories of WISEs among WISEs not mobilizing reciprocity-based resources:

* redistribution social enterprises;
* social enterprises combining market and redistribution;
* market and socio-politically embedded market sales social enterprises.

REDISTRIBUTION SOCIAL ENTERPRISES

These 11 'redistribution social enterprises' are almost wholly dependent on subsidies, which represent a minimum of 70 per cent of their resources. For these 11 enterprises, an average of 90 per cent of their total budget comes from subsidies, with sales of services, which are almost all made without recognition of their social and socio-political goals by the purhasers, accounting for 9 per cent of the total budget. These are rare examples. Most of them are German, along with some Portuguese integration companies and some initiatives in Sweden and Ireland.

There are a variety of reasons behind this strong rooting in redistribution. In the case of the German redistribution enterprises, three factors account for this resource structure: their creation by local authorities; their goal of implementation of public policies targeting the unemployed (and, more specifically, those dependent on social aid); and the 'collective interest' nature of their activities. Three of the 15 Portuguese 'integration companies' that provide services to individuals can be described as principally redistribution-based; their specific resource mix is linked to the fact that they are located in deprived regions and aim to provide services to people with very scarce financial resources. The Swedish initiatives that are heavily dependent on public funding are those whose users are mentally handicapped and for whom extensive social and therapeutic provision is required.

Table 7.5 Types of resource mobilization and distribution of WISEs among the different types (%)

	Redistribution social enterprises	Social enterprises combining market and redistribution	Market and socio-politically embedded market sales social enterprises	Reciprocity and predominantly redistribution-funded social enterprises	Reciprocity and predominantly market-funded social enterprises	Average
Market	9	**45**	**53**	9	**43**	33.5
Embedded market	0	11	**44**	16	**31**	22.2
Redistribution	**90**	**44**	4	**62**	16	36.9
Reciprocity	0	0	0	**13**	**11**	7.4
Total	100	100	100	100	100	100
No. WISEs	11 (7%)	25 (17%)	20 (14%)	**39 (27%)**	**51 (35%)**	**146 (100%)**

From a transversal point of view, a common feature of these social enterprises is that they were mainly created by public bodies or major third sector organizations that mobilize few volunteers with the purposes of integrating low-qualified unemployed persons with a very weak profile of abilities, and delivering social services to highly deprived sections of the population, for example, dependent old people with low resources. The profile of the workers accounts for the importance of redistribution-based resources in these enterprises.

SOCIAL ENTERPRISES COMBINING MARKET AND REDISTRIBUTION-BASED RESOURCES

These 25 enterprises mix market and redistribution-based resources only, with reciprocity representing under 1 per cent of their budgets. The group comprises 11 of the 15 Portuguese integration companies for which the majority of resources derive from redistribution. Integration companies in Portugal are generally created by parent associations that do not attempt to mobilize volunteers for these new projects. This group also includes most of the Finnish work centres which mobilize reciprocity only during their start-up phase, via donations for setting up the organization. The other cases are spread across the various countries and do not constitute groups identified as such by the research teams. This observation notwithstanding, there are generally strong links between these initiatives and national[3] public schemes (as in the Portuguese example) which guide the operating mechanisms of these enterprises without any allowance made for reciprocity in their mode of operation. These enterprises also hire a high proportion of low-educated unemployed persons and their main activity is the provision of social services.

MARKET AND SOCIO-POLITICALLY EMBEDDED MARKET SALES SOCIAL ENTERPRISES

This group comprises 20 enterprises for which more than 90 per cent of resources come from the sale of goods and services, with minimal reciprocity-based resources (under 1 per cent), and redistribution-based resources accounting for 0 to 9 per cent of their budgets. This group comprises five enterprises from the United Kingdom, three from Denmark, three from Spain and a handful of enterprises from six other countries.

This group includes initiatives that unambiguously operate in the market, working with public and private organizations, and practising market-rate pricing without any special support from the public authorities. The absence of public funding specifically intended to recognize integration activities is not simply the result of a desire for autonomy on the part of these social enterprises; it is also, more often, symptomatic of a lack of opportunities to forge partnerships with the authorities.

But, on average, the majority of these enterprises' sales are made to the public sector and a high proportion (higher than the average) of these purchases incorporate a recognition of the social and socio-political goals of the WISEs: the public sector accounts for 43 per cent of the total resources of enterprises in this group (as compared to an average of 19 per cent for all the enterprises), and for 45 per cent of total sales (as compared to an average of 36 per cent for all the enterprises); but the most salient feature is the fact that 44 per cent of resources originate in sales made in recognition of the enterprises' social and socio-political objectives. This recognition compensates for the absence of public subsidy.

A majority of these enterprises adopt the legal form of co-operative (UK, Italian and Finnish workers' co-operatives, community businesses in the UK). Although around 95 per cent of their resources are derived from the sale of goods and services (of which a percentage are to private individuals and the private sector), it would be wrong to underestimate sales of services by WISEs in this group to the public sector and the recognition by purchasers of the social and socio-political goals. Some of the enterprises in this group must be termed socio-politically embedded market social enterprises. About a quarter of them are active in the field of recycling. The profiles of the workers in integration are varied but there is a high representation of young high-educated unemployed persons.

A majority of WISEs mobilizing reciprocity-based resources

Ninety of the 146 WISEs surveyed, representing 62 per cent of the sample, incorporate reciprocity to an extent that may vary from one case to another but is over 1 per cent (monetary valuation) of their total budget. Two groups can be identified:

- *predominantly redistribution-funded hybrid social enterprises*, in which direct and indirect public aid accounts for a higher proportion of resources than sales. In this group, reciprocity-based resources represent on average 13 per cent of the total budget;
- *predominantly market-funded hybrid social enterprises*, the biggest group, in which sales represent a greater proportion of resources than public grants. In these enterprises, reciprocity-based resources represent on average 11 per cent of the total budget.

RECIPROCITY AND PREDOMINANTLY REDISTRIBUTION-FUNDED SOCIAL ENTERPRISE

The redistribution-based resources of these 39 enterprises (27 per cent of the sample) are higher than those generated by the sale of goods and services. Direct and indirect aid represents on average 62 per cent of their total budget, reciprocity-based resources account for 13 per cent and sales for 25 per cent, with a majority of sales recognising social and socio-political objectives (16 per cent of total resources). The WISEs in this group presented at least one of the following three characteristics: a recent start-up, the strong presence of civil society from the outset and the provision of community services.

Concerning the provision of community services, the Belgian team emphasized the contradictions that can result from pursuing the joint objectives of employing disadvantaged people and carrying out socially useful activities, notably personal services. In Ireland, where over two-thirds of WISEs are included in this category and 85 per cent of social enterprises seek to mobilize voluntary participation (against an average 34 per cent in Europe), the focus is on the importance of reciprocity-based resources and social networks, for both the emergence and consolidation of 'local development WISEs' and 'social economy WISEs', even though certain forms of reciprocity seem to be less present in the latter type of social enterprise, which has a commercial status. It is also worth noting the presence in this group of Danish enterprises with the status of associations or foundations (Hulgård and Bisballe 2004).

Various elements combine to account for the specific resource mix of social enterprises relying mainly on redistribution but also on reciprocity and on resources generated by the sale of services according to socio-politically embedded market mechanisms: a deep embeddedness in local social networks, high voluntary participation, support from parent associations, their legal form of associations or foundations, a production with multiple social goals relating to integration but also to the actual services provided, the provision of facilities for people undergoing integration who are in great difficulty, for example. These enterprises are mainly active in the field of social services and recycling, which explains the importance of the public funding mobilized. The characteristics of the workers hired vary, but these enterprises hire fewer workers in great difficulty, which can be explained by the types of service developed (such as some types of social service), which require a certain level of qualification.

RECIPROCITY AND PREDOMINANTLY MARKET-FUNDED SOCIAL ENTERPRISE

These predominantly market-funded hybrid social enterprises are the most numerous: they account for 35 per cent of the sample (51 of the 146 enterprises surveyed). These enterprises participate in the market, but also succeed in selling their products by making purchasers take their social and socio-political goals into account, which is why they can also be described as socio-politically embedded market enterprises. Redistribution is mobilized to finance their integration activities, and reciprocity, less present than among predominantly redistribution-funded hybrid social enterprises, takes on a diversity of forms and degrees. We can distinguish between two sub-categories on the basis of the nature and importance of reciprocity within these WISEs' resource mix.

The first sub-category is characterized by a strong mobilization of reciprocity (notably of volunteers and the third sector) and market-based resources, motivated by the enterprises' social and socio-political objectives for almost half the sales made. The Finnish self-help initiatives feature different forms that fall between the market and reciprocity categories: the initiatives supported by national or regional associations mobilize a type of reciprocity that takes the form of monetary donations, whereas co-operative-type initiatives tend to mobilize voluntary participation. Two-thirds of Italian social co-operatives belong to the 'reciprocity and predominantly market-funded WISEs' category. Along with Germany, Italy is the country that shows the strongest mobilization of reciprocity-based resources in our sample, notably via donations made to enterprises by other third sector organizations that exceed 10 per cent of their total budget. Reciprocity-based resources also take the form of voluntary participation, primarily provided by administrators who are motivated by charity values. Half of Italian social co-operatives are also seeking to further develop voluntary participation; this is a higher rate than the European average of 34 per cent. The total amount of reciprocity-based resources for Italian social co-operatives exceeds the total of redistribution-based resources (but it has to be remembered that redistribution-based resources are undervalued, since exemptions from social contribution are not taken into account). This embeddedness of social co-operatives in the local fabric is also reflected in their good relations with the public authorities, which is not expressed through subsidies but rather through public procurement contracts which, in three-quarters of the cases, take WISEs' social and socio-political goals into account.

WISEs of the first sub-category show a strong mobilization of reciprocity-based resources; in WISEs of the second sub-category, reciprocity is also present but volunteer investment is often seen as a constraint linked to the lack of market- or redistribution-based resources. This holds true for some of the Spanish enterprises and German market-oriented enterprises; Belgian integration enterprises are also in this category, with a predominance of market-based resources combined with redistribution-based resources financing integration goals, and reciprocity-based resources that, while present, remain limited mainly to the 'forced' voluntary participation of the workers, i.e. work carried out without being paid for in order to ensure the economic balance of the WISE.

In the final analysis, these social enterprises with a significant level of market- and socio-politically embedded market-based resources usually have co-operative legal forms; they mobilize redistribution-based resources through subsidies centred on their integration activities, and reciprocity-

Table 7.6 Characteristics of WISEs according to their resource mix

Characteristics	Resources				
	Redistribution social enterprises	Social enterprises combining market and redistribution	Market and socio-politically embedded market sales social enterprises	Reciprocity and predominantly redistribution-funded social enterprises	Reciprocity and predominantly market-funded social enterprises
Number and % in the sample	11 (7%)	25 (17%)	20 (14%)	39 (27%)	51 (35%)
Examples of enterprises	German municipally-owned social enterprises, some Portuguese integration companies and some Swedish social co-operatives	Portuguese integration companies, Finnish work centres owned by major associations	Workers' co-operatives, British community businesses, Swedish community enterprises	Belgian NPOs, Irish local development WISEs and social economy WISEs, French centres for adaptation to working life	Belgian integration enterprises, most Italian social co-operatives, German social capital-orientated WISEs, Finnish self-help co-operatives
Type of sales of goods and services	Insignificant sales, but mostly strictly market-based relations	Mostly strictly market-based relations	Varied but importance of socio-politically embedded sales (sales to the public sector in recognition of social and socio-political goals)	Socio-politically embedded market	Varied but importance of socio-politically embedded market

Characteristics of public aid	Funding of activity and/or subsidies for hiring people in particular difficulty	Significant subsidies mainly relating to integration	Almost non-existent but support from the public authorities via socio-politically embedded market sales	Funding of activity and/or subsidies for hiring people in particular difficulty	Generally limited to integration activities
Position and type of reciprocity	Launched by public bodies or large-scale associations mobilizing very little reciprocity	Strong links with public mechanisms and/or start-ups originating in large pre-existing associations mobilizing very little reciprocity	Organization set up by individual workers or groups of workers with no voluntary participation but social networks that are sometimes well-established	Mobilization of volunteers and support from the third sector linked to activity and rooted in reciprocity-based networks	Strong roots in local social networks. Mobilization of volunteers or over-investment of workers depending on the organization
Type of workers in integration	Higher proportion of workers with a low level of employability	Higher proportion of low-educated unemployed persons	Various but with a higher representation of young high-educated unemployed persons	Various but a higher proportion of workers with a stronger profile of employability	Various
Main types of production	Various	Social services (10), personal services (4), gardening (2)	Recycling (5), services to enterprises (4), building (2), restaurant (2)	Social services (9), recycling (8), personal services (3), restaurant (3), industry (3)	Recycling (12), services to enterprises (8), gardening (7), building (5)
Main legal form			Co-operative	Association (NPO)	Co-operative

based resources in various forms: mobilization of social networks, support of parent organizations, and voluntary participation by volunteers as well as 'forced' voluntary participation of employees. Many of these WISEs are active in the field of recycling, but they also carry out a significant part of their activities in the fields of services to enterprises, gardening and building. The profiles of the workers are varied.

Table 7.6 summarizes the various forms of resource mobilization and the characteristics of the WISEs according to these definitions.

Finally, it appears that this typology of WISEs is strongly linked to the activities that are undertaken. For example, among the WISEs of the third and fifth categories (respectively 'market and socio-politically embedded market sales social enterprises' and 'reciprocity and predominantly market-funded social enterprises'), which mobilize mainly market-based resources, a high proportion are active in the fields of recycling and services to enterprises. They generally adopt the legal form of co-operatives. These categories do not concentrate on the most disadvantaged workers. The difference between these two categories is linked to the fact that WISEs of the fifth category rely more on reciprocity- and redistribution-based resources. This difference can be accounted for, on the one hand, by the way in which public authorities support these initiatives (granting of direct or indirect subsidies to WISEs of the fifth category, purchase of goods or services from WISEs of the third category). On the other hand, the fact that volunteering plays a more significant role in this fifth category can be explained partly by the recognition of volunteering and the strong embeddedness in local networks which characterize co-operatives such as Italian social co-operatives.

The other three categories mobilize more public funding. There are various reasons for the mobilization of public funding. WISEs of the first category ('redistribution social enterprises') hire workers who are particularly disadvantaged in the labour market and, so to say, develop a 'sheltered labour market' requiring significant public funding. The other two groups ('social enterprises combining market and redistribution' and 'reciprocity and predominantly redistribution-funded social enterprises', which constitute the second and fourth categories, respectively) are mainly active in the fields of social services and personal services, which are partly funded by public subsidies. Moreover, it also appears that WISEs of the fourth category target workers with a higher level of training than WISEs of the other two categories; this is linked to the fact that providing social services might be difficult when hiring workers with disadvantages that are too serious. This category of 'reciprocity and predominantly redistribution-funded social enterprises' mobilizes more reciprocity-based resources thanks to its local embeddedness in social networks relying on its 'twofold' social goal: the integration of disadvantaged workers through a production activity and the provision of social services to disadvantaged individuals.

Conclusion: resource mixes models in WISEs

Given the diversity of the resource mixes among WISEs that this study has highlighted, it is necessary to go beyond an approach to the funding of these enterprises according to which WISEs only mobilize market resources (just like any other form of enterprise) and non-market resources from the public sector that purport to make up for the low productivity of their workers in integration and the specific needs of the latter in terms of support and training. Such a point of view ignores: the reality of the markets in which these enterprises position themselves thanks to the mobilization of their social networks; the existence of markets in which the social and socio-political goals of these enterprises are taken into account; the importance of the public sector as a source of resources; and the mobilization of reciprocity-based resources. These enterprises do not operate using a mix of market- and redistribution-based resources only; their resource mix is more complex and builds upon four types of economic relationship: the market and redistribution, but also the socio-politically embedded market and reciprocity.

The need to put the market into perspective

This analysis of the resource mix of WISEs challenges certain preconceptions about these enterprises on the part of public authorities and of some federations of WISEs, which tend to apprehend WISEs on the basis of their participation in the market. For example, in France the Ministry of Social Affairs and Employment considers that 'an integration enterprise through economic activity produces market goods and services in the same manner as any other enterprise ... [and] it must be subject to the same requirements for economic viability' (Ministère des Affaires sociales et de l'emploi 1988). The Charter of the National Integration Enterprise Committee states that 'the integration enterprise produces goods and services and conducts its business according to the same regulations, the same rights and with the same rigour as any other market enterprise' (CNEI 1992). Redistribution, in the form of public subsidies, is provided only to compensate for the productivity deficit of the workers in integration, their social support and training, and the intensive supervision that this entails.

While the analysis of these enterprises' budgets confirms this type of mixed economic operation, reliant on both the market and redistribution, the substantive approach allows us to apprehend in a more accurate way the various types of resources mobilized by these enterprises and the mechanisms of involvement of public authorities – which go further than simply compensating for the cost of integration; finally, it underlines the importance of an economic principle that is often ignored: reciprocity.

Reciprocity and the re-embedding of market relationships

Beyond support provided by other third sector organizations via direct or indirect aid, and beyond voluntary involvement on the part of board members, volunteers and workers, reciprocity is also expressed through the capacity to construct market economic relationships that take WISEs' social and socio-political goals into account.

The analysis of economic relationships between purchasers and WISEs shows that the former are not only motivated by the search for the maximization of their own interests. There is a will to take the other party into account in the framework of the relationship, although these are centred on the exchange of goods and services on the basis of price setting. Granovetter highlighted the importance of social networks for the building up and operation of markets, underlining the reticulated embeddedness of market relations. By highlighting the taking into account of socio-political goals in the sales of WISEs, the analysis shows that these purchases reflect not only a reticulated embeddedness of the market but also a socio-political re-embedding of the market. If, like any other enterprise, WISEs produce market goods and services and if, like any other enterprise, they are able to call upon local social networks, what seems important – and is too often ignored – is the recognition, by purchasers, of WISEs' social and socio-political goals.

These socio-politically embedded markets are not often built with households and the private sector; they are generally created with public authorities, whose purchases from WISEs are, in three-quarters of the cases, motivated by the latter's social and socio-political objectives, whether these concern simply the integration of disadvantaged workers, or whether public bodies also recognize the social benefit of their production.

These observations should not lead us to the conclusion that WISEs are not enterprises producing goods and services; they simply demonstrate that the manner in which these enterprises obtain their orders is very closely linked to their embeddedness in social networks as well as to the taking into account, by public purchasers, of their work integration objectives.

The analysis also reveals that we cannot observe any correlation between the importance of reciprocity and that of redistribution (see Table 7.7): although the quartile where redistribution is highest (41.2 per cent) shows the lowest level of reciprocity – which could lead us to suppose that redistribution gives way to reciprocity –, the quartile where reciprocity is highest shows a redistribution average reaching 36.8 per cent.

On the other hand, it is clearly observable that it is in the quartile of WISEs where reciprocity is lowest that economic relations are most often market-based (there is a 32.6 point gap between sales through the market

Table 7.7 Correlation between reciprocity and other economic principles (%)

Reciprocity quartile	Redistribution	Socio-politically embedded market	Market	Reciprocity	Total
Per cent					
≥ 9.11	36.8	19.5	20.4	23.3	100
< 9.11 and ≥ 2.9	34.9	27.0	32.6	5.5	100
< 2.9 and > 0.1	33.9	31.7	33.2	1.3	100
≤ 0.1	41.2	13.1	45.7	0	100
Average	36.9	22.2	33.5	7.4	100

and those made through a socio-politically embedded market). In the other categories, although socio-politically embedded market-based resources are always lower than market-based resources, the gap varies between 5.6 points and 0.9 point. Beyond the generation of financially valuable resources, reciprocity thus appears as an agent tending to 're-embed' market relations by requiring them to take into account WISEs' social and socio-political goals.

Democratizing redistribution

Through these purchases, as well as through direct and indirect public subsidies, the public sector is the main provider of resources to WISEs. WISEs seek to develop their economic relationships with those public bodies whose calls for tenders include clauses demanding the best social value instead of the cheapest service.

Socio-political re-embeddedness is achieved through the mobilization of redistribution-based resources that allow individuals in integration to find a job and not to be excluded from the labour market. It is also achieved through reciprocity which, beyond providing enterprises with voluntary resources, also leads to the purchase of services taking into account the social and socio-political goals of WISEs.

Faced with accusations of unfair competition by the for-profit private sector, WISEs may be reluctant to highlight their privileged relationship with the public sector and the importance of reciprocity-based resources for their economic equilibrium, although these elements appear to be vital. By 'copying' the dominant market vision, they underestimate types of economic resources that are crucial to their operation: redistribution and reciprocity.

The importance of redistribution in the resource mix of WISEs raises the question of the modes of regulation of the relationship between public authorities and social enterprises. These modes of regulation can be of three types. First, they can be based on a market logic, considering initiatives only as service providers competing with private sector or third sector providers on the basis of a market regulation in a neo-liberal perspective. The modes of regulation can also adopt a 'welfare-state' perspective, with public regulation placing the initiatives in a situation of dependence and inferiority. Finally, modes of regulation negotiated between public authorities and social enterprises are emerging (Du Tertre 1999: 213–37; Laville and Nyssens 2001: 250–1). This last type of regulation represents a means to discuss the process of allocation of public funds and, in this sense, constitutes a testimony to the political capacity of the economic principle of reciprocity to participate in a democratization of redistribution. The analysis of social enterprises based on taking into account the plurality of economic principles thus also leads to taking into account the plurality of the forms taken by democracy.

National case studies

The three national case studies that follow in the next three chapters present contrasting ways of mixing resources, depending on the country.

Irish WISEs (Chapter 8) mobilize mainly reciprocity- and redistribution-based resources, whereas resources from the market are more limited. This type of resource mix corresponds to the *reciprocity and predominantly redistribution-funded social enterprises*, which are particularly numerous among the WISEs studied.

The Spanish team (Chapter 9) highlights the importance of non-monetary resources in the economic balance of WISEs. WISEs in this country appear to suffer from a lack of public support in terms of subsidies, which WISEs overcome through non-monetary resources from indirect aid and volunteer work. As regards the sale of services, which plays a central role in the economic balance of WISEs, a distinction should be made between those WISEs that rely mainly on sales to the private sector and those whose services are primarily sold to the public sector.

In Finland (Chapter 10) the WISEs surveyed mainly mobilize resources from the market and from reciprocity, which is typical of *reciprocity and predominantly market-funded social enterprises*. A more thorough analysis of the resource mix of Finnish WISEs underlines the various forms of reciprocity that are present in these initiatives, and among others the distinction that has to be made between a form of reciprocity that takes the form of donations from supporting organizations and a form of reciprocity that originates in volunteer work.

These case studies thus allow us to illustrate and deepen the typology of WISEs based on their type of resource mix.

Review questions

• Why can European social enterprises be considered, in terms of their resources, as located in an intermediate space, between market, public policies and civil society?
• How can reciprocity influence market relationships?
• Identify, in your country, a social enterprise of each type in the typology suggested in this chapter and analyse its characteristics according to Table 7.6.

Notes

1 The situation in this country is exceptional in that the recently created integration companies (*empresas de inserção*) were set up by major associations implementing a government policy that did not involve civil society actors, and thus did not mobilize volunteering. However, the Portuguese researchers are of the view that volunteering does take place but that the associations are reluctant to acknowledge the fact:

> based on empirical knowledge of the WISEs, we must point out that, at least in some cases, voluntary work exists, even though this is not recognized as such, and of course it is not financially valuated by the WISEs. This kind of voluntary work usually refers to management or technical staff, this being usually provided by members of the promoting body.
>
> (Perista and Nogueira 2004: 12)

2 This group is over-represented as it includes the 15 Portuguese 'integration enterprises' (*empresas de inserção*) for which the absence of reciprocity-based resources noted in the analysis is the result of difficulties with the initiatives' approach rather than of a true lack of reciprocity in their operation. Excluding the Portuguese enterprises from the sample would result in the proportion of enterprises which have no reciprocity-based resources falling to only 31 per cent.

3 Or sometimes even with local public schemes in some other countries; for example, a French neighbourhood enterprise is heavily dependent on the municipality that founded it.

Bibliography

Bode, I., Evers, A. and Schulz, A. (2004) *German Report on the Resource Mix of Social Enterprises*, PERSE project research report, Liège: EMES European Research Network (unpublished).

Borzaga, C. and Loss, M. (2004) *Resource Mix in Italian Work Integration Social Enterprises*, PERSE project research report, Liège: EMES European Research Network (unpublished).

CNEI (1992) *La charte des entreprises d'insertion*, Paris: CNEI.

Denneulin, F. (1999) 'Secteur du bâtiment, état des lieux', *CNEI Mag*, Paris: CNEI, no. 7.

Du Tertre, C. (1999) 'Les services aux personnes: vers une régulation conventionnée et territorialisée?', *L'année de la régulation*, Paris: La Découverte – Recherches, no. 1: 213–37.

Goussault, A. (2001) 'Des passerelles entre insertion et marché du travail', *Territoires*, 420 (interview with Nicolas Leblanc, September).

Granovetter, M. (2000) *Le marché autrement*, Paris: Desclée de Brouwer.

Hulgård, L. and Bisballe, K. (2004) *Resource Mix in Danish Work Integration Social Enterprises*, PERSE project research report, Liège: EMES European Research Network (unpublished).

Laville, J.-L. and Nyssens, M. (2001) 'The Social Enterprise – Towards a Theoretical Socio-Economic Approach', in Borzaga, C. and Defourny, J. (eds) *The Emergence of Social Enterprise*, London: Routledge, 312–32.

Ministère des Affaires sociales et de l'emploi (1988) 'Circulaire du 20 Avril 1988 concernant le soutien aux entreprises d'insertion', *Journal officiel*, Paris.

Perista, H. (co-ord.) and Nogueira, S. (2004) *Resources Mix and WISE in Portugal*, PERSE project research report, Liège: EMES European Research Network (unpublished).

Polanyi, K. (1944) *The Great Transformation: the Political and Economic Origins of our Time*, New-York: Farrar & Rinehart.

Polanyi, K., Arensberg, C. and Pearson, H. (eds) (1957) *Trade and Market in the Early Empires. Economies in History and Theory*, New York: Glencoe, Free Press.

8 Irish social enterprises: challenges in mobilizing resources to meet multiple goals

Mary O'Shaughnessy

Overview

This chapter describes the different types of Irish WISEs. It shows that the role of volunteers, the forms of public schemes supporting these social enterprises and the emphasis on sustainability vary across these different types. After reading this chapter, the reader should:

- identify the different goals characterising Irish WISEs;
- understand the links between these objectives and the types of resources mobilized;
- understand the main differences between 'local development WISEs' and 'social economy WISEs'.

Introduction

Irish WISEs share a number of common characteristics. They are not for profit, have evolved to serve disadvantaged communities, combine the efforts and expertise of voluntary and paid workers, and create training and employment opportunities for the long-term unemployed and other groups at risk of social and economic exclusion. Historically, WISEs have emerged at various stages in Irish society, under differing social and economic conditions and policy regimes. They have evolved in the context of an extensive reliance on public labour market integration programmes essentially developed to tackle long-term unemployment.[1] The role of volunteers, the types of goods and services produced, and the emphasis on improving the employability of the workers varies across WISEs. Three types of Irish WISEs can be identified.[2]

Sheltered employment WISEs

Sheltered employment enterprises or 'workshops' constitute the first type of Irish WISE. These provide training and employment opportunities to persons with a physical disability and/or learning difficulty and are run by voluntary, non-profit organizations. They provide on-the-job training, temporary and longer-term reintegration opportunities to persons with a registered disability. This type of WISE emerged as a response by the Irish community and voluntary sector to addressing the labour market integration needs of people with disabilities. Reintegration into the open labour market is not necessarily always the goal, although it can often be an outcome, depending on the nature of the disability and the availability of suitable job opportunities.

These WISEs combine different sets of resources: from the state in the form of capital and direct employment grants, from the market place through the sale of the goods and services produced and through fundraising activities such as national lotteries.

Volunteers play a very important role in these WISEs, contributing voluntary labour and managerial skills at different levels within the social enterprise. More often than not, the volunteers are either parents or guardians of the trainees/employees within the WISE and are a significant resource in organizing events and raising funds from the public. This type of social capital represents a significant non-monetary resource for WISEs, which is often complemented by other sources derived through the development of relationships with other business and social partners.

Local development WISEs

This second type of WISE began to emerge in the mid- to late 1990s. These are community- and area-based organizations. They evolved in the context of high national unemployment levels and a national policy framework that favoured social partnership and an area-based approach to local development. These WISEs grew in response to local problems of social exclusion and combine two goals: the provision of community-based services and the creation of training and labour market reintegration opportunities for the long-term unemployed and other disadvantaged groups such as lone parents, travellers and persons with a disability. They have emerged with the financial support of active labour market programmes such as Community Employment (CE).

The role of volunteers is crucial. Local development WISEs originate through the efforts of concerned local people and combine voluntary effort with supported employment. This voluntarism is significant in providing the WISE with a formal management board which is legally constituted and accountable for the expenditure of public funds. These volunteers also contribute their labour to the production of various goods and services, thus reducing the cost of delivery. Because WISEs of this type are typically community-based, they meet the needs of disadvantaged groups who would not ordinarily be able to access such services. The strong voluntary characteristic and overtly non-profit nature of this type of WISE contributes in a major way to their ability to raise money from public donations. Their localised character also helps them to attract financial donations and other types of support such as reduced-cost premises, free legal and business advice from local professionals, and equipment (such as computers) from local businesses. This type of social capital is instrumental in sustaining such WISEs.

Social economy WISEs

The third type of WISE, which we can refer to as a social economy WISE, has a direct link to the national Social Economy Programme (SE).[3] This most recent type of WISE has similar objectives to local development WISEs; however, the WISEs that operate through SE are obliged to reflect a greater degree of professionalism and business acumen than those that operate with the assistance of measures such as CE. They must produce a detailed business plan, illustrating overhead and set-up costs, capital needs and proposed staff development, and are subject to regular auditing and review. In addition to this, these WISEs must also demonstrate their contribution to the regeneration of the local area, the extent of the involvement of employees in the management of the enterprise and the personal and life skills benefits to the workers in the WISE.

Volunteers play a strategic management role rather than contributing to the daily delivery of goods and services; many are involved in developing more formalised business relationships with statutory health boards and local authorities. Social economy WISEs offer services such as waste management, rural transport, elder and childcare and the refurbishment of houses. Public service contracts are increasingly forming a significant source of trading income for these WISEs. Because they are perceived as commercial organizations, they are less likely to attract private and public donations than the local and community development WISEs described above. Ensuring a continued trading income is vital for the sustainability of the social economy WISE.

1 Resource mix of Irish WISEs – a brief synthesis

Data derived from a series of semi-structured interviews and an analysis of the 2001 end-of-year accounts of a cross-section of 13 WISEs provide an insight into the typical resource mix of an Irish WISE.[4]

The average revenue derived from the sale of goods and services to private individuals, across the 13 WISEs surveyed, was 27 per cent of the total income; the highest level recorded was 86 per cent and the lowest was 2 per cent. The main types of services and goods sold include education, health and social care services, culture and leisure and services for enterprises. The most common type of good/services sold to private individuals and/or the private sector is education, health, and social care related. The WISEs included in this study operate in peripheral, rural locations often devoid of the type of services made available by the WISE. Therefore they generally experience no difficulty in finding customers for their goods and services. However, these customers are often unable to pay a 'market' price for these services and the WISE can experience difficulties in generating an income sufficient to pay for the services produced. This presents an enormous challenge to those WISEs that may be serving a disadvantaged community, where the consumers of their services lack the financial means to procure these services from other vendors and where public service provision is inadequate.

The average income from sales of goods and services to the public sector as a percentage of total income across the 13 WISEs is 4 per cent, but this figure masks strong variations from WISE to WISE. In fact, only 15 per cent of the WISEs studied derive an income from the sales of goods and services to the public sector. Among those WISEs, sales to the public sector represent between 4 and 27 per cent of their income. The services most commonly sold are training and educational services. In general, public authorities do not buy directly from WISEs; the common trend is for these agencies to subsidize WISEs by providing financial support to the disadvantaged groups, thus enabling them to buy directly from the WISEs.

The average share of subsidies from the public sector in the total income of WISEs is 66 per cent, with the greatest proportion of these subsidies being used to support labour market activities and the production of goods and services. The highest level of public subsidies received by one particular WISE is 98 per cent and the lowest level is 7 per cent. For the most part, these subsidies are awarded in a supervisory manner, in that there is no negotiation between the WISE and the funding agency. Indirect subsidies are uncommon across this sample of WISEs; those recorded include the provision of sites for project development and low-cost rent, each being sourced from other third sector organizations. Voluntary work accounted for an average of 8 per cent of total income of all 13 WISEs, with donations and subscriptions accounting for an average of 5 per cent across all organizations studied.

2 Irish WISEs – volunteerism and reciprocity

Irish WISEs, in particular local development WISEs, generally emerge as a result of sustained voluntary activity, often originating from citizens' concerns regarding a particular issue (e.g. inadequate service provision for a particular community). Voluntary contribution underpins the long-term sustainability of these organizations. The successful mobilization of volunteers by Irish WISEs reflects their strong roots in local social networks.

Volunteers exercise a variety of roles within Irish WISEs, including producing goods and services and providing strategic managerial direction. The organizational structure of Irish WISEs, generally encompassing a local voluntary board with a focus on addressing local needs, decreases dependence on external service providers and increases self-sufficiency within the local community. Volunteers also assist in generating local funding and in some instances are an effective sales mechanism through their development of formalised business relationships with statutory health boards and local county councils. A significant challenge facing WISEs in retaining their voluntary component is the increasing levels of bureaucracy they face in acquiring statutory financial support. The legal incorporation of WISEs places an additional responsibility on the volunteer who has to assume the responsibility of being a company director. This can be a source of anxiety and concern for an individual who may wish to demonstrate altruism in addressing a local need, but be reluctant to take on such additional responsibilities.

3 Irish WISEs – predominantly redistribution social enterprises

Public funds are the predominant resource for Irish WISEs. As non-profit organizations, combining voluntary and paid labour, and with a stated commitment to provide community-based services, local development WISEs rely heavily on state support through active labour market programmes (ALMPs). Some of these programmes have emerged as an explicit support to WISEs. However, the goals that WISEs must pursue under these measures are quite specific in terms of (a) improving the employability of the disadvantaged worker, and (b) – in the case of the Social Economy Programme – demonstrating an ability to become financially viable within a three-year period. The relationship between the public sector and the WISE is sometimes described as supervisory. Managers often exercise a limited discretion in setting the terms of reference for either obtaining or using these subsidies.

In their efforts to serve the community, especially the most socially and economically disadvantaged, Irish WISEs must provide a high-quality service at a nominal charge to clients. This nominal charge can only go so far in meeting the operational costs of the WISE. This has significant implications for the WISE. In the first instance, WISEs might seek to adopt a more strategic approach to developing and selling their services. This could include an attempt to generate additional income by providing goods or services to those members of the community who are in a position to pay a commercial rate. This option is particularly relevant in the area of elder and childcare where other options are not available. This additional income could be used by WISEs to offer services at little or no cost to the more disadvantaged service users. By adopting this approach of stratifying the market, WISEs could play a greater redistributive role within society, complementary to the goals of the public sector and in contrast to for-profit organizations.

Conclusion

The hybrid nature of WISEs stems from their ability to combine different types of resources – from the market, civil society and the public sector. However, this also makes them increasingly susceptible to a range of internal and external factors: Irish WISEs are vulnerable to the uncertainty of the market place, changes in public policies and funding mechanisms, and the availability of volunteers.

As non-profit organizations, combining voluntary and paid labour, and with a stated commitment to provide community-based services, local development WISEs rely heavily on state support through ALMPs. However, restructuring of such programmes presents a significant challenge to the long-term sustainability of these organizations.

WISEs that emerged under the national Social Economy Programme have also been faced with the additional task of becoming financially viable. This is a challenge for those whose customers lack the financial means to pay for their services. Depending on the internal and external resources available to them, WISEs may seek to achieve viability in two ways: (a) by seeking to diversify their activities in order to attract additional revenue which would allow them to continue to serve the disadvantaged; (b) by actively pursuing 'paying customers' at the expense of reducing service provision to those 'less able to pay' for those services.[5]

Irish WISEs depend on volunteers for a variety of functions – fundraising, strategic management and labour. In view of the changing life styles and regularly cited difficulty in recruiting new volunteers, many WISEs will be forced to develop new ways to attract volunteers, which might be an additional drain on often scarce resources.

Review questions

- Why are reciprocity and redistribution so important in Irish WISEs?
- Describe some of the typical challenges that face Irish WISEs. Suggest some ways by which these challenges might be met.
- What are the roles of volunteers in each type of Irish WISE?

Notes

1   Active labour market programmes (ALMPs) were introduced in the 1970s in response to rising unemployment and included the provision of subsidies to employers and training schemes targeted at the long-term unemployed. Direct Employment Schemes are one type of ALMP which provide subsidized temporary employment in the voluntary and public sectors. These schemes include Community Employment (CE), Job Initiative (JI) and a national Social Economy Programme (SE).

2   This discussion appears in O'Shaughnessy and O'Hara (2004).
3   The national Social Economy Programme (SE) was launched in 1999. This programme is designed to support social enterprises that are professionally managed and entrepreneurial, i.e. functioning in the market place.
4   These 13 WISEs represent a cross-section of local development and social economy WISEs. The sample was selected from a total research population of 69 WISEs. For the purpose of this study sheltered employment WISEs were not included.
5   This discussion appears in O'Shaughnessy and O'Hara (2004).

Bibliography

FAS (1998) *The Job Initiative Operational Guidelines*.

FAS (2000) *Social Economy Enterprise Guidelines*.

Irish Government Publications (2000) *Ireland National Development*.

National Economic and Social Council (1986) *Manpower Policy in Ireland*, NESC Report No. 82, Dublin: NESC.

O'Connell, P.J. and McGinnity, F. (1997) *Working Schemes? Active Labour Market Policy in Ireland*, Ashgate: Aldershot.

O'Hara, P. (2001) 'Ireland: Social Enterprises and Local Development', in Borzaga, C. and Defourny, J. (eds) *The Emergence of Social Enterprise*, London and New York: Routledge.

O'Shaughnessy, M. and O'Hara, P. (2004) 'Work Integration Social Enterprises in Ireland', *Working Papers Series*, 04/03, Liège: EMES European Research Network.

PLANET (1998) *The Development of a Support Framework for the Social Economy*, Dublin: PLANET.

Sexton, J.J. and O'Connell, P.J. (1996) *Labour Market Studies: Ireland*, Luxembourg: European Commission.

9 Spain: weak public support for social enterprises

Isabel Vidal and Núria Claver

Overview

This chapter analyses the resource mix of Spanish WISEs. The Spanish context is characterized by the quasi-absence of public recognition of social enterprises. Therefore, WISEs suffer from a lack of public support in terms of subsidies, which they overcome by relying on both non-monetary resources and sales. After reading this chapter, the reader should:

- understand the rationale behind the resource mix of Spanish WISEs;
- grasp the attitude of the different external stakeholders towards WISEs.

Introduction

In Spain, four types of organization that fit the definition of work integration social enterprises (WISEs) have been identified: special employment centres (*centros especiales de empleo*), sheltered employment centres (*centros ocupacionales*), enterprises that are part of the national organization for the blind (*Organización Nacional de Ciegos de España* – ONCE), and social integration enterprises for people at risk of social exclusion (*empresas de inserción*). The first three types of enterprise work with people with recognized disabilities, while, as far as the fourth type is concerned, it should be underlined that social exclusion is a type of 'disability' that is not legally recognized in Spain. For the purpose of the PERSE project, we have focused on WISEs of this fourth type (social integration enterprises for people at risk of social exclusion), as social enterprises targeted only at people with recognized disabilities have been excluded.

This chapter analyses the different resources obtained by the 15 Spanish WISEs that make up the PERSE project sample.[1] It does not restrict itself to monetary resources; on the contrary a great effort has also been made to measure the impact of non-monetary resources, since we believe that these resources, which come mainly from relationships of mutual aid and reciprocity, are of greater importance in social enterprises than in 'traditional' enterprises.

WISE profiles

The results are based on the in-depth study of 15 Spanish WISEs, selected according to two main criteria: first, they had to carry out a continuous activity of the production of goods and services; and second, the sample was constituted so as to include enterprises from various regions (territorial diversity). Most of the enterprises selected had existed for at least five years, although some recently created WISEs were also included in the sample.

Spanish WISEs can be divided into two main groups according to their goals and the strategies they employ to achieve them. Applying such a distinction to the sample produces the two following groups:

- Ten WISEs that define themselves as 'intermediate enterprises', i.e. their aim is the social integration of their participants through work. Their productive and lobbying activities are the tools that allow them to achieve this goal. They operate under a variety of legal forms (foundation, co-operative, etc.).
- Five WISEs whose main activity is productive and which trade under a variety of legal forms. Some of them have a clear 'self-employment' nature, and most of them consider themselves to be permanent employers, or may combine intermediate integration jobs with permanent ones.

In the autonomous communities with specific legalisation, WISEs must be trading companies or co-operatives founded by public or not-for-profit bodies, which must own at least 51 per cent of the share capital. The aim of legislators is to guarantee the mission of work integration in any business situation in which the WISE might find itself over the course of its history.

In the sample it is only some of the recently created WISEs that have made use of this specific legislation, and the predominant legal form is still the foundation. However, this might change in the immediate future, and the predominant legal forms for WISEs might well become the worker-owned limited company (*sociedad laboral*, or SL) and the other forms that have recently been introduced.

General trends

Of the total resources obtained by the WISEs in the sample in 2001, an average of 10 per cent is non-monetary. Non-monetary resources are an important source of income for some WISEs.

The majority of the WISEs studied state that their income is on an upward trend. A distinction should be made between:

- those WISEs that are already consolidated and whose incomes continue to increase, but more slowly or, in some cases, whose incomes have already stabilized;
- those WISEs that are in the growth stage, and whose income is rising by 15–20 per cent a year;
- the youngest WISEs, which are still in the stage of finding their place in the market and, in the first years of activity, see a slow but sustained increase in income.

Analysis of the accounts of the 15 WISEs in the sample for 2001 reveals that only two recorded losses, while 13 realized a profit. Most of these (61.5 per cent) made a profit of less than €20,000, and only one (7.7 per cent) showed a profit of over €100,000.

The WISEs surveyed give a variety of reasons for the increase in their income (and, in most cases, profits). Several mention the launch of new activities, and an increase in the number of customers is also cited. Winning contracts with the public sector is mentioned as a decisive factor for this positive trend.

As far as the use of the profits is concerned, it must be pointed out that the three co-operatives and the worker-owned limited company (i.e. four WISEs in the sample) must, by law, set aside part of their profits to compulsory reserves. Apart from this share of the profits whose use is defined by law, none of the managers interviewed could provide a percentage breakdown of use of the profits. However, the unanimous response (although with varying emphasis) was that the profits are reinvested in the WISE itself, be it to launch new projects, hire new participants or increase the number of programme users – all of which may lead to a small increase in technical staff. Another way to reinvest the profit is to purchase land, buildings and equipment suitable for the WISE's activities.

1 Sales of goods and services

1.1 The main customers and their relationship with the WISE

Table 9.1 gives an overview of the resource mix of the WISEs in the sample. Sales of goods and services represent 68 per cent of their total resources. The public sector is the main customer (38 per cent of sales), followed by private businesses (34 per cent) and individuals (23 per cent). However, if we take private businesses and individuals together, the private sector was the WISEs' main customer (57 per cent of sales) in 2001. Sales to the third sector represent only 5 per cent of the total sales of WISEs.

Table 9.1 Resource mix of Spanish WISEs (%)

Origin of resources		Share of total resources
1 Monetary resources		
Sales of goods and services		68
of which:		
to the public sector	38	
to the private business sector	34	
to individuals	23	
to the third sector	5	
Direct subsidies		17
of which:		
from Autonomous Communities	73	
from central or national government	9	
from municipal authorities	12	
from the EU	6	
Contributions, support, gifts		5
of which:		
from individuals	77	
from the third sector	19	
from the private sector	4	
Resources from shares, stocks, bonds, etc.		0
Total monetary resources		**90**
2 Non-monetary resources		
Value of in-kind donations		2
Indirect subsidies from the public sector		1
Value of volunteers' time		7
of which:*		
work carried out by ordinary volunteers	87	
work carried out by managers	9	
professional work carried out by individuals	4	
work carried out by third sector board members	0.6	
work carried out by private sector board members	0.1	
Total non-monetary resources		**10**
Total resources (1 + 2)		**100**

*The sub-total for this section comes to 100.7% owing to rounding.

1.2 Sales to individuals and the private sector

As just mentioned, individuals account for 23 per cent of WISEs' sales. The goods and services they buy are: second-hand clothing and other objects, cleaning services and, some way behind, other services, such as the collection of old furniture from homes, transport and repair. Although sales to individual customers raise no particular problems, WISEs underline the fact that these sales are not as profitable as those to companies or to the public sector.

The private business sector represents 34 per cent of all WISE sales. It purchases, almost exclusively, services: industrial cleaning, the collection of paper, scrap, furniture and used equipment, and courier services. Two enterprises were going to launch activities in ecological agriculture and gardening, but these had not yet started in 2001; they expected to sell to both individuals and the private sector.

Generally, it can be stated that the more dependent a WISE is on individuals as customers, the lower its income is. The example of a WISE making 90 per cent of its sales to individuals illustrates this: this WISE would not be economically viable without public subsidies and the support of the Catholic charity *Cáritas* (although it also has to be said that it is the youngest WISE in the sample). Most WISEs achieve economic growth by winning an important private business or governmental customer.

When asked about the motivation behind their private customers' purchases, WISE managers cannot provide any accurate answer. They do not know whether these purchases are motivated by socio-political criteria, but what they can say is that if they do not offer a good service at a competitive price, they will not have these customers at all. In general, there is no uniform type of relationship between WISEs and private businesses. Some enterprises admit that they have won customers thanks to the fact that they are WISEs, while others say that their business partners treat them like any other company. Some enterprises explain that the way they present themselves depends on the customer: in some cases, they do not reveal that they are a WISE, because it may be prejudicial to them, while in other cases they do so because it is a further point in their favour.

Private enterprises' interest in the social role of WISEs is still slight. Commercial relationships are rarely established because of the very nature of the WISE. Nonetheless, there have been some experiences of employers' associations backing WISEs.

In the case of the sale of second-hand clothing and objects to individuals, the social motivation seems to play a more important role in the decision to buy from a WISE. The General Manageress of a WISE states that the fact that their points of sale bear the name of *Cáritas*, a well-known and respected organization in the social care field, is an important factor in the motivation of some customers.

Some WISEs make financial investments that generate an income; however, they underline that the purpose of such investments is to support the start-up of other WISEs in the group, and the income generated is only a by-product.

1.3 Sales to the public sector

As already mentioned, the public sector accounts for 38 per cent of WISEs' sales. Two-thirds of these sales are to local authorities, namely, municipal councils and agencies providing municipal services. The remaining one-third of sales to the public sector are made to regional authorities which, in the case of Spain, are the Autonomous Communities. These have their own powers and a great deal of autonomy from the central government, which explains why none of the WISEs in our sample have the Spanish state as a customer.

The services sold to the public sector differ according to the level of government, since each level has its own powers. The main services provided to municipal authorities are collecting urban waste and managing sorting centres; cleaning public buildings; construction and public works; and managing and constructing socio-cultural facilities. At the regional level (Autonomous Communities), the principal services provided by WISEs are in the field of training and career guidance and, occasionally, other social services; cleaning public buildings; and construction and public works.

The general relationships between WISEs and the public authorities are good. All WISEs, in their daily activities, are in contact with the services and departments connected with their integration and productive activity: local social services, autonomous community social welfare departments, departments of public works, etc.

Public sector customers tend to be important to WISEs. Several WISEs state that winning a public tender or contract has been a decisive factor in their success. Such contracts give a WISE security and stability, but many WISEs – especially the youngest and smallest enterprises – complain of the difficulty in accessing them.

The majority of the WISEs interviewed complain that the public authorities do not take sufficient account of their social dimension when awarding public contracts. The authorities design the tender process for large companies, often including terms that do not suit the circumstances of the majority of WISEs. As a result, only the largest, most prestigious WISEs can win these contracts, and most choose to operate in the private sector. One of the main demands of Spanish WISEs is the inclusion of, and compulsory compliance with, social clauses in public contracts.

The main difficulty indicated in mobilizing resources from sales to the authorities (aside from that of winning public contracts) is the time lag between the provision of services and payment. One WISE even states that, while sales to the public sector are very profitable, the payment periods (of three to six months) force them to rely on credit.

1.4 Sales to the third sector

Sales of goods and services to the third sector only represent 5 per cent of the sales of goods and services of WISEs for 2001. The market is more limited than that for businesses or individuals but, on the other hand, WISEs have not considered focusing on this market specifically as a way of winning new customers.

Managers found it difficult to evaluate the motivations of the various categories of customer for purchasing goods and services from WISEs; they cannot usually say what percentage of each type of customer has socio-political reasons for choosing a WISE as a supplier. What does clearly appear from the analysis of the interviews carried out is that, in general, the third sector has greater socio-political motivation than other customers; indeed, some social economy enterprises establish positive discrimination criteria for social enterprises when deciding upon the purchase of goods and services.

However, all the managers interviewed state clearly that, even when such socio-political motivation exists, it is not sufficient in itself: the WISE has to offer a quality product or service at a competitive price – otherwise, even socio-politically motivated purchases will not be made. Not only is the fact of being a WISE not sufficient in itself to gain customers; in some cases, the nature of the social enterprise can even represent a disadvantage. Vidal and Claver (2003) underline how the more market-oriented WISEs decide to reveal their status as such to some customers, but not to others, since although this could in certain cases represent an advantage, in others it could be prejudicial to their interests.

With the exception of the co-operatives, whose backers are the partners/workers, the WISEs surveyed are backed by not-for-profit organizations, such as associations, foundations and the Catholic charity *Cáritas*. These bodies, in addition to backing the WISEs, are their customers and are also able to bring in other third sector customers: in other words, they can mobilize third sector resources in favour of WISEs.

2 Subsidies

2.1 Direct subsidies

This section analyses the direct subsidies granted to WISEs by the authorities – i.e. the total or partial funding of some WISE programmes or activities.

Direct subsidies provide 17 per cent of WISEs' total resources. These subsidies come mainly from the relevant Autonomous Communities, which provide 73 per cent of them, followed by municipal authorities (12 per cent), central or national government (9 per cent of direct subsidies) and, last, by the European Union (6 per cent). Only one of the WISEs received no direct subsidy in 2001.

As regards the purpose of the financing, 85 per cent of subsidies are awarded for the socio-occupational integration of the participants. More specifically, 47 per cent of them subsidize temporary jobs, i.e. the regional government subsidizes the participant's job for a specific period of time, which ranges from one to three years. After this period, participants should have acquired sufficient professional and social skills to find a job on the mainstream labour market.

The remaining 15 per cent of the subsidies are shared between the other objectives: 10 per cent subsidize the production of goods and services and 5 per cent fund general activities.

To understand the complex situation of public subsidies available to Spanish WISEs, a number of things need to be taken into account. First is the fact that, until very recently, subsidies specifically intended for WISEs did not exist in Spain, since there was no such legal entity. Second, it should be noted that, throughout 2003, the country's Autonomous Communities have taken on the task of legally regulating the field of WISEs at the regional level, since a number of attempts to pass a Spain-wide law on WISEs had not succeeded, as described in the Spanish national report for the PERSE research project (Vidal and Claver 2004). In general, regional regulation is accompanied by financing measures but, in some Autonomous Communities such as Catalonia[2] (the first Autonomous Community to pass a WISE Act) and La Rioja,[3] the law is awaiting development and no specific financing measures have yet been enacted. Other Autonomous Communities have enacted specific financing measures following the passing of a regional law on WISEs, as is the case in Aragón[4] and Madrid.[5]

In some Autonomous Communities, WISEs with the legal form of co-operatives are also entitled to subsidies if new partners join the co-operative; two WISEs in the Basque Country received such aid in 2001.

As a consequence of these circumstances, the subsidies received by the enterprises surveyed in 2001 were not specifically intended for WISEs; rather they were job-creation subsidies and aid programmes for the unemployed or those at risk of exclusion. In a majority of cases (71 per cent) the subsidies were secured under an initiative of the relevant authority (usually the regional 'Employment' or 'Employment and Training' department). This means that, following a public announcement of a subsidy scheme, WISEs submit their application and then may or may not receive it; subsequently, if the subsidy is granted, supporting documentation must be sent showing how the amount was spent, and this use must coincide with the conditions imposed by the authorities.

The three WISEs that obtained some subsidies in a negotiated manner are the three enterprises in our sample that admit having won greatest recognition, not so much from society at large as from the authorities. One of the advantages of this recognition is thus a certain ability to negotiate public subsidies.

2.2 Indirect subsidies

We also analysed indirect subsidies and exemptions – by exemptions, we understand the money that WISEs do not have to pay, owing to their status or to meeting some specific requirements.

Indirect subsidies from the public sector – exemptions and tax deductions – make up only 1 per cent of WISEs' total resources. They basically comprise social security deductions and corporation tax deductions at the central government level, and IAE[6] and other tax deductions at the municipal level.

As regards state-wide exemptions, Act 12/2001, of 9 July, establishes an exemption of 65 per cent from employer 'common contingency' social security contributions for companies and not-for-profit organizations which hire, on open-ended contracts, workers suffering from exclusions. Additionally, the co-operatives in the sample are entitled, as are all co-operatives, to a 90 per cent exemption from Corporation Tax,[7] and two WISEs are even totally exempted from this tax, as they are officially recognized as being 'entities of public utility'. WISEs are also entitled to general job creation exemptions, as is any Spanish company hiring workers meeting defined criteria, such as workers under 30, workers with recognized disabilities, etc.

The most frequent municipal exemption is the exemption from IAE, but only two of the WISEs in the sample benefit from it: one only pays 10 per cent of the tax, while the other is totally exempted. This latter WISE also benefits from a reduction in the municipal rubbish collection tax.

Public exemptions, and especially those granted by the central government, are closely monitored. Exemption percentages are established by law, and the WISE must submit supporting documentation to prove that it meets the requirements.

2.3 Difficulties in mobilizing direct and indirect subsidies

When asked about the possible difficulties in accessing subsidies, WISE managers mention that a great deal of administrative work is required, both to apply for the subsidies and to justify the expense. Additionally, the period between the award of the subsidy and its payment may be very long; it may be months, sometimes even years, before the subsidy is fully paid. This may account for the fact that the majority of WISEs try to operate without relying on subsidies. In general, subsidies represent a helping hand, but the WISE is not dependent upon them.

Direct public subsidies are thus regarded as a helping hand, a small contribution to finance the enterprise's structure. As we saw in the preceding section, specific subsidies for WISEs have not existed until very recently, and only now are financial measures in support of WISEs being implemented. Subsidies represent extra income for the majority of WISEs, not a basic source of financing; they therefore need lines of credit to finance their activities, like any other company. Only those that have a significant care and training component depend on subsidies.

Moreover, in the case of investment-related subsidies, WISEs must pay in advance and the authorities cover the cost after receiving the relevant supporting documentation. To be able to invest, WISEs must thus use resources initially set aside for other things or seek loans from backers or financial institutions, which, in the latter case, means paying interest.

3 Reciprocity-based resources

3.1 Contributions, subscriptions, donations, sponsorship and non-monetary donations

The contributions, donations and sponsorship received by the 15 WISEs in the Spanish sample represented, in aggregate, an average of 5 per cent of their total resources: 77 per cent of these were contributed by individuals, followed at some distance by the third sector (19 per cent), and the private sector (4 per cent). Individuals usually donate money. Partner and worker subscriptions and employer and management donations are of lesser importance, but the latter may be undervalued as managers sometimes prefer to make donations on an individual, anonymous basis. In one of the WISEs in the sample, technical staff voluntarily donated part of their salary (paid from public subsidies) to meet the organization's needs. This type of action can only be understood in the light of the WISE's underlying principles.

Business donations and sponsorship in monetary form is still relatively infrequent in Spain: as noted above, this sector is the one that makes the lowest contribution of this type. It should nonetheless be borne in mind that this figure may be underestimated, as some large companies and savings banks have their own foundations, and donations made by these foundations are considered in our figures as coming from the third sector. According to the WISEs surveyed, one common reason for companies to make donations (aside from social motivations) is the fact that such expenses are tax-deductible.

In 2001, non-monetary resources represented 10 per cent of the total resources of the WISEs surveyed. Generally, the goods and services donated by the backers consist of premises and offices in which to carry on the business activity, as well as commercial premises, flats, warehouses and, in the case of the public sector, land. In general, the WISE can use the premises, but does not own them. Vehicles and other fixed assets such as computers are also donated. These in-kind donations represent 2 per cent of the total resources of the WISEs surveyed. Such donations are also sometimes – although less frequently – made by individuals and by the public sector.[8] In the latter case this occurs at the municipal level, usually after negotiations with the WISE.

It should be noted that some of the WISEs that carry out recycling and restoration of used clothes and assets treat the used clothes and objects contributed by individuals as donations, whereas other WISEs consider such donations to be of nil value, given that some of the clothes cannot be used and the remainder is only of value after being recycled and restored. These consider the collection of the clothes to be more like a service they carry out.

3.2 Voluntary work

The current trend in the majority of WISEs is towards the professionalization of their workforce, with a view to eliminating voluntary work or reducing it to a residual status. To the WISE, achieving remuneration for all positions (i.e. the progressive professionalization of the organization) is a sign of progress.

Nonetheless, those WISEs backed by *Cáritas* use volunteers from their backer, which has a large network of voluntary workers, and the volunteer presence within these WISEs has a significant economic impact. By way of example, in one of the WISEs in the sample, 35 volunteers staff the shops on a part-time basis. The manager estimates that they represent the equivalent of 14 full-time staff, and thus represent a yearly saving of approximately €176,000.

On average, volunteers make up 7 per cent of WISEs' total resources, but it should be noted that, of the 15 WISEs in the sample, five have no voluntary positions, not even on their board of directors. Almost all the voluntary work is performed by people on an individual basis. This can be split as follows:

- Eighty-seven per cent of all the voluntary work is carried out by ordinary volunteers, i.e. people who contribute some of their time to working in a not-for-profit organization for personal, social or humanitarian reasons. These people receive no monetary compensation for the work they do and are present to a greater or lesser extent in six of the 15 WISEs, carrying out relatively unskilled tasks (filing, sales, etc.).
- Nine per cent of the voluntary work is carried out by managers, who work longer than stipulated in their employment contract without receiving remuneration. In the report on multiple goals and social capital (Vidal and Claver 2003) there are three 'permanent employer' enterprises with a significant self-employment component. In these cases, volunteer work performed by the managers is not motivated only by the company's social role; it is also linked to the fact that working unpaid overtime increases the survival chances of the WISE

and thus, indirectly, their chance of keeping their jobs. In one case, for example, the voluntary work carried out by the two women running the company was not remunerated; the general manageress had a part-time contract and salary but worked longer so as to meet the organization's production and social goals.

- Individuals carrying out professional work (accountancy, legal advice, etc.) on a free of charge, voluntary basis represent 4 per cent of voluntary work.

- Finally, the remaining percentages, of little significance, relate to persons representing the third sector (0.6 per cent) or the private sector (0.1 per cent) on some WISEs' boards of directors, spending only a few hours a month on this non-remunerated activity.

Conclusion

The analysis of the data collected shows that the WISEs in the Spanish sample have mixed resources: 90 per cent is monetary and 10 per cent is non-monetary, and both types of resources come from various sources. Most of the monetary resources come from sales (which represent 76 per cent of monetary resources and 68 per cent of total resources), although some WISEs are still highly dependent upon subsidies. The WISEs that are more dependent upon subsidies are, as might be expected, those whose productive activity is less developed and that are more care- and training-oriented. It can nonetheless be stated that Spanish WISEs are becoming increasingly independent of subsidies.

There are considerable variations among WISEs from the point of view of the mobilization of voluntary resources. Those whose productive activity is more consolidated rely less on voluntary work or other non-monetary resources. Within the group of WISEs focusing on productive or market-oriented activities, a distinction should be made between those whose main customers are the public administrations, both at the local level and at the level of autonomous communities, on the one hand, and, on the other, those whose main customer is the traditional private sector. For the first type, their current status is, in part, the result of the public recognition obtained and the securing of public contracts.

It should also be underlined that a WISE's main customer often determines its legal form: WISEs that are highly financially dependent on the public administration tend to adopt the legal form of a non-profit organization (association or foundation). By contrast, WISEs whose main customer is the traditional private sector often have a for-profit legal form.

In Spain, WISEs are not very numerous, and they do not form a well-delimited socio-economic sector. The strong heterogeneity that characterizes this sector is the consequence of the local environment in which each WISE has had to develop in order to survive, and this can be accounted for by the lack of institutional recognition at the national level.

Review questions

- In which category of the typology developed in Chapter 7 could Spanish WISEs be classified?
- Distinguish the motivations that different types of customer have for buying from WISEs.
- Why are resources coming from reciprocity so important in the Spanish context?

Notes

1 For more details see Vidal and Claver (2003).
2 The WISE Regulation Legislative Measures Act 27/2002, of 20 December.
3 The Socio-Employment Integration Act 7/2003, of 26 March.
4 Decree 33/2002, of 5 February, governing the creation and running of WISEs.
5 Decree 32/2003, of 13 March, governing WISEs.
6 *Impuesto de Actividades Económicas* (Economic Activities Tax). This tax was abolished in 2003, but was still applicable in 2001, at the time of the survey.
7 Corporation Tax is levied at a rate of 35 per cent on the profits of any Spanish company.
8 Note that donations made by the public sector were included in indirect subsidies (and not in reciprocity-based resources).

Bibliography

Vidal, I. and Claver, N. (2003) *Work Integration Social Enterprises in Spain: Multiple Goals and Social Capital*, PERSE project research report, Liège: EMES European Research Network (unpublished).

Vidal, I. and Claver, N. (2004) 'Work Integration Social Enterprises in Spain', *Working Papers Series*, 04/05, Liège: EMES European Research Network.

10 A plurality of logics behind Finnish social enterprises

Pekka Pättiniemi

Overview

This chapter analyses the resource mix of Finnish WISEs. While sales and resources coming from the mobilization of reciprocity are important for all of them, a more thorough analysis of their resource mix highlights the various forms of reciprocity in this sector of social enterprise. After reading this chapter, the reader should:

- understand the rationale behind the resource mix of Finnish WISEs;
- have a sense of the diversity of the resource mix of Finnish WISEs.

Introduction

On Finnish WISEs

Finnish WISEs may be divided into two main groups: on the one hand, enterprises connected to the associations for the disabled, namely work centres (*työkeskus*), together with other enterprises owned by the associations for the disabled (*muut sosiaalialan järjestöjen omistamat yritykset*); and on the other hand, co-operatives, namely labour co-operatives (*sosiaalinen työosuuskunta*) and social co-operatives for the disabled (*vajaakuntoisten osuuskunta*).

Work centres and other enterprises owned by the associations for the disabled originate from a long tradition of sheltered work – work centres and other entrepreneurial initiatives aiming to help disabled persons integrate into the labour market. The first initiatives to support enterprises for the disabled appeared in the 1890s, and a governmental measure supporting the employment in enterprises of the visually impaired was adopted in 1935. A law supporting the employment of persons with mobility disabilities was passed in 1952. In the late 1950s and early 1960s, further steps were taken to support sheltered workshops and work centres. In the period that followed these decisions, the number of work centres increased sharply (Kuotola 1988: 92–5, 360, 366; Mähönen 1998: 153–6). Today most of the organizations aiming at integration through work are owned and governed by the public sector; only some 20 initiatives are owned by private organizations.

Most of the over 200 work integration enterprises that compose the second group of WISEs – i.e. co-operatives – were established in the late 1990s, following the economic crisis and mass unemployment that hit Finland in the early 1990s. The oldest enterprises in this group are, today, about ten years old. Most of them were created as self-help initiatives: labour co-operatives were established by long-term unemployed persons, while co-operatives for the disabled were created by disabled people.

Both groups of WISEs meet the criteria of the EMES definition of social enterprises (see Table 10.1 and Chapter 1 of this book), even though, in principle, it seems that co-operative enterprises are more participative and autonomous, due to their ownership structure, than the enterprises connected to the associations for disabled.

There are considerable differences between the WISEs originating in the associational tradition and those that have adopted the co-operative form. The co-operatives, as we have seen, are new establishments, whose origins only date back to the 1990s. They do not have well-established organizations supporting them in their business activities or through lobbying. Co-operatives are mostly active in the service sector, providing services either to enterprises or to households. Work centres and other enterprises owned by the associations for the disabled have longer traditions and more experience of the markets; some of them have been active for decades. Work centres already have well-established support structures. They are active in producing goods in traditional industrial sectors, such as wood, metal and textiles.

The Finnish sample

The Finnish sample includes 15 WISEs, of which six are work centres and nine are co-operatives. The sample does not include any WISEs belonging to the group of 'other enterprises owned by the associations for the disabled', owing to the large size and small number of the enterprises of this group. Most of the co-operatives in the sample were established during the second half of the 1990s and are thus fairly young initiatives. Conversely, a couple of work centres for the disabled were established in the 1960s.

Data were collected during the spring of 2003, through interviews of the managing directors of the WISEs. All participants were asked to deliver beforehand the balance sheet for the year 2001. Only a couple of enterprises did not provide all the necessary information; missing data especially concern the subsidies received. In one case, the data on the economic results concern the year 2002, owing to the fact that the enterprise was

Table 10.1 Different types of Finnish WISE and the criteria of the EMES definition of the social enterprise

Main type of WISE	Enterprises connected to the associations for the disabled		Co-operatives	
Subgroups	Work centres*	Other enterprises owned by the associations for the disabled	Labour co-operatives	Social co-operatives for the disabled
Continuous production of goods and/or services	Yes	Yes	Yes	Yes
A high degree of autonomy	Yes in most cases	Yes in most cases	Yes	Yes
A significant level of economic risk	Often not	Yes	Yes	Yes
A minimum amount of paid work	Yes	Yes	Yes	Yes
An initiative launched by a group of citizens	Yes in most cases	Yes	Yes	Yes
A decision-making power not based on capital ownership	No	No	Yes	Yes
A participatory nature, which involves the persons affected by the activity	No	No	Yes	Yes
A limited distribution of profits	Yes in most cases	Yes in most cases	Yes	Yes
An explicit aim to benefit the community	Yes	Yes in most cases	Yes in most cases	Yes in most cases

*Private work centres under the Invalid Care Act.

Source: Pättiniemi 2004.

established in late 2000 and the balance sheets for 2002 were more representative of the WISE's activities.

1 Economic performance of Finnish WISEs

The turnover varied considerably among the enterprises in the sample. The highest turnover was about €5.8 million and the lowest about €8,000. The average turnover was about €880,000, but a more realistic picture is obtained if these highest and lowest cases are excluded; the figure obtained then is about €500,000.

Total income varied from a maximum of €7.2 million to a minimum of €32,000. Non-monetary resources varied from nil to almost €1.5 million. The average figure if we exclude the highest and lowest cases was about €28,000.

The 'work centre' type of WISE had, on average, a higher turnover than WISEs of the 'co-operative' type: work centres' turnover ranged from €130,000 to €5.8 million, and their average turnover amounted to €2.2 million, while labour co-operatives' turnover ranged from €50,000 to €815,000, with an average of about €310,000.

In terms of turnover, eight enterprises had grown substantially during the three years preceding the survey; in six enterprises the growth had been weak or there had been no growth at all, and only one enterprise had experienced a decrease in turnover.

The main reasons cited to explain the growth were increased visibility in the market place and increased demand for the services produced. Growing experience and professionalism in running a social enterprise was also mentioned as a reason for growth. A factor that positively influenced the evolution of enterprises providing services to the public sector was their capacity to strengthen their trust relationship with public sector authorities.

Those which had not experienced growth in the last three years cited, as the main reason for this, the fact that they were running at full capacity. Three other reasons were mentioned to explain the absence of growth: difficulties in training employees; the difficulties in finding competent workers; and the after-effect of a period of rapid growth in the late 1990s. The only enterprise whose turnover had decreased explained it by its own 'incompetent work'.

Out of the 15 social enterprises surveyed, 11 made profits and only four made losses. The biggest profit/surplus amounted to about €100,000 and the heaviest losses were about €40,000. The average result was a profit of €8,600.

Surplus was used mostly to renew technical equipment; five enterprises used their surpluses totally or partially to this purpose. Other important purposes were investment into working capital and overhead equipment. In one enterprise surpluses were distributed to employees as dividends, in another as production bonuses to all employees in the enterprise, and in one case the profits were donated to fund the owner association's general activities.

2 Sales

2.1 *Private sector and individual customers and their relation to WISEs*

Sales to private persons, which represented on average 28 per cent of total sales, consisted mostly of domestic services (cleaning and minor renovations). The share of sales to individuals varied significantly among the enterprises surveyed, from nil (in seven WISEs) to 85 per cent of total sales.

Sales to the private sector (enterprises) represented on average one-third (36 per cent) of total sales. This share varied from nil (in only two enterprises) to 98 per cent of the total sales of WISEs.

Finnish WISEs seem not to experience any special problem in selling their goods or services to the private sector. In the enterprises where sales to the private sector represented less than 20 per cent of the total sales, the products and the production line were not aimed at this type of customer; the production of goods and services was, instead, directed to private persons, to the third sector or in some cases exclusively to the public sector.

Three of the 15 managers interviewed estimated that, as far as sales to private persons were concerned, the social purpose of the WISE positively influenced the choice of the social enterprise as a provider; in only one case was the effect of the social purposes felt to be negative.

Regarding sales to private enterprises, the experiences of the managers were divided into two groups. On the one hand, some managers considered that the social purpose played a positive role in the customers' choice of the WISE as a provider, or at least that it had some positive effect on sales. One manager considered that: 'The smaller the client organization, the more positive is the effect of the social purpose.' On the other hand, the other group of managers felt that the social purpose had a negative effect. They argued that according to their experience, customers were suspicious regarding the quality of products or services when they knew that the enterprise producing these was employing people with difficulties.

In general, using the social connotation as a means of building contacts was regarded as a possibility when approaching a new market; for several WISEs, the first contacts with customers were brought about with the help of the social purpose, but the importance of the latter as a marketing tool seemed to decrease with the development and growth of the enterprise.

The most important resource in building relationships with both customer groups (individuals and private enterprises) was managers; both professional managers and voluntary members of the managing board were mentioned. In most cases, relationships with current customers originated in relationships that already existed before the creation of the WISE, and were personal in nature. However, in cases where the WISE had been operating in a market for a longer period, the most important commercial relationships could be described as traditional. Finally, in the cases where there was a strong association or other support organization backing the WISE, the latter played a very important role in creating commercial and financial relationships.

None of the enterprises in the Finnish sample received any significant resources from shares, stocks, bonds or such investments.

2.2 Sales of goods and services to the public sector

The share of sales to the public sector represented about 23 per cent of the total sales of Finnish WISEs; its importance in the various enterprises in the sample ranged from nil to 100 per cent of sales. The main customers were regional and municipal public organizations, which together represented, on average, 15 per cent of total sales.

Most of the sales (92 per cent) to the public sector were not motivated by the social and socio-political activities of the WISE; in other words, only 8 per cent of the sales to the public sector were motivated by the social nature of the enterprise.

About 80 per cent of the sales to the public sector were industrial products. The other sales to the public sector were split among the following categories: building industry (7 per cent of the sales to the public sector), health and social services (about 6 per cent, provided by a single enterprise) and 'other private or public services' (7.5 per cent).

The sales to the public sector were based, in most cases, on 'normal' business contracts. As in the case of sales to private individuals and enterprises, the business relationships with the public sector were mainly established by the managers. Initially these relationships may have been motivated by the social activities of the WISE, but after a trial period and the formation of trust in the quality of the goods or services and in the capacity of the WISE to deliver the products, the relationships evolved into normal business contracts. This transformation was generally considered as positive; it was seen as allowing the WISE to increase its sales while minimizing the idea that to buy from the WISE was an act of charity. The only case in which the choice of the WISE as a provider was clearly connected to its social purpose was that of a WISE active in the health and social sector.

3 Subsidies

Nine per cent of the total income of the WISEs in the Finnish sample came from direct subsidies. The main direct subsidies received by WISEs were the 'employment subsidy' and the 'employment and combined subsidy for employing unemployed or disabled persons', which are both delivered through the Employment Offices of the Ministry of Labour. Municipal subsidies for employing disabled persons were also used, especially by WISEs of the work centre type.

Finnish WISEs derive 6 per cent of their total income from national direct subsidies and 3 per cent from municipal direct subsidies. It should be noted that, in the present study, the subsidies delivered through the Employment Offices were considered to be national, because these offices are officially ministerial; however, in practice, they are actually local actors, usually municipality-based, with good relations to the local labour markets. WISEs of the work centre type were practically the only ones to receive subsidies from the municipal level. Relations with municipalities were traditional and well established and run by the managing directors, board members and other directors.

In a couple of cases, the managers interviewed were reluctant to separate subsidies from other income from the sale of goods and services to the public sector, because they considered (which is a defensible point of view) that these subsidies were assimilable to an income derived from selling employment services to the public sector.

Practically all subsidies were negotiated, which means that they were the result of negotiations between governmental agencies and the organization and that the WISEs were not supervised (at least no more than in any normal business relationship) when using them. This is also confirmed by the fact that, according to the managing directors interviewed, most WISEs had a totally free hand in choosing their workers.

Non-monetary aid (personnel secondments and loans of equipment) from the public sector was entirely directed to 'labour market activities'. Owing to their importance for local employment, some WISEs of the co-operative type had also managed to establish good relations with municipal authorities and to obtain resources from them. These resources mainly took the form of free or cheap workspace in municipality-owned buildings.

4 Resources from reciprocity

4.1 Non-monetary aid

Most of the non-monetary aid (which, as just mentioned, can take the form of equipment loans or personnel secondments) came from the private sector and the third sector. The bulk of these resources was allocated to the general activities of the WISE and was in the form of personnel secondments. In some cases, private persons or enterprises had donated non-monetary resources such as office furniture, old personal computers and other office equipment for general purposes. All forms of non-monetary aid were based on negotiated agreements between the WISE and the donors, in the framework of relationships in which the personal contacts of the managing director or chairman of the board with the donating bodies played an important role.

Only a few enterprises (mostly WISEs of the work centre type) benefited from non-monetary aid. For one of the enterprises this represented the main source of income. In most cases the donor and the WISE belonged to the same interest group, and the donations were thus assimilable to a 'mutual help' type of aid. In some cases, donations and non-monetary aid rose to considerable amounts and were vital to the organizations. The importance of donations and non-monetary aid was of special significance when the WISE was in its start-up phase or was experiencing a difficult period of change.

4.2 Voluntary work

The value of voluntary work was estimated using the wages that volunteers would have been paid if they had carried out paid work. This research took into account – assessing its monetary value – the work performed, for example, by voluntary board members and by persons attending non-obligatory information meetings after work hours. This type of voluntary work was present in nine of the 15 enterprises in the sample.

Voluntary work was carried out mainly by employees, members and managers of the WISEs. In practice, no 'ordinary' volunteers were used. The assessed value of voluntary work varied widely from one WISE to another: in two cases, voluntary work was equal in value to other resources; by contrast, in another case it represented only 2 per cent of total resources. It seemed to be more important in the start-up phase of the enterprises than in later phases. In some cases, it was stated that without voluntary work, it would have been impossible to conduct any activities, but although all nine enterprises declared that the voluntary work was important to the success and economic well-being of the enterprise, only two of them were interested in developing it and/or were trying to increase its amount. In general, WISEs sought to get rid of voluntary work rather than to increase it. The reasons for this seemed to be that the burden of voluntary work was heavily concentrated on a few persons, usually managers or workers in specialized positions.

Conclusion: the resource mix of Finnish WISEs

The WISEs in the Finnish sample can be divided into three main groups (as already mentioned, no WISE in the group of 'other enterprises owned by associations for the disabled' was included in the sample): (1) labour co-operatives (co-operative self-help initiatives); (2) work centres (owned by major national or regional welfare associations or foundations); and (3) social co-operatives (self-help initiatives supported by national or regional associations for the target group).

The resource mix of the WISEs surveyed varied considerably among these three groups:

- In the first group (labour co-operatives), the major source of income was the market. Subsidies and non-monetary aid only represented, on average, 3 to 4 per cent of income: the share of subsidies in the income of the WISEs in this group varied from nil to 14 per cent, and non-monetary aid was important in only two enterprises, in which it represented, respectively, 4 and 21 per cent of the total income. Donations and grants amounted, on average, to 5 per cent of the enterprises' resources, while voluntary work was worth 10 per cent of the total monetary resources. For the WISEs in this group, voluntary work was an important means of financing, especially in their start-up phase. Voluntary work was also considered important in raising the awareness of the general public of the social goals and aims of these WISEs.

- The second group (work centres) was constituted mainly by well-established enterprises with long traditions in their industry. Subsidies were important for all enterprises in this group; they represented, on average, about 19 per cent of their income, ranging from 3 to 61 per cent of their resources. Another important resource, especially for newly established WISEs, was donations; in two cases, donations and similar resources were equal to income from the market. In general, public sector subsidies were a vital part of the resource mix of these traditional and well-established WISEs. The subsidies and other income from support measures were taken into account by the WISEs in planning and organizing their entrepreneurial activities.

- The third group (social co-operatives) were heavily dependent on donations and similar resources; in these WISEs' resource mix, they represented, on average, twice the amount of income from the market (from 92 per cent to over 400 per cent). All these donations and similar resources came from private sources – mainly from supporting organizations. Without these donations the activities of these enterprises would have been impossible.

On average 70 per cent of the resources of Finnish WISEs were monetary resources and 30 per cent were non-monetary resources. Over 90 per cent of the monetary resources came from sales, the most important customers being private sector enterprises and private persons; in aggregate, these two categories of customers represented 64 per cent of the sales. Public sector sales represented 23 per cent of the sales, and the third sector 13 per cent of the sales.

Review questions

- What is the role of socio-politically motivated sales in Finnish WISEs?
- How can one differentiate between the resource mix of work centres, that of social co-operatives and that of labour co-operatives in Finland?

Bibliography

Kuotola, U. (1988) 'Johtopäätökset', in Kuotola, U., Tšokkinen, A. and Vartio, E. *Suomen näkövammaisten ja näkövammaistyön historia*, Helsinki: Näkövammaisten Keskusliitto.

Mähönen, H. (1998) *Omin voimin yhteistoimin – Invalidiliitto 60 vuotta*, Hämeenlinna: Invalidiliitto.

Pättiniemi, P. (2004) 'Work Integration Social Enterprises in Finland', *Working Papers Series*, 07/04, Liège: EMES European Research Network.

Part III

Profiles and trajectories of workers in work integration social enterprises

11 Profiles and trajectories of participants in European work integration social enterprises

Carlo Borzaga and Monica Loss

Overview

After a general examination of the place of WISEs in the European land-scape of active labour market policies targeted at low-qualified people, this chapter analyses the data that have been collected regarding the profile and trajectory of 949 disadvantaged workers who entered European WISEs in 2001. After reading this chapter, the reader should:

- be aware of the diversity of profiles of beneficiaries in European WISEs;
- identify the different integration paths of beneficiaries;
- have an understanding of the different impacts of WISEs on the workers;
- be aware of the influence of public schemes on the integration paths of beneficiaries of WISEs.

Introduction

This chapter is dedicated to the analysis of the 'profiles and trajectories' of the workers employed by WISEs, on the basis of the data collected through the interviews of the PERSE sample of managers of European WISEs. The relationships of WISEs with social and labour market poli-cies are also considered, and characteristics of target groups and different models of integration of disadvantaged workers are highlighted.

We analysed individual benefits through a 'target-oriented evaluation research' (Schmid *et al.* 1996) approach adopting a bottom-up perspective, which entails viewing policy impacts from the angle of the people to whom the policy is addressed. This work aims to provide a picture of the situa-tions within different countries in terms of the individual benefits, both monetary and non-monetary, gained by disadvantaged workers during their experience inside WISEs.

After sketching the general framework of the situation regarding unemployment in Europe and of policies implemented to fight it, with special focus on the role of social enterprises (Section 1), this chapter presents the main results of the 'individual benefits' analysis. A description of the methodology adopted and of the sample constituted is provided in Section 2. Section 3 describes the personal profiles of the disadvantaged workers in the European sample. The description is enriched by a classification of the profiles of the workers, based on characteristics regarding their personal and professional condition. Section 4 is devoted to the description of the identified trajectories of the workers; the analysis distinguishes between those who were still employed in the social enterprise at the time of the survey and those who had left it. In the following three chapters, the analysis is illustrated by three country cases: Portugal, Sweden and Belgium.

1 General framework

1.1 Unemployment and active labour market policies for disadvantaged workers

Since the 1970s, unemployment rates have been rising in all European countries; the growth of unemployment started declining only at the end of the 1990s, but unemployment rates remained high. The rise in unemployment was due to various factors, among which the most important ones were the economic crisis that followed the oil shocks (1973–4 and 1979) with the associated increases in production costs, the slowing down of productivity growth and, finally, globalization and computerization, which shifted the economic balance in favour of skilled workers (Bertola *et al.* 2001). Besides, other key factors – such as the evolution of demographic trends and the increase in female participation in the labour market – contributed to the labour market crisis; welfare systems and policies put in place before the 1970s were unable to cope with these changes.

At the end of the 1990s the unemployment rate stopped rising, but it remained stable at high levels. If unemployment was initially mainly a problem affecting low-skilled workers, during the 1990s long-term unemployment became the most relevant aspect. Among the unemployed, at this time, the average duration of joblessness was around 22 months and it increased with age: 13 months in the 15–24 age group, but 20 months in the 25–29 age group.

Long-term unemployment and non-participation in the labour market have different causes in the various parts of Europe. Long-term unemployment is partly a consequence of a 'skill mismatch', due to the structural decrease of the labour demand for low-skilled workers. This phenomenon is attributed to deindustrialization, skill-biased technical progress, or the growth in international trade and the consequent competition with low-wage countries. Unemployment of low-qualified people can also be explained by the 'ladder effect': in a context of lack of jobs, more skilled workers take the jobs of the least skilled, who then have a greater probability of being unemployed. Low-qualified people can also be trapped in inactivity when the monetary benefits (net wages minus cost of transport, childcare, etc.) and the non-monetary ones (quality of job, for example) they can obtain from working are too low compared to what they obtain when unemployed (social benefits, time for the family and so on). In fact, enormous sums are spent on passive policies, such as long-term benefits, which may sometimes encourage inactivity and social exclusion, generating unemployment traps and poverty. Finally, another cause of long-term unemployment is disability; disabled workers have even fewer opportunities than able workers to get a job and can rely on unemployment benefits for a longer period of time.

Traditional policies designed to assist the unemployed, and especially disadvantaged and very low-qualified people, do not seem to be very effective (Martin and Grubb 2001), partially owing to a decrease in employment opportunities and to the increasingly selective demand for labour. The problem is even more complicated and difficult to solve when unemployment is associated with certain kinds of disadvantage, such as social exclusion, disability, low skill level, etc.

This inefficiency of passive labour market policies in combating unemployment, experienced by all European countries in recent years, has led them to encourage, during the last decade, the development of 'active labour market programmes' (European Commission 2004). However, the percentages of GDP designated for these measures are, in many European countries (except for the Scandinavian countries, Germany and Belgium) lower than 1 per cent and always lower than the percentages allocated for passive measures (European Commission 2004).

A cursory look at existing programmes in the various countries reveals that very few new programmes and policies have been designed for the most disadvantaged workers. For example, notwithstanding the fact that persons with mental illness may represent a majority of those referred to as 'persons with a disability', only a very small number of structural programmes exist and are adapted to the needs of this group, as compared to programmes for people with physical or sensory disabilities (Harnois and Gabriel 2000: 30).

It is in this context that initiatives of a new type, which have subsequently been recognized as a tool of labour market policy in many countries, have been set up: work integration social enterprises (WISEs). The following sections will describe them.

1.2 The specific place of WISEs in the fight against unemployment

In recent years, confronted with the difficulties experienced by traditional employment policies in combating long-term unemployment, some grassroots initiatives launched by civil society actors started to deal with the problem of the social and occupational integration of disadvantaged people. The organizations that have been identified by the PERSE research as WISEs belong to this group of initiatives. WISEs are promoters of alternative programmes (such as on-the-job training) which are close to active employment strategies. They aim to help poorly qualified unemployed people and other people affected by one or more kind(s) of disadvantage, who are at risk of permanent exclusion from the labour market; they integrate them back into work and society in general through productive work activity. They thus combine social and productive goals, trying to adapt jobs and job environments to the needs of the workers, and to cope with a reduction in productivity without losing their competitiveness in the market.

The specific goal of WISEs can be either the stable integration of disadvantaged people inside the organization (particularly for those affected by certain types of disadvantage, such as mental disabilities), or to act as a springboard to the normal labour market. In this latter case the WISE helps its workers achieve the skill level necessary to (re)integrate into the mainstream labour market. Certain characteristics of these organizations allow them to be identified as tools of active labour market policies, which are effective in the work integration of disadvantaged workers.

Social enterprises are production-oriented organizations but, simultaneously, they are firms that can have a 'shock absorber' effect. In fact, social enterprises are 'elastic' organizations that welcome and motivate; they have rules that are not excessively strict and which can withstand prolonged or frequent absences; they modify the job environment to suit the personal needs of the workers; they are, therefore, not only workplaces – they also become places of relationship and rehabilitation as well as organizations contributing to the creation of jobs.

As a consequence, social enterprise might be a starting point for disadvantaged people in the process of regaining independence, in both economic and social terms, leading them to develop new strategies for dealing with daily life. Having an occupation might improve the personal status of the workers, in terms of good relations with their colleagues and family and in terms of better managing their everyday life.

According to Borzaga (2000), WISEs help to improve the profiles of the most disadvantaged workers. WISEs contribute to a better allocation of human resources in society by the selection they operate, the low-cost training they provide, as well as through the work integration of persons who are potentially productive, but who would otherwise be excluded from the labour market. The causes of this exclusion are a problem of information asymmetry about their real abilities and the institutional constraints on the appropriation of the benefits resulting from the investments in training and selection of these workers: the results of the work integration benefit the disadvantaged workers and society as a whole, whereas the costs and the risks are supported mainly by the employers. WISEs have a comparative advantage – due to their inner characteristics – regarding the integration service they provide: the training and the hiring of disadvantaged workers. Combined with other forms of intervention, they seem to be a good tool to integrate disadvantaged workers through work and to give people the incentive to become economically active.

Social enterprises do not offer only job opportunities and on-the-job training; they also work with disadvantaged people to help them overcome their condition of disadvantage. These models of work integration offer disadvantaged people the opportunity of work and social inclusion, through membership of an organization that can, at the same time, be productive, compensate for the weaknesses of this type of labour force and give support to people taking part in an integration scheme.

Finally, by developing activities in new fields, social enterprises contribute to the creation of new employment opportunities. In some local contexts and for some kinds of people (people with mental health problems, for example), social enterprises constitute the main opportunity for social inclusion and, often, the sole opportunity for work integration.

These organizations, therefore, have a fundamental role, not merely from the point of view of work and income redistribution, but also from the perspective of a better allocation of community resources. Examples of such work and income redistribution policies include increasing individual options for labour market participation, facilitating the school-to-work transition and increasing employment opportunities for 'hard-to-place' jobseekers. However, research on the outcomes of work integration programmes and on the results of WISEs in terms of employment is currently relatively scarce. One of the aims of the present study was thus to provide data and analysis on this subject.

2 Methodology

For each of the 11 European countries surveyed, a sample of approximately 15 WISEs was investigated (see Table 11.1). For each WISE, a sample of approximately seven disadvantaged workers who had joined the social enterprise in the year 2001 was constituted. However, the flow of workers who had joined social enterprises during the year 2001 varied among countries, and in some cases it was not possible to consider only the year 2001, as the flow was too small; in such cases, the period was lengthened to include the years 2000 and 2002. As a consequence, a majority of the workers in the sample joined the social enterprise in the year 2001, and a minority joined the WISE in the previous or following years.

Managers were interviewed about the situation of these workers approximately two years after their joining the WISE. The database created on the basis of the questionnaire filled in by each country team includes data on a total of 949 disadvantaged workers employed in WISEs. All the results

Table 11.1 Research sample

Country	Number of WISEs	Number of workers interviewed
Belgium	15	103
Denmark	8	50
Finland	11	71
France	10	81
Germany	9	79
Ireland	15	91
Italy	14	84
Portugal	15	105
Spain	12	83
Sweden	15	98
UK	15	104
Total	139	949

presented in this chapter refer to this sample. Nevertheless, it has to be noted that, in some cases, the manager interviewed found it difficult to answer some questions (especially regarding the income level of the workers before they joined the WISE, and their training path). As a consequence, some results refer to a smaller number of workers.

The methodological instrument used for the entire analysis was a closed questionnaire, which was submitted to the manager of the social enterprise, but not directly to the workers. It was considered that managers may be better informed than others about the personal situation of the disadvantaged workers employed in their organization.

3 Personal profiles

In this section, we explore the socio-economic characteristics of the disadvantaged workers, investigating some of their socio-demographic characteristics (such as age, gender, level of education, household condition and types of disadvantage) and their employment experience and conditions previous to their joining the social enterprise.

3.1 The socio-demographic status of the beneficiaries

At the European level, disadvantaged workers employed by WISEs are equally distributed between men and women (52.5 per cent of the disadvantaged workers of our sample are men), and are typically middle-aged, with a low level of education. As far as the type of disadvantage is concerned, they are mainly long-term unemployed or people with social problems, most of whom are hardly considered as employable by the managers interviewed.

As far as gender is concerned, the analysis by country reveals some marked contrasts. In some countries, the majority of the workers surveyed are women: 83 per cent in Portugal, 69 per cent in Ireland and 61 per cent in Germany. Conversely, in other countries, the majority of workers are men: approximately 80 per cent in the UK and 75 per cent in Italy. It seems that the main explanation is to be found in the type of production carried out by the WISE: in Portugal, for example, WISEs are active in the area of personal services, a sector that employs a mainly female labour force.

As far as the age of the workers surveyed is concerned, the picture at the country level is also quite differentiated. The largest age group is middle-aged workers, i.e. those between 36 and 45 years old. Generally speaking, the workers in the sample are quite young: over 70 per cent are under 45. The percentage of over-55s is quite low – only 9 per cent of the sample. There are some countries in which the highest percentage is young workers – in the UK, for instance, the largest group is the under-25s – while in other countries (Finland and Sweden) the largest group is workers between 46 and 55 years old.

As regards education, the average level of formal education is very low: almost 70 per cent of the workers have at most a lower secondary education. A significant proportion of workers (11.7 per cent) have no formal education at all.

Higher levels of education correspond to young workers (see Table 11.2). In the UK, where more than 60 per cent of workers are under 35, 75 per cent have a secondary school qualification. Conversely, in Finland, where over 65 per cent of the workers surveyed are over 46, 55 per cent have only a primary education qualification.

Managers were asked what, in their opinion, was the main obstacle to the employment of the disadvantaged workers (see Table 11.3).[1] Among the workers in the sample, long-term unemployment seems to be the main cause (48 per cent) and it is also the prevailing disadvantage (34 per

Table 11.2 Level of education by age group (%)

| | Age group | | | | |
Level of education	*18–25 years*	*26–35 years*	*36–45 years*	*46–55 years*	*55+ years*
No formal education	10.6	9.9	13.5	11.0	15.1
Primary education	32.6	27.0	30.7	38.5	45.3
Lower secondary education	37.1	39.7	37.6	25.3	26.7
Upper secondary education	18.9	19.0	14.6	19.7	7.1
University degree	0.8	3.6	3.6	5.5	5.8
Not known	–	0.8	–	–	–
Total	100.0	100.0	100.0	100.0	100.0
(N)	(132)	(252)	(274)	(182)	(86)

Table 11.3 Types of disadvantage of the workers (%)

| Type of disadvantage | All* | Prevalent** | |
		Male	Female
Long-term unemployed	47.8	26.2	43.4
Person with qualification problems	27.7	8.8	14.2
Young participant (under 25)	8.6	2.9	1.8
Old participant (over 55)	3.9	1.8	1.8
Officially disabled person	10.7	7.0	6.5
Person with other social problems	29.8	27.2	12.4
Immigrant	7.0	5.5	2.5
Person with mental problems	12.0	10.6	7.2
Refugee	2.5	1.8	0.4
Other (prisoner, adult outcast, etc.)	14.5	8.2	9.9
Total		100.0	100.0
(N)	(949)	(489)	(445)

*Since this table is the result of a question with multiple answers, summing the percentages of this column would not make sense.

**Type cited as the unique or first cause of disadvantage.

cent).[2] People with other social problems (former drug addicts, alcoholics, homeless people or people with family problems) account for 30 per cent of the sample. The low qualification level also appears as a major cause of integration problems (in 28 per cent of cases) and a significant minority of workers (12 per cent) seems to be affected by mental problems. Other types of disadvantage are the fact of belonging to an ethnic minority and being an ex-prisoner or a prisoner on probation.[3]

Men are mainly affected by social problems (27 per cent) and long-term unemployment (26 per cent), while women are mainly long-term unemployed (43 per cent) and low-qualified (14.2 per cent).

In the framework of the questionnaire the managers were asked to evaluate the disadvantaged workers' level of employability at the time they joined the social enterprise. Most are defined as hardly employable (40.5 per cent) or partially employable (40.8 per cent). Analysis by gender shows that men are judged to be hardly employable more often than women.

Cross-tabulation of the data on the prevalent type of disadvantage of the workers with that on their estimated level of employability produces quite interesting results (see Table 11.4).

Disabled workers and workers with mental problems are, to a large extent, deemed 'hardly employable' by managers. Immigrants and young participants, as well as workers with other types of disadvantage (mainly ex-prisoners, as mentioned above) are considered as partially employable. There are no categories of disadvantage in which the majority of workers is defined as 'easily employable' by the managers interviewed.

Table 11.4 Level of employability by prevalent type of disadvantage

| | Level of employability (%) | | | | |
	Easily	Partially	Hardly	Total (%)	(N)
Long-term unemployed	26.5	36.4	37.1	100.0	(321)
Persons with low qualification	17.0	44.3	38.7	100.0	(106)
Young participant	36.4	54.5	9.1	100.0	(22)
Old participant	11.1	38.9	50.0	100.0	(18)
Officially disabled person	9.8	27.9	62.3	100.0	(61)
Person with other social problems	16.9	37.0	46.0	100.0	(189)
Immigrant	24.3	64.9	10.8	100.0	(37)
Person with mental problems	11.8	28.2	60.0	100.0	(85)
Refugee	9.1	36.4	54.5	100.0	(11)
Other	24.1	39.8	36.1	100.0	(83)
Whole sample	18.7	40.8	40.5	100.0	(933)

A first conclusion emerges from the data analysed so far on the characteristics of the workers: the social enterprises in the sample deal with workers who are, in a majority of cases, hardly or partially employable.

3.2 Previous employment experience and income level

Before joining the social enterprise, most of the workers were unemployed and receiving unemployment benefits (28 per cent); the second most numerous group was that of the unemployed not on benefit (20 per cent). Only a little more than 10 per cent of the workers were employed (with fixed-term or open-ended, full-time or part-time contracts) before joining the WISE, 6 per cent were housewives or students and approximately 10 per cent were inactive (see Table 11.5).

According to the data collected on the income of the workers before joining the WISE (which were unfortunately not available for all workers, because of problems incurred in collecting the data), 9.6 per cent of the workers in the sample had an income of between approximately €250

Table 11.5 Status of the workers before joining the social enterprise (%)

	Share of workers
Employed	10.6
Trainee	6.3
Unemployed or inactive	58.2
Housewife, student	5.9
Other (sheltered work, prison, refugee, etc.)	17.7
Not known	1.3
Total	100.0
(N)	(933)

Table 11.6 Total income of the disadvantaged workers just before joining the WISE (%)

	Share of workers
No income	22.0
Not known	18.7
Missing	15.2
Less than €250	0.8
€250–500	9.6
€500–750	8.7
€750–1,000	6.2
€1,000–1,250	6.2
€1,250–1,500	5.2
More than €1,500	7.4
Total	100.0 (946 workers)

and €500 a month, while 22 per cent had no income before joining the social enterprise and 33.7 per cent earned more than €500 per month (see Table 11.6).

Since fewer than 10 per cent of the workers were employed before joining the WISE, most of their income came from public subsidies. Differences between countries appear more clearly as regards the workers' income before joining the WISE (see Table 11.7) than for other aspects investigated by the research. The welfare systems of some countries (such as Denmark and Sweden) include a strong income protection system, whereas in some other countries (such as Portugal and Spain), the degree of social protection is weaker, and this also affects income.

3.3 WISEs' target group

Analysis of the profiles of workers upon joining the WISE reveals that it is not possible to define a common profile. The 'typical worker' joining a WISE does not exist in the population, which is actually quite heterogeneous. However, we have been able to divide the sample of 949 workers – through multiple correlation analysis and classification analysis – into six broad categories, using a set of variables for each worker (age on joining, gender, household situation, level of education, employment experience, main disadvantage,[4] level of employability,[5] level of abilities, status just before joining and channel of arrival).

The different categories that resulted from the classification (and whose characteristics are summarized in Table 11.8) are the following:

- high-educated and easily employable adult men (group 1);
- adult low-educated unemployed (group 2);
- young high-educated unemployed (group 3);
- low-educated women without unemployment benefits (group 4);

Table 11.7 Distribution of workers (%), in each country, by income just before joining the social enterprise

Total income	Belgium	Denmark	Finland	France	Germany	Italy	Ireland	Portugal	Spain	Sweden	United Kingdom
No income	12.6	–	2.8	45.7	8.9	35.7	–	65.7	47.0	4.1	7.7
Less than €250	–	2.0	1.4	–	5.1	3.6	2.2	8.6	4.8	–	21.2
€250–500	24.3	–	14.1	8.6	19.0	1.2	3.3	7.6	20.5	5.1	29.8
€500–750	36.9	2.0	9.9	2.5	16.5	–	4.4	–	1.2	18.4	5.8
€750–1,000	13.6	2.0	2.8	–	7.6	–	–	–	–	12.2	5.8
€1,000–1,250	1.0	12.0	2.8	–	3.8	–	1.1	–	–	9.2	1.9
€1,250–1,500	–	–	–	–	1.3	–	–	–	–	3.1	–
More than €1,500	–	–	5.6	–	–	–	–	–	–	10.2	1.0
Missing data/unknown	11.6	82.0	60.6	43.2	37.8	59.5	89.0	18.1	26.5	37.7	26.8
Total	100.0	100.0	100.0	100.0	100.0	100.0	100.0	100.0	100.0	100.0	100.0
(N)	(103)	(50)	(71)	(81)	(79)	(84)	(91)	(105)	(83)	(98)	(104)

Table 11.8 Summary of the main characteristics of the workers by group

	Average age/Employment experience	Level of education	Former status	Gender	Abilities/Employability	Country well represented*
Group 1 (213)	38/Long term	High	Social help, at work	Men	High/Easy	Italy, Finland
Group 2 (279)	43/Long term	Low	Unemployed	Women	High/Middle	Germany, Finland, Portugal
Group 3 (86)	32/Short term	High	Unemployed	–	Low/Middle	Ireland, UK
Group 4 (105)	34/Short term	Low	Unemployed, housewives, students	Women	Medium/Middle	Portugal, Sweden
Group 5 (119)	28/Short term	Low	Trainees	–	Low/Hard	Belgium, Sweden
Group 6 (147)	32/Short term	Very low	Inactive – social help	Men	Extremely weak/Very hard	Denmark, France, Italy

*All countries are relatively well represented in each group.

- hardly employable trainees (group 5);
- the most precarious men, generally inactive (group 6).

These different groups are in different positions regarding the labour market. The last two groups clearly suffer from a serious lack of skills, so they might be unable to find a job because of shortages of jobs adapted to their profiles. The question is, therefore, whether the WISE can either develop their human capital sufficiently to allow them to find a job in the normal labour market or create stable jobs adapted to their profiles. At the opposite end of the spectrum, the first and the second groups seem easily employable; they most probably suffer from temporary unemployability. Short-term subsidies could be a springboard to enable them either to reintegrate into the normal labour market or to stay in the social enterprise without any public financing. The diversity of the profiles of workers in WISEs makes it clear that public schemes (in terms of length and level of public financing) cannot be uniform for all these groups.

4 Trajectories of the beneficiaries

This section analyses the channels via which disadvantaged workers join WISEs, the types of integration schemes in the framework of which they are hired, the duration of stay that they can expect upon joining the WISE and the training offered by WISEs. We also analyse the profiles, characteristics and trajectories of WISEs' disadvantaged workers by means of a 'before and after' approach,[6] distinguishing between those who were still employed in the social enterprise at the time of the survey and those who had already left it.

4.1 Channels of entry

In most cases the workers surveyed had benefited from some kind of help in their search for a social enterprise that could hire them. At the European level, the main channel of entry into social enterprises is referrals from social services or local authorities (29.2 per cent) or labour offices (28.4 per cent). Self-initiated applications represent 19.7 per cent of cases, while 9.9 per cent and 4.1 per cent of the workers were sent by other third sector organizations or by other units of the same WISE, respectively (see Table 11.9).

Cross-referencing these data with those on the kinds of disadvantage the workers surveyed suffer from reveals that people affected by long-term unemployment are almost exclusively referred by labour offices, while most persons affected by problems of social exclusion are sent to the social enterprise by social services. Self-initiated application also represents a significant percentage of cases (typical in this regard are Ireland and Finland, where 40 per cent of the workers joined the social enterprise as a result of self-initiated application): these workers are mainly long-term unemployed, but also people with other social problems. Finally, it should be noted that immigrants are directed to the WISE mainly by other third sector organizations.

The channels of entry of disadvantaged workers are quite strongly influenced by the relationship between the social enterprise and local services. Table 11.9 shows the importance of the links and relationships existing between local or national authorities and WISEs in the different countries. This gives a clear picture of the roles played by the various actors concerned in the work integration of disadvantaged workers. Table 11.9 shows, for example, the 'non-role' of the Italian local labour offices as a 'channel of entry' into WISEs (no worker joined a WISE through this channel) and, conversely, the strong role that these offices play in Germany and in the UK (where they represent the main channel of entry into WISEs). This is linked to the fact that in some countries (such as Germany or the UK) WISEs are recognized as tools of labour market policy while in other countries (such as Italy), they are seen mainly as actors in social policies.

4.2 Types of integration scheme

The data collected also give indications about the types of integration scheme social enterprises provide for their workers. Not all social enterprises have the same purpose: some aim to stably integrate disadvantaged workers by creating jobs, while other WISEs only aim to provide workers with the basic tools that will enable them to (re)integrate into the mainstream labour market. Logically, the aim of the WISE influences the types of employment contracts it offers to its workers; these can be normal contracts or specific types of contracts linked to integration programmes (employment schemes). The results of the survey show that, on the whole, the social enterprises in the sample in most cases (54.1 per cent) use employment schemes, while 25.7 per cent of workers are hired in the framework of regular employment contracts (Table 11.10). There is also a low percentage of workers who are integrated through training schemes. The remaining workers might, for example, receive an allowance from the social enterprise for their working activity.

The analysis by country shows that in some countries, such as Portugal, Germany and Belgium, an overwhelming majority of workers are hired in the framework of employment schemes (98 per cent, 96 per cent and 86 per cent, respectively). In Finland the prevailing category is that of normal employees (79 per cent), while in Sweden the majority of workers are hired through vocational training schemes (53 per cent).

4.3 Employment prospects of the workers

As far as the duration of the contracts (which we refer to, in this chapter, as the 'employment prospects' of the workers) is concerned, the social

Table 11.9 Channels of entry into the social enterprise by country (%)

Channel of entry	Belgium	Denmark	Finland	France	Germany	Ireland	Italy	Portugal	Spain	Sweden	United Kingdom	Average
Social services or other local authority	33.0	54.0	15.5	41.3	30.8	1.1	57.1	33.3	20.5	44.8	2.0	29.2
Labour office	6.8	26.0	38.0	23.8	50.0	45.1	–	35.2	3.6	33.3	49.0	28.4
Self-initiated application	30.1	8.0	38.0	23.8	9.0	40.7	2.4	23.8	14.5	12.5	9.8	19.7
Other third sector organization	21.4	2.0	1.4	3.8	5.1	13.2	13.1	3.8	37.3	–	3.9	9.9
Other unit of the same WISE	3.9	4.0	4.2	2.5	–	–	4.8	3.8	21.7	–	2.0	4.1
Other (advert, etc.)	4.9	6.0	2.8	5.0	5.1	–	22.6	–	2.4	9.4	33.3	8.7
Total	100.0	100.0	100.0	100.0	100.0	100.0	100.0	100.0	100.0	100.0	100.0	100.0
(N)	(103)	(50)	(71)	(80)	(78)	(91)	(84)	(105)	(83)	(98)	(104)	(947)

Table 11.10 Types of integration scheme by country

Country	Type of integration scheme (%)				Total (%)	(N)
	Regular employees	People in employment schemes	People in vocational training schemes	Other		
Belgium	9.7	86.4	3.9	–	100.0	(103)
Denmark	16.3	59.2	2.0	22.4	100.0	(49)
Finland	78.9	4.2	1.4	15.5	100.0	(71)
France	26.3	50.0	6.3	17.5	100.0	(80)
Germany	2.6	96.2	–	1.3	100.0	(78)
Ireland	53.8	45.1	1.1	–	100.0	(91)
Italy	28.6	52.4	19.0	–	100.0	(84)
Portugal	–	98.1	1.9	–	100.0	(104)
Spain	28.8	51.3	11.3	8.8	100.0	(80)
Sweden	28.6	8.2	53.1	10.2	100.0	(98)
United Kingdom	19.8	35.6	10.9	33.7	100.0	(101)
Average	25.7	54.1	10.9	9.4	100.0	(939)

enterprises surveyed give different employment prospects to their workers: 35.4 per cent were hired on open-ended work contracts, while another 30 per cent were expected to stay for a limited period of time, namely until the end of their fixed-term contract. As far as the remaining workers are concerned, managers explained that the duration of their stay in the WISE was not defined in advance, but that it could be defined in the course of their working experience. Asked to indicate the duration of this period, managers gave a duration ranging from a minimum of one to a maximum of four years. The highest percentage among this group is expected to stay for two years.

Analysis of the national situations reveals significant differences between countries regarding the duration of employment in the WISEs surveyed (Table 11.11): in several cases (Sweden, Belguim, Italy and Finland), most workers are hired on open-ended contracts. In these countries, indeed, some WISEs aim to provide stable jobs for the disadvantaged workers they employ. Germany and Portugal are at the other end of the spectrum: respectively 100 per cent and 98.1 per cent of the workers are expected to stay only until the end of the programme under which they were hired.

The employment prospects are obviously influenced by the type of disadvantage. The cross-tabulation shows that, for instance, 37.9 per cent of the long-term unemployed and 50 per cent of the young participants and immigrants are expected to stay only for a fixed period in the WISEs (whose duration depends on the length of the programme under which they have been hired), while a large majority (76.2 per cent) of the disabled are hired with no projected time limit; this is also the case for 43.9 per cent of people with mental or social problems.

Table 11.11 Employment prospects of the disadvantaged workers at the time of their joining, by country

	Employment prospects (%)			
	To stay for a fixed term	To stay with no time limit	Total (%)	(N)
Belgium	29.2	70.8	100.0	(73)
Denmark	52.0	48.0	100.0	(50)
Finland	49.3	50.7	100.0	(71)
France	87.7	12.3	100.0	(81)
Germany	100.0	–	100.0	(78)
Ireland	88.5	11.5	100.0	(91)
Italy	35.7	64.3	100.0	(84)
Portugal	98.1	1.9	100.0	(105)
Spain	77.1	22.9	100.0	(83)
Sweden	23.5	76.5	100.0	(98)
United Kingdom	68.6	31.4	100.0	(102)

4.4 Training

WISEs often emphasize the fact that training – both formal and on-the-job – is one of their major goals. Data collected in the PERSE project confirm the importance of the training role of WISEs: only 10 per cent of the workers did not receive any kind of training. In other words, for an overwhelming majority of workers, some kind of training was provided during their stay in the WISE. Thirty-two per cent of the workers benefited from some kind of training organized inside the social enterprise and 23.4 per cent from training organized by external institutions, mainly training organizations. Over 40 per cent of the workers received training within 'working groups', in the form of work together with a person in charge of their training.[7]

4.5 Profiles, characteristics and trajectories of the workers

The methodology of the research was to classify the workers in two groups, those who had left the social enterprise by the time of the survey, on the one hand, and those who were still employed in the WISE at the time of interview, on the other. The majority (58.5 per cent) of the workers in the sample were still employed in the social enterprise at the time of the survey.

Cross-tabulating the situation of the workers at the time of the survey (by 'situation of the workers', we mean whether they were still employed in the WISE or had left it) with their age, sex, working status before joining the WISE, level of education, type of disadvantage and level of employability reveals that, surprisingly, none of these factors has an impact. It seems that the important factor in explaining the situation of a worker is the type of scheme through which he/she joined the WISE. For example, it appears that the percentage of workers employed in employment schemes is higher among those who had left the social enterprise (60.6 per cent) than among workers who were still employed by the WISE (54.3 per cent).

Unsurprisingly, in Belgium, Italy or Sweden, where a high proportion of people have the prospect of staying in the WISE indefinitely, a higher proportion of workers were still in the WISE at the time of the survey.

Workers still employed in the WISE at the time of the survey

Analysis of the trajectories of the beneficiaries still employed in the social enterprise at the time of the survey shows that most of these workers were stably integrated inside the WISE; they had been trained during the integration path; their income level was significantly higher than before (see Table 11.12); and their personal abilities had improved during their time in the WISE. Approximately 46 per cent of these workers still employed in the WISE had an open-ended contract, and among these the majority had a full-time contract. This can be interpreted as a successful result as regards the integration objective.

Cross-tabulating the data on present work status and that on employment experience, for the workers still employed in the WISE at the time of the survey, reveals that workers employed with an open-ended contract (either part-time or full-time) had, before joining the WISE, more than five years of employment experience, while trainees and workers with fixed-term, part-time contracts did not have previous employment experience.

It is also interesting to analyse, for the workers still in the WISE at the time of the survey, the connection between their status and the work

Table 11.12 Distribution of the workers still employed in the WISE according to their level of income before joining the social enterprise and at the time of the survey

Income at the time of the survey	Income before joining							(N)
	<€250	€250 to 500	€500 to 750	€750 to 1,000	€1,000 to 1,250	€1,250 to 1,500	>€1,500	
Less than €250	2	1	–	–	–	–	–	(3)
€250–500	9	14	–	–	–	–	–	(23)
€500–750	10	12	10	1	1	–	–	(34)
€750–1,000	4	16	5	4	1	–	–	(30)
€1,000–1,250	2	5	9	7	8	1	1	(33)
€1,250–1,500	4	7	10	9	2	2	–	(34)
More than €1,500	1	3	7	2	10	5	21	(49)
(N)	(32)	(58)	(41)	(23)	(22)	(8)	(22)	(208)

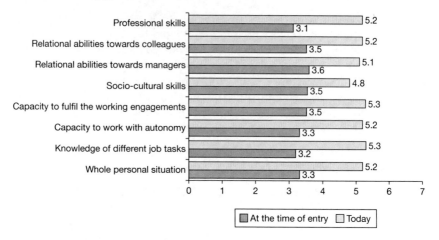

Figure 11.1 Improvement of workers' abilities (workers still employed in the WISE at the time of the survey)

prospects they had at the time they joined the social enterprise. Over 60 per cent of the workers on open-ended contracts had started the integration programme with no time limit, while the balance, nearly 40 per cent, started working in the WISE with a fixed-term contract but subsequently switched to an open-ended contract. This is not the same for those hired on a fixed-term contract, whose expectation was to stay for a fixed period of time.

Capability and autonomy in daily life and relationships had significantly improved. The workers' abilities were studied through various items, to which the managers were asked to give a score of between 1 and 7. The managers estimated that the abilities of the workers had improved by at least two points for over half the ranked items, as shown in Figure 11.1. In all the countries in the sample, the individual condition of the workers had improved thanks to their employment experience inside the WISE. The best improvements were in abilities related to employment: scores that improved by approximately two points concern, in fact, professional skills, relationships with managers and colleagues and knowledge of different job tasks. Socio-cultural skills, on the contrary, had improved only to a limited extent.

Workers who had left the social enterprise at the time of the survey

The number of workers who had left the social enterprise at the time of the survey is 391, which represents 41.5 per cent of the sample. When asked to indicate the reasons for the workers' departure,[8] the reason most often cited by managers is the end of the project (19.7 per cent), followed by leaving before the end of the contract or of the project because of the

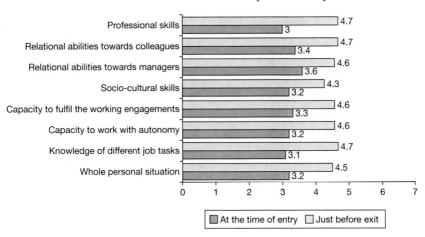

Figure 11.2 Improvement of workers' abilities (workers who had left the WISE at the time of the survey)

prospect of a new job (18.9 per cent) – which is a very positive element for evaluating the integration programme – and the end of a fixed-term contract (18.2 per cent). This is coherent with the profile, in occupational terms, of the group of workers who had left the WISE: most of them were employed in an employment scheme with the prospect of staying in the WISE until the end of their fixed-term contract. Other reasons cited include leaving without the prospect of a new job, dismissal, and resignation because of health problems (which account respectively for 13.8 per cent, 11.8 per cent and 5.9 per cent).

The evolution of the personal condition and abilities of the workers who had left the WISE was analysed in the same way as for the workers still employed in the WISE (see Figure 11.2); their personal abilities improved noticeably, although the average level of improvement was a little higher for the workers still in the WISE than for those who had left it.

Conclusion

Social enterprises are a widespread and not a marginal phenomenon, and are particularly relevant as regards employment. WISEs employ a significant number of people: in the year 2001, the 139 WISEs surveyed employed over 5,000 disadvantaged workers.

The survey conducted on the personal characteristics of a sample of 949 disadvantaged workers allows us to draw up a profile of the European sample as consisting of middle-aged workers, equally distributed between the two sexes, with low qualifications and a low level of education. Almost all workers employed by WISEs, according to the personal information collected, could be defined as disadvantaged in a strict sense. This disadvantaged condition was linked, for some of them, mainly to their labour market situation (long-term unemployed or low-qualified workers), and for others, mainly to their personal condition (problems of social exclusion, family problems or physical/mental disability); in many cases, the workers surveyed were disadvantaged in both senses.

Most workers hired by social enterprises were unemployed or inactive in the period just before joining the WISE. A high percentage of workers had quite a long employment experience (over five years), even though their status before joining the WISE was, in most cases, long-term unemployed. Notwithstanding this quite long employment experience, 40.5 per cent of the workers were defined as hardly employable.

It also appears that WISEs' target groups are those one might have expected, given the different models of WISEs active at the European level and national labour market and social policies. WISEs are often able to support or, in some cases, to replace public authorities in solving social and employment problems, and their target groups can differ depending on public programmes. Within the different models of social enterprise that aim to help disadvantaged workers and to relieve or overcome social and/or employment exclusion, different objectives, related partly to public policies and partly to the organizations themselves, can be highlighted. The main objective may be the stable integration of the disadvantaged workers inside the WISE, especially if the WISE is a tool of social policy; or, if the organization is a labour market tool, the WISE may mainly aim to provide job tools to the disadvantaged workers, through training and/or temporary employment.

Most of the long-term unemployed and young participants have the prospect of staying in the WISE for a limited time; however, among officially disabled people or people with other social problems, the prevailing prospect is of remaining in the WISE indefinitely. Country analysis reveals that the work prospects of the workers (the expected duration of their stay in the WISE) is correlated with the different countries' policies in favour of disadvantaged persons.

In some countries, where labour market policies prevail, as in Germany, most workers are supported by specific programmes designed to help the long-term unemployed. In other countries, the access systems to social enterprises are quite strongly influenced by the relationship between the social enterprise and the social services, which are the privileged channel for the integration of disadvantaged people.

In order to evaluate WISEs' activities correctly, we must keep in mind at least three important aspects:

•   The aim of the enterprise varies from one WISE to another; in some cases its main goal is to provide a temporary alternative to a situation of need, while in some other cases the mission is to re-include people into the labour market and society. When evaluating the effectiveness of the integration paths, this distinction should be kept in mind, and the evaluation should not be based only on the number of workers who found a job in the mainstream labour market after their experience inside the WISE.

- The level of employability of some of the workers is hardly influenced by their stay in the WISE. The personal profiles and employment experiences of these disadvantaged workers suggest that their chances of finding a job outside the social enterprise are very low, and this is confirmed by their status before joining the WISE and by the path they follow after they leave it. Before joining the social enterprise, most disadvantaged workers were not able to find and keep a job in a normal enterprise. Furthermore, when they exit the social enterprise, they can return to being unemployed.
- The relationship between WISEs and labour market policies plays an important role. In many countries, WISE experiences have spread and developed rapidly, and their effectiveness in tackling the employment difficulties of a target group of workers has increasingly led to their being considered as successful tools of active labour market policies.

These premises have been taken into account in the analysis of the results of the survey. Outcomes of the stay in the WISE have been classified (see Table 11.13) distinguishing between positive outcomes, negative ones, and neutral ones – the latter referring to situations for which the available data did not allow us to determine whether the outcome was positive or negative for the worker.

For a majority of workers, the stay in the WISE had a positive outcome: 58.6 per cent of the workers were still employed in the WISE at the time of the survey and 7.7 per cent had found a job outside the social enterprise.

Table 11.13 Outcomes of the integration path

	(N)	%
Positive outcomes of the integration path		
Still employed in the WISE	552	58.6
Left with prospect of new job	73	7.7
Negative outcomes of the integration path		
Left without prospect of new job	53	5.6
Dismissed	45	4.8
Resigned because of health problem	23	2.4
Other (*WISE closed, etc.*)	51	5.4
Neutral outcomes of the integration path		
End of the project	76	8.1
End of fixed-term contract	70	7.4
(N)	(943)	100.0

For a small percentage of workers, the stay in the WISE resulted in a negative outcome: 5.6 per cent left the programme without the prospect of a new job, and a probable interpretation of this could be that they gave up because of problems of different kinds. Some other workers (4.8 per cent) were dismissed, and 2.4 per cent resigned because of health problems. Finally, the stay of the remaining workers concluded with the end of the project (8.1 per cent) or the end of the fixed-term contract (7.4 per cent) – neither of which outcomes can, in themselves, be considered as positive or negative. Overall, the effect of the stay in a WISE can be positively evaluated.

For those still employed in the WISE, levels of income had increased thanks to the employment experience inside the WISE; their personal abilities had also improved, thus helping these people in the process of gaining or regaining autonomy. For those who had left the WISE, our data indicate that their human capital had also increased significantly through their stay in the WISE, although this improvement was more pronounced among the persons who were still in the WISE than among those who had left it.

Besides these conclusions relating to the profiles and trajectories of the workers, some comments can also be made as regards the situation of the WISEs themselves. Notwithstanding the rapid development of the work integration social enterprise phenomenon in many European countries, it appears that some of their needs remain unmet.

First, the analysis highlights the fact that WISEs are a good tool for helping people at risk of labour market and social exclusion, but that, in many European countries, they are still not very well known and are not always adequately recognized by policy makers and traditional enterprises. Some things could be done to support and stimulate the development of these organizations. For example, our results tend to show that the types of public programmes available to social enterprises are not sufficiently linked to the actual profiles of the workers. And these programmes strongly influence the trajectory of the workers: if we cross-tabulate the situation of the workers (whether they are still employed in the WISE or have left it) with data about age, sex, working status before joining the WISE, level of education, type of disadvantage and level of employability, it appears that, surprisingly, none of these factors has an impact. The main factor influencing the situation of the workers seems to be the type of integration scheme, defined by the labour market authorities in order to support certain kind of workers, under which the workers are engaged.

WISEs are in many cases, as just stated, closely linked to public integration schemes; the fact of being the tool of specific programmes for disadvantaged workers can drive the organization towards sustainability risks. When programmes end, what is the future of both participants and the social enterprise? The need not only for trust but also for financial support by the public authorities is evident for many types of work integration social enterprises. The case study of Portugal, for instance, highlights the difficulties that Portuguese WISEs faced because of requirement after three years to sell their services in the competitive market without any support from public bodies to compensate for the workers' low productivity (see Chapter 12 of this book).

Notwithstanding the fact that social enterprises pursue a social aim (which is, for WISEs, to provide job opportunities for disadvantaged workers), these enterprises simultaneously have to deal with a business aim – namely, the economic sustainability of the enterprise. WISEs thus face a challenge, and they have to improve and strengthen their management and entrepreneurial framework in order to become viable in financial terms.

The purpose of this analysis was to identify the European context in which WISEs operate. However, the study has also revealed that the situation of WISEs differs from country to country, sometimes quite strongly. The analysis of the workers' profiles and trajectories presented in this chapter can thus usefully be enriched by a deep analysis of some country studies. The following three chapters go into some distinctive elements of three countries involved in the PERSE project: Portugal, Sweden and Belgium. These countries have some characteristics, compared to the European standard, that are interesting to highlight.

Sweden has a well-established system of active labour market policies; the author explains how WISEs reveal some of the limitations of these policies for some vulnerable groups. This contrasts with the case of Portuguese WISEs, created in the framework of quite recently introduced active labour market policies, as an answer to the priorities of the national strategy to fight poverty and social exclusion. The case of Belgium is characterized by a long-term tradition of collaboration between public bodies and the third sector in implementing labour and social policies.

Review questions

- How do European WISEs contribute to a better allocation of community resources?
- Which outcomes could be evaluated as positive or negative results of European WISEs regarding the integration path of participants?
- Which data reveal the different patterns, across countries, of relationships between WISEs and public bodies?

Notes

1   In the questionnaire, managers were asked to rank, by order of decreasing importance (from rank 1 to rank 3), the types of disadvantage by which the workers were affected.

2   The 'prevalent' cause is either the only cause cited for a worker or, in the case of a worker with more than one cause, the one that is considered the most important. The 'main' cause is the cause that was cited most often, regardless of its 'rank' of importance.

3   This factor has also often been indicated as a 'social problem'; it is quite relevant for some countries, such as Italy.

4   Managers were asked what they considered as the main disadvantage of the workers regarding their integration into the labour market.

5   Managers were asked to evaluate the levels of employability and of ability of the disadvantaged workers at the time of their joining the social enterprise, on a scale from hardly employable to easily employable, with an intermediate stage of partially employable. These judgements are related to various aspects: skills, working experience and types of disadvantage.

6   In the absence of a control group, we are aware that we were not able to capture the net effects of WISEs. Indeed, we can measure the number of participants to the programme and the gross placement rate at the end of it, but we cannot know what would have happened to the beneficiaries of the programme if they had not participated to it. The net effect of WISEs on the beneficiaries' trajectory in the labour market is thus difficult to measure because we know that selection bias (resulting from the 'creaming' behaviour of operators and from self-selection by the participants) is important. However, for the Belgian sample, a control group was built and a net effect could be calculated (see Chapter 14 of this book).

7   A worker could receive several forms of training.

8   Several possible answers.

Bibliography

Acemoglu, D. (2001) 'Human Capital Policies and the Distribution of Income: a Framework for Analysis and Literature Review', *Treasury Working Paper*, 01/03.

Adnett, N. (1996) *European Labour Markets: Analysis and Policy*, London and New York, NY: Longman.

Atkinson, T., Cantillon, B., Marlier, E. and Nolan, B. (2002) *Social Indicators, the EU and Social Inclusion*, Oxford: Oxford University Press.

Bertola, G., Boeri, T. and Nicoletti, G. (2001) *Welfare and Employment in a United Europe, a Study of the Fondazione Rodolfo Debenedetti*, London: MIT Press.

Boeri, T., Layard, R. and Nickell, S. (2000) 'Welfare-to-Work and the Fight against Long-term Unemployment', document presented by Tony Blair and Massimo D'Alema to the *European Council of Lisbon*.

Borzaga, C. (1994) 'La cooperazione sociale di inserimento lavorativo: una analisi empirica dell'efficacia e dei fattori di successo', in *Rivista della Cooperazione*, 18, September–October.

Borzaga, C. (ed.) (2000) *Capitale umano e qualità del lavoro nei servizi sociale. Un'analisi comparata tra modelli di gestione*, Rome: Edizioni Fondazione Italiana per il Volontariato.

Borzaga, C. and Defourny, J. (eds) (2001) *L'impresa sociale in prospettiva europea*, Trento: Edizioni 31.

Borzaga, C. and Loss, M. (2002a) *The Socio-economic Performance of Social Enterprises in the Field of Integration by Work*, PERSE project intermediate research report, Trento: ISSAN (unpublished).

Borzaga, C. and Loss, M. (2002b) 'Work Integration Social Enterprises in Italy', *Working Papers Series*, 02/02, Liège: EMES European Research Network.

Borzaga, C. and Loss, M. (2003) *Labour Integration, Social Enterprise and Local Development*, Trento: Agenzia del Lavoro.

Borzaga, C. and Santuari, A. (eds) (1997) *Servizi sociali e nuova occupazione: l'esperienza delle nuove figure di imprenditorialità sociale in Europa*, Vol. 1, Trento: Regione Trentino Alto-Adige.

Borzaga, C., Gui, B. and Povinelli, F. (1997) 'L'inserimento lavorativo di soggetti svantaggiati: il ruolo delle organizzazioni nonprofit specializzate', *Working paper*, Trento: Università di Trento.

Borzaga, C. and Zandonai, F. (2002) 'I contenuti del terzo rapporto sulla cooperazione sociale', in *Comunità cooperative*, Turin: Edizioni della Fondazione Giovanni Agnelli.

Centro Studi CGM (ed.) (1997) *Imprenditori sociali. Secondo rapporto sulla cooperazione sociale in Italia*, Turin: Edizioni della Fondazione Giovanni Agnelli.

Demozzi, M., Loss, M. and Valenti, G. (2000) *The Work Integration of Disadvantaged People*, PERSE project research report, Trento: ISSAN (unpublished).

European Commission (2004) *Employment in Europe*.

Fazzi, L. (2003) *Costruire Politiche Sociali*, Milan: Franco Angeli.

Giudici, C. and Guarneri, A. (2004) *La qualità del lavoro nell'Europa allargata: evidenze dalla European Values Studies Survey*, Rome: Università La Sapienza.

Hansmann, H. (1996) *The Ownership of Enterprise*, Cambridge, MA: Harvard University Press.

Harnois, G. and Gabriel, P. (2000) *Mental Health and Work: Impact, Issues and Good Practices*, Geneva: WHO/ILO. Available at www.ilo.org/public/english/employment/skills/disability/publ/index.htm/

ISTAT (2001) *Le istituzioni nonprofit in Italia. I risultati della prima rilevazione censuaria. Anno 1999*.

Loss, M. (1999) *Active Employment Policies and Labour Integration for Disabled Persons: Estimation of the Net Benefits*, research report, Trento: ISSAN (unpublished).

Loss, M. (2004) *The Individual Benefits for Disadvantaged Workers Employed in Work Integration Social Enterprises. European Analysis*, PERSE project research report, Liège: EMES European Research Network (unpublished).

Maiello, M. (1997) *La cooperazione sociale di inserimento lavorativo*, in *Imprenditori sociali*, Turin: Edizioni della Fondazione Giovanni Agnelli.

Marocchi, G. (1999) *Integrazione lavorativa, impresa sociale, sviluppo locale*, Milan: Franco Angeli.

Marocchi, G. (2002) 'L'inserimento lavorativo nelle cooperative social', in *Comunità cooperative*, Turin: Edizioni della Fondazione Giovanni Agnelli.

Marocchi, G. (2005) *Le traiettorie di sviluppo della cooperazione sociale italiana in Beni comuni, Quarto rapporto sulla cooperazione sociale in Italia*, Turin: Edizioni Fondazione Giovanni Agnelli.

Martin, J.P. and Grubb, D. (2001) 'What Works and for Whom: a Review of OECD Countries' Experiences with Active Labour Market Policies', *Working paper*, 2001–14, IFAU Office of Labour Market Policy Evaluation.

Meager, N. and Evans, C. (2001) *The Evaluation of Active Labour Market Measures for the Long-term Unemployed*. Available at www.ilo.org.

Modigliani, F., Fitoussi, J.P., Moro, B., Snower, D., Solow, R., Steiner, A. and Sylos Labini, P. (1998) 'Manifesto contro la disoccupazione nell'Unione Europea', in *BNL Quarterly Review* (September).

Paggiaro, A. (1999) 'Lavoro e disoccupazione: questioni di misura e analisi, Un modello di mistura per l'analisi della disoccupazione di lunga durata', *Working paper*, 12, 1999, Dipartimento di Scienze Economiche e Statistiche, Università di Padova.

Schmid, G., O'Reilly, J. and Schoemann, K. (1996) *International Handbook of Labour Market Policy and Evaluation*, Cheltenham, Brookfield, VT: Elgar.

Spear, R., Defourny, J., Favreau, L. and Laville, J.-L. (eds) (2001) *Tackling Social Exclusion in Europe*, London: Ashgate.

12 Work integration social enterprises in Portugal: a tool for work integration?

Heloísa Perista and Susana Nogueira

Overview

The emergence of WISEs in Portugal is closely related to the priorities of the national strategy to fight poverty and social exclusion. This chapter shows how these social enterprises have contributed to the work integration and to the improvement of the skills and abilities of their disadvantaged workers. After reading this chapter, the reader should:

- be able to identify the goals of Portuguese WISEs;
- identify the outcomes and the drawbacks of the public scheme in the framework of which Portuguese WISEs have developed;
- be aware of the 'top-down' process at work in the development of Portuguese WISEs.

Introduction

The Portuguese third sector covers a wide range of organizations, including *misericórdias* (charitable organizations closely related to the Catholic Church), mutual benefit associations, private institutions of social solidarity (*Instituições Particulares de Solidariedade Social*, or IPSS) and co-operatives.

The role of third sector organizations in Portugal has to be understood within a national context in which the high incidence of poverty and social exclusion goes along with a late and slow development of the welfare state. Full juridical and institutional acknowledgement of the Portuguese social security system came only after the Portuguese Revolution of 1974, with the enlargement of social rights and the state's assumption of a central role in providing social protection to citizens. This occurred in a broader context of national and international economic recession and of crisis of the welfare state.

The Portuguese social security system[1] is based on a model in which responsibilities are shared between the state – through public bodies, including local authorities – and the non-governmental and non-profit sector.[2] According to the principle of complementarity, it recognizes the articulation among the various forms of social protection – public, social, co-operative, mutual and private for-profit organizations – in developing, replacing or complementing state initiatives for social security purposes and, especially, for social action.

The activity of private institutions of social solidarity is regulated, fiscally controlled and financially supported by the state, through co-operation agreements. In 1996, for the first time, a 'Covenant on Co-operation for Social Solidarity' was signed, setting out a common strategy of co-operation between institutions of the third sector that pursue social solidarity-oriented aims, the central administration, and the local and regional administrations. In the 2003 Protocol between the state and these social solidarity institutions, a new 'Programme of Co-operation for the Development of Quality and Safety in the Social Answers' is mentioned – this was launched in March 2003 and it will be in force until the end of 2006.

WISEs emerged in Portugal quite recently, in 1996, with the creation of a specific public scheme, the so-called 'Social Employment Market', partly under pressure from the 'National Action Plan for Employment' developed in the framework of the European Employment Strategy. Portuguese WISEs – 'integration companies' (*empresas de inserção*) – are only weakly embedded in the social fabric, and the public framework in which they were created has been developed through a 'top-down' process. The main beneficiaries of the measure are the long-term unemployed and the unemployed who are at a disadvantage in the labour market (alcoholics in rehabilitation, guaranteed minimum income beneficiaries, the disabled, etc.). Eighty per cent of the wages of the workers in integration are funded by public authorities for a limited period. The law also provides that WISEs can only develop products that are 'additional' to existing products and services, i.e. they are not already provided either by the state or by a market actor. This leads WISEs to explore and test new concepts and products, with a low profitability but with a collective dimension, such as social services or services linked to the environment. But, paradoxically, no specific financing is provided, in the framework of the public scheme, for this 'production goal', in spite of it being somehow, indirectly, 'imposed' on WISEs. As a result, WISEs often face serious problems when the period of subsidy is over, and workers have to leave the WISE, with a low probability of finding a job.

1 Labour market and social situation in Portugal in recent years

The Portuguese labour market has gone through two distinct periods in the last few years: a first period, until 2000, characterized by significant economic growth and rising employment; and a second one, since 2001,

marked by economic slowdown and rising unemployment. The employment rate was still falling at the beginning of 2003, reaching 67.2 per
cent.[3] The employment rate of Portuguese women, however, increased
more rapidly than the male one and did not reflect as much as that of
men the effects of the labour market crisis following 2001. In 2001, the
female employment rate had already overshot the targets defined for the
female employment rate in the European Union of 57 per cent by 2005
(Stockholm Summit), and of 60 per cent by 2010 (Lisbon Summit); in
2002, the female employment rate in Portugal was 61 per cent.[4] Nonetheless, the female unemployment rate remains persistently higher than
the male one.

It is important to stress that having a job in Portugal is not synony-
mous with not being poor. Exclusion from the labour market is, in fact,
only one of the many dimensions of poverty and social exclusion, and the
situation of the 'working poor' in Portugal shows that the poverty risk
extends beyond access to employment. This raises the issue of the persistence of structural fragilities in the country, related to a low level of
education associated with high rates of school failure and early drop-out,
a low skill level of large sectors of the working population, together with
low participation in life-long learning, low wages, low-quality employment
and low productivity. In Portugal, the situation regarding poverty and
social exclusion remains worrying: in 2001, 20 per cent of the population
was exposed to the risk of poverty, and 15 per cent to the risk of persistent
poverty.[5]

2 WISEs in Portugal: the case of the integration companies

The emergence of WISEs in Portugal is closely related to the priorities of
the national strategy to fight poverty and social exclusion. In 1996, within
the framework of that strategy, the so-called 'Social Employment Market'
(*Mercado Social de Emprego*) was launched as part of a set of measures aiming
at the work integration of people with specific social difficulties or vulnerable groups, such as the disabled, the long-term unemployed, former drug
addicts and young people looking for a first job. The Social Employment
Market provides several measures, among which is the creation of integration companies, occupational programmes for the unemployed, sheltered
employment (*emprego protegido*) and workshop-schools (*escolas-oficina*).

Referring to the definition of WISEs adopted for the purpose of
the present study (Borzaga and Defourny 2001), we identified two types
of WISE (both part of the Social Employment Market) currently
operating in Portugal: sheltered employment and integration companies.
Both types may be run/promoted by different third sector organizations,
namely *misericórdias*, mutual benefit associations, private institutions of social
solidarity (IPSS) and co-operatives. However, due to the methodological

Table 12.1 Integration companies – number of structures and beneficiaries
1998–2001*

	1998	1999	2000	2001
No. of integration companies created by year	67	308	107	82
No. of beneficiaries	555	2,640	3,109	4,236

*Unfortunately, reports on the Social Employment Market were only published until 2001. In spite of our efforts, it was impossible to update this information.

Source: *Mercado Social de Emprego*, Relatórios de Actividades 1998–2001.

option taken in the PERSE project not to include sheltered employment, the present national study focuses on integration companies only.

The 'Integration Companies programme' was created in 1998 within the Social Employment Market. It aims to develop a new social entre-preneurial spirit, thus contributing to the resolution of problems of unemployment, training, poverty and social exclusion through the creation of jobs and economic activities addressing unsatisfied social needs such as home care, proximity services, the improvement of green spaces, and the rehabilitation and restoration of buildings. As already mentioned, the main beneficiaries of integration companies are the long-term unemployed and the unemployed who are at a disadvantage in the labour market, namely alcoholics in rehabilitation, minimum income (currently referred to as the 'integration social income' – *Rendimento Social de Inserção*) recipients, the disabled, former convicts, young people at risk, lone parents, people with psychiatric disorders in rehabilitation, the homeless, drug addicts in rehabilitation and prostitution victims.

Table 12.1 presents some data on the situation of integration companies in Portugal.

Most of the 564 integration companies created during the period for which information is available were launched in 1999. These structures involved 4,236 beneficiaries in 2001.

3 Comments on the main research results

3.1 Gender differentiation: the over-representation of women

Women are significantly over-represented among the disadvantaged workers on whom we have collected detailed information; in fact, nearly 83 per cent of the workers surveyed are women.

The high female share has to do, on the one hand, with the sectors of activity in which most Portuguese WISEs are operating, namely home-care support for elderly people or laundry and cleaning. On the other hand, women are also over-represented among the main target groups of the integration companies, such as low-qualified workers and the long-term unemployed. As underlined above, even in the context of low and decreasing unemployment (compared to the European Union average) which prevailed until 2001, the unemployment rate remained higher for women (5.1 per cent in 2001, compared to 3.2 per cent for men).[6] After 2001, with a significant increase of unemployment (still in progress), the greater vulnerability of women to unemployment remained (women's unemployment rate was of 6.1 per cent in 2002 and 7.3 per cent in 2003, compared to 4.2 per cent and 5.6 per cent, respectively, for men).[7]

3.2 Integration schemes

Considering the most relevant type of disadvantage of workers upon entering the WISEs (each worker could cumulate several types of disadvantage), we can conclude that most disadvantaged workers were long-term unemployed (54.4 per cent), whereas persons with other social problems represented 19.4 per cent of the workers surveyed and persons with qualification problems 13.6 per cent.

The long-term unemployed are mostly women (59.3 per cent), while persons with other social problems are mostly men (52.9 per cent). The percentage of workers with qualification problems is higher among male workers (17.6 per cent) than among female ones (12.8 per cent).

Throughout the duration of the programme, and according to the main purposes of the integration companies, the disadvantaged workers in integration are supposed to develop their professional skills as well as their personal and social capabilities in order to improve their employability in the open labour market. Therefore, the integration companies must combine a training period with the development of a professional activity for each disadvantaged worker following the integration path. Integration companies are thus supposed to develop a relevant component of professional training. However, in a large majority of the cases (87.2 per cent), this training was on the job.

Ninety-eight per cent of the disadvantaged workers had the status of employees in employment schemes; this result is not surprising, integration companies having been created in the framework of an employment scheme.

3.3 Monetary benefits

In order to be hired by an integration company, the worker must be registered at an Employment Centre of the Institute for Employment and Professional Training (*Instituto do Emprego e Formação Profissional*, or IEFP). They can be beneficiaries, for instance, of unemployment benefits, integration social income or disability allowances.

If we consider the actual occupational status of the disadvantaged workers just before entering the WISE, most of them were not employed (irrespective of the age group): 62.9 per cent were unemployed and not receiving unemployment benefits; 9.5 per cent were unemployed with unemployment benefits; and 12.4 per cent were inactive. The workers had been in the same situation for over one year in 54.3 per cent of the cases, while 17.1 per cent of the disadvantaged workers had been in the same situation for more than three years before entering the WISE.

Moreover, these disadvantaged workers generally had limited work experience before entering the WISE: 41 per cent had work experience totalling less than one year, and 23 per cent had no experience at all. Men had, on average, a longer experience than women: 39 per cent and 19 per cent, respectively, had more than five years of experience.

Before entering the WISE, the average monthly income level of these disadvantaged workers was rather low. A high proportion of workers did not answer this question. However, the data collected reveal that 46.2 per cent had an income lower than the national minimum wage; most workers received their income via social services grants. Unemployment benefits and other sources of income seemed to ensure a slightly higher income.

During their stay in the WISEs, disadvantaged workers have a regular income, co-funded by public support. When training (with a maximum duration of six months) is part of the individual integration plan, trainees are entitled to a training grant corresponding to 70 per cent of the national minimum wage – this amount is covered by the IEFP. As for the workers in the integration process, wages are paid taking the national minimum wage as a reference; the IEFP funds 80 per cent of the wages and the other labour costs.

Compared to the income of the disadvantaged workers before entering the WISE, and in spite of the scarcity of the data we were able to collect from the managers on this issue (data on 47 workers), it appears that the workers still employed in the WISE by the time of the survey showed a significant increase in their income level, although 93.6 per cent of them receive less than €500 a month (2.1 per cent of the workers earned between €500 and €750 per month, and 4.3 per cent had a monthly income of between €750 and €1,000).

The main goal of WISEs is the integration of the disadvantaged worker into the open labour market at the end of the programme. In the cases where this is not possible, the jobless people are entitled to unemployment benefits, integration social income or other social benefits.

3.4 Benefits in terms of workers' abilities

WISEs aim to improve their workers' abilities. According to the evaluation done by the managers or social workers (see Figure 12.1),[8] the abilities of the disadvantaged workers who were still employed in the WISE at the

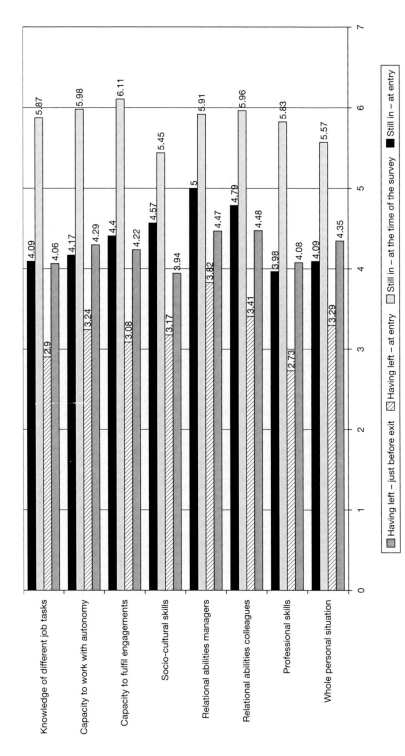

Figure 12.1 Improvement of the disadvantaged workers' abilities – workers still in the WISE and workers having left it at the time of the survey

time of the survey had improved significantly in all aspects, in particular regarding their professional skills, their capacity to fulfil work commitments, their capacity to work autonomously and their knowledge of different tasks. The improvement in terms of relational abilities and socio-cultural skills was less significant, which might have limited, to some extent, the improvement of the whole personal situation of the disadvantaged workers.

The result is similar regarding the disadvantaged workers who had already left the WISE by the time of the survey: their situation improved for all the items listed, although these workers tend to score lower, on average, both at entry and at the time of the interviews, than the disadvantaged workers who were still there.

3.5 Reasons to exit the social enterprise

From a total of 105 disadvantaged workers, 44.8 per cent were still in the WISE at the time of the interview, while 55.2 per cent had already left it. Most of the male workers in the sample (55.6 per cent) were still in the WISE by the time of the survey, while most women (57.5 per cent) had already left – 39 of the 50 women surveyed were unemployed at the time of the interview. As for the 58 disadvantaged workers who were no longer employed in the WISE, 71.4 per cent had started working in the integration company more than 24 months before, and none of these workers had started working there less than 18 months previously.

The interviewees were asked to choose among several categories of reasons for the workers to leave the WISE. When considering the reason cited as the most important one for each worker who had left the enterprise, it appears that the main reasons to leave the WISE (see Table 12.2) were either the 'end of a fixed-term contract' or the 'end of the project supporting

Table 12.2 Reasons for leaving the WISE, for each gender (%)

	Gender		All
	Male	*Female*	
End of project	28.6	20.0	21.1
Interruption without prospect of new job	–	24.0	21.1
Interruption with prospect of new job	14.3	6.0	7.0
Dismissed	42.9	–	5.3
Resigned because of health problems	–	8.0	7.0
End of subsidy	–	–	–
Enterprise closed or restructured	–	–	–
End of fixed-term contract	14.3	34.0	31.6
Other	–	8.0	7.0
Total	100.0	100.0	100.0
(N)	(7)	(50)	(57)

labour integration inside the integration company'. However, it is also important to notice that 21.1 per cent of the disadvantaged workers – all women – decided to leave before the end of the project, with no prospect of a new job. Eight per cent of women, but no men, resigned because of health problems. On the other hand, only male workers were dismissed.

Although the number of cases here is too low to allow conclusions to be drawn, it is also interesting to point out that the disadvantaged workers who resigned because of health problems were long-term unemployed, while the disadvantaged workers who were dismissed were persons with other social problems. On the other hand, those with mental problems decided to leave without the prospect of a new job.

Conclusion

According to the data collected through the interviews of our sample of WISE managers, we can conclude that entering a WISE proved beneficial for the disadvantaged workers. Indeed, the overwhelming majority of the workers hired by WISEs – most of whom were long-term unemployed, and nearly all women – saw their situation improve, in terms both of their professional status and of their capabilities, after entering a WISE.

Considering their working situation, 47 out of the 105 disadvantaged workers surveyed were still working in the WISE at the time of the interview. It is, of course, difficult to anticipate what their professional future will be. As to the workers (58) who had already left the WISE by the time of the interview, 32.8 per cent had found a new job (13.8 per cent with an open-ended, full-time contract and 19 per cent with a fixed-term, full-time contract). Taking into account the low educational level, the lack of work experience and the low employability which characterize these disadvantaged workers, this may be considered as a positive outcome.

It is also important to stress that, although it is quite common for disadvantaged workers to return to unemployment after their period in the WISE, in most cases their situation nevertheless seems to improve: a situation of unemployment without benefit is often replaced by one of unemployment with benefit. Focusing our analysis on the workers who had already left the WISE at the time of the survey, it appears that just before entering the WISE, 60.3 per cent of these were unemployed without unemployment benefit and only 10.3 per cent were unemployed with unemployment benefit; by contrast, after their stay in the WISE, only 6.9 per cent were unemployed without unemployment benefit and 17.2 per cent were unemployed with unemployment benefit.

As far as monetary benefit is concerned, this seems to be particularly important, since all the disadvantaged workers who were still employed in the WISE at the time of the interview had a wage income, which was not the case before their entry for most of them. Nevertheless, this monetary benefit may be only temporary and their income might easily fall at the end of the project or if they leave the WISE.

In short, in spite of all the difficulties, Portuguese WISEs are, in fact, contributing to the work integration and to the improvement of the skills and abilities of their disadvantaged workers. This positive effect is particularly obvious as regards the improvement of their professional skills and abilities and their capability to work autonomously.

In Portugal, WISEs emerged thanks to the creation of a specific public scheme, partly under pressure from the 'National Action Plans for Employment' developed in the framework of the European Employment Strategy. These WISEs are only weakly embedded in the social fabric and rely on a public scheme that appears somewhat artificial.

The choice of the kind of production is imposed by the public scheme regulating these social enterprises, which states that WISEs can only develop products that are 'additional' to already existing types of products and services, i.e. that are provided neither by a state actor nor by a market actor. In most cases, this leads WISEs to explore and test new concepts and products, with a low profitability but with a collective dimension: for instance, social services and services linked to the environment. However, paradoxically, no specific financing is provided for this 'production goal' in the framework of these policies.

Considering these data, one might reasonably fear that Portuguese WISEs will have to face serious challenges at the end of the subsidy period.

Review questions

- Which outcomes could be evaluated as positive or negative results of Portuguese WISEs regarding the integration path of participants?
- Why are women over-represented in Portuguese WISEs?
- Why might one fear that Portuguese WISEs will have to face serious challenges at the end of the subsidy period?

Notes

1 Cf. *Lei de Bases da Segurança Social*, Law no. 32/2002, of 20 December.
2 It was our decision to refer to the different legal and policy sources using their own wording: third sector, non-governmental and non-profit sector, social economy, etc. These different terms may reflect the ambivalences and the ongoing discussion about the meaning and the contents of the concept of social enterprise in Portugal.
3 INE (2003), annual average.
4 Eurostat data, based on the *European Community Labour Force Survey* for 2002.

5   According to Eurostat, ECHP data, efforts made to fight social exclusion have brought the poverty risk rate down (from 23 per cent in 1995 to 20 per cent in 2001). Nevertheless, Portugal still has one of the highest rates in the EU, 5 per cent above the EU average (Commission of the European Communities 2003).
6   INE (2001), annual average.
7   INE (2002–03), annual average.
8   Interviewees were asked to give, for each worker, a score of 1 to 7 for each of the aspects mentioned in the graph.

Bibliography

Borzaga, C. and Defourny, J. (eds) (2001) *The Emergence of Social Enterprise*, London and New York: Routledge.

Commission of the European Communities (2003) *Joint Report on Social Inclusion, Summarizing the Results of the Examination of the National Action Plans for Social Inclusion (2003–2005)*, Brussels: Commission of the European Communities.

Eurostat (2002) *European Community Labour Force Survey 2002*.

Instituto Nacional de Estatística (2001) *Estatísticas do Emprego 2001*.

Instituto Nacional de Estatística (2002) *Estatísticas do Emprego 2002*.

Instituto Nacional de Estatística (2003) *Estatísticas do Emprego 2003*.

Mercado Social de Emprego (undated) *Relatório de Actividades 1998*, Lisbon: IEFP.

Mercado Social de Emprego (undated) *Relatório de Actividades 1999*, Lisbon: IEFP.

Mercado Social de Emprego (2001a) *Cinco Anos de Acção criando Emprego e Inclusão (1996–2001)*, Lisbon: IEFP.

Mercado Social de Emprego (2001b) *Relatório de Actividades 1º semestre 2001*, Lisbon: IEFP.

Mercado Social de Emprego (2001c) *Relatório de Actividades 2000*, Lisbon: IEFP.

Perista, H. and Nogueira, S. (2004) 'Work Integration Social Enterprises in Portugal', *Working Papers Series*, 4/06, Liège: EMES European Research Network.

13 Sweden: social enterprises within a universal welfare state model

Yohanan Stryjan

Overview

The Swedish model of the universal welfare state is based on a basically corporatist division of tasks between organized sectors of society: the state, the business community and popular movements. The last two decades have been marked by a growing awareness of the shortcomings of existing active labour market policies, and a gradually increasing openness to new initiatives such as social enterprises. After reading this chapter, the reader should:

- understand that Swedish social enterprises appear as an original actor that tackles the deficiencies of a well-institutionalized model;
- have an understanding of the goals pursued by Swedish WISEs;
- identify both formal and informal relationships between WISEs and public authorities.

Introduction

Sweden's 'active labour market policy' (ALMP) is a central element of the Swedish model. It has played a decisive role in shaping today's labour market and, indirectly, contemporary Swedish society as a whole. The institutions of the labour market set the baseline for the operation of emergent WISEs, and define the opportunities and constraints for their formation and action. A brief introduction to the Swedish model is therefore necessary to understand the field.

Full employment and universal welfare, the societal goals that historically stand at the core of the Swedish model,[1] were to be pursued by the business community and the state in concert, with popular movements (civil society's formalised aspect) as a bargaining partner with strong consultative voice (Stryjan and Wijkström 1996). Within the division of tasks between organized sectors of society, wealth creation (and thus, job creation) was entrusted to the 'business community' (*näringslivet*; cf. Erixon 1996), while the state administered (re)distribution and maintained optimal (ideally frictionless) functioning of the labour market. With time, this division of tasks evolved into a public monopoly over both welfare provision and labour market administration, linked to a tacit understanding that the state should not involve itself in the creation of (production) jobs. Organized civil society was not assigned any direct role in the operation of the labour market. The emergence of WISEs, as discussed in this chapter, constitutes a marked departure from this tradition (Stryjan 2001).

The institutional (and conceptual) separation of the spheres of production and redistribution, and the subsequent re-linking of the two into a functioning and conceptually coherent whole, are the Swedish model's most distinctive feature. The model's production-centred spirit (Esping-Andersen 1994) and labour market policy's central role are seldom discussed by economists, who mainly focus on its redistributive features. The ALMP was, in fact, entirely separated from welfare, and conceived as an element of the model's *economic* sphere (Hedborg and Meidner 1984; see Meidner 1997). The two spheres were linked through the labour taxation nexus. Opting for full employment enabled the Labour Movement to sidestep the choice between Bismarckian (employment-related) welfare and universal welfare, turning full employment into something of a normative keystone (enshrined in the Basic Law Proclamation 1974: 52) that links the two spheres into a functioning whole. Both the model's spectacular success throughout the 1950s and 1960s and the difficulties it encountered from the 1970s onwards are intimately connected to this institutional make-up. The model was push-propelled (national wage-negotiations precluded competition for labour) and facilitated the phasing out of the least efficient firms and industries, and the channelling of the labour force that was made redundant in the process towards growth sectors, while keeping inflation in check. The strong emphasis on the collective pursuit of group interests, the *Arbetslinjen* ethos of integration through the mainstream labour market institutions (requiring individuals 'to stand at the labour market authorities' disposal'; Axelsson 2002), and the array of mobility enhancement measures, contributed to the model's internal consistency and stability. Mobility was enhanced through retraining, whenever required, and the social overheads of mobility were reduced by income maintenance schemes and mobility grants (von Otter 1980). Time spent between employments was to be made as brief, productive and painless as possible.

Initially, the problem of 'less employable' people was perceived as an engineering problem of ALMP flow management, rather than a matter of social justice. This 'functional sediment' was treated stratum-wise: (a) less productive individuals were allotted wage subsidies so as to enhance their reabsorption into the labour market; (b) those capable of low-skill regular work were accommodated by a network of state-run sheltered workshops, *Samhällsföretaget* (later incorporated as *Samhall*), which mainly contracted simple menial tasks from Swedish multinationals; (c) a residual group, judged unsuited to the discipline of a workplace, was defined out of the labour market (and employment statistics) altogether, through measures such as prolonged sick leave, disability pension or (until the 1980s) hospitalization in closed institutions. This group was exempted from labour market policies.

The Swedish model was designed for a homogeneous society in (Fordist) industrial expansion, where productivity gains directly translate into increased demand for labour in growth sectors. Those assumptions, formed in the 1940s, became increasingly untenable in a post-industrial economy in which profits, investments and mass industrial employment are not directly linked. The previously well-integrated elements of the labour market policy started drifting apart, as it were, under the pressures of social and economic change: traditional business no longer generated a demand for the industrial manpower that the ALMP tools were designed to provide, and the supply of labour churned out by its institutions did not match the (increasingly fragmented and selective) demand in new growth sectors. The least 'attractive' groups formed a growing sediment of permanently unemployable people. The public tools of integration, which were supposed to accommodate this sediment, faced a different sort of crisis: as industry relocated its production facilities to low-wage countries, the sheltered workshop system (*Samhall*) was caught between a shrinking demand for low-skilled tasks on the one hand, and a declining volume of state commissions[2] on the other (Stryjan and Laurelii 2002).

In the absence of viable exit options, redundant labour was left circulating in training programmes. This, in turn, prompted overuse of administrative and quasi-medical labelling (early pension, health leave, etc.) initially designed to dredge up obstructions from (less sluggish) labour flows. The number of persons labelled as permanently unemployable (such as recipients of early pensions) passed the half-million mark in 2004, and now constitutes about two-fifths of the growing group not covered by ALMP measures. Their subsistence is ensured by social transfer payments, but they may not seek employment, at peril of losing this income. Moreover, growing groups of potential entrants (youth, immigrants) remain at the threshold, cut off altogether from the (employment-linked) elements of labour market and transfer systems, and dependent on (municipally financed) social help.

Broadly speaking, we have to consider (at least) two different categories of participants, whose problems lie beyond what the mainstream ALMP system can deliver. These two categories are:

• Those constitutionally unable to reach the level of qualification required in the present labour market. Adjusting jobs in the economy (and, by extension, enterprises that create such jobs) to suit their capabilities is a task that lies outside the scope of ALMP, which primarily integrates individuals into a predefined labour market.

• Persons who fail to gain a foothold in the increasingly selective labour market (Swedberg 1995) owing to a lack of appropriate social skills and social capital (in the Bourdieu'esque sense of the term) – a handicap that an employment system geared for mass allocation cannot remedy. This problem group increased progressively from the mid-1990s onwards, as a result of the labour market's increasing selectivity, and of the fact that employment agencies cannot, by their nature, handle the piecemeal allocation of non-standard manpower to non-standardized small business.

Awareness of the deficiencies of existing labour-market policies triggered new initiatives in this field, both by those directly involved, and by committed members of the community. This development was pioneered by social co-operatives (*sociala arbetskooperativ*) established and/or run by the participants themselves, which emerged in the wake of mental health care reforms in the late 1980s (Stryjan and Wijkström 1996). The prime target group was 'work seekers' who lacked ALMP entitlements. Community enterprises (*grannskapsföretag*), which are constituted by local stakeholder coalitions with social integration of the marginalized included in a broader community agenda (Stryjan forthcoming; Stryjan and Laurelii 2002), emerged in the mid-1990s. All these actors enter a field that was previously exclusively held by state agencies. A variety of hybrid forms that combine participant involvement with active support of community actors now also exists. The availability and specific structure of EU programme financing have shifted the balance between central policies and local initiatives yet further, and paved the way both for new initiatives and for new financing channels for the established ones.

1 The sample

The organizational population of WISEs dealt with in this chapter is rather young and dynamic. We are dealing with an interstitial phenomenon that emerges, as it were, in the cracks of the old system, and evolves in a rapidly changing institutional framework. Thus, newly established enterprises reflect the problems and opportunities of the time and region they were created in. Those may differ from the problems and opportunities encountered by an enterprise created in the previous or following year or in the neighbouring municipality. Organizational features thus vary considerably from one WISE to another. The sample that is reviewed in this study consists of 15 enterprises, and was assembled to reflect the population's diversity. The two dominant organizational forms in the sample are social co-operatives and community enterprises. The sample also includes one (live-in) collective and one charity-oriented enterprise, though both forms are relatively rare. The WISEs selected vary in terms of age (from 3 to 15 years[3]), geographical location (north and south, urban and rural) and size (from €0.06 to €1.9 million turnover; and from 2 to 69 participants). The different indicators may co-vary, but do not always do so. The two indicators of size chosen are often linked, but both turnover and employment figures may also be misleading (Stryjan 2003a), since some of the participants and staff in the WISE may lack a formal employment position, and not all services delivered by the enterprise are formally invoiced. The correlation between size and age seems to be weakly negative.

At the time of the survey (2003), the organizations surveyed provided work to 361 participants and 67 staff members. Gender-wise, recruitment is slanted towards male participants, since 61 per cent of participants and 63 per cent of staff members are male. One of the largest enterprises (a residential drug-rehabilitation collective) has an all-male participant group, which tips the gender balance somewhat, but on the other hand, women participants constitute the absolute majority in two other WISEs.

2 Personal profile of the disadvantaged workers

The common denominator for WISE participants is the failure of the established ALMP system to deal with their situation. The omnibus label of 'disadvantaged', while politically correct and meaningful financing-wise, obscures substantial differences between the sub-categories, both in terms of resources and of limitations. Sixty-five per cent of the participants were labelled by our respondents as long-term unemployed. Since people who are permanently excluded from the labour market or never entered it would not be classed as 'unemployed' in the Swedish institutional terminology, we may assume that a large portion of the remaining 35 per cent lacked employment for a prolonged time but were not eligible for unemployment insurance.

A detailed study of individual benefits, carried out on a sample of participants (amounting to about 23 per cent of the total workforce), gives a general idea of the labour market status of persons entering/joining the WISE:

- only 3 per cent of participants were employed directly prior to joining the WISE, and a further 1 per cent were self-employed;
- 56 per cent were unemployed or inactive, the latter being a euphemism for the 'undeserving non-employed', who are excluded from the labour market insurance system;
- the remainder (40 per cent) participated for longer periods in publicly financed training or in public employment measures. Being directed to the WISE was, in their case, something of a last-resort measure.[4]

Seventy-three per cent of the participants were judged by the managers to be 'hardly employable'. Only 8 per cent were considered 'easily employable'.

Depending on ideological and material considerations, different WISEs address different segments of the pool of the marginalized. As would be the rule for any enterprise, the profile of the participants working in a WISE is shaped by the enterprise's recruitment policies and by the resources and manpower within the enterprise's reach.

As far as their formation is concerned, Swedish WISEs fall into roughly two categories: worker co-operatives started by prospective participants, and enterprises started by other parties, either on behalf of the disadvantaged, or with a broader aim in sight. The way in which the enterprise's original participants were recruited is influenced by the different modes of formation, which also tend to set the WISE's recruiting pattern for years to come. Thus, enterprises that were formed by the participants themselves tend to rely to a higher degree on self-referral/voluntary entry, and to maintain a more homogeneous participant group (in terms of the participants' handicaps or disadvantages), while those founded by other actors tend to rely on referral/placement by authorities, and (not least because the authorities' agenda is seldom consistent over time) are often less homogeneous. Enterprises within both categories may, however, resort to selective recruitment strategies.

Broadly, it is possible to distinguish between 'generalist WISEs', which aspire to address different integration/exclusion problems in their community, and may branch into a wide range of participant mixes and activities (from picture-painting to scrap-metal salvage within one enterprise), and 'specialist WISEs', which focus on a single distinct participant group. The most typical examples of the second category are:

* *Basta*, a rehabilitation collective for drug addicts (Hansson and Wijkström 1997, 2001);
* The *Sign-Language Centre* (SLC), a worker co-operative started by hearing-handicapped and deaf-mute persons; and
* *Danviksport*, a social co-operative for the mentally handicapped that strives to spread IT-literacy among the mentally handicapped.

Specialization can be explained by a favourable combination of normative commitments and financing possibilities. Typically, *Basta* and SLC primarily take in people who apply of their own volition, an ambition that is somewhat less realistic in the case of the mentally handicapped. The line of business pursued by the *Sign-Language Centre* necessitates continued recruitment of persons from the same group. Most of the WISEs show, however, some tendency to diversify over time. Both demographic change (the disappearance of, or emergence of, alternative solutions for the original target group) and economic considerations (opting for groups whose rehabilitation is paid for) may play a role in this diversification process.

3 The paths of rehabilitation

3.1 Entry

> *Somebody has to be willing to pay for [the person's rehabilitation] for one year. [The person] should say what they are willing to contribute to Basta in order to come in. We have to believe that they really have the will.*

The quote describes screening procedures in *Basta*, a collective that is strongly dependent on both participant commitment and on external (municipal) financing, and neatly sums up the key elements whose interplay shapes the recruitment process: will, trust and economics, and the three key actors – the enterprise, the authorities, and the participants themselves. Depending on the enterprise's character, the strategy it pursues and its situation, participants would either apply of their own volition, be recruited by the WISE, or be directed by the authorities. As will be discussed in more detail below, joining the WISE may take different forms, some temporary and some permanent. Generally, authorities have considerable influence over temporary placements, while the enterprises have the last say on long-term or permanent placements. Labelling, i.e. assigning would-be participants to different categories of disadvantage (health, unemployment or social disadvantage), is a central element in the admission process. Authorities' budgetary preferences change quite often, and labelling is largely a matter of finding a category that is both broadly appropriate and opens access to financing at a given moment.

Voluntary joining is noted as an important recruitment mode in nearly half of the enterprises. WISEs may also promote recruitment by spreading information about themselves through available networks; such recruitment cannot be clearly separated from voluntary joining. In most cases, those applying of their own volition would be admitted only if financing (primarily of training and supervision) could be secured. Some worker co-operatives (in which work and membership are largely decoupled from formal employment), however, do not take external financing into consideration when admitting new members (a step made possible by the fact that the participant's living expenses are taken care of by the welfare system), while more business-minded co-operatives may approach the authorities to 'refer' to them a person who has already been recruited.

Most prospective participants are directed to the WISE by authorities. The prime sources of referrals are the labour market authorities,[5] which is hardly surprising, considering the dedicated funding for rehabilitation purposes at their disposal. Interestingly enough, municipal social services and the health insurance funds (*försäkringskassan*) – which lack budgetary resources for labour market activity under the Swedish welfare's rule system – were also ranked by the WISEs as important sources (second and third respectively) of referrals. Obviously, these actors perceive needs and are, at times, able to divert funding for the purpose. Other channels mentioned (twice each) were the prison service, schools and special schools. In keeping with the Swedish traditional division of roles, third sector involvement is quite low.

A referral would commonly be backed up by a financing solution that is negotiated between the parties concerned. Generally, such solutions would take the form of assigning the individual in question to a category for which funding is available at a given moment. There is some anecdotal evidence of authorities (names withheld) bending the rules for the purpose. Since the existing rules and available channels were not designed with cross-sector collaboration in mind, specific labels that would be affixed to different persons, job positions or financing forms reflect an authority's financing prerogatives, rather than a person's position in the WISE organization or his/her long-term rehabilitation prospects. Thus, a succession of short-term placements of one and the same individual may indicate that long-term funding was not available, a 'medically-worded' diagnosis would indicate financing by health authorities, etc. In certain cases, authorities may sign a blanket contract for a set number of places (for rehabilitation, assessment or temporary placement) from a WISE, to be filled as they find fit.

The formal and informal procedures that surround the process of joining a WISE are summarized in Table 13.1.

In this set-up, placement becomes somewhat of a log-rolling compromise between two partners that often have different conceptions of each other's mission, and the negotiation aspect is central to the entire process. The manager of *Medvind*, a successful community enterprise, states: 'The advantage is that we are free: we are not recipients of grants, we supply and sell services'. The relation is perceived as a partnership between equals.

Table 13.1 Joining a WISE: formal and informal procedures

	The WISE	*The authorities*
Formal rules and organs	Voting in members by the board, or by the general assembly. Decision by management on permanent (or temporary) employment.	Direct referral for temporary placements. 'Renting' of rehabilitation or day-care places. Labelling/assessing individuals' eligibility for subventions/financing. Time-limited rehabilitation contracts.
Informal criteria and processes	Social compatibility, assessment of future prospects and/or available alternatives. Members 'taking in friends'. Tutors' (often informal) judgement and influence.	Negotiations, assessing degree of trust in the WISE's capabilities. Joint discussion to find the right label and to tap available financing sources.

There is a substantial amount of continuous, ongoing negotiations: about the municipal financing level and financing forms, the employment status of participants and their grant eligibility – but also about issues that may lie outside the business relation itself – such as participants' housing situation and other elements of the social services they receive. While the perception of freedom and of championing their own agenda is fairly strong in all WISEs, the balance of power between the WISE and the authorities is often less favourable for the WISE.

3.2 Forms of participation

Once admitted into the enterprise, the participant's status may assume a variety of forms. The position may be permanent or temporary. It may – but need not – involve membership in the co-operative or voluntary association that runs the WISE, and it often *does not* entail an ordinary employment contract. Generally, it is possible to distinguish between core participants and transitory ones. This distinction and the range of combinations of work, employment and membership it may cover are most manifest in the case of worker co-operatives. Generally, a co-operative would have an organizational core of participant-members who regularly work in the co-operative, whose member status is made contingent on regular work participation and not on formal employment status. Members are normally voted in after a trial period.[6] Depending on economic considerations, some – but not all – of these members may obtain a formal employment status. Many do not, though. A striking example is provided by the person who held the position of finance controller in *IC Samproduktion*, from his release from a 25-year stay in a closed psychiatric ward, in the late 1980s, until his retirement in 2003: this person was on a disability pension throughout the period. Formally speaking, his entire working life was a voluntary contribution. This unconventional strategy probably was economically advantageous for the enterprise, and perhaps to himself as well.

The 'core staff' of tutors, foremen and administrators may consist of formally employed, externally recruited professionals (this is largely the case in community enterprises) or be elected by the participant member group from among themselves. Staff in the latter category need not necessarily be formally employed.

Besides members and aspirants for membership, a variety of other, more transient categories could be present in a WISE, such as trainees or people on observation placements, directed by social or health authorities, whose time-limited stay in the co-operative is underwritten (by wage subsidy, or as a purchased service, or within a project) by the authority in question, with the specific aim of rehabilitation and social integration in mind. Other excluded people may use the premises as a day centre. Such day-care places may be provided as a business activity – as in the case of *Danviksport*, which besides its regular business operations also provides (on contract) day-care places for twice as many persons who are gravely mentally handicapped. In some cases, day-care places may be offered out of an ambition to maintain a meeting place for friends and acquaintances of the participants. The WISE's commitment towards such day-guests is limited beforehand (in time, content or both), and does not include participation in the WISE's governance.

Generally, the recruitment, selection and retention of participants are the product of a complex negotiating process, in which administrative labelling, the nature of the individual's organizational affiliation to the WISE, the extent and form of financing available, the individual's aspirations and the WISE's perception of its task are defined, redefined, and balanced with each other. Nearly all WISEs accommodate a varying mix of persons from the groups outlined above, though the proportions of core and 'periphery' may vary. Participants' member role in community enterprises and other hybrid co-operative and association forms, whose organizational core is often dominated by employed staff, is less pronounced than in worker co-operatives.

3.3 Business activity, rehabilitation and integration

While all WISEs engage in a business activity that generates workplaces for the participants, the relationship between the business activity of the WISE and the personal characteristics (the nature of the disadvantage) of the participants is not a clear-cut one. Some examples, such as a personal computer reconditioning workshop largely run by mentally handicapped workers or a family recreation outfit run and managed by former drug-addicts[7] provide extreme illustrations of the gap between the line of activity that would intuitively be expected and the one actually chosen. The *Sign-Language Centre*, established by people with hearing impairments, is the only case in the sample in which the business idea is clearly linked to the participants' handicap. Inasmuch as the centre's activity uses individuals' resources (sign-language skills) rather than their limitations, the choice has also commercial merit.

Some of the enterprises demonstrate an ambition to diversify activities whenever feasible so as to fit new entrants' abilities and needs,[8] while others strive to prove a symbolic point with their choice or to satisfy social aspirations. Worker co-operatives tend to establish themselves in niches that involve contacts with, or services to, households and individuals in the community. Examples include horse-riding lessons and rental, graffiti removal, running a workplace canteen or a cafeteria in an industrial park, etc. Community enterprises, on the other hand, mainly concentrate on business-to-business activities (Stryjan forthcoming). Besides their core business activity, enterprises of both types often sell training places and rehabilitation services. Community enterprises appear to encounter fewer problems in managing such purchaser-provider relationships with municipalities and social authorities.

A recurring theme in the interview material is the quest for a right balance between production and integration, with advocacy placed as a distant third. The aggregate ranking presented in Table 13.2 was obtained in response to a request to rank the enterprise's goals.

While integration (not necessarily in the mainstream labour market) is perceived as the enterprises' central goal, daily routine is dominated by the actual production of goods and services to a much higher extent than this ranking would suggest. Only six of the 15 WISE managers interviewed find that production is subordinated to integration; three consider that production dominates over work integration. Since presence on the market and business-mindedness distinguish WISEs from therapeutic activity and are essential for bestowing dignity and meaning on the participants' activity, the respondents do not perceive this seeming contradiction between the rankings as problematic.

Individual rehabilitation is only one of the possible trajectories that may be chosen by a WISE. This is most evident in the case of the worker co-operative WISEs and their members. The range of conceivable strategies in this special case would include:

- Individual rehabilitation/integration, with the co-operative as a 'halfway house' from which an individual advances to employment on the ordinary labour market. This strategy would mean, in effect, that the best workers leave first – a problematic retention strategy from a strict business perspective.
- Collective rehabilitation, with the enterprise as a common vehicle: the ambition is that the entire co-operative (which often starts from a marginal position) would graduate to the status of an ordinary enterprise, i.e. generate sufficient revenue to offer its own members an ordinary employment contract. The personnel strategies adopted in this case would aim at retaining the best workers.
- A combined strategy, in which the co-operative, in parallel with other business activities, sells rehabilitation places as a part of its business

Table 13.2 The enterprises' goals

| Goal | Ranking | | | | |
	I	*II*	*III*	*IV*	*No rank*
Integration	**13**	1	1	–	–
Production	–	**12**	3	–	–
Advocacy	–	1	**9**	3	2
Other (rehabilitation and personal development, respectively)	2	–	–	–	–

concept. Thus, high (personnel) turnover is reconciled with retention of a core group for whom jobs are created within the co-operative, enhancing economic performance, and maintaining recruitment channels. Addition of new members may go hand in hand with the creation of new branches. In this mode, integration is closely linked with job creation.

There is evidence on record that all three strategies are being pursued, in varying mixes, by enterprises in the population studied. In at least one case in the sample, the launching of a private enterprise by one of the participants was actively supported.

3.4 Outcomes

Most WISEs in the sample were started in order to create a more supportive environment for (and at times to have such an environment created by) their prospective participants. Work (in the broad sense of the term) is but one – albeit crucial – element of this concept. Five of the enterprises were planned, from the outset, to provide a permanent workplace (or a live-in community) for a group of participants. The enterprises in the sample explicitly devote themselves to the development, empowerment and integration of excluded and/or disadvantaged groups. Other goals (including labour market integration) are generally perceived as subservient to this end.

Beyond this general orientation, the WISEs in the sample do not have a uniform policy as to the desired individual outcomes of the rehabilitation process, owing in no small measure to the substantial differences among the sub-populations that they cater to. Roughly, it is possible to speak of two alternative career paths: the internal path and the external one. These are balanced in varying fashions by the different enterprises. The prime internal advancement path is from the periphery towards the core, i.e. from temporary placement to membership and/or regular employment in the enterprise. As already noted, worker co-operatives would tend to emphasize the work and membership dimensions rather than formal employment contracts. Some of the participants (in all types of WISEs) may advance to a tutor/supervisor position that is often linked to a permanent employment contract.

A large portion of the participants 'graduated' from the ALMP institutions and their extensive schooling programmes. Formal teaching, therefore, plays a secondary role in the WISEs' rehabilitation programme. Only 33 per cent of the participants in the sample are said to have received any formal teaching during their stay (divided evenly between instruction within the organization, and by other agencies). Formal schooling, wherever it is introduced, may be due to external specifications imposed by the financing authority, rather than being an element in the WISE's rehabilitation policy proper. The chief emphasis of WISEs' work is, instead, on social skills, managing routines, reliability and self-discipline, and, inasmuch as work involves contacts with members of the community, on providing the participants with social resources. PERSE data for Sweden also indicate that improvement in social and group proficiencies is generally stronger than that on directly work-related skills.

Social co-operatives, which put a premium on a stable work environment for the participants, tend to avoid a too rapid expansion of their core group, and often pursue a conservative business policy. Other WISEs, which aspire to provide permanent employment to core participants, often pursue a conscious policy of expansion, creating new jobs, and branching out into new fields of operation. This is more often the case in WISEs that are located in sparsely populated areas, with a weak labour market. *Basta* follows a highly structured and explicit way of balancing the two approaches: participants are taken in for a stay of one year's duration, which is financed by a rehabilitation contract signed with their (respective) municipality. On the completion of the contract period, the participants may either apply to the co-operative to be admitted as aspirants (and eventually become members, if admitted), or leave the co-operative. Those who wish to stay are encouraged to develop their own business ideas or to contribute to existing ones, so as to earn their own keep.

The survey returns also show a clear improvement in earnings, though such data should be treated with some caution. A comprehensive evaluation of the institutional context of rehabilitation (FRISAM 2000)[9] concluded that direct net *economic* benefits of successful rehabilitation/integration to an individual are marginal, at times outright negative, owing to the rules that govern transfer systems, and to employment-related private expenses (that may not have been taken into account by the respondents). Individuals' prime gain is enhanced life-quality rather than income improvement. From the evidence that is available, demand for rehabilitation and the motivation to complete it successfully are not clearly correlated with an expectancy of economic gain.

Conclusion

Generally, Swedish WISEs have a tendency to focus on personal development and rehabilitation, and on qualitative – rather than instrumental – improvements. The interest in following those who depart after a fixed-term contract stay is low. Metaphorically, the attitude is somewhat reminiscent of a family-run bed and breakfast that attends to its guests while expanding the family and keeping it afloat, both economically and socially. This seemingly self-centred attitude ought to be understood in its broader institutional context: the 'active labour market' paradigm that forms the backdrop of our case should be perceived as a piece of social engineering par excellence, bent on the 'upgrading' of its subjects to a level of performance at which they could be picked up and allocated by market mechanisms and, implicitly, on the weeding out of those whose upgrading is not judged feasible. The present group of excluded is, thus, being generated and reproduced by the selfsame institutions that generate and reproduce the mainstream labour force. WISEs emerge in a highly institutionalized field of manpower flows, between programmes and public agencies, whose prerogatives are safeguarded by legislation or by tradition. A limited portion of these flows is diverted (or finds its own way) to WISEs, and most participants return, after the completion of their stay, to the fold of the mainstream system. Those who stay do so because the organization can handle their problems and needs better than mainstream institutional solutions would. Whether the solution devised entails a formal employment relation or not would depend on the individual and on the enterprise's economic considerations and possibilities.

Though subject to the rules and institutions of ALMP, the WISE population cannot be considered a genuine component of the system. Certainly, none of the enterprises would consider itself a mere policy tool (called into being by, and expected to serve, social authorities) or would be willing to adhere to their definitions of integration or career. The point can be proven by a simple mental exercise: as an extension of the existing labour market institutions, a WISE would have been expected to 'process' the marginalized, so as to supply the employment agency with easily allocable labour. This task is neither realistic for part of the target population, nor would be considered desirable by any of those involved. Instead, the WISEs studied chose to concentrate on those aspects of integration that are not, and by their nature cannot be, provided by public authorities and formal programmes – namely, helping to create social networks, improving individuals' skills for handling them and, to some extent, underwriting them with the enterprise's own social capital. In this they move gradually towards employment mediation/allocation proper (a field that was, until recently, barred by law to non-public agencies). Unlike a public employment agency, however, labour offers to prospective employers are mediated by WISEs' business networks, based on their own personal and local knowledge and backed by their own reputation.

This development is championed by the younger enterprises in the sample, and reflects the gradual evolution of the institutional field and of the population of WISEs. The first WISEs arose as a response to gaps in an otherwise comprehensive labour market policy system. They addressed a population that was exempted from labour market policy measures, and provided a service (the possibility of engaging in meaningful work) that did not contest labour market organs' allocation monopoly over regular employment. Later cohorts were established by better-endowed actors, and emerged within a system whose erosion has progressed further. Consequently, they tend to adopt a considerably more proactive attitude and engage to a growing extent in labour market measures proper, as partners and initiators of joint projects (Stryjan 2003b), as subcontractors – and at times even as outright competitors to the public policy organs (e.g. to *Samhall*) that, besides subcontracting for schooling and practice places as mentioned earlier in this chapter, increasingly tend to outsource core tasks.[10] For the time being, the question of whether this involvement revitalizes the mainstream system or hastens its demise remains open. Whatever the case, WISEs' contribution to the well-being of their participants is certain.

Review questions

- Which failures of the active labour market policies system does the development of Swedish WISEs reveal?
- How do public policies and public bodies take into account the diversity of profiles of participants joining WISEs?
- How could one differentiate between the objectives, the dynamics and the type of participants in Sweden's social co-operatives, on the one hand, and those in its community enterprises, on the other?

Notes

1 See the Labour Movement's post-war programme (*Arbetarrörelsens efterkrigsprogram*) of 1945.
2 *Samhall*'s contracted employment volumes in millions of work-hours per year declined from 33.6 in 1992 to 27.5 in 2003 (*Dagens Nyheter*'s economic supplement, 18 January 2003).
3 *ICS* and *Gräsdalen* are among the first WISEs created in the country.
4 In a sobering illustration of the authorities' view of such persons' future prospects, the target set for a public project entrusted to a WISE in the sample was that one in 10 participants should obtain a job within the year, and 2 in 10 should start studies or vocational training.
5 Labour authorities were rated as the most important channel in seven cases, and as the second in importance in three cases; social services were ranked most important in five cases, and as second in importance in three cases.
6 In some co-operatives, membership is not mandatory, and some regular workers decline to apply, staying on as non-member workers. The status of non-member supporters, or supporting members, may be awarded to persons who come to work on a less regular basis than members.
7 This case, described in the ELEXIES study (Stryjan and Laurelii 2002), was not included in the PERSE project's sample.
8 The most unconventional example is the decision by *EcoTeck*, which otherwise specializes in forestry and scrap metal, to start a painting studio for an amateur painter – an initiative that was a commercial success.
9 The evaluation instrument, *Sampop*, was developed by the *Samhall* corporation. It includes and balances the gains and expenditures for individuals, local government and social care organs. Two of the cases surveyed by the team were included in the PERSE study. See also Statskontoret (1997).
10 Thus, Nordanstig administers the employment of some of the sheltered workshop employees, outsourced by *Samhall* to a neighbouring municipality.

Bibliography

Axelsson, C. (2002) *Arbetslinjen i storstadsarbetet. En studie av insatser i Stockholm, Södertälje och Huddinge*, Research report 3/02, Södertörns högskola.

Erixon, L. (1996) *The Golden Age of the Swedish Model. The Coherence between Capital Accumulation and Economic Policy in Sweden in the Early Post-war Period*, Stockholm: Department of Economics, University of Stockholm.

Esping-Andersen, G. (1994) 'Jämlikhet, effektivitet och makt', in Thulberg, P. and Östberg, K. (eds) *Den svenska modellen*, Lund: Student litteraturen, 75–106.

FRISAM (Samverkan inom rehabiliteringsområdet) Interdepartmental team (2000), *Samhälsekonomiska effekter vid rehabilitering*, Report 2000: 11.

Hansson, J.-H. and Wijkström, F. (1997) '"Basta!" Beskrivning och analys av Basta arbetskooperativ', *Sköndalsinstitutets arbetsrapportserie*, Report 3, Stockholm: Sköndalsinstitutet.

Hansson, J.-H. and Wijkström, F. (2001) 'Civilt samhälle, social ekonomi eller non-profit? Fallet Basta arbetskooperativ', *Sköndalsinstitutets skriftserie*, Report 19, Stockholm: Sköndalsinstitutet.

Hedborg, A. and Meidner, R. (1984) *Folkhemsmodellen*, Stockholm: Rabén and Sjögren.

Laurelii, E. (2002) *Sociala arbetskooperativ*, report commissioned by Socialstyrelsen, Vinnova, NUTEK and Arbetslivsinstitutet.

Meidner, R. (1997) 'The Swedish Model in an Era of High Unemployment', *Economic and Industrial Democracy*, 18: 87–97.

Statskontoret (1997) *Perspektiv på rehabilitering*, report 1997: 2.

Stryjan, Y. (2001) 'Sweden', in Borzaga, C. and Defourny, J. (eds) *The Emergence of Social Enterprise*, London and New York: Routledge, 220–36.

Stryjan, Y. (2003a) 'Social Cooperatives in Sweden. Etudes in Entrepreneurship', *Meji Business Review*, 50, 1: 209–24.

Stryjan, Y. (2003b) 'Social Democracy, the Labour Market and the Third Sector: the Swedish Case', in Yamaguchi, J., Miyamoto, T. and Tubogo, M. (eds) *Posuto fukushi kokka to soshiaru gabanansu*, Tokyo: Minerva Publishing, 303–23.

Stryjan, Y. (forthcoming 2006) 'The Practice of Social Entrepreneurship: Notes Towards a Resource-Perspective', in Steyeart, C. and Hjorth, D. (eds) *Entrepreneurship as Social Change*, Cheltenham: Edward Elgar.

Stryjan, Y. and Laurelii, E. (2002) 'National Profiles of Work Integration Social Enterprises: Sweden', *Working Papers Series*, 02/08, Liège: EMES European Research Network.

Stryjan, Y. and Wijkström, F. (1996) 'Co-operatives and Non-profit Organisations in Swedish Social Welfare', *Annals of Public and Co-operative Economics*, 67, 1: 5–27.

Swedberg, L. (1995) *Marginalitet*, Lund: Studentlitteratur.

von Otter, C. (1980) 'Swedish Welfare Capitalism: the Role of the State', in Scase, R. (ed.) *The State in Western Europe*, London: Croom Helm, 142–63.

14 Profiles of workers and net effect of Belgian work integration social enterprises

Marthe Nyssens and Alexis Platteau

Overview

This contribution highlights the variety of profiles of the workers hired by Belgian WISEs, who thus have different relations to the labour market. By cross-analysing the data collected during the PERSE project with those from the Walloon regional placement office, a matching procedure could be designed that allows the net effect of WISEs to be worked out. After reading this chapter, the reader should:

- know what would have become of the beneficiaries of WISEs, had the WISEs not existed;
- be aware that Belgian WISEs have extremely heterogeneous clienteles;
- identify the different goals of Belgian WISEs.

Introduction

Work integration social enterprises (WISEs) contribute to (re)integrating individuals who have been excluded from the labour market for a long period of time. These enterprises are unique in that they are specifically intended for individuals whose labour market record is relatively unstable or who experience so-called 'unemployability' (i.e. difficulty in obtaining employment, owing to the deterioration of their skills following their extended absence from the labour market) but who also have a number of skill-related and social problems. Consequently, several objectives must be pursued simultaneously for this kind of person: helping them find a job, but also developing social capital, human capital and other abilities.

Given the numerous legislative differences among Belgian regions in the area of employment policy, we decided to focus our study on only one of Belgium's three regions, namely, the Walloon Region. We first describe the institutional setting in which WISEs in the Walloon Region operate.

Next, we examine the socio-economic profiles of the workers who constituted the focus of our study, noting their diversity. We then analyse the labour market trajectories of these individuals, comparing them to the trajectories followed by their peers in a control group, not employed by WISEs. Last, we examine the contribution made by WISEs in terms of developing the human and social capital of their beneficiaries.

1 Public policy and integration social enterprises

The first social enterprises in Belgium were launched by civil society groups in the 1970s and 1980s[1]; they questioned conventional social policies, which they considered too limited. These groups took root in various fields of social work, dealing with individuals whom society had marginalized. At the time of their emergence, these groups, as already stated, challenged public policies, and they remained relatively independent of the state. However, they also helped revitalize social policies in the fight against exclusion. This resulted in the emergence of a second generation of projects, based on co-operation and open to collaboration with other actors, especially governments.

Indeed, when these projects began to grow, during the first half of the 1980s, governments decided to recognize them and provide them with specific public schemes (see Box on p. 224). Legal recognition, in turn, led to a further increase in the number of projects (for an estimate of the number of accredited work integration social enterprises and of people employed in them in 2004, see Table 14.1). Other WISEs, mostly associations, became active though without applying for public accreditation. In addition, 'self-accreditation' (i.e. independent classification) and enterprise net-working practices developed alongside legal institutionalization. For some enterprises, 'self-accreditation' is the most important form of identification; for others, it is secondary, since they consider their legal framework more important.

Table 14.1 Estimate of the number of accredited WISEs and of people employed in them in 2004

	EI IB	ETA BW	EFT AFT	SW
Number of social enterprises	143	142	81	109
Total number of employees in the target group	±1,000 full-time equivalent	±21,000	±2,800 (trainees)	2,113 full-time equivalent

Source: regional administrations and federations of social enterprises.

Accreditation of work integration social enterprises in Belgium

Aside from the *entreprises de travail adapté* (ETAs, accredited sheltered workshops in the Walloon Region and in the Region of Brussels-Capital) and the *beschutte werkplaatsen* (BWs, sheltered workshops in the Flemish Region), which were designed for on-the-job integration of individuals with disabilities, the field of work integration in Belgium also includes *entreprises de formation par le travail* (EFTs, accredited on-the-job training enterprises in the Walloon Region, which are named *ateliers de formation par le travail* – AFTs, accredited on-the-job training workshops – in Brussels). The distinguishing feature of these enterprises is their objective, i.e. to train a target population by providing them with a productive activity over a limited period of time. By contrast, the goal of the *entreprises d'insertion* (EIs, accredited integration enterprises in the Walloon Region and in Brussels) and *invoegbedrijven* (IBs, integration enterprises in the Flemish Region) is to create temporary or long-term employment for their target population through a productive activity. The subsidies for these jobs decrease gradually over four years. Finally, the *sociale werkplaatsen* (SWs, social workshops in the Flemish Region) aim to create long-term employment in a sheltered work environment for very unstable jobseekers with serious socio-professional disabilities.

Since WISEs have embarked on a long process of institutionalization, the question of their legal recognition should be studied within the context of evolving public policy. Since the end of the 1990s, the concept of the 'active social state' has been central in the field of labour policies. In this concept, the state is supposed not only to guarantee a sufficient level of income, but also to develop a policy mix that will encourage individuals to become more active, and especially to (re)enter the labour force. For their part, social beneficiaries must take advantage of the opportunities they are given. There are several risks linked to this type of policy: on the one hand, there is a risk of making marginalized individuals face the difficulties of job insecurity and work integration alone while, on the other hand, the responsibility of other socio-economic actors might be obscured. Another potential risk is that of sliding into a logic based exclusively on the social control and monitoring of marginalized groups, who are likely to become permanently dependent on integration services, notwithstanding the fact that the integration mechanisms are designed to be more or less temporary for those who use them (Liénard 2001). Since WISEs work within the framework of the active social state, they represent an instrument for implementing active employment policies. Consequently, their institutionalization has allowed public authorities to recognize their role in the labour force integration of persons who are at risk on the labour market. In the process, these enterprises have gained greater public visibility, legal recognition and, above all, more secure access to the public resources needed to pursue their objectives.

Working within the framework of the PERSE research, we focused our analysis on WISEs in the Walloon Region whose objective was to create jobs for workers who were at risk of exclusion from the labour market. The research sample consisted of ten enterprises to which the Walloon authorities had granted accreditation as 'integration enterprises' (see Box on p. 224) and five other social enterprises (four non-profit organizations and a co-operative), that had not applied for accreditation but were, in fact, WISEs in that their objective was to create employment for an unstable target population. We constituted a total sample of 103 workers using the methodology proposed by Loss and Borzaga (see Chapter 11 in this book). In 85 of the 103 cases, we were also able to interview the workers themselves.

In the Walloon Region, legal recognition of 'integration enterprises' (*entreprises d'insertion*, or EIs) dates back to 16 July 1998 (the legal framework was revised in 2004). The mission of EIs has been identified as job creation for 'particularly hard-to-place jobseekers' (defined as individuals who do not hold a certificate of upper secondary education and who are unemployed). Recognition by the regional government gives these enterprises access to public funding for an initial period and according to the number of disadvantaged workers hired. One of the things the 2004 revised version of the decree on EIs provides for is the subsidising of a social support worker to assist individuals in the integration process. Less productive workers are supposed to complete the training within four years; after this period, the workers can leave the enterprise or they can continue working in it, but they no longer receive subsidies. EIs must adopt the legal form of 'social purpose company' (*société à finalité sociale*, or SFS).[2] EIs must comply with all standards in effect in their respective sectors, including those dealing with wages.

Obviously, the enterprises that do not receive accreditation as EIs are not eligible for subsidies specifically intended for recipients of this accreditation, but they can apply for subsidies originating with other public policies, especially those linked to the 'second market programme' (see Chapter 17 in this book). These are longer-term subsidies that fund jobs in projects considered to have significant social value. These programmes for fighting unemployment are somehow 'halfway' between traditional social policies and employment policies, since the idea behind them is to finance, with public funds, the creation of jobs for the unemployed in areas of 'collective interest' ignored by both the market and traditional forms of public intervention.

2 Workers in integration programmes: taking into account the differentiated effects of inequalities and tackling them

A single standard profile of workers in the WISEs surveyed did not emerge. WISEs in the Walloon Region, be they accredited or not, have extremely heterogeneous clienteles. However, statistical classification analysis[3] allows us to define five main groups.

Category 1: Long-term unemployed workers with many years of experience (34 workers, of whom 23 were in accredited EIs) The average individual in this category, whether Belgian or European, is 38 years old, lives with his/her partner and has many years of work experience, which has facilitated the acquisition of significant work skills. In spite of these skills, this individual has lost his/her job and found it difficult to find another one. A possible hypothesis is that employers view his/her low level of formal training (often a lower secondary school diploma) unfavourably. Consequently, this person is relegated to the ranks of the 'chronically unemployed', a label that further handicaps his/her chances on the labour market. His/her prime motivation for entering a WISE is to maintain his/her social contacts (with his/her career behind him, his/her objective might not be of a purely 'professional' nature), especially since he/she tends to have social problems (drug dependence, domestic problems, homelessness, alcoholism, etc.).

Category 2: Qualified and experienced recipients of minimum social assistance benefit (17 workers, of whom 13 were in accredited EIs) This is the category with the greatest number of women. On average, the worker in this group is 43 years old, and is generally single and living alone. She has at least two years of work experience and a high-level diploma (a certificate of upper secondary education or even a higher education diploma). It is not surprising, therefore, that she belongs to the group of workers who, in the view of WISE managers, has the most stable profile (easily employable, very capable). However, something happened that made her lose her claims to unemployment benefits. Thus, the social assistance office referred her to the WISE so that she could, at least, regain her right to unemployment benefits thanks to a minimum period of work. Consequently, she views her own transfer to the WISE as temporary, since her ultimate objective is to find work in an ordinary establishment.

Category 3: Young, hard-to-employ trainees or students (21 workers, of whom 14 were in accredited EIs) The typical worker in this category is young (25 years old), Belgian, male, still lives with his parents and has had major learning difficulties (he generally has no more than an elementary school leaving certificate). Two paths of entry into the WISE are possible: he either followed a training programme in an on-the-job training enterprise (EFT) before entering the WISE or entered the enterprise directly after finishing his studies. According to the managers of these enterprises, he belongs to the category of workers with the least stable subjective profile (difficult to employ and unskilled) and lacks work experience (no more than six months). However, he has a desire to prove that he is worth more than his limited educational achievements would suggest and to increase his income.

Category 4: Foreign diploma holders without work experience (26 workers, of whom 14 were in accredited EIs) The average individual in this category is a single foreigner, fairly young (30 years old) and inexperienced. After obtaining a relatively advanced diploma (at least lower secondary school), he/she left his/her country. However, since his/her diploma is generally not recognized in Belgium, he/she had difficulty in finding a job. In addition, the fact that he/she is an immigrant (sometimes even a refugee) does not help his/her cause, especially since enterprise managers consider his/her skills inadequate. It therefore takes him/her at least a year to find a job, in spite of his/her desire to work (he/she arrives in the WISE after making an unsolicited application and expresses a desire to be useful to society).

Category 5: Working males (five workers, all in accredited EIs) The typical worker in this category is a male who has inadequate skills (holding only a primary or lower secondary school diploma) and finds work in a sheltered workshop (ETA). This enterprise allows him to acquire significant work experience that, over time, proves sufficient for working in another type of establishment, but not in a 'classic' enterprise. This is what leads him to the WISE.

WISEs in the Walloon Region, whether accredited or not, serve a very heterogeneous population. However, the decree on EIs provides for a form of integration based on the 'trampoline approach', providing workers with sufficient experience over a four-year period to facilitate their future entry into the ordinary labour market, or their stay in the WISE without subsidies; accredited enterprises (EIs) should thus hire workers with a similar profile – namely, workers close to entering the labour market. However, the experience of EIs reveals that the populations actually hired do not always have this profile and that the labour market requirements of the individuals using their services vary enormously. Indeed, the problem of these workers is not simply low 'employability'; they may have a variety of problems, such as a lack of skills, mental disabilities or social problems, all of which can have long-lasting effects on their productivity. The temporary nature of the subsidies can, therefore, lead to a phenomenon of skimming, i.e. there are incentives for the enterprises to hire only the workers most likely to be 'cost-effective' by the end of the project and/or to retain only those who have attained this level of 'cost-effectiveness' when the subsidized period ends.

The non-accredited WISEs seem to hire individuals whose profile is somewhat more stable. This can be explained by the fact that these organizations combine the goal of on-the-job integration with that of creating social services. A strained relationship between these two goals (i.e. integration and production) may occasionally surface, and in order to ensure the quality of the service provided, an enterprise may be more selective in its hiring criteria.

3 Worker trajectories

Sixty-seven workers were still working in the WISEs surveyed at the time of the survey, but this figure is obviously influenced by the fact that the subsidized period had not yet ended, at least for accredited EIs. It is difficult to determine if working in this type of enterprise for a long time is a positive or negative sign. The goal of numerous enterprises is to keep their workers as long as possible; this occurs mainly when the latter succeed in adapting to the enterprise. Other enterprises favour a turnover of workers and their reintegration into the mainstream labour market as soon as they are ready. The situation of the 36 workers who had already left the WISE by the time of the survey is, of course, much easier to analyse. Either they found work, in which case we can consider them 'reintegrated', or they are inactive. We were able to collect data on the trajectories of 34 of these 36 workers. Only ten of them had found another job. It seems that the workers who were the most motivated (walk-in WISE applicants and those who no longer wanted to depend on the social welfare allowance) or who had improved their skills significantly found work more often than did the others. Thus, 76 per cent of the individuals were employed at the time of the survey, whereas 5 per cent were employed before entering the WISE. Surprisingly, we did not observe a significant difference between the different categories of workers (described above) in terms of continuing to work in the WISE or leaving it.

What would have happened to these people if they had not entered a WISE? In order to answer this question, we worked out the net result of WISEs, i.e. we measured the proportion of workers who had a job thanks to the WISE and its integration programme. In practice, the net result is equal to the gross result minus the 'deadweight' effect (the workers who would have found employment in any case). To obtain this net result, we adopted the exact matching method.[4] The Public Employment Service provided us with the database used to constitute the control group (the database with the work trajectories and socio-economic characteristics of all individuals registered as jobseekers in the Walloon Region). The variables we used to carry out the matching were the following: age, sex, diploma obtained, length of work experience, nationality and status before entering the WISE (unemployment, minimum social assistance benefit or without status), including the seniority of this status (more or less than one year). This method allowed us to retain, on average, 15 'individual-matches' per subject in the study. Our approach had certain biases, as is always the case, but it is reasonable to think that these biases are not overly important and that, for the most part, they probably tend to cancel each other out.[5]

Thirty-two per cent of the workers in the control group had found a job at the time of the survey. Therefore, if the gross effect is 79 per cent,[6] the net effect is 47 per cent, which means that among the workers in our sample, nearly one out of two was employed, in the WISE or in another enterprise, at the beginning of 2003, and would not have been so without the WISE. In the light of Belgian or European research assessing the net effect of active labour market policies, this is an impressive result (Martin and Grubb 2001; Calmfors *et al.* 2002). Cockx *et al.* (2004) have evaluated two types of Belgian active labour market policies. The net result, although calculated differently from ours, of the so-called 'Advantage to Employment Plan' programme (*Plan Avantage à l'Embauche*) is 37 per cent for men and 32 per cent for women, whereas the net result of the 'Guaranteed Income Benefit' programme (*Allocation Garantie de Revenu*) for women is 13 per cent.[7] However, as both the method and the timing of an evaluation have a considerable effect on the results obtained, we must use these results cautiously.

We also computed the direct fiscal impact of hiring a disadvantaged worker in an accredited EI. The direct fiscal impact is the difference, as it affects the public sector, between the costs and benefits resulting from two distinct situations: that in which the person is hired by the EI, on the one hand, and that in which this same person would be without the EI (hired by another enterprise or in receipt of social assistance, unemployment benefits, etc.) on the other. The comparison carried out takes into account all the variations linked to fiscal and para-fiscal benefits (direct and indirect taxes, social contributions, etc.) and costs (social benefits, work subsidy, etc.). It appears that supporting the EI does not generate any cost for public bodies, on the contrary: the net benefit for public bodies is between €267.47 and €720.12 per worker and per month (Grégoire and Platteau 2005).

Thus, our data demonstrate that the employment rate achieved in our sample was remarkable (even though, admittedly, the subsidy period had not yet expired for a number of the workers, and this is likely to have influenced this figure upwards). However, some workers who had left the enterprise ended up inactive. As we have already pointed out, while a limited term of employment in a sheltered environment allows some groups of workers to re-enter the classic labour market, it is not enough for other groups. The highly unstable profiles of certain workers have a long-lasting effect on their productivity. This raises serious questions about the temporary nature of the subsidies, and leads to the conclusion that integration subsidies should be differentiated according to the population targeted, allowing some workers to keep their 'sheltered' work. However, Belgium has not yet taken this path: only WISEs that are not part of a specific public scheme (see Box above) are in a position to offer various types of work contracts (some temporary, of varying duration, and others permanent), and they accomplish this by using a wide array of active policies, available to them through sources other than subsidies specifically intended for EIs.

4 Beyond labour market integration

As far as income is concerned, among the workers who had already left the WISE at the time of the survey, 15 people (i.e. 68 per cent of those who were unemployed) were receiving unemployment benefit. By contrast, only 43 per cent of those who were unemployed when they began working at the WISE were eligible for unemployment benefit. If we include employed individuals – inside the WISE[8] or elsewhere – for whom, presumably, income increased, the financial circumstances of the workers surveyed improved considerably.

Although the Walloon Region decree on EIs stresses re-entry into the labour force, the interviews with social entrepreneurs reveal that they value other objectives as well, such as developing the workers' human and social capital (by 'human capital', we mean the workers' skills relating to the labour market, whereas 'social capital' refers to a person's level of integration into a social network). The analysis of the available data reveals that the disadvantaged workers' skills improved significantly[9] during their stay in the WISE. The improvement was greater for those individuals 'with the most unstable subjective profile'. This is not surprising, since these workers start with a lower level of skills and thus have more to learn. The skills of the workers who were still present in the WISE at the time of the study increased the most. This might suggest that only the least productive workers left the enterprise; however, this is hard to believe, since a significant proportion of them left with the prospect of a new job. But several other explanations are possible. On the one hand, the relationship between the worker and the enterprise may have ended unpleasantly. This would probably prompt the director to assess the worker negatively in the ex-post evaluation. On the other hand, it is likely that since the worker was no longer present in the enterprise, the manager might be inclined to underestimate his or her abilities. Regarding social capital, most social entrepreneurs also emphasized the need to increase it. The fact that social problems topped the list of 'weaknesses' experienced by individuals when they started working in the enterprise confirms this need. Social capital also tends to increase,[10] though it does not seem to increase as much as human capital.

The workers displayed a high level of satisfaction with their experience within the WISE.[11] They felt that the development of social contacts in the social enterprise was more important than anything else – even the job, the training and the salary. Although two-thirds of the workers were working when the survey was conducted, only a minority of these workers cited as a positive element of their WISE experience the fact of having a job or being in more comfortable financial circumstances. In the absence of empirical evidence on the matter, we can put forward several possible hypotheses to explain this fact: (i) their uncertainty concerning the future; (ii) their comparatively low salary, despite the fact that the latter was much higher than the social allowances most workers relied on when they started; or (iii) the fact that they were very satisfied with the social integration, which made these other aspects seem less important by comparison.

The workers still working in the WISE at the time of the survey stressed the importance of social contacts, training and self-confidence. The workers unemployed at the time of the survey placed more emphasis on work experience, perhaps because this was precisely what they lacked. Not surprisingly, the jobless workers viewed their experience in the WISE nega-tively; most of them declared that they had experienced problems related to mental health (harassment, mental fatigue), relationship problems or a decline in household income compared to their previous situation. Indeed, the increased revenue following the transition from social beneficiary to wage earner sometimes fails to meet travel costs, children's day care, clothing and so on. In addition, their new status can lead to the worker's partner losing his/her revenue (the unemployment office might consider that his or her status has changed).

Thus, the data show that human capital and (to a lesser extent) social capital both increase significantly during the workers' term in the WISE. This result can be explained by the fact that social enterprises, in serving individuals who find themselves outside the pale of society, do not pursue only pure 'labour integration' goals; they also attempt to pursue several socio-professional integration objectives. There is actually a very high posi-tive correlation between the fact that they are working (either in the WISE or elsewhere), their level of human capital and their level of social capital.

The decree on EIs stresses the objective of re-entry into the labour force. But, as already mentioned, social entrepreneurs also value other objec-tives, regarding the well-being of their beneficiaries, and it is important that the regional authorities take this into account as well. The 2004 revi-sion of the decree on EIs, which deals with subsidies for social support workers assisting individuals in integration services, is undoubtedly a sign of the gradual inclusion of the social integration objective alongside the work integration objective.

Conclusion

We have noted a wide diversity of worker profiles – from very unstable or vulnerable profiles to the profiles of workers almost ready for the non-sheltered labour market. Labour market instability is often associated with a lack of skills; however, it can also relate to social problems and mental health problems. Nonetheless, the Walloon decree on EI only adopts one perspective: that of workers rapidly developing their employability in a non-sheltered work environment.

Sixty-seven of the 103 workers in our sample were still in the WISE two years after they started working there. These workers gave primary importance to the social contacts they established in the social enterprise, considering these contacts even more important than having a job or a salary. Thirty per cent of the workers who had left the social enterprise had found another job by the time the survey was conducted. As regards the workers who had then left the social enterprise, their level of motivation had an impact on their labour market integration. As regards the 'deadweight' effect, it appears that only 32 per cent of the workers in our sample would have been working if they had not had the opportunity to work in a WISE. Therefore, the analysis of the trajectories of the workers in our sample reveals that almost one out of two workers who was working in early 2003 would not have found work, had they not gone through the WISE programme. This is an impressive result in comparison with other active employment policies. It also appears that there is a net fiscal benefit for public bodies supporting EIs. Unsurprisingly, unemployed individuals were the least satisfied with their experience within the WISE.

Nevertheless, getting people back to work is not the sole objective of WISEs; they also try to improve their workers' human capital and social capital. Our data indicate that human capital, and to a lesser extent social capital, increased significantly while workers were in the WISE. The increase in human capital was greater among individuals who had weak skills upon entering the WISE, and the increase had a positive influence on their labour market entry when they left the social enterprise. We actually found that there was a very high positive correlation among the attainment of the three main goals identified: thus the workers with a job (in a WISE or in another enterprise) were those who were most successful in improving both their human capital and social capital.

This analysis of the trajectories of the beneficiaries of the WISEs highlights, therefore, the multiple-goal nature of WISEs regarding their beneficiaries. Moreover, it should be remembered that, as regards the objectives of WISEs, some WISEs provide goods and services of a collective nature (recycling, services for a disadvantaged population, etc.). These social enterprises thus have a twofold social objective: to integrate vulnerable individuals and to develop collective services. This multiple-goal nature brings into question the process of public institutionalization through the Walloon decree on EIs, which, strictly speaking, covers only the labour market integration of the beneficiaries.

Review questions

- Which outcomes could be evaluated either as positive or negative results of Belgian WISEs regarding the integration path of their participants?
- How could one explain the strained relationship between the goal of integration and the goal of production in some Belgian WISEs?
- How can one explain the fact that supporting a Belgian WISE does not generate any cost for public bodies?

Notes

1 Well before this period, several associations had already pioneered the development of social enterprises designed to create employment for unskilled persons.

2 The 'social purpose company' (*société à finalité sociale* or SFS, in French; *vennootschap met en sociaal oogmerk* or VSO, in Dutch) is not, strictly speaking, a new legal form; in fact, article 2 of the 'reparative law' enacted on 13 April 1995 stipulates that as of 1 July 1996, all types of business corporations (be they co-operatives, joint stock companies, limited liability companies, etc.) can adopt the 'social purpose company' label, provided they 'are not dedicated to the enrichment of their members', and their statutes comply with a series of conditions. Thus, SFS statutes must stipulate that 'the members seek little or no return on investment'. The articles must also define a 'profit allocation policy in accordance with the enterprise's internal and external purposes'. In the event of liquidation, it must be stipulated that 'after the discharge of all the liabilities and the repayment of their investment to the members, the liquidation surplus shall be allocated in a manner as close as possible to the entity's social purpose'. If the company abandons its legal status as a social purpose company, 'the existing reserves may not be distributed in any form whatsoever'. These last two prescriptions are intended to protect the enterprise from any attempt to realize substantial capital gains. In addition, the social purpose company also introduces a certain type of democracy into the organization. Thus, its articles must provide for 'procedures allowing each employee to acquire the capacity of member within one year after his/her hiring by the enterprise'.

3 Using the following variables: age, gender, household situation, nationality, level of education, employment experience, former status, level of employability, capabilities and handicap in the job market.

4 The matching method works as follows: using a database made up of individuals not participating in the policy under consideration, we isolate those who most closely match those benefiting from the policy (using the variables at our disposal). Next, we compare the trajectories of the individuals selected in this way with those of the individuals being examined. The observed difference represents the policy effect. However, there are various methods for selecting individual-matches. Exact matching uses all variables, and only those individuals for whom the observation distance is considered nil are selected (thus, the two individuals are alike). In this way, we are certain that the individual-matches will be highly comparable to the individuals being examined. Nevertheless, the number of individual-matches is not the same for each observation, and this must be taken into account (Todd 1999).

5 Possible biases include the following: (1) The use of quarterly data implies that the individuals in the control group who would have found a new job between the date of the entry of the subject observed in the WISE and the end of the quarter in question were not taken into account. However, we feel that the quarterly data are acceptable and that this bias is relatively harmless. (2) It is possible that the individuals selected for the control group themselves began working in the WISE during the period in question. Nonetheless, having taken into account a sufficient number of 'individual-matches', we believe that these cases should probably be merged with the others, especially since the WISEs do not, in general, hire many workers. (3) The Public Administration is not entirely certain of the path taken by many of the individuals, which forces us to make certain assumptions about them. Still, these assumptions seem reasonable and should not overly skew our results. (4) We are faced with a selection bias that we are unable to take into account: clearly, there are other variables, aside from the six taken into consideration (social problems, motivation, etc.), that influence both access to WISEs and individual trajectories.

6 Seventy-nine per cent and not 76 per cent, given that the sample that was suitable for a comparison with administrative data did not include all the workers of the surveyed sample.

7 Nevertheless, it has to be mentioned that the authors are cautious in their interpretation of these results.

8 Regarding the workers who are still active in the WISE, the gross monthly income increased from an average of €586 per month before joining the WISE to €1,357 in early 2003.

9 For the methodology used, see the chapter by Borzaga and Loss (Chapter 11 in this book). In our sample, human capital increased from an average value of 3.09 upon entering the WISE to 4.31 upon leaving (on a scale of 1 to 7).

10 Social capital showed, on average, a slight increase.

11 The average satisfaction level is 5.99 (on a scale of 1 to 7).

Bibliography

Calmfors, L., Forslund, A. and Hemström, M. (2002) *Does Active Labour Market Policy Work? Lessons from the Swedish Experiences*, IFAU Office of Labour Market Policy Evaluation, Working paper 2002–4.

Cockx, B., Göbel, C. and Van der Linden, B. (2004) *Politiques d'activation pour des jeunes chômeurs de longue durée sans expérience de travail. Une évaluation*, Politique Scientifique Fédérale, Gent: Academia Press.

Grégoire, O. and Platteau, A. (2005) 'L'impact budgétaire de l'engagement de demandeurs d'emploi dans les entreprises d'insertion', *Revue belge de la sécurité sociale*, 3.

Liénard, G. (2001) 'L'ambivalence des politiques d'insertion', in Liénard, G. (ed.) *L'insertion: défi pour l'analyse, enjeu pour l'action*, Sprimont: Mardaga, 181–212.

Martin, J.P. and Grubb, D. (2001) *What Works and for Whom: a Review of OECD Countries' Experiences with Active Labour Market Policies*, IFAU Office of Labour Market Policy Evaluation, Working paper 2001–14.

Todd, P. (1999) 'A Practical Guide to Implementing Matching Estimators', *Mimeo*, Santiago, Chile: IADB Meeting, October.

Part IV

Public policies and social enterprise

15 Work integration social enterprises in Europe: can hybridization be sustainable?

Ingo Bode, Adalbert Evers and Andreas Schulz

Overview

The multifaceted nature (multiple stakeholders, multiple goals, multiple resources) of European social enterprises may be experienced as a particular asset, but also as a potential weakness. Given this hybrid character, social enterprises risk facing a precarious existence and hence changing their structures and missions over time. This contribution proposes an analytical framework to grasp the historical dynamics of the organizational field of WISEs. After reading this chapter, the reader should:

- be aware that European WISEs have grown up drawing on a diversity of traditions;
- identify the elements that help social enterprises to preserve their missions within dynamic environments and the elements that impede them from doing so;
- understand why the institutional models that give WISEs a firm place in the landscape of a given society are not exempt from drawbacks.

Introduction

Organizations that aim to bring disadvantaged people (back) into 'ordinary society' through social business have become widespread across Western Europe. Historically, however, they appear as quite a recent societal phenomenon. It was not until the late 1970s that such 'work integration social enterprises' (WISEs) grew in number and variety, drawing on a diversity of traditions such as sheltered workshops, the co-operative movement, models of mutual self-help and social and charitable work carried out by associations. A major factor in the background to this evolution was the rising unemployment in Western Europe, together with a growing segmentation of labour markets and the experience of social exclusion. Key impulses came from citizens with a social work background or with links to charitable associations. These citizens aimed to respond to social exclusion and unmet societal needs through grassroots economic organizations in fields such as the recycling of goods, personal services and cultural work.

WISEs emerged, then, with a strong reliance on civil society, before public policies contributed to the further expansion of this organizational field.[1] As pursuing the goal of social integration through economic activities appeared (and still appears) a somewhat strange activity from the point of view of major political and economic forces, public authorities have often hesitated to provide a more solid backing to these organizations. Concomitantly, WISEs have been colonizing new, unstable markets. And as is shown in other chapters of this book, they depend on a mix of resources including the sale of goods or services, volunteering, public subsidies and civic support. Given their disadvantaged workforce and the sometimes volatile flow of resources, a firm economic base is difficult to achieve, compared to standard public, private and traditional non-profit organizations. Thus, there are good reasons to suggest that, owing to their hybrid character, WISEs are prone to live a precarious life and to modify their structures and objectives over time. Therefore, it is important to explore if, and under which conditions, their particular approach to social integration does endure. The question is: can the hybridization of goals, resources and outputs as practised by WISEs be sustainable?

This chapter deals with this question by comparatively retracing the history of the organizational field in a wide range of Western European countries. It is largely based upon reports written by the national teams of the PERSE research project,[2] out of which this book has grown. These reports (for which precise references are given in the bibliography) have drawn on case study evidence and some hard data, in addition to a review of the existing literature. Before summing up their findings, we will provide some theoretical reflections on the particular evolutionary problematic of WISEs. Thereafter, we will briefly sketch the empirical evidence, by figuring out the paths WISEs have taken in different national settings. Finally, we will draw lessons from our overview concerning the role of contexts, cross-country driving forces of organizational change and those factors that endorse and impede WISEs in preserving their missions within dynamic environments.

1 Some theoretical reflections on the evolutionary problematic of WISEs

Previous research on social enterprises has shown that these organizations operate on shaky foundations (Laville 1996; Spear *et al.* 2001; Borzaga and Defourny 2001), and face risks of decay or subversion, linked to various factors. For-profit enterprises may be inclined to lobby against public regulations conferring fiscal advantages on WISEs engaged in markets in which they are, or intend to become, active themselves. Public authorities purchasing services from these organizations may overlook the particular constraints the latter are exposed to, e.g. the fact that they take care of the social problems of their employees. Moreover, the flow of civic resources into these organizations may vary over time. Finally, WISEs that have successfully entered into niche markets may discover that, from the moment these markets become more stable, private competitors (with fewer social concerns and constraints) are keen to make money in them as well.

Given this precariousness, it makes sense to examine the evolution of what can be referred to as the sustainability of the *institutional design* of these organizations. There is, however, some 'confusion over the distinction between organizations and institutions' (Rowlinson 1997: 87). Most agree that 'organizations can be said to be embedded in institutions' but many contend that 'actors are able to change the routines and rules, that is, the institutions, within which they organize' (ibid: 88–9). Obviously, institutional forms are produced outside and inside organizations. If it comes to the question of WISEs maintaining or abandoning their characteristics over time, an interesting research perspective then is *through which mechanisms* the institutional design of these organizations becomes (trans-)formed.

To provide answers to this question, one might draw on the concept of *institutional isomorphism*. This goes back to Max Weber's theory of modernization (Weber 1968). In Weber's view, the modern world is affected by an overall bureaucratization. Organizations are said to have a tendency to resemble each other in the long run since both the capitalistic economy and state administration favour a certain kind of behaviour based on hierarchical control and on instrumental rationalization. Weber's model has been modified by a seminal article of two scholars defending the so-called neo-institutionalist approach of organizational theory (DiMaggio and Powell 1983). Organizations in a given field are assumed to be shaped by a broad set of institutional influences rather than pure economic rationales: they can be a means to define and follow a collective mission, or a vehicle to give life to particular social norms. Hence, they are not just tools for running human activities efficiently.

It is argued that if populations of organizations become more homogeneous or subject to *isomorphism* over time this is due to the influence of symbols and norms that provide for legitimacy, and not (so much) to the pressure from economic competition.[3] One important mechanism of isomorphism consists of organizations coping with uncertainty by imitating their peers. 'Uncertainty is . . . a powerful force that encourages imitation. When organizational technologies are poorly understood . . ., when goals are ambiguous . . ., organizations may model themselves on other organizations' (DiMaggio and Powell 1983: 151). Uncertainty may also constitute a problem in *defining* efficiency, given the fact that the latter may be considered in shorter or longer terms, with a reference to hard business data or with a broader perspective including external social effects, and by ignoring or by accepting incompatible elements. The aforementioned authors identify three overall mechanisms that are conducive to an assimilation of institutional features of organizations (e.g. similar structures, languages, styles of management, etc.): 'coercive isomorphism' (mainly by legal constraints), 'mimetic processes' (in the case of organizations modelling themselves on other organizations, with the aforementioned background), and 'normative pressures' (exerted mainly by professions). Such evolutions of 'institutional isomorphism' are said to lead to homogeneous organizational forms independently of efficiency records or given structures of social power.

The concept of institutional isomorphism appears useful when investigating WISEs. The hypothesis of these organizations abandoning their original features over time, however, implies that they adopt characteristics from organizations that exhibit *different* societal functions and rely on *distinctive* stakeholder structures, such as those of for-profit firms or public bureaucracies. Yet, in the eyes of DiMaggio and Powell, isomorphism is 'a process that forces one unit *in a population* to resemble other units that face the *same* set of environmental conditions' (DiMaggio and Powell 1983: 149, emphasis added). As WISEs represent an organizational population of their own (subject to particular policy regulations, pursuing particular goals, operating with a specific resource mix, etc.) and do not face the same set of environmental conditions as ordinary statutory or private sector organizations do, the question underlying our analysis refers to *intersectoral isomorphism* rather than to institutional isomorphism such as that understood by DiMaggio and Powell.

An interesting point is professional, normative or coercive pressures *spilling over* from one sector to another. WISEs are facing competitors from other sectors in different sorts of markets: first, they produce goods or services for regular commercial markets (second-hand shops, selling of craftwork, etc.). In this case, they may tend to adapt their routines to those of their private sector competitors, not just because they have to offer competitive prices but also because a certain 'business look' is commonly expected on a given market. Second, WISEs operate in quasi-markets in which governmental bodies devolve the delivery of public services to providers, among which are social enterprises. This may concern the productive business of WISEs or work integration activities themselves, with WISEs being a contract partner of welfare bureaucracies purchasing counselling, placement or training services for the socially disadvantaged. If particular patterns of governance or accountability shape the inter-organizational relations prevailing in such markets, institutional characteristics can spill over from one sector to another. This is typically discussed with respect to New Public Management (see e.g. Clarke *et al.* 2000).

Yet is intersectoral isomorphism inevitable? A huge body of organizational theory makes the case for collective actors changing their goals as a 'response to changing external selection pressures, including not only a deteriorating resource base and shrinking niche but also the declining legitimacy of an organization's current goals' (Aldrich 1999: 180). However, other approaches predict organizational inertia, especially in a situation of insecurity (Hannan and Freeman 1984). To this may be added the fact that the experience with many (young) not-for-profit agencies seems to contradict the isomorphism thesis. Bound to specific constituencies such as social movements or political entrepreneurs, non-profit organizations are supposed to preserve some kind of autonomy and distinctiveness.[4] As WISEs resemble this type of organization, the question rather concerns the conditions under which their distinctiveness persists. At any rate, it appears reasonable to allow for some intermediary patterns of organizational evolution, between continuity and change. Four evolutionary configurations can be distinguished:

- *Organizational stability*: WISEs maintain their hybrid character by linking social, economic and political goals to some extent, through mixing different kinds of resources, and by producing multiple outputs, the latter ranging from work integration through social capital building or socio-political networking to the production of goods or services (in the public interest). Hybridization as practised by these organizations proves sustainable, and this hybridization is what enables them to provide social integration.
- *Institutional flexibility*: WISEs respond to environmental pressures to some degree. This may occur in a logic of *'instrumental isomorphism'* (Osborne 1998: 187) – a symbolic reinterpretation of the organization's mission without really changing its content – or as *pragmatic, inter-organizational imitation*;[5] both patterns are similar to what DiMaggio and Powell refer to as 'mimetic processes'. In this case, hybridization is still at work, albeit less visibly and in danger of becoming destabilized.
- *Organizational metamorphosis*: WISEs operate a programme shift without altering the core of their institutional 'constitution'. This may be reflected in an intra-organizational transfer of energy into action fields that are highly valued by environments, such as concepts of businesslike management proliferating in the non-profit sector as a whole (Dart 2004). The hybrid character of the organization is subject to latent transformation, undermining basic potentials of hybridization in the long run.
- A fourth possibility is *institutional isomorphism*: WISEs run through a radical transformation entailing a new goal set and/or a completely different kind of activity and, in the most extreme cases, a shift in institutional form (such as a social enterprise becoming a for-profit organization). The hybrid character of the organization is lost. For our investigation, this configuration mostly serves as a hermeneutic device since the sample from which the case studies were selected rarely embraced organizations that had adopted an organizational form that was inconsistent with those characteristics that have been found to be

(more or less) typical of WISEs. Rather, there may be the first steps towards institutional isomorphism within existing WISEs, materializing for instance in a given project of 'business re-engineering' or in the creation of a commercial branch splitting off from the original enterprise.

The scheme sketched so far can be used as an analytical fundament upon which to base the study of WISEs' evolution. Moreover, it allows for working out both the mechanisms through which an organization is exposed to isomorphistic pressure and its potential to resist this pressure.

2 The history of European WISEs

In this section, we will briefly sketch the organizational field and its evolution for each of the countries under review.[6] To begin with, we consider those countries in which social enterprises have been given a quasi-institutional status. Depending on the country, this status can take the form of a specific public scheme or even a specific legal form.

This is the case of Belgium, for instance. In this country, social enterprises emerged from the 1970s onwards; they were launched mostly by social workers but also by unions or members of civic groups outside any specific public scheme. Things changed when the state (more precisely, regional authorities) announced a new public scheme that led to an overall institutionalization of the field, as the author of the Belgian country report expounds (Lemaître 2003). With new employment policies aiming to integrate the unemployed into the labour market (through occupational training programmes, job subsidy programmes, etc.), statutory regional authorities made most social enterprises subject to a scheme providing temporary subsidies (over a three-year period) for a job contract. While a range of WISEs remained outside this system, many adopted one of the institutional models that now existed, among which the 'integration enterprise' (*entreprise d'insertion*) is quite an important one. As to the characteristics of WISEs, case studies illustrate the way the organizational field has been restructured over the course of time. First of all, they reveal how WISEs have developed within a complex network based on various social ties to administrative, political and civic actors. A major tendency was the gradual broadening of these ties, as the organizations became established. However, while the basic conditions within which the latter were built still persist (some economic risk, formal organizational autonomy, the production of goods and services), the influence public schemes exert on the organizations' activity has changed in nature. Before the (current) public scheme was launched, WISEs relied on public subsidies that were 'looser', while for the WISEs that have chosen to enter this framework, subsidies are much more strictly linked to rules concerning the organizations' activity. These 'recognized' WISEs have also experienced a move towards professionalization and some decrease of voluntarism.

In France, too, the starting point of WISEs was initiatives anchored in local grassroots movements driven by political motives or alternative concepts of social work. Their core idea was to promote innovative patterns of working and living, together with providing the disadvantaged with new chances of social integration. Again, public policies then provided for an institutional framework to which many of the existing social enterprises subscribed, and again, the movement dynamics faded away to a considerable extent. The current regulation, which distinguishes between a range of institutional forms – the most important being the 'work integration enterprises' (*entreprises d'insertion*) and the 'intermediate voluntary organizations' (*associations intermédiaires*) – has created particular fields of organizations that receive public subsidies for employing long-term unemployed people and are at the same time active in local (service) markets. These enterprises are confronted with growing pressure to remain competitive in their markets, and though the state has generalized its supportive regulations, there is an increasing tendency on their part to adapt through evolving towards models of private business. As the French report (Gardin 2003) expounds, however, some of the WISEs have managed to stick to their original concept by defending their freedom to run activities of social integration outside the existing regulations. In the case of the so-called 'neighbourhood enterprises' (*régies de quartier*), this often became possible through resources they received from housing associations and municipalities as a reward for activities of estate management and neighbourhood regeneration. A certain number of WISEs active in the field of local recycling have managed to keep some autonomy by negotiating contracts with local authorities to take on tasks of waste management. The general movement towards contracting out such services, however, goes along with a more managerial approach to public policies. Authorities have, indeed, begun to redesign their contract strategy, working through competitive tenders that widely disregard the social functions of the WISEs involved.

Interestingly, the case of Ireland is similar to the preceding ones. Again, civic groups laid the groundwork for the emergence of the organizational field, and again, the state established an institutional regime which intertwined Irish WISEs with public programmes. According to the author of the Irish report (O'Shaughnessy 2003), the pioneering initiatives were managed by religious orders, particularly in the field of sheltered workshops, before local community initiatives in the field of social services began to flourish, with support coming from public labour market policies and the EU. A scheme of 'Community Employment' was created, in which disadvantaged populations could work as 'participants', on the basis of a part-time contract and with formal supervisory guidance. Many WISEs emerged with the support of this Community Employment scheme which, at the time, was one of the rare public support mechanisms open to the voluntary sector. Hence, the sector of local initiatives providing social services took up the goal of work integration primarily in order to obtain the subsidy. Moreover, another public scheme was created: the 'Social Economy Programme'. With an emphasis placed on 'measurable outputs' of work integration, 'social economy WISEs' are required to become financially viable within a three- to five-year period. They are obliged to produce a detailed business plan and are subject to regular auditing and review. Though public stakeholders continue to expect them to make a contribution to the social regeneration of the local area, these WISEs increasingly adopt the goals of the for-profit sector. Altogether, the volunteer base is very different from that of the NPO relying on the Community Employment programme; it remains important for the strategic direction of a WISE, but its contribution to the actual delivery of services to the community has been shrinking.

Italy is a special case. The enterprises depicted by the Italian report (Borzaga and Loss 2003) have their roots in civil society, too. It was, among others, church-related groups that invented co-operative enterprises with the goal of covering unmet community needs and giving work to disadvantaged populations, especially those who had been discharged from mental health institutions. Yet the emerging institutional setting was a particular one, as was the entrepreneurial approach of the WISEs. Italian law gave these organizations the legal form of 'B-type social co-operatives' (*cooperative sociali di tipo b*). These co-operatives were given priority in the allocation of contracts to deliver public services on condition that at least 30 per cent of their workers are publicly 'certified' disadvantaged workers. Moreover, the regulation provided for an exemption from social security contributions for these workers (similar to the position in other countries). The core idea was to encourage conventional enterprises to hire a high proportion of deprived people and, apparently, this model has proved rather sustainable. On closer examination, however, some change is under way here as well. This concerns the preferred provider status of the co-operatives. The traditional 'gentlemen's agreement' between public authorities and B-type social co-operatives has gradually been replaced by real tenders, though this is not yet the case everywhere to the same degree. As a result, many WISEs have changed their strategy in order to become competitive with for-profit firms. To this may be added the evolution of the markets in which the co-operatives operate. Obviously, it has appeared necessary to offer high quality products. One general response has been diversification, including the creation of units training disadvantaged workers for employment outside the organization. In the same run, many co-operatives have begun to focus their core activity on the commercial market. Concerning the characteristics of the WISEs, there is a stronger emphasis than elsewhere on managerial discretion (instead of decision-making by general assemblies), though the governance remains based on a multi-stakeholder structure and the contribution of volunteers to the management process subsists as an important organizational resource. With stronger environmental pressure (especially the changing contracting strategy of public authorities), however, there is a growing risk of scaling down to some extent the aim of social integration.

In other parts of southern Europe, the organizational field is still in its infancy. WISEs in Portugal exhibit some traits to be found elsewhere, but they have appeared only as the result of a public programme. Indeed, most Portuguese WISEs came into being from the end of the 1990s onwards, after the state had instigated special programmes for labour market integration.[7] The launching of the 'Employment Social Market' in 1996 was a major milestone. Moreover, a 'Covenant on Co-operation for Social Solidarity' created the framework for public–private partnerships. A scheme for 'integration companies' (*empresas de inserção*) was started in 1998, paving the way for fixed-term, subsidized jobs in the field of local social development. Over a three-year period, 80 per cent of the wages are paid by the state; the remaining share of the costs has to be covered mainly by sales and fees for services. Some of the emerging initiatives have been embedded into intense relationships with public bodies or advocacy groups, these networks proving an important support in running the businesses (though volunteering seems to be less important). To date, it is difficult for integration companies to achieve economic autonomy, since they are not equipped to compete in the for-profit service market. Many workers lack the necessary skills at the beginning, and supervisory personnel are often inclined to leave the enterprise after a short period of time. Hence, the further evolution of the field depends heavily on public policy.

In Spain, the organizational field appears to be more mature, though for a long time it did not develop on a broad scale. The first WISEs appeared during the 1980s; they were launched by social workers or members of Catholic charities. In spite of limited backing from national public bodies, the movement accelerated in the 1990s. As the Spanish report points out (Vidal and Claver 2003), public assistance to the initiatives was mostly confined to the local level, including technical support for applying to development programmes of the EU. The dominant form of public backing was contracts with local authorities (e.g. in industries such as waste collection and recycling). Networking with local social services has always been important. Spanish WISEs have benefited from their embeddedness in existing (e.g. charitable) non-profit contexts. Furthermore, extensive volunteering at the management level proved crucial, though it was also sometimes a source of internal quarrels. Spanish WISEs have been experiencing considerable economic instability, given the weak institutionalization of the organizational field (though their dependence on markets is variable). More recently, some regional public bodies have officially recognized social enterprises as a particular form of non-profit undertaking, via 'Autonomous Community legislation'.[8] WISEs are conceived as firms founded by a non-profit entity but with a trading legal form (including that of a private company with limited liability). The new partnerships between WISEs and public bodies also materialize in yearly contracts for job training, conferred on WISEs by local authorities. Some WISEs have not followed this path of co-operating with labour market policies. The economic development of these more autonomous organizations has proved highly variable, with some quite successful enterprises and other organizations in which employment turned out to be quite precarious because of volatile markets and a reduced capacity to bid for public contracts.

At the other end of Europe, in Finland, WISEs have come into existence mostly in the form of self-help groups engaging in economic activities (in some ways similarly to what occurred in southern Italy and Spain). The country had long lacked a specific legal form, but a 'Law on Social Enterprises' has recently been passed. The Finnish report (Pättiniemi 2003) notes that the early founders of WISEs were local civic groups or established non-profit organizations. The dominant types of WISEs are labour co-operatives for the unemployed and workshops for people recovering from mental illness. While the workshops – which, through links to major national welfare associations, exert considerable political influence – are bigger in size and are active in producing goods, labour co-operatives mostly operate in service sectors. From their onset, many labour co-operatives pursued a strategy of hiring out the labour of their full-time personnel to other firms and serving de facto as a transitional labour market for the disadvantaged. To a considerable extent, they recruited, and still recruit, their staff by using services and subsidies granted by public labour offices. There is also collaboration between these labour co-operatives and the public labour offices in the field of vocational training. Thus, a kind of public–private partnership has evolved in Finland, too. Yet with the public labour offices themselves starting operations to hire out the labour of unemployed people, the co-operatives had to face a new competitor in the domain of work integration. Finnish WISEs are often confronted with problems in finding suitable workers to realize their business goals. As a consequence, some of them have evolved into for-profit co-operatives, with a high proportion of 'standard' workers and a firm commercial orientation. In these cases, the goal of work integration has become ancillary to economic viability. To this may be added a clear tendency towards professionalization, with a crowding out of the original vision of co-operative democracy as an inevitable consequence.

So far, we have dealt with countries in which WISEs have achieved, or are in a state of achieving, a (quasi-)institutional status as non-profit organizations employing disadvantaged people in the framework of a social business. Even though these institutionalized enterprises coexist with others that have not adopted this status, the distinctiveness of these national configurations remains. In other European countries, such a status is totally missing or is, at least, very fuzzy. WISEs thus have to establish themselves in the framework of legal forms or public schemes that are not specific to them, drawing on particular voluntary sector traditions, but also on conventional business models. This is particularly evident in the case of the United Kingdom. With the exception of the small number of so-called 'Intermediate Labour Market (ILM) organizations', there is no clear organizational domain of work integration, strictly speaking (though a new legal form, the 'Community Interest Company' (CIC), which might be used for such purposes, has recently been created). Rather, the British report (Spear and Aiken 2003)[9] presents an enormous variety of practices of work integration, including those community businesses in which work integration is just seen as a collateral effect. Enterprises engaging in work integration were often founded by other non-profit organizations, sometimes in partnership with government agencies. Volunteering was often fundamental at the start-up stage, but it subsequently seemed to lose importance. The evolution of the field can hardly be associated with national public policies. It is true that, for a couple of years, public policies have addressed voluntary organizations as temporary employers of jobless people ('New Deal' programmes); yet British WISEs rarely concentrate on these programmes. Some organizations that have a role that comes near to our definition of a WISE operate through commercial contracts rather than through a mix of income streams such as grants and subsidies, while other quasi-WISEs, combining social and economic goals, effectively use a mix of public (service) contracts and commercial resources. Contracts with public authorities are often negotiated in fields such as recycling and public transport. In some cases, the financial base is 'unsteady' in the sense that the WISE relies on few contracts (or grants in some cases), which means that the loss of one can substantially affect the viability of the organization. For these WISEs, then, political networking proves quite important. WISEs involved in contracting with public purchasers also experience growing stress because the latter increase their pressure on costs or performance measure in quite blunt terms. Moreover, given the generally limited public budgets for social integration, the overall evolution is shaped by a move towards commercialization, with some organizations being seduced into creaming off their clientele (hiring the most skilled instead of the most needy workers) in order to improve their business (see Chapter 16 of this book).

The situation in Germany is not fundamentally different. While the idea of a social economy has lost most of its visionary attraction since the Second World War, a comparatively solid field of WISEs can nonetheless be discerned in this country. Faced with rising unemployment in the 1970s, engaged citizens (especially students and practitioners in the field of social work) created enterprises to produce goods and services in order to steadily employ socially disadvantaged workers. The welfare state rapidly came in, creating the framework for a 'second labour market' in which public bodies quite generously subsidized WISEs. Subsequently, civic action became increasingly professionalised, and larger organizations (especially the big welfare associations and the municipalities) took centre stage as managers of social enterprises. With the end of Keynesian policies, the organizational field was re-tailored towards the temporary employment of the most unfortunate. All in all, labour market policies proved the driving force of organizational change. During the late 1990s, public administrations such as the employment or social assistance offices redefined their role as sponsors; as the German country report (Bode *et al.* 2003)[10] explains, the dominant reasoning became to subjugate subsidized employment to rigid efficiency norms in terms of successful placements into the regular labour market. In many places, WISEs entered into competition with each other and with newly created for-profit training and placement agencies. This evolution occurred in East Germany, too, albeit with some delay and after an intermediary period in which a considerable amount of public money was spent 'feeding' the 'second labour market' there. Even though a new programme subsidising jobs in the non-profit sector has recently been set up, the overall trend remains to make the social and productive aims of WISEs ancillary to successful job placement, whereas the idea of combining economic and social integration has gone out of fashion in both politics and civil society.

This appears similar to the situation in Denmark. WISEs have come into existence there through grassroots initiatives or through projects run by more traditional actors of civil society (e.g. trade unions). Over the course of time, public (labour market) policies have proved the most important vector of development, though the Danish report (Hulgård and Bisballe 2003) states that many WISEs follow an economic vision of their own. As in Germany, Danish WISEs sell 'integration services' to public bodies. In a number of cases, this is linked to a micro-economic vision underlying concepts of business re-engineering, and this vision marginalizes the original social economy approach of the undertaking. Moreover, it appears that the social movement dynamics that stood behind the upswing of WISEs has often been replaced by a staff-led professionalization, with a more managerial approach towards what is regarded as a promising way to run a social enterprise. Those organizations – whose main activity is based on 'workfare' contracts with public bodies – operate under growing competitive pressure. Being obliged to deliver detailed accounts on their short-term 'integration performance', many of them tend to give the 'integration business' prevalence over their original community-oriented goals.

3 Variety, change and sustainability: a comparative view

A comparative analysis of these national portraits provides general insights concerning the evolutionary dynamics of WISEs. The country reports illuminate the cultural background of international variation (Section 3.1). We then address the question of the existence, over and above this variation, of cross-border driving forces of change (Section 3.2). Finally, we study whether and under which conditions WISEs, as hybrids, can remain stable notwithstanding precarious environments (Section 3.3).

3.1 The impact of varying national contexts

The national contexts in which the organizational fields of WISEs have developed differ in some important respects. However, the differences in the national institutional landscapes overlap only slightly with variations in what are usually called 'welfare regimes'. A widespread grid of comparative analysis[11] would have predicted clear-cut differences between the Anglo-Saxon countries, the continental nations, the Nordic countries and southern Europe. Yet in our field there is much disparity *across* welfare state families. The organizational landscape of WISEs in France and Germany, for instance, is shaped by diverging institutional logics, and the British and Irish frameworks differ in that WISEs face a much stronger dependence on labour market policies in Ireland. The situation in the southern countries exhibits considerable international variation as well, for instance with respect to the degree and the pattern of institutionalization. Finally, the classic prevailing understanding of the non-profit sector in the Nordic countries would exclude productive activities motivated by social goals being run by organizations other than public bureaucracies – while this is exactly what is happening in many instances.

The main dividing line might be drawn between countries in which WISEs *as such* have achieved a quasi-institutional status and those in which this is not (yet) the case. This would imply roughly distinguishing a south-western axis from the rest of Europe. In particular, the dominant *raison d'être* of WISEs appears not to be the same across this axis. As stated above, a good many of these organizations emerged as initiatives devoted to the 'public benefit' and in domains such as proximity services, recycling or collective transport. However, there is considerable variation in the *role attached to economic activities* as such. In many cases, the latter have been conceived of as the main purpose of the organizations, e.g. in the UK, France, Ireland, Portugal and Italy. Elsewhere, WISEs were instigated for (or increasingly confined to) the very aim of providing vocational training or temporary work to disadvantaged people. This is the prevailing situation in Denmark and Germany, for instance.

There appears to be some overlap between the nature of the dominating organizational approaches in a given country, on the one hand, and the 'third sector legacy' to be found in this country, on the other. On the one hand, throughout Europe, the emergence of the organizational field has certainly been the result of charitable and civic initiatives as well as alternative social work projects. Yet concomitantly, on the other hand, we can discern a de facto revitalization of antecedent approaches of collective economic action run by co-operatives or mutual societies, e.g. in Italy, Spain and France. In several countries, we see a coexistence of both traditions, as in the UK and Finland. It seems that the countries where a particular institutional label for WISEs has emerged are those in which the 'social economy sector' has maintained some of its original features or cultural identity. Conversely, the demise of the consumer co-operative sector in Germany, for example, has impeded WISEs from becoming a model with an identity of its own (see Bode and Evers 2004).

This being said, WISEs have developed in some countries *without* being perceived as a particular type of enterprise, too. This is especially the case of countries in which traditional voluntary or welfare associations have grown into the role of a mere transmission belt of labour market policies (e.g. Germany, Denmark and, to some extent, Ireland, Belgium and France as well). In cases where civic environments continue to provide for a stream of intangible resources, and when public strategies leave some discretion to the integration 'business', WISEs may develop on quite a solid base here as well. In the UK, for example, some voluntary organizations have adopted the 'transmission belt' role (especially within the 'New Deal' framework), yet on the whole, we deal here with a 'jungle' of dispersed types of organizations.

3.2 Driving forces of change: convergence beyond dissimilarity

There are some important cross-country driving forces of change in the organizational fields under study. *Public policies* are one of these; their role proves quite important in all the countries surveyed (see also Chapter 17 of this book). Their effects are two-faceted. On the one hand, public support has clearly contributed to the growth of WISEs. At least indirectly, it has protected them from potentially hostile environmental influences (from for-profit firms or public administrations). Throughout Europe, the field has been expanding, with the young enterprises facing little economic risk and considerable freedom in caring for their clientele. This has held especially true where active labour market policies were rolled out and, later on, led to the creation of a particular institutional status (e.g. Italy, France, Belgium and Ireland). Yet this has not been the sole mechanism of expansion, as the German case illustrates: in this country, WISEs became entitled to subsidies without such a status ever being created. Some British and Danish WISEs benefited from the direct involvement of public actors in their boards. An additional source of stabilization has been public service remits handed over to these organizations as 'preferred' contract partners.

On the other hand, throughout Europe, both labour market programmes and public service policies have put WISEs under strain. Of special importance in this regard is the way in which public services are contracted out – or, more broadly, the style of public governance. While it holds true that the handing over of services has initially provided WISEs with a (sheltered) market in which disadvantaged people could experience real work settings, public bodies have increasingly devolved economic risks upon private agencies. As some country reports (Italy, UK) point out, the practice of competitive tendering, applied to markets in which WISEs are active, has obliged the latter to behave more like their for-profit competitors and to risk neglecting their social missions. Changes in funding rules have also proved crucial. Almost everywhere, there have been cuts in public subsidies. Moreover, grant aid and unconditional subsidies have come under scrutiny while WISEs have, in the same vein, been directed to quasi-market schemes for work integration (with less likelihood of being selected as service providers). These developments make WISEs increasingly operate according to a short-term return-on-investment logic. In some places, besides their original aims, they have simultaneously been required to fulfil predefined roles in new 'workfare' regimes, with shrinking operational flexibility in the enterprises' business approach as a major result.

Against this ambivalent public policy background, *civic backing* is of critical importance. The transformation of civic endorsement, with WISEs being ever more exposed to the volatility of markets and public programmes, constitutes a second, albeit weaker, convergence in the development of the different national organizational fields under study. All country reports clearly show the role of intangible resources, and all of them show that WISEs have emerged and persist because of their ability to build links to civic constituencies that sympathise with them. These constituencies consist of local consumers of goods and services, of municipal administrations and of citizen groups concerned with the public good. Civic inputs also arise from social capital acquired through networking and political agency, sometimes at the level of umbrella organizations.

This being said, the evolution of the social capital element within the overall composition of WISEs proves variable. There is evidence of network ties thinning out over time, e.g. when the influence civic stakeholders exert on local policies decreases. In many cases, moreover, tangible voluntary commitments are changing. While they seem to remain vivid where volunteers are active in management or networking, voluntarism at the rank and file level is often shrinking. Many longer-established WISEs face problems in finding new and young volunteers. Besides, a 'dark side' of voluntarism sometimes materializes in internal quarrels concerning the future strategy or the degree to which the aim of social integration shall be given priority over business issues. A further general tendency is professionalization, though founders or civic stakeholders have sometimes insisted on the original grassroots rationale when it comes to the question of a transition towards a more commercial style of management.

3.3 The sustainability of hybridization: endorsements and obstacles

Throughout Europe, the organizational fields have undergone changes as the result of evolutions in both public policies and civil society. What does this imply concerning the sustainability of the hybrid character of these organizations? Evidence from the country reports confirms the hybrid character of WISEs. In most cases, the concept of providing social integration through running productive activities has attracted a wide range of stakeholders (see Chapter 2 of this book), be they public bodies, individual users, civic organizations or philanthropic entrepreneurs. WISEs have come into existence as a 'public benefit arena' of their own, even though some of them have defined themselves as conventional businesses.[12] Moreover, WISEs have grown using a mix of resources and through simultaneously interacting with markets, public authorities and civil society.

Yet to what extent are these enterprises affected by subversive organizational change that saps the potentials of hybridization? Which factors support, and which factors impede such an evolution? These questions lead us back to the typology of scenarios of organizational change as presented in Section 1 of this chapter, and based upon the theoretical distinction between the tendencies towards 'organizational stability', 'institutional flexibility', and 'organizational metamorphosis'. As argued above, organizational stability refers to a continuity of the hybrid character of WISEs, while organizational metamorphosis indicates that this hybrid structure is under pressure or in danger. Regardless of the very different configurations in which WISEs have developed and still do develop, there is almost everywhere a growing tension between the micro-economic rationale and the social orientation. WISEs have to find new balances between social integration and productive purposes, though in different forms and to varying degrees:

Organizational stability is ensured most clearly when initial approaches have been reconfirmed after being challenged by internal or external impulses, as for example in some Italian and Spanish WISEs. The still young Portuguese WISEs also seem to be sailing in quite untroubled waters, though this may be due to the fact that they are still in their highly subsidised period. With respect to their 'market position', one might consider the situation of many organizations as stable, too (e.g. in Belgium). WISEs may even expand their scope of activities through innovation (e.g. in the UK). In all these cases, WISEs can actively corroborate their hybrid character and secure both a practice of social integration and economic sustainability. This being said, the possibility of a hidden agenda of change, materializing under the surface, has to be taken into account.

This change can adopt the form of *institutional flexibility*. Some WISEs stick to their multiple goal orientation despite making considerable modifications to their organizational practice (see Chapter 2 of this book). This, for instance, seems to be the case with German WISEs which – through permanently seeking prestigious social projects supported by local authorities and others – withstand the mainstream tendency to reduce their role to being merely an instrument of managerial labour market policies. Similarly, some Irish WISEs succeed in maintaining vivid links to community groups though using a more 'managerialist' public programme. Those Italian WISEs that diversify without creaming off their personnel, as well as those Spanish WISEs that preserve strategic discretion while participating in specific programmes of regional labour market policies (training courses) also belong to this category.

There is *organizational metamorphosis* under way in many other cases, though. A first observation is that there is a widespread tendency towards professionalization, together with a shrinking role of voluntarism. While this evolution has different reasons and adopts various forms from one case to another, it is also often a reaction to growing pressure to adopt forms of economic accountability known from private business, including a focus on measurable short-term efficiency. This may result from WISEs being increasingly exposed to ordinary markets, but also to a business culture proliferating in the public and social welfare sector. Especially in the latter case, WISEs are hit by normative pressures as suggested by DiMaggio and Powell. A good example is provided by Danish WISEs that feel caught in the middle between running their business according to mainstream productivity expectations and hiring ever more disadvantaged workers. Thus, the social integration element in the multiple goal structure is put under strain.

The same holds for WISEs that find themselves obliged to hire more qualified (and less disadvantaged) workers in order to cope with changing patterns of stakeholder support or with a market niche opened to intersectoral competition. Commercially oriented British WISEs competing in open service markets do not see themselves as being in a position to employ large cohorts of disadvantaged workers. A similar effect applies where WISEs need to counteract detrimental policy shifts and no social capital resources are available to compensate for economic losses. Cases from Germany, Ireland and Belgium are quite instructive here: managers think that it would be necessary to hire more qualified people as a possible response to the stream of public subsidies running dry. This evolution reveals coercive isomorphism insofar as public regulations squeeze WISEs into markets that do not reward social integration activities.

This may also make WISEs offer a job quality that is inconsistent with their initial social economy approach, as in the case of those Spanish initiatives that depend upon spot markets for personal services and have to accept quite modest working conditions for their workers. The social economy approach is also endangered where WISEs – as in Italy – delegate their integration activities to specific organizational departments (which use temporary personnel instead of employing them) or – as in Germany – disengage from producing socially valuable goods or services.

In sum, the evidence is mixed. Full *intersectoral isomorphism* is hardly visible. An interesting case, however, is that of the Finnish labour co-operatives, which have tended to transform themselves into for-profit enterprises quite rapidly after their inception. In Ireland and Germany, some WISEs have abandoned the organizational field by retreating from labour market policy programmes or by leaving their business to commercial sub-departments. This being said, there is no overall tendency towards isomorphism, understood as an evolution in which WISEs completely lose their hybrid character. Across all countries under study, it has certainly proved difficult for numerous WISEs to fully preserve their original approach, that is, to provide for the long-term social integration for disad-vantaged groups, to solidly establish different sorts of economic activities that are beneficial to the community, to keep relying on strong civic stake-holders, and to empower employees through workplace democracy and broad social support. Obviously, the economic and political conditions have led the enterprises to a more managerial approach, which focuses on economic productivity. One might interpret this as a process of stream-lining the organization towards those accountability standards that exist in the private sector or in new public management contexts. Yet many WISEs have shown a capacity to resist such external pressures. After having succeeded in making themselves a firm societal reality, including through exerting a strong influence on public policies, they have found ways to adjust themselves to new environmental challenges without selling their soul. Seen through this lens, the hypothesis of isomorphism is not confirmed by our research.

As the evidence is variable, though, it is interesting to know what makes hybridization sustainable and what hinders WISEs from sticking to their initial approach(es). A further inspection of the previously outlined tension between social and economic aims serves as a proxy to tackle this ques-tion.

This tension grows *stronger* in a range of particular configurations. To begin with, a *decrease of social capital resources* may prove problematic, espe-cially if these resources are needed to defend a sheltered market or to compensate for the loss of material resources. If voluntarism was important in the beginning and subsequently decreases, or if public policies have been influenced by social movements (including local ones) that have faded away, dependence on market income or on contracts with adminis-trative bodies under the new public management regime grows stronger. When WISEs that lose social capital see themselves obliged to adapt their organizational identity to a purely commercial service culture, they risk abandoning their socio-political role in the public sphere.

A second source of tensions for WISEs is linked to their *dependence on public regulations*, especially those linked to labour market policies. More encompassing activities of social support are impeded in cases where public support is made conditional on measured and quantified recorded outcomes regarding work integration. To this may be added the fixed-term character of many work integration missions devolved upon WISEs, and the often imposed rotation of workers that harms the economic sustainability of the undertaking. The more economic self-sustainability is required, due to the decline of public subsidies, the more WISEs serving disadvantaged clienteles run the risk of neglecting the general interest, for instance by raising user fees too high for poor consumers or by creaming off their workers.

Third, tensions occur when WISEs move into *volatile markets*, combining limited resources for work integration and limited support from civil society. This often means squaring the circle of competing with commercial for-profit firms, on the one hand, *and* providing the (really) disadvantaged with opportunities for social integration, on the other. With very flexible, unsteady contracts, limited resources for training and social counselling, little scope is left for those which present the most acute social problems. Rather, a tendency towards creaming off is quite probable under these conditions. The pressure rises if the number of customers who appreciate the social mission of the WISEs, and accept, for example, higher prices in return, declines.

Conversely, our evidence also suggests that there can be mechanisms that *ease the tension* between economic constraints and social goals. An important element preserving WISEs from isomorphism is the existence of *market niches* that remain free of for-profit competitors. This has often been the case of activities in the domain of person-related social services. A WISE from the (British) building sector provides an example in another field of activity; it demonstrates that a WISE can overcome labour markets dilemmas in some market niches, by up-skilling workers and directing them to sectors of production and service work in which even the less fortunate are given a new chance.

Second, many WISEs have experienced a *balanced dialogue with public bodies*, e.g. with regard to how to create and shelter an economic domain in which social integration can take place. A preferred provider status in a system of public service contracts is one example of this configuration. More generally, with public backing becoming more solid, WISEs have managed to build economic reserves and to thereby consolidate their business. A similar effect occurs with WISEs having a permanent access to subsidies for running their own training schemes: this not only increases their overall reputation as enterprises for social integration but also helps them to recruit suitable workers (possibly after having helped them to overcome their social troubles).

Last but not least, *social capital* can be gainfully used even when broader movement support is missing. For instance, the building of linkages with local community activists helps to raise the reputation of the goods and services a WISE is providing. Moreover, improving relations with influential political or civic actors enables a WISE to make its approach known to a wider audience, with more institutional backing as a possible consequence. The same holds true in cases where WISEs extend their networking by participating in umbrella organizations.

Conclusion

Hybridization can be sustainable in the organizational fields of work integration through social business, albeit under specific conditions. As WISEs live in precarious environments, one might finally be tempted to search for the best national model or, in other words, to ask in which country hybridization is most sustainable and potentially conducive to high(er) impacts of social integration. Analysis of the evidence shows that there are no clear answers to this question. Our comparative findings suggest that, in every country, more than one single pattern of social, political and economic embeddedness can be discerned. In each country we find WISEs that manage to stick to their multiple goal approach, even in hard times, and even though the trend of rising tensions between social and economic goals is obviously an international one, with some national organizational fields being shaped by state interference to a comparatively high extent and others tending more towards commercial business. It is noteworthy that those institutional models that give WISEs a firm place in the institutional landscape of a given society are not exempt from drawbacks, and that WISEs have been able to emerge and evolve even in institutionally unfriendly settings. It remains that, while national peculiarities matter, the movement of WISEs has been (and still is) international – with all its ups and downs.

Review questions

- What makes hybridization sustainable and what hinders European WISEs from sticking to their initial identity?
- Why do public policies have ambivalent effects on the development of European WISEs?
- Why is civic backing of critical importance for the development of European WISEs?

Notes

1 The notion of 'organizational field' has been introduced by DiMaggio and Powell (1983). It addresses areas of organizational action that contain the same 'key suppliers, resource and product consumers, regulatory agencies, and other organizations that produce similar services' (ibid.: 148).
2 For more details about the PERSE project, see Chapter 1 of this book.

3 The authors draw on Meyer and Rowan, who argue that organizations 'which exist in highly elaborate institutional environments and succeed in becoming isomorphic with these environments gain the legitimacy and resources needed to survive' (Meyer and Rowan 1977: 352; see also Dart 2004: 415–17).

4 For the relevant body of theory, see DiMaggio and Anheier (1990), Evers (1993) or Laville (1997).

5 By this, we mean the use of routines known from other organizations, without a modification of final goals (cf. Miner and Raghavan 1999).

6 Note that the field of pure sheltered workshops has been excluded from the sample since it is subject to a history of its own and to specific social regulations in most of the countries surveyed.

7 As the Portuguese report points out (Perista and Nogueira 2003), it appears difficult to retrace organizational and institutional change for the short period for which WISEs have existed in this country. Some rough tendencies can nonetheless be made out.

8 Note that there is still no quasi-institutional status at the national level.

9 See also Chapter 16 of this book.

10 See also Chapter 18 of this book.

11 A very influential comparative scheme was suggested by Esping-Andersen (1990). As to different points of view in, and a summary of, the relating debate see Arts and Gelissen (2002).

12 Even in the cases where WISEs have tackled markets which usually do *not* belong to the 'public benefit economy', they can follow a logic of public benefit, e.g. by raising the interest of the building industry in low-skilled workers (this is an example taken from the British country report).

Bibliography

Aldrich, H. (1999) *Organisations Evolving*, Thousand Oaks, CA: Sage.

Arts, W.A. and Gelissen, J. (2002) 'Three Worlds of Welfare Capitalism or More? A State-of-the-art Report', *Journal of European Social Policy*, 12, 2: 137–58.

Bode, I. and Evers, A. (2004) 'From Institutional Fixation to Entrepreneurial Mobility? The German Third Sector and its Contemporary Challenges', in Evers, A. and Laville, J.-L. (eds) *The Third Sector in Europe*, Cheltenham: Edward Elgar, 101–21.

Bode, I., Evers, A. and Schulz, A. D. (2003) *The Evolution of Work Integration Social Enterprises in Germany. The Isomorphism Study*, PERSE research paper, Liège: EMES European Research Network (unpublished).

Borzaga, C. and Defourny, J. (eds) (2001) *The Emergence of Social Enterprise*, London and New York: Routledge.

Borzaga, C. and Loss, M. (2003) *The Evolution of Work Integration Social Enterprises in Italy. Isomorphism Study*, PERSE research paper, Liège: EMES European Research Network (unpublished).

Clarke, J., Gewirtz, S. and McLaughlin, E. (eds) (2000) *New Managerialism, New Welfare?*, Buckingham: Open University Press.

Dart, R. (2004) 'The Legitimacy of Social Enterprise', *Nonprofit Management and Leadership*, 14: 411–24.

DiMaggio, P.J. and Anheier, H.K. (1990) 'The Sociology of Nonprofit Organisations and Sectors', *Annual Review of Sociology*, 16: 137–59.

DiMaggio, P.J. and Powell, W.W. (1983) 'The Iron Cage Revisited: Institutional Isomorphism and Collective Rationality in Organisational Fields', *American Sociological Review*, 48: 147–60.

Esping-Andersen, G. (1990) *The Three Worlds of Welfare Capitalism*, Cambridge: Polity Press.

Evers, A. (1993) 'The Welfare Mix Approach. Understanding the Pluralisms of Welfare States', in Evers, A. and Svetlik, I. (eds) *Balancing Pluralism. New Welfare Mixes in Care for the Elderly*, Aldershot: Avebury, 5–31.

Gardin, L. (2003) *Rapport national sur l'évolution et l'isomorphisme – France*, CRIDA, PERSE research paper, Liège: EMES European Research Network (unpublished).

Hannan, M. and Freeman, J. (1984) 'Structural Inertia and Organisational Change', *American Sociological Review*, 49: 149–64.

Hulgård, L. and Bisballe, T. (2003) *The Evolution of Danish Work Integration Social Enterprises Over Time*, PERSE research paper, Liège: EMES European Research Network (unpublished).

Laville, J.-L. (ed.) (1996) *L'économie solidaire. Une perspective internationale*, Paris: Desclée de Brouwer.

Laville, J.-L. (1997) 'L'association: une organisation productive originale', in Laville, J.-L. and Sainsaulieu, R. (eds) *Sociologie de l'association. Des organisations à l'épreuve du changement social*, Paris: Desclée de Brouwer, 75–89.

Lemaître, A. (2003) *Country Report about Evolution over Time and Isomorphism. The Case of Wallonia*, PERSE research paper, Liège: EMES European research Report (unpublished).

Meyer, J.W. and Rowan, B. (1977) 'Institutionalized Organisations: Formal Structure as Myth and Ceremony', *American Journal of Sociology*, 83: 340–63.

Miner, A.S. and Raghavan, S.Y. (1999) 'Interorganisational Imitation: A Hidden Engine of Selection', in Baum, J.A.C. and McKelvey, B. (eds) *Variations in Organisation Science*, Thousand Oaks, CA: Sage, 35–62.

Osborne, S.P. (1998) *Voluntary Organisations and Innovation in Public Services*, London: Routledge.

O'Shaughnessy, M. (2003) *Evolution over Time Report. Ireland*, PERSE research paper, Liège: EMES European Research Network (unpublished).

Pättiniemi, P. (2003) *Development of Work Integration Social Enterprise Sector in Finland*, PERSE research paper, Liège: EMES European Research Network (unpublished).

Perista, H. and Nogueira, S. (2003) *The Evolution of Work Integration Social Enterprises in Portugal*, PERSE research paper, Liège: EMES European Research Network (unpublished).

Rowlinson, M. (1997) *Organisations and Institutions. Perspectives in Economics and Sociology*, Houndmills, Basingstoke: Macmillan.

Spear, R. and Aiken, M. (2003) *Evolution: In-depth Cases. PERSE UK Country Report*, PERSE research paper, Liège: EMES European Research Network (unpublished).

Spear, R., Defourny, J., Favreau, L. and Laville, J.-L. (eds) (2001) *Tackling Social Exclusion in Europe. The Contribution of the Social Economy*, Aldershot: Ashgate.

Vidal, I. and Claver, N. (2003) *The Development of Spanish WISEs. In-depth Case Studies*, PERSE research paper, Lige: EMES European Research Network (unpublished).

Weber, M. (1968) *Economy and Society*, translated and edited by Roth, G. and Wittich, C., New York: Bedminster Press.

16 Towards market or state? Tensions and opportunities in the evolutionary path of three UK social enterprises

Mike Aiken

Overview

There has been a historical lack of distinctive legal frameworks, dedicated income sources or clear recognition for UK social enterprises. More recently, there has been central government encouragement to accelerate their development. Social enterprises evolve in an increasingly marketised environment. In order to understand the isomorphic pressures operating, three distinctive types of social enterprises engaged in work integration are distinguished according to the type of market on which they rely. After reading this chapter, the reader should:

- be aware of the lumpy character of the landscape of social enterprises in the UK;
- identify the different markets on which British social enterprises are present;
- understand the different pressures that British social enterprises face, according to the kind of market environments in which they are operating.

Introduction

This chapter briefly describes the variegated social enterprise sector in the UK and sketches some of the policy changes relating to the delivery of social welfare services. In a context of increased marketisation of social provision, it explores the isomorphic pressures on social enterprises. It is suggested that an examination of the kind of market in which social enterprises are operating will give a clearer picture of whether they are being drawn towards either commercial or state ways of operating. Three cases of social enterprises, operating in three different market environments, are presented.

1 The social enterprise field in the UK

The social enterprise field in the UK has been characterized as 'lumpy'. There has been a historical lack of distinctive legal frameworks, dedicated income sources or clear recognition, even within the wider third sector. It is against this background that a plethora of social enterprise initiatives have emerged with differing origins, characteristics and values.

In the field of work integration, social enterprises in the UK have been considered to include worker co-operatives, intermediate labour market (ILM) organizations, some voluntary organizations, social firms and community businesses (see Spear and Aiken 2003).

The wider social enterprise field also includes, according to Social Enterprise London,[1] credit unions and local trading networks such as LETS[2] (Social Enterprise London 1999: 5). An important Scottish-based network of organizations and individuals seeking to support social enterprise also adds Development Trusts and employee-owned businesses; the trading arms of large charities are often considered to be social enterprises too (Community Business Scotland 2003).

There is no one agreed definition of social enterprise in the UK. This conceptual uncertainty has meant that attempts to measure the size and scale of the sector in any straightforward way have, unsurprisingly, only offered confusing outcomes (see ECOTEC 2003). Legal structures have offered little in the way of clarification. Despite the emergence of a new legal form in 2005 (the Community Interest Company), which is likely to offer benefits to some organizations in the field, there is little evidence to suggest that all organizations that could be considered social enterprises will find this a suitable vehicle. The definitional issues are not considered further in this chapter; however, in general, Borzaga and Defourny's (2001: 16) nine criteria[3] for social enterprises were used as an analytical framework to describe the social enterprises discussed in this article.

2 Policy background

The policy shifts to engage the third sector in combating social exclusion since 1997 have meant the organizational and environmental context for third sector organizations has changed considerably. There has been central government encouragement to accelerate the development of a social enterprise sector; in the autumn of 2001 the Department for Trade and Industry launched its Social Enterprise Unit. This has come alongside moves to further contract out existing state services in a realigned welfare state. To illustrate the current flow of state resources, research and analysis from the Charities Aid Foundation (Pharoah 2004) showed that around 2 per cent of all state expenditure in England, or around £67 billion (€95.75 billion),[4] goes to the voluntary sector. The Charities Aid Foundation identified an extremely wide variety of statutory income sources used by third sector organizations.[5]

The changed policy focus has been on developing more horizontal local connections between those organizations engaged in combating poverty and disadvantage. This can be seen in cross-cutting initiatives to bring the arenas of health and care together; partnerships involving different providers of social projects; and a move from 'reducing poverty' to the more complex idea of 'combating social exclusion', which has implied a more extensive range of local actors being involved in planning services (Kendall 2003: 59). This has meant a wide range of initiatives: for example, local 'compacts' to agree the principles and roles involved in the relationship between local government and the voluntary sector (Craig *et al.* 2005); the growth of partnership arrangements to map and deliver local services through Local Strategic Partnerships; area-based initiatives around employment and urban regeneration (including the New Deal for Communities and Neighbourhood Renewal programmes). Stoker (2004) suggests there may be as many as 5,000 such partnership bodies now operating in the delivery of public services. All of these developments have brought extended roles for many third sector organizations involved in both local policy development and the delivery of social welfare services.

These policy shifts have led to an increasingly marketized UK environment for welfare delivery. Third sector organizations have begun to act as providers for some of the many government programmes now available, although sometimes with mixed results for their users (Spear and Aiken 2003). Overall, this evolution towards the contracting out of welfare services has meant a higher level of managerial relations between the state and third sector organizations in managing and regulating the delivery of such services to a given contractual specification.

Social enterprises have, like the other organizations making up the third sector, been affected by such an evolution. In the following section, we will discuss the particular effects that this evolution has had on social enterprises operating in what could be termed 'social welfare markets' and those operating in other contexts (commercial markets and mixed markets).

3 Social enterprises and markets

In order to understand the dynamics of change affecting social enterprises in this new context, social enterprises are examined in relation to the kind of market environment within which they are operating, with a view to analysing the different kinds of isomorphic pressures that are affecting their operations and development paths. Two particular kinds of market environments are envisaged here: social welfare markets, on the one hand, and 'commercial markets', on the other. It can also happen that social enterprises' activities lead them to operate significantly in both markets at the same time; this can be considered as a third kind of environment, mixing characteristics and features of the first two kinds.

Le Grand and Bartlett (1993) made the broad distinction between the nature of commercial markets, on the one hand, and the quasi-markets within the public sector, on the other, and Moore (2000) expanded on the differences between the ways these two markets work, with much more state influence in delivery in the latter case. Making this distinction is useful when examining the characteristics of quasi-markets in their more recent extension: the contracting processes third sector organizations engage in to provide mainstream public services and also special programmes for disadvantaged groups. What is referred to as 'social welfare markets' in this chapter can then be seen to be a particular case, or subset, of the quasi-market phenomenon. Activities such as the provision of employment, childcare and housing services usually take place in the context of these *social welfare markets*; the specificity of these markets lies in the fact that they are fed by monies from public sector programmes designed to benefit targeted disadvantaged groups. The social enterprise operating in this kind of market develops tenders to bid for these pieces of work and, if successful, gains a contract to deliver to a certain specification. There is usually a significant degree of involvement of the public authority in managing and monitoring such work. Macintosh (1998: 227–38) described this kind of resource environment as similar to a 'franchise' offered by the state whereby a 'voluntary specialist organization' becomes 'a public supplier subject to higher levels of formal functioning'.

Other social enterprises may be engaged in activities such as recycling, building works and gardening projects or selling refurbished consumer goods and running shops in niche markets, such as wholefoods. These activities tend to be located in a different kind of market environment, resembling the private commercial sector, where goods or services are sold on businesslike terms to individuals, private companies, voluntary organizations or public authorities. This will be referred to here as a *commercial market* environment.

As already mentioned, a third type of social enterprise may be operating in both of these markets. A social enterprise may have activities, such as integrating disadvantaged workers, which enable the enterprise to gain resources, in a quasi-market environment, from public sector social exclusion programmes; simultaneously, the enterprise might be undertaking other activities – such as building works or landscape gardening – which are sold to individuals or organizations (whether in the private or public sector) on a commercial trading basis. This will be referred to as a *mixed market* environment.

The distinction between these three types of markets is used here to explore and understand the differing impacts and pressures social enterprises face. It is not suggested that these markets have fixed boundaries and do not change over time, nor that the distinction proposed is the only possible one; for example, some voluntary organizations operate within a grants market. This could be distinguished from the social welfare market in that in the case of grant funding, the outputs, targets and beneficiaries are generally less rigidly specified and monitored than in the contracting relationship of social welfare markets.

In the following section, three cases are presented with a view to offering differing perspectives on the isomorphic pressures social enterprises face, depending on their income mix – the latter having been taken as an indicator of the kind of market in which the enterprise is operating. The hypothesis put forward is that the nature of the pressures facing such organizations will differ according to the kind of market environments in which they are operating (Aiken 2002: 239).

4 Social enterprises operating in different markets

4.1 Social welfare market: Childcare Works

Childcare Works represents an elegant solution to two social exclusion issues: a lack of trained childcare workers (and childcare places) in poor neighbourhoods of Glasgow, on the one hand, and the large number of unemployed people (mainly women) in those same locations, on the other. Childcare Works aims to train people in childcare, within community-based core projects, and then gain them places in other childcare organizations in that area. Childcare Works is not itself an organization but a strategic *programme* which is manifested at different geographic sites and owned by a complex set of organizations in Glasgow. A key worker at Community Enterprise Strathclyde in Glasgow spends part of her time on development work for Childcare Works, thus playing an important role in the overall development of the programme; she wrote several of the funding bids for the individual core projects. Childcare Works effectively operates out of the office of Social Enterprise Glasgow, a social enterprise incorporated as a not-for-profit company limited by guarantee. Childcare Works' origins lie in a pilot project, operating within Social Enterprise Glasgow, concerned with intermediate labour market (ILM) opportunities, which was undertaken with European Social Fund (ESF) funding and emerged as a functioning entity in 1999.

There are now seven core projects where Childcare Works operates. Each of these projects develops its own training, support structure and recruitment process. Each is unique, responding to the needs of its area. The aim is to build different kinds of childcare provision, relevant to different groups, and to reduce the number of unemployed people by providing them with training and so allowing them to reach a level where they can get a permanent job within the core projects or with other childcare providers.

The funding for Childcare Works comes from a range of public sector sources including the European Social Fund and Glasgow City Council, matched by Social Inclusion Partnership Funding. Childcare Works supports the development of childcare within existing projects that have their own income. In a development programme of this size, fees and grants play a minor role; the vast majority of income is derived from public sector funding programmes at city, region, state or European level. These funding programmes operate as contracts within a strong regulatory framework. Public bodies are, in effect, purchasing a training programme that also offers an increased provision of childcare. The total worth of the Childcare Works programme was estimated at around £2.2 million (€3.14 million) in 2001; during the same year, the seven core projects together created 150 jobs.

A persistent pressure on Childcare Works is the increasing demand that it should be more 'real' and move towards self-sufficiency by 'paying its way'. This misses, according to its development worker, an awareness of the overall added value these projects provide, and illustrates how an over-simplified view of a detached and financially self-sufficient social enterprise fails to take into account the wider 'investment' that the programme is creating in disadvantaged areas.

A key issue for Childcare Works is the rules and regulations that are attached to the public sector contract funds it receives. The conditions attached to these monies tend to distract attention from the central issues of addressing exclusion and providing training, so that 'the programmes, instead of being client-focused, become funder-focused'. Childcare Works attempts to keep the beneficiaries in mind while staying within the bounds of what funders require, always negotiating back carefully. However, the loss of flexibility and conflicting demands of different funders can be detrimental. As a development worker argues: 'Public sector partners can hold us back from delivering the best service to clients.'

Childcare Works is not so much concerned about growth and economic success as about combining social and economic goals effectively, using a mix of public sector contract resources. There is, however, a heavy demand on professional staff time in researching, applying for, and then servicing the monitoring of this number of complex public sector funds.

4.2 Commercial markets: ECT Group

Ealing Community Transport (ECT) originated within the third sector. It was an initiative formed by local voluntary organizations, such as Age Concern[6] and youth groups, who were concerned about transport issues in the London borough of Ealing. It was established in 1979 within a local second-tier umbrella of voluntary organizations (the Ealing Council for Voluntary Services); in 1987 it became an independent organization with the legal form of an industrial and provident society (IPS). Today there is a network of over 250 voluntary and community organizations involved in the community transport part of the operation, which in 2001 had a total income of £675,515 (€965,021).

However, rather like a small village surrounded by a growing urban conurbation, the community transport voluntary organization is now dwarfed by the social enterprise it owns. This is an expanding collection of not-for-profit companies, called ECT Group. ECT Group, in turn, owns several further not-for-profit organizations: ECT Engineering, ECT Recycling and ECT Bus. Around 300 people are employed in the ECT Group. About 50 people who could be described as disadvantaged are working in ECT at any one time. There is a reasonable turnover of staff, which means about 20 to 30 disadvantaged people start work there during any one year. The ECT Group and its subsidiaries comprised, by 2002, a business with a £10.5 million (€15 million) income. It retains social values but asserts that these can best be met by ensuring an efficient business that generates sufficient surplus to deliver social outcomes. A senior manager described the implicit benefits they offered with a successful enterprise being the key:

> For ECT some of the social benefits come in a collateral way ... I think we do more good by being more successful than being desperately anxious – for example – compromising our recruitment strategy. Targeting disadvantaged groups would mean a huge extra cost. But most of our workforce is in fact disadvantaged – usually young men with low education who can't read very well.

The group operates kerbside recycling contracts, engineering operations and a bus route, and is active not only in several London boroughs but also increasingly nationwide. Overall, ECT claims its recycling services cover over a million people. Nearly 98 per cent of the group's income now comes from commercially won contracts with the public sector. The trend has been for a steady growth, about 20 to 25 per cent per year, and ECT Group has become highly successful in its market operations. ECT is now considering creating a charitable foundation so that it can covenant surpluses for the community transport charity.

A senior worker emphasized that the lack of shareholders and the balance of goals were crucial to the organization.

> Ownership is crucial – ECT is a social enterprise and so all the resources within are focused on the organization – there is no dividend. The organization is not for sale ... because of the ethos which underpins it [there is a] balance between financial, social, environmental considerations.

In summary, thus, for ECT the work integration of disadvantaged groups is not an explicit goal. Commercially successful social enterprises such as ECT can be characterized as opportunistic, entrepreneurial and aiming for growth with implicit social goals.

4.3 Mixed markets: Necta

Necta originated in 1998, growing out of a community campaign by residents to build a neighbourhood centre and create jobs for local people. Its primary aim is enabling people to gain work, but developing building services is also very important, as is lobbying on construction industry issues. Key partners have included umbrella organizations such as Social Economy East Midlands, a body supported by the Regional Development Agency. Through networks such as this Necta is involved in one of seven UK pilot projects in social exclusion being examined by the Department of Work and Pensions. Necta's yearly income in 2001/2002 approached £1 million (€1.4 million). The income streams included social inclusion contracts from public sector programmes (New Deal would be one example); such contracts made up around 50 per cent of the income, with commercial building contracts representing the other half.

Necta has been in existence for less than ten years, yet it has already noticed significant shifts in its relations with community organizations, both public and private. First, the organization is much less tied to community organizations and the grassroots, according to a lead worker there, while it has become much more aware of the needs of the local building industry. Second, it has been highly influenced by government programmes arranged via Job Centre Plus offices (the government agency in every town which seeks to move the unemployed into work).

The overall income has been increasing each year and Necta was anticipating a turnover approaching £2 million (€2.9 million) in 2003. However, the balance between public funds (for social inclusion work with disadvantaged workers) and income from commercial building contracts has remained close to 50/50 since the organization's inception.

A senior staff member described the programme funding this way:

> The four or five funding regimes that Necta has been under in the last four or five years have dictated the flavour of what we have been doing . . . Now we are button and bean counting – every single action and activity of the organization . . . has to be measured, quantified and recorded.

Additionally the changes in funding programmes affected the service delivered to trainees. These changes meant that the training period, which originally lasted one year, was shortened to six months – and with the mix of monies and targets this, in effect, meant that Necta had to get people into work within 11 weeks. This contradicted their main aim of targeting the most needy or excluded.

The changing rules within funding regimes generated pressures on costs and changing priorities. These shifts of public sector priorities necessitated internal adjustments – such as changes in staff teams, revision to the depth of support that could be offered to the beneficiaries and alterations to internal procedures – in order to meet evaluation criteria, particularly in measuring the work integration social enterprise's (WISE) performance.

As discussed earlier, roughly half of Necta's income came from contracts with public programmes and the other half from private or public building contracts; the WISE thus operated in a mixed market. It was in a position to influence agendas for funding and programme monies at a local level through partnership working in committees and project groups around the social inclusion parts of its activities. However, substantial areas around some of the national programme regimes remained problematic.

For Necta, the pressure to achieve large-scale commercial success did not seem present, perhaps because it was a relatively small and local operation. The speculative question for Necta in the longer term may be more about commercial survivability with a disadvantaged workforce, which might lead to pressures to split the organization into a commercial wing with a 'business logic' and a social inclusion side with a 'welfare logic', with only limited crossover between the two sections. Alternatively, the arrival of public procurement policies that favour more socially orientated organizations could give Necta a competitive advantage in tendering processes. The public sector funding pressures on Necta were towards requiring the WISE to deliver 'job-ready' people quickly, which forced a tendency towards 'creaming' – taking on less disadvantaged people so as to maintain funding.

5 Isomorphic tendencies

Spear and Aiken have argued elsewhere (Spear and Aiken 2004) that the UK social enterprise scene is characterized by organizations with different configurations of resource mixes, which can be seen as proxies for defining their market environment. What are the differing pressures social enterprises face according to the kind of market they are operating in?

For organizations involved wholly or partially in social welfare markets, one threat is the dominance of techniques from the public sector managerialist model (Waine and Henderson 2003: 49), which can be introduced by programme funding mechanisms at local, regional, national or international level. These may clash with the preferred methods and culture of a social enterprise. The effects of these isomorphic tendencies were being acutely felt and, where possible, resisted strongly by Necta in some of its programmes. Without care and attention to their values and purposes, organizations operating in social welfare markets face a risk of morphing into quango-like organizations. Childcare Works experiences these pressures too, but it may be that the size of its operation enables it to dilute some of these effects by having more organizational resources, which make it possible to move users across programmes flexibly. However, for both Childcare Works and Necta there was a noticeable access to policy-makers, often at quite senior levels in government departments.

The wide range of programmes utilized by organizations such as Childcare Works does impose high managerial maintenance and infra-structure costs. However, it can also allow such organizations more internal flexibility in how they arrange placements. This, coupled with a high quality of professional practice, may enable social enterprises to resist some of the worst pressures arising from public sector managerialism. Similarly, Aiken (2002: 220) has suggested that organizations such as St Mungo's, a charity for street homeless people, which may derive up to 90 per cent of their income from public funds, might also be able to preserve their prac-tices and values through their unique knowledge and expertise of a particular client group – knowledge and expertise that are needed by the statutory sector.

Viewing this from the framework presented by Bode, Evers and Schultz (see Chapter 15 of this book), Necta, operating in mixed markets, faces a fork in the road. It shows signs of moving from organizational stability – where the combination of social and economic goals is more or less main-tained – in the direction of organizational metamorphosis. Here the path splits, with dangers in both directions: pressures exerted from the social welfare markets may engender a shift in purposes towards becoming a passive agent of state programmes; alternatively, in seeking to avoid this, Necta may try to increase its income from commercial markets and lose some of the strength of its social purpose with disadvantaged workers in order to compete with other for-profit builders.

Childcare Works, operating almost exclusively in social welfare markets, but with a larger set of resources to juggle, shows signs of movement towards organizational flexibility – outwardly appearing to adapt to the demands of public welfare programmes while inwardly maintaining its core purposes.

For the larger and commercially successful social enterprises such as ECT, which are operating mainly in commercial markets (whether they are trading with individuals, private companies or public bodies), in head-to-head competition with commercial operators, the challenges are differ-ent. For them the danger is of moving too readily to an over-commercialized private sector business model, with loss of essential values and purposes – in other words, organizational metamorphosis in the direction of a busi-ness model where social purposes become merely symbolic or historic. Possibilities that the social purposes may be occluded remain. Organizations such as ECT have, to some extent, recognized this danger of 'simple' com-mercial success by making attempts to valorise the social purpose. ECT, for example, had begun, at the time of the research, to investigate the creation of a charitable foundation from trading surpluses. However, the commercial success also had positive effects: it offered freedom from the ideological pressures of shifting public programme demands and detailed monitoring that are characteristic of organizations operating in social welfare markets. For workers at ECT there are the dual advantages of entry-level work requiring few initial skills being offered in an environment closer to the more conventional world of work.

Social enterprises, as hybrid organizations, face an essential challenge: strategically managing the tensions presented above. However, there are a number of drivers that may help them to maintain or reproduce their value base (Aiken 2002: 251). These consist of internal aspects (such as the role of a vigilant organizational membership or key guardians of the values within the organization), external aspects (good and close intelligence about their field, or a role as having a perceived 'expert' status in their field) and inter-organizational aspects (links to a social movement or communities of practice).

Conclusion

Simple ideas of financial sustainability need to be treated with caution: it is likely, for example, that severely disadvantaged workers will always need to be in organizations where there is some form of public support for a training and orientation programme and for compensating for lower productivity. Highly disadvantaged workers are, therefore, most likely to be in social enterprises whose resource mix includes some degree of social welfare funding. Less disadvantaged workers may be taken on and given productive work by social enterprises trading in commercially orientated markets.

It is suggested here that there will be differing pressures towards distinctive evolutionary paths for social enterprises depending on their specific resources mix, considered here as an indicator of their market location. Nevertheless, social actors within organizations are themselves a resource that can resist unwelcome pressures from commercial or social welfare markets.

In European states with an emerging social enterprise sector and where social enterprises are faced with similar shifts in welfare state regimes, there may be comparable experience. For example, Bode and Aiken (2004) suggested there was some convergence between the welfare regimes in Germany and the UK – although, in the UK, there was less emphasis on the corporate and social solidarity model of Germany and more on a marketised model with local level partnerships. Social enterprises, when viewed as delivery agents, are positioned at the sharp end of such changes, whether they are operating in social welfare, commercial or mixed markets.

Review questions

- What are the signs of isomorphic tendencies in British social enterprises?
- Which drivers may help British social enterprises to maintain their value base?
- Give examples of British social enterprises which are either present in the social welfare market or in the commercial market. What are the respective pressures they face?

Notes

1   Social Enterprise London (SEL) is a not-for-profit organization that aims to improve business support and access to finance for social enterprises in London as well as improving understanding of the sector.
2   LETS (Local Exchange Trading Systems) are neighbourhood alternative 'currencies' through which members trade their skills or tools (e.g. babysitting, plumbing) with each other in a mutual exchange system (see Croall 1997).
3   On the definition of social enterprise, see Chapter 1 of this book.
4   Based on the exchange rate during 2002 of €1 = £0.7.
5   These sources included central government fees, contracts and grants for services; local authority fees, contracts and grants for services; fees, contracts and grants for services from the National Health Service; income from other government agencies, e.g. Regional Development Agencies, Local Skills Councils, Fire, Police and Ambulance services; other 'quangos', e.g. Big Lottery Fund, Arts Council; special programme funds, e.g. Single Regeneration Budget (SRB), Landfill Tax, Sure Start (childcare); tax exemptions; sector infrastructure funds, e.g. Futurebuilders, Phoenix; European funds.
6   A national charitable organization concerned with older people, which provides advocacy and direct services.

Bibliography

Aiken, M. (2002) 'Managing Values: the Reproduction of Organisational Values in Social Economy Organisations', unpublished PhD thesis, Milton Keynes: Open University.

Aiken, M. (2005) 'Social Enterprise in Social Economy: UK Experience in the European Tradition and Context', *Trzeci Sektor*, Warsaw, Poland, 2005, 2.

Bode, I. and Aiken, M. (2004) 'Non-profit Organisations Tackling Unemployment in Germany and the UK: Vigorous Independent Enterprises Meeting Social Needs or the Emergence of "Entrepreneurial Not-for-profits with Limited Social Liability"?', paper presented at the *VSSN Conference*, Manchester University, 12 May 2004.

Borzaga, C. and Defourny, J. (2001) *The Emergence of Social Enterprise*, London and New York: Routledge.

Community Business Scotland (2003) 'Social Enterprise Development and the Social Economy in Scotland: a Report by the Bridge to the Social Economy Project

July 2003'. Available at www.ssec.org.uk/index.php?SK=e9ef7e2e2a956c88df480 b615a3f296a&W21ID=146 (7 November 2004).

Craig, G., Taylor, M. and Carlton, N. (2005) *The Paradox of Compact: Monitoring the Implementation of Compacts*, Home Office Research Development and Statistics, online report 02/05.

Croall, J. (1997) *Lets Act Locally: the Growth of Local Exchange Trading Systems*, London: Gulbenkian Foundation.

DiMaggio, P.J. and Powell, W.W. (1991) 'The Iron Cage Revisited: Institutional Isomorphism and Collective Rationality in Organizational Fields', in Powell, W.W. and DiMaggio, P.J. (eds) *The New Institutionalism in Organizational Analysis*, London: University of Chicago Press.

ECOTEC (2003) *Guidance on Mapping Social Enterprise: Final Report to the DTI Social Enterprise Unit*, ECOTEC Research and Consulting Ltd 6–8 Marshalsea Rd, London SE1 1HL.

Kendall, J. (2003) *The Voluntary Sector*, London: Routledge.

Le Grand, J. and Bartlett, W. (eds) (1993) *Quasi Markets and Social Policy*, Basingstoke: Macmillan.

Macintosh, M. (1998) 'Social Markets', in Macintosh, M., Brown, V. and Costello, N. (eds) *Economics and Changing Economics*, Milton Keynes: Open University.

Moore, M. (2000) 'Competition within and between Organizations,' in Robinson, D., Hewitt, T. and Harris, J. (eds) *Managing Development: Understanding Inter-Organizational Relationships*, London: Sage.

Pharoah, C. (2004) 'Main Government Funding Sources to the Voluntary Sector in England', West Malling, Kent ME9 4TA: Charities Aid Foundation (unpublished paper).

Shaw Trust (2001) *Annual Report*, Trowbridge: Shaw Trust.

Social Enterprise London (1999) *Social Enterprises in London: Case Studies in Economic Participation*, London: Social Enterprise London.

Spear, R. and Aiken, M. (2003) 'Gateways into Employment: Third Sector Organisations Working with People Disadvantaged in the Labour Market', *NCVO Research Conference*, University of Central England, Birmingham, 2–3 September 2003.

Spear, R. and Aiken, M. (2004) 'Where Does the Money Come from? Lessons from Research into the Income Streams of UK Social Enterprises', paper presented at the *Social Enterprise Research Conference*, Open University Milton Keynes, 2–3 July 2004.

Stoker, G. (2004) *Transforming Local Governance*, London: Palgrave.

Waine, B. and Henderson, J. (2003) 'Managers, Managing and Managerialism', in Henderson, J. and Atkinson, D. (eds) *Managing Care in Context*, London: Routledge.

17 Public policies and social enterprises in Europe: the challenge of institutionalization

Jean-Louis Laville, Andreia Lemaître and Marthe Nyssens

Overview

The objective of this chapter is to sketch the different types of public policies that have contributed to shaping the institutional environment of European social enterprises. A central assumption is that social enterprises are characterized by socio-political embeddedness. Indeed, these public policies are the results of interactions between the promoters of social enterprises and representatives of the public bodies. However, the accommodation between the views of social enterprises and those of public bodies on the contested nature of the mission of WISEs seems not to be simple. After reading this chapter, the reader should:

- be aware of the different analytical viewpoints available to grasp the nature of relationships between public policies and organizations;
- understand the different ways for public bodies to support the mission of European WISEs;
- identify the impacts of public policies on the goals of European WISEs.

Introduction

This chapter provides an overview of the different types of public policies that have helped shape the institutional environment of work integration social enterprises (WISEs). It demonstrates that policy models are various, and that different models can coexist within one country.

A central assumption is that WISEs, and more generally the third sector, are characterized by social and political embeddedness. Stated differently, WISEs, which are economic institutions, develop from social constructions embedded in society in general, and in the political context in particular. They therefore reflect the changing regulatory role of the state. Public policies, for their part, develop from interactions among social actors, particularly interactions between WISE entrepreneurs and public authorities.

The chapter is divided into two parts. The first part (section 1) deals with the question of institutionalization and embeddedness, with a view to defining more accurately the analytical framework that has been chosen. The second part (sections 2–5) tests, on the example of WISEs, the heuristic value of this framework.

1 Analysis of organizations and institutions

The relation between economic initiatives and their context raises theoretical problems that we have summarized in three parts (Sections 1.1 to 1.3), each of which corresponds to a distinct conceptual approach.

Historically, researchers have approached this topic through organization theory. From the standpoint of both neo-classical economics and sociology, the choices made within this framework have two limits. First, they view the context as an environment whose pressure is assimilated to a contingency; in this perspective, organizations have no influence on their environment. Second, in a contract perspective, they reduce the subject to an actor whose behaviour within the organization is only strategic.

On a theoretical level, so-called 'neo-institutionalist' approaches improve on organization theory, especially with regard to our present concern, i.e. these approaches analyze the link between organizations and public policies. For example, as Bode *et al.* demonstrate in this book (Chapter 15), the goals and practices of organizations are influenced by requirements linked, among others things, to legal frameworks that encourage the homogenization of organizations.

However, it is important, when analyzing the interactions between community-based organizations and public policies, to include more complex forms of relations that allow for the possibility, however limited, of creativity in public policy making. From this point of view, the socio-political dimension of embeddedness constitutes a relevant concept, in that it allows the analysis to go beyond examining the impact of legal frameworks on forms of reproduction within organizations (an impact that is studied in Chapter 15 of this book). Such an approach, which could be termed the political embeddedness approach, also allows us to consider the role and the limits of democratic innovation – in the present case, democratic innovations supported and brought about by WISE entrepreneurs in the field of public policies.

We will now present a more detailed analysis of the strengths and limits of each of the conceptual approaches that we have just sketched; the third approach will then be tested on WISEs and will constitute the analytical framework of this chapter.

1.1 Analysis of organizations, contingencies and contracts

Neo-classical economics focuses on the analysis of markets and consumers' behaviour. It reduces the role of the firm to its simplest expression, as a function of maximizing profit under the constraint of the production function. In this framework, organizations are a black box. Until recently, economic theory thus left very little room for organizations. Recent developments of contract theory (Eymard-Duvernay 2004) analyse relations among economic agents within organizations. In this type of analysis, organizations and standards can be reduced to a set of contracts, held together, within a framework of imperfect information, by the balance of interests among economic agents. While contract theory allows us to analyse a vast array of interactions among individuals, it assumes, at least implicitly, that no institution is required beyond these contracts, which de facto constitute an extension of the market sphere into these organizations. The same system of reference is adopted in strategic analysis, which focuses on 'a set of power relationships expressed as games within the frame-work of which relatively autonomous actors pursue divergent interests and negotiate their contribution to the whole' (Crozier and Friedberg 1977). However, we need to ask ourselves where the rules of the games originate, and how they are chosen and implemented.

As Bélanger and Lévesque (1992) note in their synthesis, the sociology of organizations emerged as a response to a Marx-inspired sociology of work that dealt with the enterprise in the light of class struggle, with capital ownership dictating the organizational form. For Crozier, for example, what had to be underlined was the autonomy of the system of organizational action such as it emerged from the daily efforts to 'create effective co-operation among the members of an organization within the framework set by certain technical and economic constraints' (Crozier 1989: 46). Finally, sociological analyses of organizations explain that a social system of enterprise is the result of complex collective responses to a contingency: that of its external environments.

With regard to these external environments, the research school dealing with contingency sheds light on the ways organizations confront 'environments that force them to change and adapt' (Piotet and Sainsaulieu 1994: 79). Works on organizational responses to technical and market constraints (Burns and Stalker 1961; Lawrence and Lorsch 1973; Mintzberg 1983) show that contextual variables 'of course allow for the possibility of structural variations, but however establish certain limits to the possible combinations' (Piotet and Sainsaulieu 1994: 83). Contingency analysis focuses on 'the reactions of organizations faced with environmental constraints'. It has two underlying premises: (i) the issue of adaptation to an environment is considered to be a factor that is, by definition, external to the firm, and (ii) it interprets the environment primarily in technical and market terms.

Piotet and Sainsaulieu point out the difficulties inherent in methods employing these types of orientation: they show how the concept of environment inadequately conveys the situations of the public sector and, more generally, of organizations that are highly regulated by legal mechanisms.

Societal dimensions of the environment are also mentioned, and it is noted that 'analysis of the environment is not limited to the analysis of the product's market within a competitive economy' (Piotet and Sainsaulieu 1994: 111). These observations do not prevent the authors from concluding with a diagnosis of structural adaptation in which understanding of the environment remains focused on techniques and markets, and leads to 'the hypothesis of a possible optimisation between the organization and the environment' (Piotet and Sainsaulieu 1994: 112).

Thus, there are two limits to the explanatory capacity of organization theory: (i) the idea of adaptation in contingency analysis, which implies that organizations have no influence on their environment and which, in addition, focuses principally on technical and market environments, and (ii) the autonomy broached in terms of contracts and power games, which fails to take into account the consistency of subjects capable of reflection and action.

Neither economics nor the sociology of organizations resolves questions on the relationship between organizational forms and society. Answering such questions presupposes a shift in focus from organizations to institutions; such a shift is at the core of the new sociological and economic approaches.

1.2 Neo-institutional approaches, networks and reproduction

The so-called 'neo-institutional' approaches converge around a few points, such as assigning to institutions a major role in economic life or contributing to defining behavioural routines (Rizza 2004: 76–7). According to North (1996), institutions can be defined as the humanly devised constraints that structure human interactions. They are made up of formal constraints (rules, laws, constitutions), informal constraints (norms, conventions, and self-imposed codes of conduct), and their enforcement characteristics.

The 'new institutional economy' creates a rupture in the economic analysis of contracts. First, by developing concepts such as limited rationality[1] (following Simon 1996), it calls into question the premise of perfect rationality on the part of individuals. Second, it recognizes that the environment is essentially uncertain. Last, it acknowledges that the market is not the only mechanism for allocating resources. According to Williamson (1975), the enterprise provides an alternative approach to market co-ordination. In this framework, the theory of transaction costs analyses which organizational forms minimize transaction costs among the various stakeholders (see Chapter 1 of this book) in a context of incomplete information (Nyssens 2000). This is an essentially comparative approach, since it asks which institutions are most efficient in reducing uncertainty and transaction costs.

As Eymard-Duvernay (2004: 48) notes, 'the approach of the economics of transaction costs is at a crossroads: it can be based on a contractualist approach framework ... it can underline the institutional dimension of transactions'. As a matter of fact, while it moves away from contractualist theories by postulating the extreme uncertainty of the socio-economic environment and by recognising institutional diversity, it resembles these theories in its utilitarian conception of the actor.

The description of institutions introduced by Coase (1937) and taken over by Williamson (1975, 1985), who uses transaction costs to explain them, has been criticized by Granovetter. The latter maintains that enterprises are not more efficient than markets and underlines that, as is common with functionalist analyses, these two authors implicitly assume that every problem raised has a solution, without spelling out which mechanisms make this possible. They only deal with the question of 'Why are they institutions?', but not with the question of 'How do they emerge?' (Granovetter 2000: 214).

Faced with this economism, sociological neo-institutionalism and the new economic sociology defend their conception of institutions as social constructions, emphasising their constitutive dimension, especially through resorting to the polysemic term of embeddedness. Granovetter develops the concept of embeddedness within networks of personal relationships. Reticular embeddedness is based on the social construction of markets and social networks. The aim is to clarify the individual and collective choices and trajectories, within the framework of the market economy. Individual choices are relative to the choices and behaviours of other individuals, and to the personal relationships prevailing in networks; the latter are defined as an ongoing set of contacts or social relationships among individuals or groups of individuals. Embeddedness can be broached from two angles: the 'relational' aspect focuses on 'personal relationships'; the 'structural' aspect is centred on 'the structure of the general network of these relationships'. The second aspect allows us to analyse segments of the social structure that do not belong to primary groups. From this standpoint, far from constituting the unique and necessary solution to problems of efficiency, institutions are constructions of human history. Thus, an institution cannot really be understood without studying the process from which it emerged. Each institution has several potential histories; it results from the crystallization of certain particular personal relationships. Thus, network analysis must be used to understand the factors explaining institutional formation since, for Granovetter, institutions can be defined as 'congealed social networks'.

However, network analysis must not overshadow the contexts within which these networks exist. The phenomenological approach in neo-institutional sociology has examined the relationship between economic action and cultural order. It highlights 'the impact of cultural interpretations on the everyday behaviour of economic actors' (Magatti 2004: 49). This anti-utilitarian and constructivist institutionalism takes into account systems of meaning and symbolic frameworks, and the cultural registers associated with social practices (De Léonardis 2001). Economic action is framed through practices and standards associated with beliefs, roles, scenarios and habits – and sometimes even myths. 'Institutions establish cognitive and normative regularities', and organizations rely on legitimate and socially accepted institutional models (Rizza 2004: 95).

While obliged to respect efficiency criteria, organizations are integrated into environments that are characterized by the presence of institutions exerting a continuous action of standardization on their activities. The institutions accomplish this by communicating criteria of legitimacy that define the operating procedures and margins of success for these activities. This is what DiMaggio and Powell (1983) have demonstrated through the concepts of organizational field and institutional isomorphism. The organizational field is made up of the various actors (such as enterprises, public organizations, associations, unions) that provide reference standards and introduce beliefs influencing various dimensions of the life of each organization. Institutional isomorphism refers to the trend toward homogenization within a given field, (i) by imitation of the prevailing modes of operation, (ii) by pressures exercised through organizations and networks or (iii) by coercion, within the framework of legal rational domination (see Chapter 15 of this book).

With the notion of institutional isomorphism, DiMaggio and Powell (1983) focus on institutional reproduction, which is reinforced by numerous routines and identified at the level of productive units. They contribute significantly to understanding how an organization is ultimately influenced by its environment, irrespective of the organization's originality or the impetus for change it initially supports. Nevertheless, their framework is of limited use for apprehending the differences between organizations – which may persist, at least to a certain degree – and the emergence of innovations.

Neo-institutional sociology is thus primarily concerned with reproduction phenomena at the micro level. However, it may be complemented by another 'level of institutionality', as Magatti would put it (2004), which is more macro since it is based on the type of historical analysis developed by Polanyi.

1.3 Political embeddedness

For Polanyi (1944), political embeddedness refers to the way the economy is integrated into the political order. The economy is an institutionalized process in the sense that political rules control the forms of production and circulation of goods and services. Polanyi viewed modernity as the trend towards disembeddedness of the economy, which shows through the autonomization of the economic sphere, assimilated to a self-regulating market. Viewing the market as self-regulating, i.e. as a mechanism that matches supply and demand through prices, leads to overlooking the institutional changes that allowed its emergence and to forgetting the institutional structures that make it possible. In reality, the integrating factor constituted by the system of prices does not emerge only from economic exchange, but from an institutionalized process, i.e. it is socially organized.

The rationalistic and atomistic premises of neo-classical economics regarding human behaviour allow us to study the economy using a deductive method. This method uses the aggregate of individual behaviours in the market. Neo-classical economics excludes non-market phenomena from the analysis, except for explaining them – as does neo-institutional economics – as being the result of market failures; other institutional solutions (such as organizations, state intervention, the third sector) are only understood as 'complementing' the market, which is considered the first solution (Nyssens 2000). Political embeddedness is a fertile research concept since it differentiates itself from such an approach, embracing an analysis of institutions that does not reduce them to their supposed efficiency, but also emphasizes their role in the constitution of a democratic framework for economic activity.

The question of the relationship between economy and democracy cannot be regarded as secondary; Polanyi suggests a problematization of this question that extends the research initiated by the founders of economic sociology on the relationship between economy and society. Its originality may be summarized as follows.

In pre-capitalist societies, markets are limited and most economic phenomena that can be isolated are embedded in norms and institutions that predate and shape them. The modern economy distinguishes itself by its propensity for disembeddedness, i.e. by the autonomization of the economic sphere, which is assimilated to a self-regulating market. However, this propensity, because it disrupts society, generates a reaction of the latter, implying different forms of 're-embedding'. Real markets give way to various forms of political embeddedness.

In addition, the expansion of the market does not necessarily entail the end of economic forms based on redistribution and reciprocity. Redistribution and reciprocity endure in modern economies, in which the very structure of government redistribution demonstrates a certain embeddedness of the economy in politics (see Chapter 7 of this book). Thus, economic disembeddedness is only a general trend; indeed, the existence – besides the numerous market relationships – of non-market and non-monetary economic poles in the economy bear testimony to the persistence of many forms of embeddedness. Consequently, despite the significant impact of the project of a market society, the political embeddedness of the economy has not disappeared – and can be studied – in contemporary society. This political embeddedness is expressed, among other ways, through social rights and legislative and regulatory mechanisms, such as collective bargaining. Market autonomy is a liberal chimera that is periodically updated and thwarted through the creation of regulatory institutions. Societal initiatives emerge as a response to deregulatory pressures, ensuring that the functioning of the economy is embedded in rules bearing testimony to the respect of the democratic framework.

Thus, if we dialectize Polanyi's approach, we can hypothesize that economies in modern democracies are characterized by two trends. The first is the trend toward disembeddedness, the economy being reduced to a self-regulating market and to a single form of enterprise. The second is the opposite trend: a trend towards the political re-embedding of the economy. Relying on this interpretation with a view to explaining the relationship between third sector organizations and public policies, this chapter is thus based on a conceptualization expressed in terms of political embeddedness of economic activities. It approaches political embeddedness of the third sector though interactions with public authorities – interactions whose mutual effects vary considerably in terms of intensity and modalities over time.

The notion of the political embeddedness of economic activities thus seeks to shed light on all relations between public policies and third sector organizations. While the third sector cannot be apprehended without analysing the public regulation to which it is subject, government regulation alone does not determine the forms that the third sector has taken. We cannot fully understand the social construction of the third sector through an approach that analyses public policies as a separate, autonomous field. Historically, this social construction has been influenced by projects initiated by various social actors who, through their existence, have helped shape public regulation. Thus, the construction of this field cannot be considered as the mere product of a 'public' construction. Rather, it is the result of interaction among heterogeneous third sector organizations and public policies.

We will now refer to this framework of political embeddedness in order to test its heuristic relevance for the field of WISEs in the European Union.

2 The pioneering initiatives

In the European Union, the pioneering WISE initiatives were launched in the late 1970s–early 1980s, without any specific public scheme to support their objectives. In a context of increasing unemployment and social exclusion, social actors did not find public policy schemes adequate to tackle these problems. Initiatives thus emerged as a protest against established public policies and pointed at the limits of institutional public intervention practices towards those excluded from the labour market: long-term unemployed people, low-qualified people, people with social problems, etc.

Most pioneering WISEs were founded by civil society actors: social workers, associative militants, representatives of more traditional third sector organizations, sometimes with the excluded workers themselves.

Table 17.1 Distribution of some types of WISE in the European Union according to type of founders

Groups of citizens, with a general interest objective (1980s)	Excluded persons, with a self-help objective (1990s)	Public–community partnership
COSO Italy	STO Finland	LV Denmark
EFT, ES Belgium	WCO UK	KB Germany
EI, AI France	EI Spain	RQ France
BLUI Germany	SK Sweden	SF UK
EI Spain	EIN France	CB UK
LD Ireland		

Note: See Chapter 1, Appendix 2, of this book for legend.

Most of these initiatives were launched by persons whose main objective was to help persons excluded from the labour market, i.e. they were created in a perspective of general interest. In some countries with a tradition of co-operative entrepreneurship, some pioneering initiatives were launched by the workers themselves, relying on a self-help dynamic. Sometimes, the groups launching the WISEs were linked to public bodies and, in countries such as Germany or Denmark, probably reflected the fact that the third sector and the public sector were closely interwoven. Different types of initiators of WISE can coexist in the same country. In France, for example, 'work integration enterprises' (*enterprises d'insertion*) and 'intermediate voluntary organizations' (*associations intermédiaires*) have been launched by groups including both social workers and associative militants, whereas 'long-term work integration enterprises' (*enterprises insérantes*) rely on a self-help dynamic and some 'neighbourhood enterprises' (*régies de quartier*) have been supported through a partnership between the inhabitants and local public bodies (see Table 17.1).

3 WISEs and public policies

The processes of institutionalization of WISEs should be studied in the context of the boom in active labour market policies. During the 1980s, public bodies, faced with high rates of unemployment and a crisis in public finances, developed policies that aimed to integrate the unemployed into the labour market (through professional training programmes, job subsidy programmes, etc.), instead of relying only on passive labour market policies based on a system of allocation of cash benefits to the unemployed. In this context, it seems that WISEs have increasingly represented a tool for implementing these active labour market policies – a 'conveyor belt' of these policies. Indeed, they were pioneers in promoting the integration of excluded persons through a productive activity. The first WISEs actually implemented active labour market policies before they came into institutional existence.

However, we can observe, at least at the beginning of these processes of public institutionalization of WISEs, that some countries, such as Sweden and Denmark, which are characterized by a long tradition of social policies, used programmes other than employment programmes to sustain such pioneering initiatives; one example is the 'Social Development Programme' in Denmark. In other cases, WISEs whose main target groups are disabled people have also been recognized through traditional social policies.

In some countries, such as the United Kingdom or Spain, where welfare spending in general is low and labour market policies in particular are underdeveloped, pioneering initiatives received little, if any, public support. This also seems to be the case, in all the countries surveyed, for initiatives that rely more on a self-help dynamic. Indeed, public bodies seem to consider that workers developing their own initiatives should be considered as carrying out 'normal business' and do not need to receive any special support, even though they are at risk in the labour market regarding their profiles of employability.

3.1 The 'second labour market' programmes

At the beginning of the 1990s, in some countries, such as Belgium, Germany, France and Ireland, WISEs used programmes offering intermediate forms of employment, between employment policies and social policies; the so-called 'second labour market' provided for a substantial reduction, funded by the state, in employer costs. These programmes were based on the observation that, on the one hand, a number of unsatisfied social needs existed and, on the other hand, a large number of people were unemployed. These second labour market programmes thus tried to encourage the creation of new jobs in areas where they could satisfy social needs, as a means of both creating jobs for unemployed persons and curbing mainstream social spending. Examples of such programmes include the 'unemployment reduction programmes' (*programmes de résorption du chômage*) in Belgium, the 'employment-solidarity contracts' (*contrats emploi-solidarité*, or CES) in France, the 'work creation measures' (*Arbeitsbeschaffungsmassnahmen*, or ABM) in Germany and the 'Community Programme' in Ireland.

In these countries, this framework opened for many WISEs a space in which they could pursue their multiple mission, namely creating jobs for unskilled workers and carrying out a productive activity, and sometimes also producing social services. But the limitations of this kind of programme now appear quite clearly. The major problem from the point of view of the public bodies has been the gradual emergence of a second labour market which did not provide the real 'bridge' between unemployment and employment that the policies' designers had intended to create (Martin 2000). Indeed, evaluations have shown that the probability of finding a 'conventional' job is actually lower for workers who have benefited from these programmes than for those who have not. This is linked to a second problem, at least for WISEs engaged in production with a collective dimension, such as social services meeting needs left unmet by traditional organizations, be they public or private. Indeed, job integration and the provision of collective services are coming to be regarded as one and the same. This 'social management' of unemployment is a mechanism that leads to the devaluation of the jobs created, generating a range of perverse and unintended effects for the promoters of the projects and for users alike.

3.2 From the 'second labour market' to 'activating' labour market policies (after 1994–5)

We have witnessed, across all European countries, an evolution over time in the kind of active labour market policies public bodies have developed; this evolution has reflected the changing regulatory role of the state. Since the end of the 1990s, there has been a tendency to give unemployed persons more responsibility for improving their own individual employment opportunities. If the first generation of active labour market policies was a kind of mix between employment and social policies, the second generation of policies – which could be referred to as 'activating' – targets much more the employment goal. We have seen the development of a wide range of temporary subsidies conditional on hiring persons belonging to groups who are 'at risk in the labour market'; simultaneously, direct job creation through the second labour market has been declining. These 'second generation' measures are generally open to all kind of firms (for-profit, public or not-for-profit), developing a quasi-market logic in this field. The objective of this kind of measure is to facilitate the transition between unemployment and the 'first' labour market through temporary subsidies aimed at helping the workers overcome their 'temporary unemployability'.

Activating labour market policies find their most significant expression in the different kinds of 'integration contracts'; these are agreements between persons registered as unemployed and the Labour Offices. These contracts include an agreement on the rights and duties of both parties with a view to ensuring the quickest possible integration into the first labour market according to the profile of the unemployed person. If the unemployed person refuses to co-operate, for example by rejecting reasonable employment offers, the labour administrations can reduce social benefits.

In some cases, this 'active welfare state', which suggests a return of the concept of responsibility in the field of social and employment policies, has fostered co-operation with social enterprises, especially at the local level. Indeed, we have to underline the increasing responsibility of local public authorities, whose autonomy to organize training and design and implement work-integration paths has increased. This seems especially to be the case in countries such as Germany, Denmark or Sweden. In this framework, social enterprises, for-profit enterprises and public organizations are on an equal footing as regards 'integration contracts' and, therefore, a quasi-market logic is de facto implemented.

3.3 The accreditation of WISEs

In some countries, WISEs are officially recognized and a specific public scheme supports their mission at the national level (this is, for example, the case in Portugal, France, Ireland and Finland) or at the regional level (for example in Belgium, Spain and Italy).

This legal recognition, by public authorities, of the mission of integration through work performed by WISEs allows, in most cases, a more stable access to public subsidies, but in a very specific way. Indeed, some temporary subsidies are granted to start the initiative and to make up for the 'temporary unemployability' of the workers. In fact, these public schemes are a tool of active labour market policies. In this sense, they recognize and support the actions of WISEs and, at the same time, they influence their objectives and target groups, as we will develop below.

In some cases, these 'labelled' social enterprises must adopt a new company legal form reflecting their social purpose, such as the form of 'social purpose company' (*société à finalité sociale/vennootschap met sociaal oogmerk*) in Belgium or that of 'community interest company' in the UK.

3.4 WISEs and public policies: a typology

As we see in Table 17.2, different models can coexist within one country. However, the analysis of the general patterns of labour market policy expenditures (see Figure 17.1) allows us to construct a typology of the countries surveyed.

The first group (which includes Denmark and Sweden) is characterized by a high level of active labour market policies (ALMP) and of welfare expenditure in general. In these countries, no public schemes specific to WISEs have been developed, but there is an increasing collaboration between WISEs and public bodies to implement 'activating labour market policies'. As Stryjan stresses for Sweden, the current Swedish labour market is, to a significant extent, the product of active labour market policy. In this context, WISEs are not the result of a shortage of active labour market policies but are, rather, a response to the fact that such facilities either cannot reach significant portions of the population, or are ineffective for certain groups (see Chapter 13 of this book). This is quite a new phenomenon for these countries, where the third sector is traditionally viewed as having an advocacy role and not that of a service provider. This first group corresponds to the 'universalist' group of Esping-Andersen's typology – a group in which welfare has traditionally been delivered by the state

Table 17.2 WISEs and public policies in the European Union countries

Public policies	1980s–	mid-1990s mid-1990s	2000s
Nothing	Worker co-ops (S)		
Social policies	Social development programme (DK)		
Active labour market policies			
Second labour market programme	CES (F)* PRC (B)* ABM (G)* Com. prog. (IRL)*		
'Activating policies'	–	Everywhere in Europe	
Specific WISE policy schemes 'Public accreditation'	COSO (I)**	EI (F) (B)**	Social ent. (FIN) EI (P)** SEW (IRL)**

*CES = 'employment-solidarity contracts' (*contrats emploi-solidarité*), France; PRC = 'unemployment reduction programmes' (*programmes de résorption du chômage*), Belgium; ABM = 'Work creation measures' (*Arbeitsbeschaffungsmassnahmen*), Germany; Com. Prog. = 'Community Programme', Ireland.

**See Chapter 1, Appendix 2 of this book for legend.

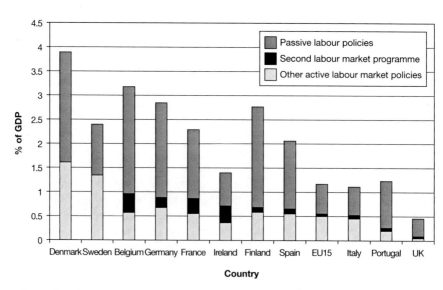

Figure 17.1 Expenditure on labour market policies in the European Union countries in 2001 (percentage of gross domestic product)

Source: Eurostat.

(Esping-Andersen 1999). But, even if there is no official accreditation for social enterprises in Sweden and Denmark, there is in these countries a tradition of a co-operative movement. So it is not surprising to see that there is now a Swedish Minister of the Social Economy rooted in this co-operative movement, and that there are linkages and lines of communication between the co-operative movement and new social enterprises.

The countries in the second group (Belgium, Germany, France and Ireland) still have relatively high levels of expenditure on active labour market policies (although lower than the countries in the first group) and large second labour market programmes. The first WISEs in these countries relied heavily on this latter kind of programme. All these countries, except Ireland, belong to the 'Bismarckian' tradition or the 'corporatist' group of countries, i.e. in these countries, intermediate bodies are important not only for the management of social insurance but also for the delivery of social services (Esping-Andersen 1999). Indeed these countries (Salamon *et al.* 1999) are characterized by a significant presence of not-for-profit private organizations, mainly financed by public bodies, in the field of social services. Not surprisingly, it is in these countries that the 'second labour market programmes' emerged; they relied on this kind of organization. The inclusion of Ireland in this second group may seem rather odd as it does not belong to this Bismarckian tradition. Nevertheless, Ireland has one of the highest shares of employment in the non-profit sector, which relies heavily on public funding. Actually, some research has shown that Ireland is a borderline case between the 'liberal' and the 'corporatist' state (Hicks and Kenworthy 2003). In the 1990s, the countries in this second group adopted public schemes specific to WISEs; the only exception is Germany – which probably reflects the decline of the co-operative movement in this country. In the other countries, the persistence of a social economy sector or a co-operative sector that still maintains some of its original features influences the environmental perception of WISEs and the building of organizational identities within this tradition (see Chapter 15 of this book).

A third group (Finland, the United Kingdom, Portugal, Spain and Italy) appears to be much more eclectic than the other two, but the countries composing it are characterized by a low level of expenditure on active labour market policies and, more fundamentally, by the (near) non-existence of a second labour market programme. Regarding the development of a public scheme specific to WISEs, Italy – as already mentioned – played a pioneering role in the European Union, thanks to the action of its strong co-operative movement. In the countries of this group that do not have such a historical heritage, the situation is in rapid evolution at the moment, due among other factors to the increasing number of interactions – and probably a certain homogenization – between European Union initiatives and national public policies. Portugal and the UK are now experimenting with an increase in their ALMP, and public schemes specific to WISEs viewed as an ALMP tool have recently been adopted in these countries, as well as in Finland.

3.5 Support to WISEs through public contracts

Another way for public authorities to support the mission of WISEs is through the contracting out of the provision of goods or services. Indeed, public bodies can organize their purchases in different ways: that of traditional market purchases (when the bid with the lowest price, for the level of quality required, is chosen) and that of purchases motivated by social or socio-political criteria (see Chapter 7 of this book).

Socio-politically motivated purchases can be made, on the one hand, when small amounts are involved, in which case public bodies are allowed to contract directly with WISEs without issuing a call for tender. The purchases occur in a discretionary way: when they have to buy a product or service, the (usually local) public bodies simply 'privilege' WISEs they know in order to support them and their social mission. On the other hand, in the case of larger purchases, when for instance the public bodies have to issue public calls for tenders, some social dimensions can be included in these public procurement procedures, for example in the form of social clauses that take into account types of criteria other than market ones, such as the importance of integrating disadvantaged workers. These are ways – formalised or not through regulations – to support both the production and the work integration goals of WISEs.

Figure 17.2 illustrates the share of sales to public bodies in the total resources of the WISEs of the PERSE project sample in 2001 as well as the motivations for these sales. Irish and Portuguese WISEs' resources are not very dependent on contracts with public bodies, whereas a relatively important part of the resources of Danish, Italian and Spanish WISEs is constituted by sales of goods and services to public bodies.

In Spain, public-sector customers tend to be important to WISEs, for whom winning a public contract has been, on a number of occasions, a decisive factor in the WISE's success, but the majority of these sales are on a traditional basis. In Denmark and Italy, public contracts are very important for WISEs and, conversely to what happens in Spain, the majority are motivated by socio-political criteria. In Italy, where active labour market policies were not as developed as in other European Union countries (see Figure 17.1), the mission of social co-operatives has long been sustained by public contracts. Indeed, the Italian case is the oldest in the European Union concerning the introduction of a social dimension into public purchasing: in 1991, a law was passed which reserved certain public markets to social co-operatives. But this law had to be re-examined following objections from the European Commission; as we will see in the next section, it is at the level of European legislation that the principal debate in this matter occurs today.

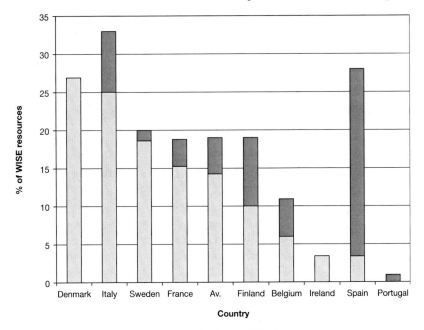

Figure 17.2 Sales of WISEs to public bodies in 2001*

Black: traditional contracts with public bodies for the sale of goods or services.
Grey: contracts with public bodies for the sale of goods or services motivated by socio-political criteria.
Av.: average of the results for the sample of the PERSE project.
* In nine of the eleven countries of the PERSE research project; for the two remaining countries, data were not available.
Source: Eurostat.

The main difficulties WISEs experience relate to their need to combine specific social purposes, such as creating jobs for disadvantaged persons, with the need to generate financial resources from the market. It thus sometimes seems difficult for WISEs to compete in the market with for-profit companies solely on the basis of financial criteria, and some WISEs demand that public authorities take their social dimension into account when awarding public contracts. The practice of inserting social criteria in public contracts is not yet very extensive in the European Union. They do not exist in countries such as Ireland, Portugal, the United Kingdom and Spain; legislation is evolving in other countries (such as Belgium), which are considering introducing social clauses into public tenders. National and regional practices in this matter are relatively diverse across the European Union.

3.6 The role of European public policies

What is the role of the European Union, if any, in supporting the development of WISEs? The share of WISEs' subsidies that comes from the

European Union level is quantitatively low, ranging from 0 to 10 per cent of the total resources of the WISEs in the PERSE project sample; such subsidies come mainly from the European Social Fund.

Although quantitatively quite low, European subsidies have in some cases constituted an important factor in the emergence and development of WISEs, sometimes opening new channels of resource mobilization at the national level. The influence of the European Commission also appears through the elaboration of the 'National Action Plans for Employment', in which active labour market policy recommendations occupy a major place and explicit reference is sometimes made to social economy organizations in the field of work integration. This has contributed, in some countries (such as Portugal or Ireland), to the development of public schemes for WISEs.

Social clauses in public tenders are regulated by different rules inside the European Union (Navez 2005). Below certain thresholds, national law prevails, but must respect the general principles of the Treaties, such as non-discrimination, freedom of circulation, etc. Above these thresholds, the Member States have to apply the European directives for intra-community purchases and the Agreement on Government Procurement, concluded within the framework of the World Trade Organisation, for other purchases. The debate in the European Commission seems to be underpinned by the general idea that the interest of public bodies is to follow strict value-for-money criteria when choosing a provider. The Commission does not prohibit any ethical, social or environmental consideration but the pre-eminence of short-term financial aspects strongly limits the possibilities of taking social criteria into account. Since March 2004, the main debate has concerned the evolution of the European legislation and the possibility of taking social and ethical dimensions into account in public procurement. More particularly, the issue concerns the latitude that the new European directives will leave to the diverse national practices and legislations in this matter.

4 Institutionalization paths: convergences and divergences in national contexts

When talking about the political embeddedness of WISEs, we refer both to their contribution to the development of public policies and, conversely, to the influence of public policies on their development.

The first wave of European WISEs emerged in contestation of traditional public policies, in some countries with no WISE-specific public scheme and with no public support, and in other countries with support obtained through social policies or second labour market programmes. Generally, these pioneering WISEs relied on a wide mix of resources: market resources, resources coming from reciprocity and an eclectic range of public subsidies. As we have also already noted, in the 1980s WISEs played a pioneering role in developing active labour market policies. In Italy, for example, the level of expenditure in the field of active labour market policies was near zero at the beginning of the 1980s and nowadays is still quite low; social co-operatives can be considered to have implemented, through a bottom-up process, the first active labour market policies.

In a second phase, of 'dialogue', the development of some pioneering initiatives led, in some countries (such as Italy, France and Belgium), to new public schemes specific to WISEs. We can underline again the pioneering case of Italy, where a new legal form, the 'social co-operative', was recognized in 1991, beside the traditional legal forms of commercial companies, co-operatives and non-profit organizations. The really innovative feature lies in the recognition of a legal business form with a social purpose, rather than in the amount of public money received in itself. Indeed, these social co-operatives receive de facto much less public financing than some WISEs in other countries. If some pioneering initiatives led to the public recognition of WISEs, at the same time, this recognition stimulated a boom in these initiatives.

However, this phase of dialogue has not always been smooth. Indeed, the accommodation between the views of WISEs and those of public bodies on the contested nature of WISEs' mission does not seem to be easy (see Chapter 15 of this book). This explains, on the one hand, why some pioneering initiatives chose not to use these WISE-specific public schemes; this is, for example, the case of the 'local development' initiatives in Ireland, which did not adopt the 'social economy' framework. On the other hand, it should be noted that, if public schemes encourage some initiatives, they also exclude others. In France, for instance, the institutionalization process recognized and favoured initiatives launched by professional and associative militant actors aiming at the integration through work of disadvantaged populations, whereas the initiatives originating from these populations themselves were, in most cases, neglected.

In other countries, such as Portugal, WISEs emerged as a result of a specific public scheme, partly under the pressure of the 'National Action Plans for Employment' developed in dialogue with the European Commission. These WISEs are only weakly embedded in the social fabric and rely on a public scheme that appears to be somewhat artificial (see Chapter 12 of this book).

In other countries still, no public schemes and/or legal forms of this kind were set up. It seems that particular cultural experiences in these countries (such as, for example, the decline of the co-operative movement in Germany) impeded WISEs from becoming a model with an identity of its own. The situation in these countries contrasts with that in countries such as Italy, France, Spain and Belgium, where the idea of a social economy or a co-operative sector that co-exists with a for-profit sector is widely acknowledged.

Beyond the existence or non-existence of public schemes specific to WISEs, we can observe, in every country surveyed, the increasing influence of activating labour market policies that are used by WISEs. These schemes, as explained, tend to give temporary subsidies to compensate for the temporary 'unemployability' of the workers and are, generally, open to all kinds of enterprises. They locate, de facto, WISEs in a quasi-market logic of placement of target groups in the 'normal labour market'. We will analyse the impacts of this kind of public scheme on WISEs in the next section.

Quite often, we observe that WISEs use a mix of different public policies to pursue their multiple-goal mission. For example, a WISE can take part in a WISE-specific public scheme and receive the public money attached to it and, at the same time, hire some workers in the framework of other active labour market schemes and mobilize social policies to sustain its mission, whether of social integration or otherwise.

Finally, it should be noted that a 'private' path of institutionalization can coexist with the public one described above; it works through self-accreditation and self-networking processes outside any legal framework. In this case, a group of WISEs develop, among themselves, a set of criteria to be fulfilled in order to be accredited.

5 Public policies and the goals of WISEs

Social enterprises usually have a complex mix of goals (see Chapter 2 of this book). For WISEs, we have distinguished between the goals linked to the work and social integration of their target groups and those linked to the production of goods and services.

What are the impacts of public policies on these goals? Indeed, if public policies recognize the existence of WISEs and some of their roles, public regulation also entails a risk of reducing the autonomy and the innovation capacity of WISEs.

5.1 Regarding the work and social integration goal

The dominant model of public policies tends to recognize only one kind of benefit, namely those benefits linked to the work integration goal, in the framework of active labour market policies. The final goal of all these measures is the placement of the worker into the 'normal labour market'. In this sense, the goal of the social integration of the workers does not fit well into this kind of measure.

Given the temporary character of public support, WISEs tend to provide transitional jobs, supported by temporary subsidies, and/or try to create permanent self-financed jobs, after a possible temporary subsidy. The temporary nature of the subsidies can lead to the phenomenon of skimming. This means that there is an incentive for the enterprises to hire only the workers most likely to be 'cost-effective' by the end of the project and to retain only those who have attained this level of 'cost-effectiveness' when the subsidized period ends. With the process of institutionalization, WISEs would tend to adopt a single-goal structure, with the (re)integration of their workers into the normal labour market becoming their only aim.

However, we have underlined (see Chapter 11 of this book) the diversity of the profiles of WISE beneficiaries. There are some workers who most probably suffer from 'temporary unemployability'; for those workers, short-term subsidies can be a springboard either to integrate into the normal labour market or to stay in the social enterprise without any public financing. But other groups may suffer from a variety of problems that have long-lasting effects on their productivity. These people might be unable to find work because of a shortage of jobs adapted to their profile. The question is then whether the social enterprise can either develop their human and social capital sufficiently to allow them to find a job in the normal labour market or develop stable jobs corresponding to these workers' profiles. This diversity in the profiles of the workers targeted by WISEs leads to the conclusion that the types of public scheme (length and level of public financing) supporting the work integration goal cannot be uniform for the different groups of workers.

There remain, in the European landscape, WISEs targeting the most disadvantaged groups in the labour market; public bodies accept that they should give these WISEs permanent subsidies in the framework of a specific public scheme. However, this is a residual model in the landscape of WISE-specific public schemes. In this case, WISEs are operating in a 'sheltered labour market', and they are better able to socially integrate their workers.

5.2 *Regarding the production goal*

WISEs value their production goal, at least as a means of support for their work and social integration objective. Indeed, carrying out a continuous activity of production of goods and services, facing a certain level of economic risk and pursuing the integration of their workers through a productive activity are all parts of WISEs' identity (see Chapter 2 of this book). 'These tasks allow the disadvantaged people to work under conditions close to those of the "first labour market" – in comparable work situations, fulfilling meaningful tasks, but with a recognition of their disadvantages' (Davister *et al.* 2004). All WISE-specific public schemes valorise this mission of WISEs – the production goal – as the main support for work integration.

Moreover, a subset of WISEs also provide quasi-collective products (for example, social services) and valorise this kind of production in itself, as being important for the collectivity, not only as a means of achieving their integration goal. The choice of this kind of production is sometimes indirectly imposed by public schemes regulating these social enterprises (as in the 'integration companies' in Portugal or in the 'Social Economy Programme' in Ireland), which state that WISEs can only develop products that are 'additional' to already existing types of products and services, i.e. that are not provided by a state actor nor by a market actor. In most cases, this leads WISEs to explore and test new concepts and products, with a low profitability but with a collective dimension: social services, services linked to the environment, etc. But public schemes do not generally recognize this collective dimension of WISEs' production and these policies provide no specific financing for this type of production goal.

To overcome this problem, WISEs develop practices of partnership with local public authorities for the contracting out of public services. In some countries, these sales to public bodies, as we saw, are important and are a sign that public bodies recognize WISEs for their productive activity and not only through active labour market policies (see Figure 17.2). But, as underlined in Chapter 15, the way of contracting out these services – or, more broadly, the style of public governance in this arena – has changed the rules of the game for many WISEs. 'While it holds true that the handing over of these services has initially provided WISEs with a (sheltered) market in which disadvantaged people could experience real work settings, public bodies have increasingly devolved economic risk upon private agencies. As some country reports (Italy, UK) point out, the practice of competitive tendering, applied to markets in which WISEs are active, has obliged the latter to behave more like their for-profit competitors and to risk neglecting their social missions' (Chapter 15, pp. 250–1). This points to the importance of developing a socio-political motivation in public bodies' contractual relations with WISEs.

Conclusions

The concept of embeddedness put forward by the new sociological approaches to the economy enriches the potential of research, as compared to contingency analysis. This is particularly true when studying the third sector which, since it is the result of different forms of interaction processes between heterogeneous initiatives and public policies, cannot be studied without taking the analysis of the public regulation into account. That is why we followed Polanyi's problematization of the relations between economy and democracy – which cannot be considered as secondary. Polanyi suggests a conceptualization in terms of the political embeddedness of economic activities, the latter being defined as the set of interactions between public bodies and initiatives, interactions that lead to mutual effects whose intensity and modalities vary over time.

The study of WISEs in the European Union has confirmed their embeddedness in the political context. We have analysed the multiple interactions between WISEs and public policies through the progressive institutionalization of these organizations; the nature of the interactions between public bodies and WISEs has proved a key element in WISEs' development.

The first European WISEs emerged 'in contestation' of traditional public policies, in some countries with no WISE-specific legal scheme and with no public support, and in other countries with support obtained by mobilizing social policies or second labour market programmes. They played a pioneering role in developing active labour market policies in the 1980s, implementing the latter before their institutionalization.

In a second phase, of 'dialogue' between public policies and WISEs, some countries developed new public schemes specific to WISEs. But such dialogue has not always been smooth and has not resolved the debate about the contested nature of WISEs. If public schemes encouraged some initiatives, they also excluded others, for instance the WISEs characterized more by a self-help dynamic in France. More generally, active labour market policies increasingly constituted the framework in which WISEs developed and which, to some degree, framed their objectives and actions. WISEs are thus socio-politically embedded organizations, and as such they reflect the changing regulatory role of the state – including the development, since the end of the 1990s, of so-called 'activating labour market policies'. These have in some cases fostered the co-operation of the public bodies with WISEs.

As has just been mentioned, accommodating the views of WISEs with those of public bodies on the nature of the mission of WISEs does not seem to be easy. We can understand, then, why some WISEs choose not to embark upon such a path of institutionalization, but prefer to take private paths of institutionalization that can coexist with the public one.

Review questions

- Why does the embeddedness concept permit us to enrich the potentialities of research compared to the contingency analysis?
- Why has the dialogue between social enterprises and public bodies not always been smooth?
- In your country, which are the different channels through which public bodies support the mission of WISEs?

Note

1   That is, the limits to human mental capacity that make it impossible to predict all possible contingencies and to determine, for each of these contingencies, the optimal behaviour (Milgrom and Roberts 1992).

Bibliography

Bélanger, P.R. and Lévesque, B. (1992) 'Éléments théoriques pour une sociologie d'entreprise', *Cahiers de recherche sociologique*, 18–19, Université du Québec à Montréal.

Burns, T. and Stalker, G.M. (1961) *The Management of Innovation*, London: Tavistock.

Coase, R. (1937) 'The Nature of the Firm', *Economica*, 4: 386–405.

Crozier, M. (1963) *Le phénomène bureaucratique*, Paris: Le Seuil.

Crozier, M. (1989) *L'entreprise à l'écoute*, Paris: Interéditions.

Crozier, M. and Friedberg, E. (1977) *L'acteur et le système*, Paris: Le Seuil.

Davister, C., Defourny, J. and Grégoire, O. (2004) 'Work Integration Social Enterprises in the European Union: an Overview of Existing Models', *Working Papers Series*, 04/04, Liège: EMES European Research Network.

De Léonardis, O. (2001) *Le istituzioni*, Rome: Carocci.

DiMaggio, P. and Powell, W.W. (1983) 'The Iron Cage Revisited: Institutional Isomorphism and Collective Rationality in Organizational Fields', *American Sociological Review*, 48, April.

Esping-Andersen, G. (1999) *Social Foundation of Postindustrial Economies*, New York: Oxford University Press.

Evers, A. and Laville, J.-L. (2004) *The Third Sector in Europe*, Cheltenham: Edward Elgar.

Eymard-Duvernay, F. (2004) *Economie politique de l'entreprise*, Paris: La Découverte.

Granovetter, M. (2000) 'L'ancienne et la nouvelle sociologie économique: histoire et programme', in Granovetter, M., *Le marché autrement*, Paris: Desclée de Brouwer.

Hicks, A. and Kenworthy, K. (2003) 'Varieties of Welfare Capitalism', *Socio-Economic Review*, 1: 27–61.

Laville, J.-L. and Nyssens, M. (2000) 'Solidarity-Based Third Sector Organizations in the "Proximity Services" Field: a European Francophone Perspective', in *Voluntas, International Journal of Voluntary and Nonprofit Organizations*, New York: Kluwer Academic/Plenum Publishers, 11, 1, March: 67–84.

Laville, J.-L., Caillé, A., Chanial, P., Dacheux, E., Eme, B. and Latouche, S. (2001) *Association, démocratie et société civile*, Paris: La Découverte.

Lawrence, P. and Lorsch, J. (1973) *Adapter les structures de l'entreprise*, Paris: Éditions d'Organisation.

Linhard, D. (1991) *Les torticolis de l'autruche. L'éternelle modernisation des entreprises françaises*, Paris: Seuil.

Magatti, M. (2004) 'Après la nouvelle sociologie économique. Quelques pistes théoriques et de recherche', in La Rosa, M. and Laville, J.-L. (eds) 'La sociologie économique européenne. Une rencontre franco-italienne', *Sociologia del Lavoro*, Supplément spécial 93, Milan: FrancoAngeli, 45–61.

Martin, J. (2000) 'What works among active labour market policies: evidence from OECD countries experiences', *Economic Studies*, 1, 30: 79–113.

Milgrom, P. and Roberts, J. (1992) *Economics, Organization and Management*, Englewood Cliffs, NJ: Prentice-Hall International.

Mintzberg, H. (1983) *Structures et dynamiques des organisations*, Paris: Éditions d'Organisation.

Navez, F. (2005) 'Marchés publics et éthique: évolution des directives européennes et du droit belge', paper presented to the *ISTR-EMES Conference*, Paris, April.

North, D. (1996) 'Epilogue: Economic Performance Through Time', in Alston, L., Eggertsson, T. and North, D. (eds) *Empirical studies in Institutional Change*, Cambridge: Cambridge University Press, 342–55.

Nyssens, M. (2000) 'Les approches économiques du tiers-secteur, apports et limites des analyses anglo-saxonnes d'inspiration néo-classique', *Sociologie du travail*, 42: 551–65.

Piotet, F. and Sainsaulieu, R. (1994) *Méthodes pour une sociologie de l'entreprise*, Paris: Presses de la Fondation Nationale des Sciences Politiques, ANACT.

Polanyi, K. (1944) *The Great Transformation: the Political and Economic Origins of our Time*, New York: Farrar and Rinehart.

Rizza, R. (2004) 'Néo-institutionnalisme sociologique et nouvelle sociologie économique: quelles relations?', in La Rosa, M. and Laville, J.-L. (eds) 'La sociologie économique européenne. Une rencontre franco-italienne', *Sociologia del Lavoro*, Supplément spécial 93, Milan: FrancoAngeli, 76–98.

Salamon, L., Sokolowski, S. W. and List, R. (1999) *Global Civil Society: Dimension of the Nonprofit sector*, Baltimore, MD: Johns Hopkins University.

Simon, H.A. (1996) *Models of My Life* (reissue), Cambridge, MA: The MIT Press.

Williamson, O. (1975) *Markets and Hierarchies*, New York: Free Press.

Williamson, O. (1985) *The Economic Institutions of Capitalism*, New York: Free Press.

18 Where do we go from here? The unfinished story of work integration social enterprises in Germany

Ingo Bode, Adalbert Evers and Andreas Schulz

Overview

This chapter presents the history of German WISEs by retracing several periods, each of them indicative of a distinctive agenda of public policies and organizational development. This history was marked by a shift towards using WISEs for the mere management of jobless people, thus increasingly marginalizing the theoretical and material foundations most WISEs had built on originally, namely combining the generation of income, training, job creation and services for the public good. After reading this chapter, the reader should:

- identify the different contexts in which German WISEs have developed;
- understand the impacts of these different contexts on the goals of German WISEs;
- be aware of the specific nature of East German WISEs.

Introduction

In 2004, in Germany, the so-called 'Hartz reforms', named after the head of a commission on labour market reforms, triggered massive protests. These reforms cut back the rights of the long-term unemployed and introduced institutional reform, which, while promising individualised case management support in the future, in fact brought in, above all, more administrative control and hardships for the unemployed. The protests concentrated in the new *Länder*, where the average level of unemployment (about 20 per cent) was twice as high as in the old *Länder*, and where many considered these reforms to be part of a broader context characterized by a general feeling of being left facing an insecure and depressing economic and social future. The reforms implemented a new system in which the long-term unemployed (i.e. those who had been unemployed for more than one year) were no longer guaranteed a special status regarding their entitlement to allowances and the conditions linked thereto; in this respect they are now treated according to social assistance rules. To some extent, the protests were also fuelled by the fact that changes in labour market administration and in social entitlements were not seen to remedy the huge job deficit. With an eye on this, the Minister for Economic and Labour Affairs announced, during the heated debate on the Hartz reforms, plans to create about half a million 'one-euro jobs'. He thereby suddenly pushed to the foreground an element that had been a non-issue in the whole concept of the Hartz reforms and in government policies of the previous years: the creation of job opportunities outside the mainstream labour market. The new programme provides that the long-term unemployed (and especially the young ones among them) are to be placed in various areas of public utility (such as gardening, care work, etc.); the symbolic amount of money (one or two euros per hour) they receive for that work is in addition to their social assistance allowance.

Those who are expected to employ these 'one-euro jobbers' – namely, public sector agencies and third sector organizations – look with mixed feelings at this offer from the government, and so do many of the long-term unemployed. The idea of subsidising employment outside the ordinary labour market is by no means new, and the prevailing experience was that the conditions under which such employment could be provided had considerably worsened. In recent years, it had been considered that more effective labour market policies of placement and activation would be sufficient; generating work opportunities through the creation of additional jobs was left to private labour markets, economic recovery and general growth policies. Programmes aiming to create such additional work opportunities through (co)financing time-limited jobs were judged to be economically ineffective, and the organizations that had co-operated with such programmes – among them work integration social enterprises (WISEs) – were seen as outdated. At present, it seems that these organizations are being rediscovered as – at least politically and socially – useful instruments. The one-euro jobs have brought them back onto the agenda – although in a different form. The overall message is that something has to be done to give long-term unemployed citizens not only some money but also access to gainful employment outside the existing labour markets, and that public authorities should support the creation of such work opportunities. The government hopes that in various areas of public utility, voluntary organizations and public bodies will create such jobs, but special agencies such as WISEs will probably be needed to structure the fields and projects.

The story is still unfinished, but the tale so far will be told in the following. This chapter first portrays a quite representative German WISE, the *Diakoniewerk Arbeit & Kultur*; by so doing, it illustrates the complex evolution linked with a changing policy environment. Thereafter, it presents the history of WISEs by retracing several periods, each of them indicative of a distinctive agenda of public policies and organizational development. It will be shown that the history of WISEs was marked by some high hopes in the beginning and a shift towards using WISEs for the mere management of jobless people in later times, increasingly marginalizing the idea and material foundations most WISEs had built on originally: namely, combining income, training, job creation and services for the public good, with support from public policies.

1 An example from the field: The *Diakoniewerk Arbeit & Kultur*

Four main types of social integration enterprise active in the field of labour market policy in Germany have been identified on the basis of the EMES criteria: social firms and co-operatives, set up by unemployed people to create their own job; municipally owned social enterprises, which mainly aim at the integration of the local long-term unemployed; social enterprises organized by welfare organizations, which aim at reducing poverty and social exclusion; and social enterprises set up by local initiatives, which share these objectives but also aim at bettering local cultural and social services, integrating migrants, or providing other services of special local importance. The *Diakoniewerk Arbeit & Kultur* (DW), which is situated in the Ruhr area, belongs to the category of social enterprises organized by welfare organizations, but its profile (or, in other words, the scope of its activities) makes it quite representative of many German WISEs and it is in fact part of a new generation of more autonomous social service agencies. The DW is involved in work integration schemes and it has been developing various activities deemed to be for the public good, ranging from retailing recycled goods (especially cloth and furniture) via cultural activities to distributing food to the poor. Various training measures are also carried out.

During the 1980s, the DW began to run employment programmes funded by the regional labour office. This was originally done on a provisional basis and with one or two dozen employees working in a recycling project located in a dilapidated building. In 1993, the umbrella organization sought to extend this activity and appointed a new manager. From that moment on, the DW has expanded rapidly. At the end of the 1990s, it employed as many as 170 workers and was engaged in several businesses. Thousands of euros were invested in modernising the building; four second-hand shops were opened, and the management team was expanded to include professionals in training and placement. The core idea of the DW has always been to fight unemployment by offering temporary work in occupational fields supposed to serve unmet social, ecological and cultural needs. Now at the end of the 1990s the concept was given a thorough underpinning by the social enterprise initiative. The organization's civic mission became its guideline for the choice of new products and services, such as the sale of recycled furniture and clothes or providing handyman and other services to private households. The organization further reinforced this emphasis in 2001 by launching a food distribution project: it adopted the concept of the so-called 'Tafel' (dinner-table), which consists of recovering unused food from local firms and supermarkets and delivering it to social agencies and individuals in need. Another element of this strategy was the creation of a 'culture shuttle' for elderly people with an interest in cultural events, this service being linked to subsidized tickets for those who cannot afford to pay the admission. There have also been growing efforts to use the enterprise's central premises as a meeting point for local inhabitants, for instance, by organizing festivities or running a café.

The DW has always relied heavily on public employment (and training) programmes. The decision to expand and professionalise the business was built on an agreement concluded in the framework of local social policy networks. However, the fixed-term character of the employment has always been perceived by the organization as a constraint on its mission, since part of the DW's clientele is considered as unemployable in the first labour market in the short run; moreover, the workers still preserve some influence on the type and scope of their activities. This vision has become ever less realistic, though. In recent years, the organization has begun to adapt its formal structures to what the labour office and public authorities have been requiring ever more urgently, i.e. a rapid placement of the clientele wherever. A sub-department for placement has been created, and the internal arrangements for training and social work have been adjusted to the aforementioned demand. Moreover, the policy has been adopted of being severe with those workers who do not fully respect the rules of the (placement) game. The organization reports a growing tension in its relations with the labour office. While shaped in the past by a high degree of informal communication, the organization now faces strict standards of accountancy.

Yet the organization is not powerless. The manager is rooted in the municipal policy establishment and maintains good relations with the Church which sponsors the organization (the *Diakonie* is the welfare organization associated with the protestant Church in Germany), despite the fact that the DW has recently become formally independent. The manager thus has a good deal of social capital at his disposal, which allows the DW to exert significant local influence; it was, for example, able to counteract initiatives by local politicians who wished to move all subsidized employment to private firms. As a matter of fact, some private firms had been critical of the DW because they were afraid to lose market share, for instance in the handyman field. However, the organization managed to find a compromise, by agreeing to cease advertising its services. With old-style second labour market policies being abandoned in the DW's area as well, the organization found new ways to preserve its business. Nowadays, for instance, social assistance recipients work in the DW on the basis of the aforementioned 'one-euro jobs'. The manager, however, asserts that the organization does not accept workers who are forced into these jobs by the labour market administration.

On the whole, the DW has succeeded in upholding some operational flexibility. This is also due to a flow of 'market' income that still makes up 20 per cent of its budget, even though some second-hand clothes shops had to be closed down owing to constant losses. Given its focus on activities deemed to contribute to the economic well-being of disadvantaged customers, its contribution to local welfare and its emphasis on the social empowerment of the employed clientele, it can be considered that the DW has not completely left the course it adopted at the outset. The organization continues to lobby for policies that conform to its social mission. However, the placement rationale and the challenge of making money in the market have become increasingly important in the everyday business, and the original approach of linking work integration to the delivery of social welfare is put under serious strain.

2 Pathways and contexts of non-profit work integration

The evolution of the example sketched above and of whole generations of WISEs cannot be understood without exploring the broader context of social and institutional change in which these organizations have grown up. The wave of WISE start-ups reached its highest level during the 1980s. Since then, the movement has slowed down considerably. While the numbers of jobs and services provided have only slightly decreased, there have been successive changes in the dominant approaches in the non-profit sector (to which most WISEs belong), in the make-up of civil society, and in the strategy-set of the welfare state. Drawing upon the literature concerned with work integration agencies (including Evers and Schulze-Böing 2001; Bode 2003, 2005; Evers 2003), we propose to retrace the history of WISEs by distinguishing several periods; these are sketched in Table 18.1 and explained in more detail in the following sections.

2.1 Independent projects and civic concern – WISEs in their foundation period

The early stage in the development of WISEs was largely shaped by actors rooted in the new social movements. With the start of the crisis in the labour market and the growing exclusion of young people from (vocational) training, it was basically students and practitioners of social work who fashioned new concepts of democratic learning and collective enterprise, with a particular attention to the most disadvantaged (Reisch 2001). Many of the social enterprises created at that time were based on

Table 18.1 Dynamics in and around the organizational field of WISEs

Evolutionary stages of WISEs	Dominating rationale			
	Civil society	*Third sector*	*Welfare state*	*Employment policy*
Foundation period	New social movements	Socio-political approach	Keynesian corporatism	Using work integration agencies for the creation of a second labour market and as 'shock-absorbers'
East Germany	*Eastern avant-gardism and 'civil society import' from the West*	*Transitory welfare approach*	*Reunification-related interventionism*	
Settling	Institutional-isation of movements and new domains for 'traditional' forces	Socio-administrative approach	Post-Keynesian corporatism and 'activation' policies	Using work integration agencies for transitional employment
East Germany	*System integration*	*Institutional-isation*		
Normalization I (East and West)	Professional-isation	(Social) business approach	Post-corporatist managerialism	Using work integration agencies for improving employability and for placement
Present – Normalization II?	?	?	?	?

independent projects and had an identity of their own. They promoted unconventional ways of producing goods and services with a steady work-force. The welfare state rapidly came in, yet without interfering much with the organizations' activities at this point: funding non-profits for services largely specified by their providers proved a well-established routine of the Keynesian–corporatist partnership that prevailed until the end of the 1970s. This routine was now applied to the public promotion of a 'second labour market'; the latter was deemed to be a remedy for rising unemployment. Against this background, the new non-profit actors could unfold their socio-political approach of practising collective self-help and advocating institutional change at the same time.

2.2 Work integration as (contracted-out) public service – institutionalizing WISEs

In a second period, beginning in the early 1980s, WISEs settled in the landscape of the German third sector as well as in the realm of local authorities. As with other branches of the new social movements, the civic element was evolving towards institutionalization; the most obvious expression of this trend was the entry of green-alternative politicians into municipal politics. With the enduring crisis in the labour market, the municipalities had a growing interest in bringing recipients of social assistance back into salaried work (and thereby onto the contributions registers of unemployment insurance); the enormous burden social assistance payments implied for the municipal budgets did much to promote work integration initiatives. The more traditional components of the German non-profit sector, namely welfare associations, also became involved in this organizational field and the setting up of a new generation of social services (the example of the DW sketched above is telling). Their concern was to prevent poverty by providing work and social support to the least fortunate. The overall result was the creation of non-profit–public partnerships in the field of work integration. Many organizations were set up with the aim of providing temporary employment for the most disadvantaged in the labour market. 'Employment enterprises' (*Beschäftigungsgesellschaften*) were founded under the co-presidency of the municipalities, traditional non-profits, and local trade unions (Heinrichs and Hild 1995). These enterprises worked together with the social assistance departments of the municipalities and with local offices of the labour market administration, which offered quite generous funding.

Generally, the welfare state's strategies moved from interventionism towards post-Keynesian austerity, this shift setting clear limits to a further expansion of the organizational field under consideration. However, the idea of a 'second labour market' persisted (Schmid 2002: 235–319), but in times of austerity there was less money for subsidising projects creating new or better services and additional jobs. The programmes that were channelled through the local labour offices and the funds from the municipal social assistance departments became increasingly targeted at the most disadvantaged and considered as a means to support transitional employment – they should lead back to 'real work', hopefully to be found in the private labour market, as soon as possible. Obviously, the way of measuring the performance of time-limited jobs changed, with the latter being evaluated according to their ability to help unemployed persons gain the qualifications needed to subsequently obtain another job. Funding was increasingly confined to wage subsidies (instead of 'complete' jobs). Moreover, these subsidies were reduced, with a decrease of material incentives to participate in a WISE as a result. The results were not those aimed at by the new policies: the rate of transfers to the ordinary labour market was low. The prevailing approach became a socio-administrative one that put the emphasis upon sheltering vulnerable people and using social assistance for 'employment therapy'. In the then existing population of WISEs, the vision of collective self-help and political agency became, by and large, marginalized.

2.3 Managerial politics of activation – normalizing WISEs

During the 1990s, a third stage crystallized. The WISEs, which were in some ways 'different', were increasingly forced to follow the standard routines of public bodies. The initial informal bargaining and co-ordination based on good will and civic engagement gave way to the attempt to treat these organizations like any other 'social business' interacting with public authorities. The organizational development of WISEs was emblematic of the evolution of the whole non-profit sector, where practices shifted from amateurism and volunteering to the hiring of salaried 'practitioners' and 'experts'; in the mobilization of civic support itself, business rationales gained more importance (fundraising, market-like recruitment of volunteers, etc.).

To this was added a transformation of the concept of the welfare state. The discourse of activation, as it developed in Germany – a special version of the 'enabling state' model – lost its links with 'activating civil society'. For the jobless this meant that access to social programmes was made conditional on agreeing to do the utmost to fit with what labour markets required. Practices began to shift towards workfare. A further point was the reform of public administration, largely inspired by Anglo-Saxon concepts of New Public Management. The emphasis was put on a much more controlling and restrictive attitude towards the workers in integration programmes, on efficient service delivery by the WISEs that had been contracted with and on benchmarking public or publicly subsidized welfare. Concerning labour market policy, the 1990s also saw the arrival of for-profit training and placement agencies under public contract (Helbig 2001: 33–40). Moreover, experts, in tune with the *Zeitgeist* of public policy, began to advocate a far-reaching transformation of the rules guiding non-profit work integration (Eichhorst 2001; Schulze-Böing 2002). The core idea was to subjugate subsidized employment to rigid efficiency norms in terms of successful placements of the workers in integration, the latter being conceived as 'customers' choosing their 'integration provider', potentially within a voucher system.

A growing part of the non-profit sector (WISEs included) tended to adopt a business-oriented approach, stressing economic accountancy and measurable outputs. Up to this point, the interrelations between the public authorities and the labour market administration on the one hand, and organizations such as WISEs on the other, had been marked by negotiations, with both sides having their own concepts and visions. Now in a managerial logic and in a context of centrally induced reform of labour market services, in many places the partnership became dominated by public bodies subcontracting predefined tasks to enterprises that were denied the possibility of being anything more than mere business partners. As WISEs continued to heavily rely on (quasi-)public resources, and because social movement dynamics in this specific field of social action tend to run dry, they tended to comply with the new welfare state culture, based on quasi-market competition and 'soft' workfare (Eick *et al.* 2004). As the above-sketched example of the DW illustrates, some room remained for social entrepreneurship, but non-profit ventures transcending mere collaboration with the new workfare state were put under considerable economic strain.

2.4 WISEs as social shock absorbers – the special story of East Germany

The evolution of work integration in East Germany follows a particular course (see Table 18.1, italic rows). After reunification in 1990, a major concern of federal social policies was to buffer the economic demise of the East. Over a couple of years, the instruments inherited from Keynesian corporatism were revitalized. An enormous flow of resources from the West to the East was set in motion, based on a new 'solidarity tax'. A special feature of this period was the setting up of a huge number of programmes and organizations providing time-limited employment. The Labour Offices proved quite generous in funding the 'employment enterprises' which spread after the run-down of East-German industries (Hild 1997; Birkhölzer and Lorenz 2001; Braun 2001). The main goal of these enterprises was to rapidly create temporary jobs in domains such as ecological renewal or cultural work, but later on also on the fringes of local social services (kindergartens, family support services, etc.). All sorts of social entrepreneurs were invited to present projects, with a high chance of obtaining funding.

In parallel, trade unions and welfare associations – which in fact were 'imported' from the Western part of Germany – advocated the creation of community-related economic ventures. In many cases, this was achieved through collaboration with representatives ('shop stewards') of firms that were closing down; the new ventures were to use parts of their facilities as well as taking over some of their staff. This period was clearly an era of transition. Employment programmes had an important role and an immediate effect in 'getting people off the streets'.[1] The East German welfare sector (i.e. the non-statutory and non-profit sector) was profoundly transformed; it was rebuilt on the basis of the Western model, with a strong involvement of West German organizations. Given the enormous disruptions in East German society at this time, a major role conferred on the sector was to provide for transitional welfare.

By the mid-1990s, the institutionalization of the non-profit sector was, by and large, achieved. The 'big' players of the West had 'conquered' the

East, albeit without being rooted in related civic milieux, as had been the case in the West. The welfare state's strategy was still to cushion the economic impacts of reunification, yet there were new limits to state interventionism. For instance, the amount of resources spent on public employment schemes (and related wage subsidies) was considerably reduced. This also brought into question exceptionally big WISEs, with some hundreds or even thousands of employees, run by municipalities. This was the case in Leipzig, for example, where the municipality-run WISE had on its payroll several thousand 'employees', who worked mainly in various sectors of municipal public services. Overall, the conditions under which East German WISEs were operating turned out to be widely assimilated to the situation in the West. However, some particularities persisted; for example, the clientele remained different, in that the proportion of 'hard cases' among the workers was far more limited in the East than in the West, while the rate of unemployment in the East reached twice that in the West.

2.5 WISEs and the latest trend in labour market policies

As depicted above, the overall landscape in which non-profit work integration operates in Germany has significantly changed. In general, profiling and placement can be expected to become the preferred activity of all non-statutory agencies concerned with work integration. These agencies are supposed to compete in quasi-markets, with public authorities selecting those that best fulfil their requirements. In 2002, these ideas were taken up by the para-governmental 'Hartz Commission' on reform of the labour market services and administration, which had until then been organized in a nationwide hierarchical top-down fashion (Schmid 2003). The government progressively implemented the bulk of the commission's proposals – arriving in summer 2004 at 'Hartz IV'. This was the last of four reform parcels containing among other things the substitution of time-limited employment programmes by jobs paying about one euro per hour, and an organizational reform involving co-operation between the municipalities and their social assistance bureaux, on the one hand, and the local labour offices, on the other. This led to the heated debates and protests mentioned at the beginning of this chapter. These reforms implied a changing institutional framework for, and a much more managerial approach towards, WISEs:

• Local labour offices (which have since been renamed labour agencies) take direct responsibility for all the long-term unemployed (many of whom were previously under the responsibility of municipal social assistance departments). They co-operate in this with the municipalities, but it seems that the still rather hierarchical labour market administration gets more say compared with the municipalities. As a result, WISEs may lose local partners and room for manoeuvre.

- The idea of subcontracting various sharply delineated services (profiling, counselling, training, job probation) operates against the concept of WISEs, insofar as the latter try to combine various objectives (e.g. offering social support, improving skills and providing for a full work experience).
- The classification of the unemployed and the case-management-led decisions on what they should get in terms of training, work facilities, social support, etc. now fall within the competencies of labour agencies, which makes WISEs more dependent than before on predefined tasks and contracts.
- Calls for tenders for the provision of local service packages are open to wide subscriptions, in which the cheapest bidder is often preferred; this may devaluate the local embeddedness and the know-how accumulated by local WISEs.

Given the current 'managerialist' trend in labour market policies, German WISEs may be entering a new stage in their evolution. It is true that with the 'one-euro job' programme, they are invited to run employment measures on a broader scale, besides their (impossible) mission to rapidly guide unemployed people back into the ordinary labour market; yet it is far from clear whether this allows for a renaissance of their original vision. On the whole, their dependence on the new contract business appears to be of crucial importance, even though some room for manoeuvre is left at the organizational level. Given the overall trend, the situation of the *Diakoniewerk* sketched above may be typical of what German WISEs will experience in the near future.

Conclusions

Formally, the institutional framework in which WISEs operate has been preserved: public subsidies for the employment of selected welfare recipients, with clear limits concerning the fields of economic activity and the duration of contracts. Yet the overall approach of labour market policy has significantly changed. At the beginning, public authorities reasoned in terms of 'financing useful work rather than unemployment', and allowed the development of a second labour market, understood in a broad sense, not only as a social reservoir but also as a place where additional jobs could be prepared and useful products or services invented. However, over time, the goal of creating additional jobs vanished, and the second labour market was increasingly fashioned as an 'antechamber' to the first labour market, before finally being completely abandoned as a conceptual reference. The focus shifted to ensuring 'employability', the jobs provided by WISEs coming to be considered as 'artificial'. The policy perspective thus moved away from linking useful work with the creation of new employment towards an approach considering nothing but the adaptability of the target groups to a given social and economic environment.

The rules for public–private partnership also changed. While in the past public authorities had left considerable operational discretion to WISEs, the latter are now treated as economic agents to be rated according to their measurable outcomes (i.e. the number of placements). Goods and services produced by WISEs have increasingly become second-order issues, while only the employment-related goals have been put in the foreground.

A third observation is that the idea of a more autonomous alternative or social economy has faded away. Importantly, WISEs have not achieved an identity of their own; they have been able to argue for changes in labour market policy, but not about their own prospects. In the perception of the relevant actors themselves, there is not much room for non-profit action understood as dealing differently with economic concerns. In their early stage, some elements of such an identity emerged, drawing on the idea of 'alternative third sector organizations' linked with concepts of reform of the local economy. Yet the public benefit-related identity of municipal WISEs proved precarious from the outset, and waned rapidly when public administration was streamlined according to private sector blueprints. The fact that German WISEs never developed a strong lasting identity seems to account to a large extent for their limited ability to react to pressures towards isomorphism (see Chapter 15 of this book).

The enormous and widespread protests and demonstrations against the Hartz reforms that swept through Germany in 2004 and which even played a role in the parliamentary elections in mid-2005 show that the attempts in recent years to remove the issue of creating work opportunities for the long-term unemployed from the policy agenda have failed. The idea of creating hundreds of thousands of 'one-euro jobs', suddenly brought back into the game by the government, bears testimony to this. It is highly ambivalent.

On the one hand, these jobs are even worse at qualifying their holders for the labour market than the job programmes governments had previously axed. Many people feel that they have far more to do with 'pressure' and 'discipline' rather than with 'opportunity', and that they are a poisoned chalice. Service providers and users are looking for better funding and quality but, instead, feel that they are being used as a dumping ground for people who have a high level of needs yet at the outset have very little to give.

On the other hand, by setting up the one-euro job programme, the government has indirectly acknowledged that the earlier belief that it is enough to manage employability alone can no longer be upheld.

A future task will be the concrete shaping of this type of work opportunity and the setting up of other parallel occupational programmes which can both build a higher level of qualification and also provide a higher level of rewards. Obviously, much will depend not only on the new local labour market authorities but also on the organizations of the public and third sector that are encouraged to offer job and work opportunities.

Today's WISEs will play an important role in this regard. They still deploy energies on fronts such as social case management, services for the public good, political agency and fostering community cohesion. An institutional alternative to them is still out of sight. They will have to ask themselves whether and how they might take up such a challenge – an additional reason why their story is unfinished.

Review questions

- How have the relationships between public bodies and German WISEs evolved over time?
- How could one explain the increasingly strained relationship between the different goals of German WISEs?
- Why did the Hartz reform put social enterprises back on the public agenda?

Note

1   See the detailed study of the policies implemented in Leipzig by Guyet (2000).

Bibliography

Birkhölzer, K. and Lorenz, G. (2001) 'Germany: Work Integration through Employment and Training Companies in Berlin and its Surrounding Regions', in Spear, R., Defourny, J., Favreau, L. and Laville, J.-L. (eds) *Tackling Social Exclusion in Europe*, Aldershot: Ashgate, 145–79.

Bode, I. (2003) 'Flexible Response in Changing Environments. The German Third Sector in Transition', *Nonprofit and Voluntary Sector Quarterly*, 33, 2: 190–210.

Bode, I. (2005) *Die Dynamik organisierter Beschäftigungsförderung. Eine qualitative Evaluation*, Wiesbaden: Verlag Sozialwissenschaften.

Braun, S. (2001) 'Zweiter Arbeitsmarkt im Dritten Sektor – das Beispiel Sport', in Priller, E. and Zimmer, A. (eds) *Der Dritte Sektor – international*, Berlin: Sigma, 251–76.

Eichhorst, W. (2001) *Benchmarking Deutschland. Arbeitsmarkt und Beschäftigung*, Gütersloh: Bertelsmann Stiftung.

Eick, V., Grell, B. Mayer, M. and Sembake, J. (2004) *Nonprofit-Organisationen und die Transformation lokaler Beschäftigungspolitik*, Münster: Westphälisches Dampfboot.

Evers, A. (2003) 'Local Labor Market Policies and Social Integration in Europe: Potential and Pitfalls of Integrated Partnership Approaches', in Zeitlin, J. and Trubek, D.M. (eds) *Governing Work and Welfare in a New Economy*, Oxford/New York: Oxford University Press, 188–212.

Evers, A. and Schulze-Böing, M. (2001) 'Germany: Social Enterprises and Transitional Employment', in Borzaga, C. and Defourny, J. (eds) *The Emergence of Social Enterprise*, London and New York: Routledge, 120–35.

Guyet, R. (2000) *Innovations et limites des politiques de l'emploi dans les nouveaux Länder. Le cas de Leipzig* (2 vols), Grenoble: Université de Grenoble, Institut d'études politiques – CERAT.

Heinrichs, S. and Hild, P. (1995) *Kommunale Beschäftigungsgesellschaften im Umfeld lokaler Arbeitsmarktpolitik*, Munich/Mering: Hampp.

Helbig, C.M. (2001) *Abbau der Langzeitarbeitslosigkeit. Auswertung praktischer Erfahrungen von Einrichtungen außerhalb der öffentlichen Arbeitsverwaltung*, Frankfurt usw.: Lang.

Hild, P. (1997) *Netzwerke der lokalen Arbeitsmarktpolitik. Steuerungsprobleme in theoretischer und empirischer Hinsicht*, Berlin: Sigma.

Reisch, R. (2001) 'Ausbildung; Beschäftigung; Qualifizierung – Wohlfahrtsverbände und Dritter Sektor oder der Weg vom Projekt zum sozialen Dienstleistungsunternehmen', in Priller, E. and Zimmer, A. (eds) *Der Dritte Sektor – international*, Berlin: Sigma, 229–49.

Schmid, G. (2002) *Wege in eine neue Vollbeschäftigung. Übergangsarbeitsmärkte und aktivierende Arbeitsmarktpolitik*, Frankfurt/New York: Campus.

Schmid, G. (2003) 'Moderne Dienstleistungen am Arbeitsmarkt: Strategie und Vorschläge der Hartz-Kommission', in *Aus Politik und Zeitgeschichte*, 6–7: 3–6.

Schulze-Böing, M. (2002) 'Fördern durch Fordern – Fordern durch Fördern? Aktivierende Arbeitsmarktpolitik und die Rolle der Kommunen', in *Sozialer Fortschritt*, 7–8: 160–4.

Conclusions

19 Social enterprise at the crossroads of market, public policy and civil society

Marthe Nyssens

Overview

This chapter sums up the main conclusions that emerged from the results of the research project and suggests further lines of research. After reading this chapter, the reader should:

- be able to draw conclusions regarding the main hypotheses of the research project;
- be able to link these conclusions to policy orientations in the field of work integration;
- have a sense of further lines of research to be developed in the field of social enterprises.

Introduction

Social enterprise is widely discussed on both sides of the Atlantic. However, as explained in more detail in the Introduction to this book, this concept can cover different meanings and still appears unclear in public debate. In the US, the concept of social enterprise mainly refers to a dynamic of commercialization at work within the non-profit sector – a phenomenon of NPOs which increasingly rely on the market to finance their activity. This concept can also be associated with the dynamics of 'social entrepreneurship' developed by businesses which seek to stress the social impact of their productive activities.

In the European context, the EMES Network has defined social enterprises as organizations with an explicit aim to benefit the community, initiated by a group of citizens and in which the material interest of capital investors is subject to limits. These organizations place a high value on their independence and on economic risk-taking related to ongoing socio-economic activity (see Chapter 1 of this book).

Against this background, the objective of the PERSE[1] research project, upon which this book is built, was to further develop a theory of social enterprise through a comparative analysis of these organizations across Europe.

In order to develop this main objective, we chose an emblematic subgroup of social enterprises, which constitutes a major sphere of their activity and which therefore allows meaningful international comparisons: namely, the field of 'work integration'. The major objective of 'work integration social enterprises' (WISEs) is to help disadvantaged unemployed people, who are at risk of permanent exclusion from the labour market. WISEs offer these persons various modes of integration through a productive activity. Even though not all WISEs adopt the labels of 'social enterprise' or 'work integration social enterprise' as such, 44 different types of WISEs have been identified in the countries studied (see Chapter 1, Appendix 2), on the basis of the indicators of the EMES definition of social enterprise. It should be remembered that these 'EMES indicators' describe an 'ideal-type' rather than constituting an actual 'definition' of WISEs; they are a tool to locate social enterprises with respect to this ideal-type and with respect to each other. In doing so, they also enable researchers to define the set of social enterprises they want to consider.

To develop our research project, 162 WISEs, located in 11 European countries, were selected. The WISEs in the sample are active in a wide spectrum of activities: some provide private goods or services (such as building work or running a restaurant), while others produce quasi-public services, such as social services.[2] These 162 WISEs employed, during the year 2001, more than 6,000 disadvantaged workers across Europe. Analysis of these workers' characteristics, based on a sample of 949 participants, showed that

> [the] disadvantaged condition was linked, for some of them, mainly to their labour market situation (long-term unemployed or low-qualified workers), and for others, mainly to their personal condition (problems of social exclusion, family problems or physical/mental disability); in many cases, the workers surveyed were disadvantaged in both senses.
>
> (see Chapter 11, p. 188)

The analysis of the trajectories of these workers also revealed that a high percentage of workers were still employed in the social enterprise at the time of interview (58.5 per cent), more or less two years after their entry.

The project was articulated around three main theoretical axes, which were presented in Chapter 1 of this book. These three theoretical axes also constitute the basis upon which this concluding chapter is structured: Sections 1 to 3 sum up the main conclusions that emerged from the results of the research project regarding these axes. These conclusions lead us to the development of some policy orientations in a fourth section, and to some lines for future research in a final section.

1 The multiple-goal nature of WISEs

> Social enterprises have a complex mixture of goals. The first hypothesis put forward by the PERSE research project regarding social enterprises' missions was that they would include at least three different categories of goals: social goals, connected to the particular mission of social enterprises to benefit the community; economic goals, connected to the entrepreneurial nature of social enterprises; and socio-political goals, connected to the fact that social enterprises come from a 'sector' traditionally involved in socio-political action.

The *integration of disadvantaged workers through a productive activity* is obviously at the core of the mission of European WISEs as it is the main criterion that defines this type of social enterprise. As explained in Chapter 1, empirical results show that European WISEs express this social mission in the form of various modes of integration: stable jobs, transitional employment or traineeships, sheltered employment, etc. However, a subgroup of WISES underlined the fact that their main mission was to participate in local development, especially in disadvantaged communities, by delivering a range of goods and services; *in this process*, they created training and employment opportunities for marginalized groups in the local labour market. For this kind of social enterprise, the 'mission of integration of disadvantaged workers through a productive activity', although important, was considered as secondary to their local development mission. This is, for example, the case of local development initiatives in Ireland (Chapter 8) or community businesses in the UK (Chapter 16).

Production is part of the identity of WISEs as a support for their integration objective. Indeed, carrying out a continuous activity of production of goods and services, facing a certain level of economic risk and pursuing the integration of their workers through a productive activity are all part of WISEs' mission by definition (see Chapter 2). Moreover, it clearly appears that in a majority of cases the integration and the production objectives are strongly interwoven and fairly balanced, which seems to be a distinctive feature of WISEs.

PERSE data also highlights the fact that an important subset of WISEs provide public or quasi-public goods (such as social services or environmental goods), and add value through this kind of production in itself, not only using it as a means to achieve their integration goal. For these WISEs, the social goal is thus twofold: integration of disadvantaged workers, who are at risk of permanent exclusion from the labour market, on the one hand; and production of a (quasi-)public good, on the other hand.

Finally, regarding *socio-political goals*, different levels must be distinguished.

At the level of the enterprise, a majority of WISEs place importance on advocacy and lobbying through networking activities (see Chapter 6). However, the weight put on that activity as well as the objectives pursued vary from one WISE to another. For some of them, the goals pursued through these lobbying activities are merely strategic and instrumental to their social mission – namely, to obtain public resources for the training of disadvantaged workers – or to their productive mission – obtaining contracts. For others, advocacy activities are not only strategic but also aim to show the value added of social enterprises, which differ from other types of active labour market policy tools in the way they tackle the social exclusion of disadvantaged groups. They would, for example, emphasize the more participative decision-making processes inside the social enterprise or the development of 'socio-politically embedded markets' in which customers put a value on WISEs' social mission in their purchasing decisions (see Chapter 7).

At the level of the 'sector' of social enterprise, as analysed in Chapter 17, WISEs are characterized by political embeddedness. Indeed, public policies in this field are the result of multiple interactions between representatives of WISEs and those of public bodies as these initiatives progressively became institutionalized over time. Consequently, even though, at the level of the enterprise, socio-political goals appear to be significantly less important than social and economic goals (see Chapter 2), networks of WISEs have over time played a crucial role in raising awareness regarding marginalized groups in society, in showing the value of this kind of enterprise, and in the design of public policies supporting their activities.

These socio-political goals can be considered in a wider perspective of 'producing social capital', as networks are features that facilitate co-ordination and co-operation. The institutional approach to social capital emphasizes the complex relation between bonding social capital, embedded in strong networks among people sharing a common identity, and bridging social capital, which opens 'the possibility for co-ordination and social cohesion on the macro level based upon the existence of generalized trust' (Chapter 6, p. 88). As analysed in Chapter 17, most WISEs were founded through a partnership among civil society actors: social workers, associative militants, representatives of more traditional third sector organizations, sometimes the disadvantaged workers themselves. Local public bodies were sometimes associated with this dynamic; when this was the case, it was usually in countries where the third sector and the public sector were closely interwoven.

This dynamic of linking people with different backgrounds is also reflected in the fact that 58 per cent of the WISEs in the sample have been described as involving more than one category of stakeholder on their board (Chapter 2). Moreover, the data collected seem to indicate that 'the participation of stakeholders in these WISEs leads to the exercise of a real influence within boards', because of the 'balanced governance structure' (Chapter 2, p. 46). These characteristics – the participative nature of WISEs, and the fact that most of them were founded through partnerships – are channels for developing links and trust across different types of stakeholders and can 'consequently enhance the development of bridging social capital' (Chapter 6, p. 105). These features also highlight the collective dynamic of social entrepreneurship and contrast with the emphasis the social entrepreneurship literature generally places on individual social entrepreneurs (see Chapter 1).

The results of the PERSE project thus strongly confirm the multiple-goal structure of European WISEs (see Chapter 2).

Moreover, regarding this multiple-goal character, a second hypothesis was put forward: multi-stakeholder ownership might be an efficient way for social enterprises to achieve their overall mission, and the representation of different types of stakeholder on the board might be a way to combine the various goals of the enterprise, thanks to the various sensibilities of the stakeholders.

Empirical analysis revealed that all the WISEs in the PERSE sample, be they multi-stakeholder organizations or single-stakeholder ones, have similar multiple-goal structures (see Chapter 2). So although multi-stakeholder ownership could be a means to manage multiple-goal structures, it seems that it is not the only one: WISEs with a single-stakeholder board also find ways to manage their multifaceted goal structure. This similarity between single-stakeholder WISEs and multi-stakeholder ones regarding their multiple-goal character might be accounted for by the fact that social enterprises, independently of their single- or multi-stakeholder nature, 'are often founded on the basis of a vision, a mission and values widely shared by the stakeholders involved' (Chapter 2, p. 42).

However, it should be underlined that the PERSE project only defines and analyses the governance structure of social enterprises through their ownership structure and through their board dynamics. However, the data show (Chapter 6) that social enterprises also keep up relations with external stakeholders (the local community, clients/beneficiaries, public authorities, etc.) through informal channels, without these formally being on the board of the enterprise. This observation underlines the need for deeper research on the implication of stakeholders inside social enterprises.

2 A variety of resource mixes among social enterprises

> The third hypothesis put forward by the PERSE project was that social enterprises mobilize different kinds of market and non-market resources to sustain their multiple-goal mission; by following Polanyi and his 'substantive approach' to the economy, we argue that social enterprises mix the economic principles of market, redistribution and reciprocity, and hybridize these three types of economic exchange so that they work together rather than in isolation from each other.

The results of the PERSE research project confirm that the economic dimension of social enterprises does not necessarily mean that they achieve economic sustainability only through resources generated by commercial activities. Indeed, a social enterprise's financial viability depends on its members' efforts to secure adequate resources to support the enterprise's mission, but these resources have a hybrid character. European Union WISEs show a particular capacity to articulate resources in various ways, in order to pursue their complex set of objectives. Moreover, it indeed appears that WISEs do not rely only on a mix of market- and redistribution-based resources; they are the scene of a more complex hybridization, built upon four types of economic relationship: the market and redistribution, but also the socio-politically embedded market and reciprocity (see Chapter 7). During the PERSE project, non-monetary resources were evaluated in order to make reciprocity-based resources (such as volunteering) visible and to highlight the support given by redistribution (such as exemption from social security contributions, personnel secondments and the free provision of premises).

The sale of goods and services represents, on average, 53 per cent of WISEs' resources,[3] while direct and indirect subsidies account for 38.5 per cent of resources. Subsidies are mostly linked to goals relating to the labour market; they primarily contribute to the funding of fixed-term contract employment or traineeship opportunities. Voluntary resources, which are most probably undervalued, represent, on average, 5.5 per cent of total resources. This last kind of resource reflects the degree of embeddedness of WISEs in civic networks; social enterprises which are more strongly embedded in civic networks are better able to mobilize volunteer resources than social enterprises launched by public bodies. These voluntary resources can be important either in the start-up phase (see the case of Finland, Chapter 10) or to support the twofold social goals of some social enterprises – the integration of disadvantaged workers and the provision of goods or services to vulnerable users. Such a multiple-goal mission is generally linked to a deep embeddedness in local social networks, which is, in turn, reflected in a high level of voluntary participation (see Chapter 8).

Beyond support provided by voluntary resources:

> reciprocity is also expressed through the capacity to construct market economic relationships that take WISEs' social and socio-political goals into account. ... These socio-politically embedded markets are not often built with households and the private sector; they are generally created with public authorities, whose purchases from WISEs are, in three-quarters of the cases, motivated by the latter's social and socio-political objectives.
>
> (Chapter 7, p. 132)

However, this is an 'average' picture; reality at the level of the social enterprises is more disparate, and different logics appear in the various ways the different types of WISE mix resources (see Table 7.6). Social enterprises that produce social services for vulnerable users or those that integrate highly disadvantaged workers obviously need more non-market resources than other types of WISE. The different types of resource mix therefore have to be analysed according to the variety of goals pursued by the WISE.

3 Social enterprises and institutionalization: between social innovation and isomorphism

> Social enterprises are embedded in the political context. Public policies in the field of social enterprises are the result of interactions between their promoters and representatives of public bodies. The fourth hypothesis put forward by the PERSE project was that this dynamic of institutionalization could lead to the development of innovative public schemes and at the same time to a movement of 'isomorphism' on the part of social enterprises, towards public organizations or for-profit enterprises.

Historical analysis shows that social enterprises have contributed to the development of public policies. Indeed, they were pioneers in promoting the integration of excluded persons through a productive activity. WISEs have increasingly represented, for public bodies in most European countries, a tool for implementing labour market policies. The 1990s saw the development, in a lot of countries, of public programmes specific to social enterprises (see Chapter 17 for a detailed analysis of these schemes). When a specific public programme exists to support social enterprises financially, it often specifies which legal forms they can adopt. Most social enterprises have an associative (non-profit) or co-operative legal form. Beside these traditional legal forms, a number of national governments have created new legal forms specifically for social enterprises, with the goal of promoting their development: 'company with a social purpose' in Belgium (as early as 1995); 'social solidarity co-operative' in Portugal; 'social co-operative with limited liability' in Greece; and 'co-operative society of collective interest' in France. Most recently (in 2004), the UK approved the 'community interest company' and, in 2005, an Italian law paved the way for rules concerning the 'social enterprise'.

This dynamic of official recognition has been quicker in countries such as Italy, France and Belgium, where the existence of a co-operative or social economy sector – alongside the public and the for-profit sectors – has still maintained some of its original features and influenced the perception of these new social enterprises (see Chapter 15). The influence has been reciprocal; the emergence of these WISEs – whose official recognition was in some respects made easier by the existence of a social economy or co-operative sector – in turn, often brought new life into this sector; for example, the development of the new public programmes targeted at social enterprise in the field of work integration fostered the creation of social economy units inside public authorities at national or regional level in Belgium, France or Ireland. In Sweden, the Minister of the Social Economy – whose existence is probably linked to the tradition of a co-operative movement in this country – supports the development of new social enterprises, even though there is no official accreditation of them. Conversely, the absence of a specific programme for social enterprise in Germany probably reflects the decline of the co-operative movement in this country (see Chapter 15).

The specific public schemes or the more general activating labour market policies which WISEs used now shape – at least partially – their objectives and practices. But can we speak of 'isomorphism' on the part of WISEs, understood as a progressive loss of some of their inner characteristics under the pressure of these legal frameworks or of professional norms spilling over from the for-profit private or public sectors? Bode *et al.* conclude in Chapter 15 (p. 254) that 'there is no overall tendency towards isomorphism', understood as an evolution in which WISEs completely lose their initial identity. This being said, external pressures, however, generate *strained relations* between the different goals of WISEs. Indeed, social enterprises, as hybrid organizations, face an essential challenge: mixing different goals and managing the tensions between them.

Regarding the *social goal* of integrating disadvantaged workers through a productive activity, the philosophy of the innovative social enterprise which emerged in the 1980s clearly resided in the empowerment and integration of excluded groups through participation in WISEs whose aim was 'to offer each disadvantaged worker a chance to reassess the role of work in their lives by supporting them while they gain control over their own personal project' (see Chapter 4, p. 62). This conception implies not only giving an occupation to these persons but also developing specific values, for example through democratic management structures in which the disadvantaged workers are given a role, and/or through the production of goods and services generating collective benefits for the territory in which the WISEs are embedded. Getting workers back into the 'first' labour market was thus not the priority as such. But the progressive institutionalization of the field over the years, through public schemes increasingly linked to active labour market policies, has generated a clear pressure to make this social mission instrumental to the integration of disadvantaged workers into the first labour market (see Chapter 17). We, therefore, observe a strained relation between the mission of empowering excluded groups and the mission of integrating the beneficiaries into 'normal' jobs. This has implications for the actual implementation of the social mission of WISEs.

First, as shown by Borzaga and Loss in Chapter 11, the type of integration provided by the WISE is highly influenced by the type of integration scheme defined by the labour market authorities. These integration schemes usually consist of temporary public support intended to compensate for the 'temporary unemployability' of the disadvantaged workers. However, it appears that these schemes are not sufficiently linked to the actual profiles of the workers. The temporary nature of the subsidies can therefore lead to a phenomenon of skimming, i.e. there are incentives for the enterprises to hire only those workers who are most likely to be 'cost-effective' by the end of the project and to retain only those who have attained this level of 'cost-effectiveness' when the subsidized period ends.

Second, although the pioneering initiatives emphasized the empowerment of participants through participative decision-making processes, nowadays, daily practices are more deeply influenced by other factors, such as the extensive professionalization of the organization and the evolution of production methods towards those of the private sector (on these points, see Chapters 6 and 15). WISEs sell their products in markets in which they compete with for-profit enterprises. As a result, WISEs can be driven to adopt the norms of these for-profit competitors (see Chapter 15). Analysis of formal channels of participation such as board membership indeed shows that, on the one hand, the level of participation of disadvantaged workers is low and that, on the other hand, the staff is one of the more influential categories on the boards of the WISEs surveyed (see Chapter 2); this could be a consequence of the process of professionalization, in which participation may suffer. However, deeper investigation is needed regarding the participation of disadvantaged groups inside WISEs through informal channels potentially linking the social enterprise and its workers.

Regarding the *production goal*, the first challenge for WISEs is to find a type of production suited to the capacities of disadvantaged groups while making it possible to train these workers through the production process.

To meet this challenge, developing market niches has proven a successful strategy, but 'WISEs that have successfully entered into niche markets may discover that, from the moment these markets become more stable, private competitors (with fewer social concerns and constraints) are keen to make money in them as well' (see Chapter 15, p. 239). Here, the case of recycling is emblematic. At the European level, WISEs played a pioneering role in developing recycling services. Today, these markets are more secure and we see that WISEs have to compete with new entrants coming from the for-profit sector. Moreover, when choosing a production niche, WISEs sometimes face a trade-off between the type of production and the level of employability of the participants. For example, PERSE data reveal that the building and gardening sectors employ more workers with a weak employability profile, while – unsurprisingly – in the field of social services and education we find better qualified workers.

If most WISEs consider their goal of producing goods and services as important insofar as it supports their integration mission, some of them also pursue a production goal deemed important for society because it generates collective benefits and equity (for example, the production of social services). These WISEs face a second challenge when looking for the necessary resources to support this kind of production. Indeed, while all WISE-specific public schemes emphasize the production goal as the main support for work integration, only a few of them recognize the possibility of producing (quasi-)collective goods (see Chapter 17). Moreover, when this is the case, this collective dimension is rarely sustained by specific public financing, which makes it more difficult for these WISEs to maintain the concurrent pursuit of different collective goals – namely, the integration of their disadvantaged workers and the production of a good or service with a collective dimension – that characterizes them. As O'Shaugnessy explains (Chapter 8, p. 140), '[this] presents an enormous challenge to those WISEs that may be serving a disadvantaged community, where the consumers of their services lack the financial means to procure these services from other vendors and where public service provision is inadequate'.

Regarding the *socio-political goal*, even if WISEs have contributed to shaping public policies in the field of work integration, 'such dialogue has not always been smooth and has not resolved the debate about the contested nature of WISEs' (see Chapter 17, p. 293). Both public authorities and promoters of WISEs agree on the fact that the hiring and occupational integration of disadvantaged workers are at the very heart of WISEs' mission, but differences arise, as we just explained, regarding the way in which this integration is to be understood. The dominant model of public recognition of WISEs tends to recognize only one kind of benefit – namely, those benefits linked to the work-integration goal – in the framework of active labour market policies and with a very specific target – the integration of workers into the normal labour market. Consequently,

WISEs are pushed to adopt a single-goal structure, and this evolution entails a risk of reducing the innovation capacity of WISEs.

4 Policy orientations

These conclusions regarding the key hypotheses of the PERSE project lead us to suggest some lines for policy making in the field of WISEs.

First, our results show that WISEs serve a highly heterogeneous target group that can be broken down into several different subgroups. The situation disadvantaged workers experience, therefore, varies greatly from one person to another, and the problem some workers face is not simply 'temporary unemployability'; they may have a variety of problems (such as a lack of skills, mental disabilities or social problems) with long-lasting effects on their productivity. In this context, the concept of a 'springboard to integration' – i.e. temporary public support compensating for the period of 'temporary unemployability' before integration in the first labour market takes place – may be inadequate for some groups of workers who are especially disadvantaged.

A way of taking into account the specific nature of the various groups targeted by WISEs would be to differentiate integration subsidies according to the profile of the workers, allowing some workers to remain in 'sheltered employment' for a longer time. Such experiences exist in some countries, for example in Italy, where social co-operatives show that integrating workers with different types of disadvantage by relying on different lengths of subsidy can be an efficient solution. Sweden (Chapter 13) provides another example: in this country, the model of integration in a WISE for a specific participant is the result of both formal and informal procedures between the WISE and the public authorities that are in charge of the integration path of the participants. In any case, this established heterogeneity among workers should encourage public bodies to develop a wide diversity of integration schemes in the labour market policy field in order to allow WISEs to integrate a variety of profiles of workers.

A second key question in matters of public policy resides in the recognition of the collective dimension of the production of some WISEs, as in the case of social services. When the production is characterized by such a collective dimension, which, obviously, does not follow the logic of the market, it has to be partly financed by redistributive resources and voluntary-based resources. However, it appears in the PERSE research that most of the redistributive resources are linked to the goal of integration of the WISEs' disadvantaged workers. If WISEs are obviously entitled to this kind of public subsidy to support their integration mission, when justified by the production of (quasi-)collective goods, they should also be entitled to additional public subsidies to support this collective mission, besides public schemes linked to the employment of disadvantaged workers. The development of specific schemes that could increase the supply of, and the demand for, social and community care services could be a relevant way to support such production with a collective dimension.

A further line of interest for public policies is linked to the recognition of the resource mix upon which most WISEs are based. Indeed, empirical evidence shows that WISEs mix different resources: the market and redistribution, but also the socio-politically embedded market and reciprocity. Moreover, this mix varies from one type of WISE to another in accordance with their specific social mission. However, one of the most visible effects of the institutionalization of WISEs in the different European countries is that it pushes them to position themselves, most of the time, in the 'market economy' or, when they employ very disadvantaged workers, in the 'redistributive economy' (on this subject, see Chapter 17). The role of voluntary resources is in neither case recognized. This type of scheme puts social enterprises in 'boxes', denying one of the fundamental characteristics of social enterprise – namely, the fact that they are located in an intermediate space between the market, the state and civil society.

In this mobilization of resources, purchases motivated by social or socio-political criteria constitute an important way for public bodies to support WISEs. For small contracts, public procurement rules do not apply.[4] In this case, this kind of purchase can occur in a discretionary way: in the decision to purchase a product or service, public bodies can also take the social mission of WISEs into consideration. When the amount of the purchase is above the financial threshold established by community law, a public call for tenders has to be issued; the question is then whether social dimensions – such as the employment of disadvantaged workers – can be introduced into public tenders through, for example, social clauses. This issue is situated at the European level, with the debate concerning the evolution of European legislation and the possibility of taking social dimensions into account in public procurement. The directive on the co-ordination of procedures for the award of public contracts, published in 2004, explicitly allows social and environmental criteria. However, European legislation still appears unclear on this issue and allows for different interpretations (Navez 2005). The latitude that national legislation implementing the new European directives will leave, or not, to the diversity of national practices in this matter is also an important issue for the future development and sustainability of WISEs.

Finally, the results of the PERSE project show the key role umbrella structures play in the development of WISEs. Their role is vital in a number of different ways. First, they foster the mutualisation of resources derived from a variety of sources in a territory. They can negotiate contracts with private enterprises and public bodies, for example, as just mentioned, in public procurement with a social dimension. Umbrella organizations could develop special know-how in negotiating this type of contract on behalf of WISEs. Second, the history of the field shows how these umbrella organizations interact with public bodies to create specific public schemes.

In other words, public schemes are not the result of top-down processes only, but are created jointly by representatives of WISEs and those of public bodies. Umbrella organizations ensure that public bodies are lobbied in order that they recognize the complex set of goals of WISEs. Finally, these intermediate organizations are used to exchange best practices not only at the national level (within an umbrella organization or between umbrella organizations) but also between different countries. Fostering networking among WISEs, therefore, seems to be a relevant way for public policies to sustain the development of this field.

5 Needs for future research

5.1 Deepening research on the 'multiple-goal, multi-stakeholder, multiple-resource social enterprise model'

The PERSE project adopted the definition of multi-stakeholder social enterprises as 'multi-ownership' organizations and the analysis focused mainly on board dynamics within social enterprises. Analysis carried out in this perspective (see Chapter 2) revealed that single-stakeholder social enterprises were more similar to multi-stakeholder ones than might have been expected. Stakeholder participation, therefore, needs to be studied on the basis not only of membership of the board – as was the case in this project – but also of participation through other channels, in order to broaden the analysis by looking at informal aspects of coalitions of stakeholders, circulation of information, emergence of leadership roles, etc. Furthermore, in-depth research is clearly needed to analyse the determinants as well as the outcomes of the involvement of a variety of stakeholders both in formal structures (such as the board) and in less formal ones.

The PERSE project developed an innovative typology to grasp the variety of rationales in mixing resources according to the types of goal WISEs pursue (see Table 7.6). It would be worthwhile to test this typology on a wider sample of WISEs.

An increasing number of for-profit enterprises claim concerns for goals other than profit maximization, such as social or environmental goals. As explained in Chapter 1, the concept of social enterprise in the literature, in contrast to our approach, sometimes includes a wide spectrum of organizations, from for-profit businesses engaged in socially beneficial activities to non-profit organizations engaged in mission-supporting commercial activity. Future research should then deal with the borders separating not-for-profit social enterprise from for-profit organizations engaged in 'corporate social responsibility' practices.

5.2 Net effect of WISEs and net fiscal cost for public bodies

Chapter 14 of this book presents a first attempt, based on the Belgian sample, to assess the net effect of WISEs through the matching method, with a control group, on the basis of administrative data. Seventy-six per cent of the individuals who had entered the social enterprise two years before the survey was conducted were still at work, either in the social enterprise or in another enterprise, at the time of the survey. The matching method allows us to calculate the 'deadweight' effect, which indicates that only 32 per cent of the workers in our sample would have been working if they had not had the opportunity to enter a WISE. In other words, the analysis of the trajectories of the workers in this Belgian sample reveals that almost one out of two WISE workers who were working in early 2003 would not have found work had they not gone through the WISE programme. As always in this kind of analysis, our approach had certain biases; however, this is an impressive result in comparison with other active employment policies.

On this basis, the authors of Chapter 14 computed the direct fiscal impact of hiring a disadvantaged worker in a publicly accredited WISE (*'entreprise d'insertion'*); this impact appears to be positive. In other words, supporting the integration of disadvantaged workers in WISEs does not generate costs for public bodies; on the contrary, it allows public authorities to make savings. It would be useful to carry out this kind of analysis in other countries and with other public schemes, in order to assess the net fiscal cost for public bodies, taking into account all the variations in fiscal and para-fiscal benefits (direct and indirect taxes, social contributions, etc.) and costs (social benefits, work subsidies, etc.) for public bodies.

5.3 Extending the research to social enterprises active in the field of services of general interest

Social enterprises are active in a wide variety of fields – not only in the fight against the structural unemployment of groups excluded from the labour market, but also in personal social services, urban regeneration, environmental services, and the provision of other public goods or services. The boundaries between these areas are not always clear given that, as the PERSE project showed, some WISEs produce goods and services with a collective dimension.

After studying WISEs, it therefore seems important to extend the research on goal structure, stakeholder involvement and multiple resources to social enterprises engaged in another field of activity; the field of the provision of services of general interest would be particularly interesting. This is a key issue in the current context, with the organization of services of general interest being discussed at the European level. In-depth study is required to better understand the role of social enterprises compared to public organizations and private for-profit business in delivering, for example, social services. It would, in fact, be very relevant for the development of specific literature and for public policies to verify, for all the forms of social enterprise, features such as the presence of a multiple-goal structure, the degree of stakeholders' involvement, the enterprises' resource mix, the relationship between resources and the multi-stakeholder structure, etc.

Conclusion

The first EMES book on social enterprises concluded that

> social enterprises can be considered as new organizational forms, diffused to a varying extent, throughout the European Union. Although still in an experimental phase, and far from being a well-established reality, the development of social enterprises constitutes a dynamic and innovative trend in the European economic and social arena.
>
> (Borzaga and Defourny 2001: 365–6)

Five years later, the concept of social enterprise is now widely discussed in public debate and a lot of specific public schemes, at the regional and national levels, have been developed across Europe to provide financial support to social enterprises. In most cases, these public schemes focus on a specific subset of social enterprises – namely WISEs. The PERSE research project has underlined the specific characteristics of WISEs compared to the vast array of active labour market policies as well the numerous challenges WISEs face, both in tackling social exclusion and as they undergo the dynamic of institutionalization linked to their progressive official accreditation.

As social enterprises have become associated mainly with work integration, they are not often recognized, by public bodies, as a viable strategy in other fields of activity. In a context where the sector of services – and more specifically that of personal services – is 'on the rise', the analysis of the specific characteristics of social enterprises must go beyond the field of work integration. Indeed, personal services are provided by a variety of operators (for-profit private enterprises, traditional non-profit bodies, social enterprises and public sector organizations) which have specific organizational forms and modes of governance. The development of these services generates many expectations, based on the collective benefits they can produce (collective externalities, impact in terms of equity, creation of high-quality jobs). Therefore, it is important that the question of the value added of the model of social enterprises – which are driven by their explicit aim to benefit the community – be studied more thoroughly. Is the development of social enterprise in this field a sign of a retrenchment of the welfare state or, on the contrary, a way to enhance the collective benefits that may be associated with these services? The answer is obviously complex. The results of the PERSE research project suggest that the response will vary depending on the type of regulation that is developed. If public bodies limit their action to developing quasi-market policies, which place all types of providers on an equal contractual footing, without taking the collective benefits the providers create into account, the risk is that the social innovation role of social enterprises will be curtailed, as most probably will be their capacity to provide specific answers to these collective problems. Conversely, if public bodies recognize the specific characteristics of the social enterprise model and foster its development, social enterprises could, most probably, make their specific contribution to the public good.

Review questions

- Explain the various types of strained relations between the different goals of WISEs.
- What kind of policy orientations would you suggest in your country in the field of work integration?
- Why would it be relevant to analyse the place of social enterprise in the field of social services?

Notes

1 Let us recall that PERSE is the project's acronym; its full name is: 'The Socio-Economic Performance of Social Enterprises in the Field of Integration by Work'.
2 For an overview of the types of production of the WISEs in the sample, see Table 1.2.
3 For a detailed analysis of the resource mix of WISEs, see Chapter 7.
4 On this point, see Navez (2005).

Bibliography

Borzaga, C. and Defourny, J. (2001) 'Conclusions – Social Enterprises in Europe: a Diversity of Initiatives and Prospects', in Borzaga, C. and Defourny, J. *The Emergence of Social Enterprise*, London and New York: Routledge: 350–69.
Navez, F. (2005) 'Marchés publics et éthique: évolution des directives européennes et du droit belge', paper presented at the *EMES-ISTR Conference*, Paris, April.

Index

Pages containing relevant figures and tables are indicated in *italic*.